MW00612125

DECEPTION

THE ANCIENT MYSTERY THAT HOLDS
THE SECRET OF NEWGRANGE

PAUL BOGGS

silvanus
publishing, inc.

***DISCLAIMER: The following information and opinions are not a substitute for professional medical prevention, diagnosis, or treatment. Please consult with your physician, pharmacist, or health care provider before taking any home remedies or supplements or following any suggestions in this book. Only your health care provider, personal physician, or pharmacist can provide you with advice on what is safe and effective for your unique needs or diagnose your particular medical history. The information in this book does not contain professional advice (e.g., financial, legal, etc.) While my sincere conviction is to provide readers with truthful, straight-forward facts surrounding the topics found inside of this book, there is never a time when anyone [other than God] knows everything. Therefore, the potential for error is ever present when communicating information. Both the author and publisher assume no responsibility for damages that may arise to those using the information found inside of this book or damages alleged to have occurred as a result of the content found inside of this book. This book is not endorsed by any of the individuals, companies, products, etc. mentioned in this book.

FAIR USE NOTICE: This book may contain copyrighted material, the use of which may not have been specifically authorized by the copyright owner. The writer of this book is making such material available in his effort to advance understanding of environmental, political, human rights, economic, democracy, scientific, and social issues, etc. This constitutes 'fair use' of any such copyrighted material as provided for in section 107 of the US Copyright Law.

DECEPTION: The Ancient Mystery That Holds the Secret of Newgrange
Cover Design and illustrations created by Silvanus Publishing, Inc.
All biblical quotes are taken from The King James Holy Bible (Charles of the Scottish James Family).
Typography by Silvanus Publishing, Inc.
Copyright © 2014 by Silvanus Publishing, Inc.
Published by Silvanus Publishing, Inc.

All rights reserved. No portion of this book may be reproduced, stored in a retrieval system, or transmitted in any form or by any means – electronic, mechanical, photocopy, recording, scanning, or other – except for brief quotations in critical reviews or articles, without the prior written permission of the publisher.

Boggs, Paul 1971 – DECEPTION: THE ANCIENT MYSTERY THAT HOLDS THE SECRET OF NEWGRANGE
by Paul Thomas Boggs
384 pages
ISBN: 978-0-9969165-0-9
1. Religion. 2. Elite (Social Sciences)—United States. 3. United States—Social Policy. 4. Body, Mind, Spirit: Occultism. 5. Body, Mind, Spirit: General

"Ministering spirits, I loose you in the Name of Lord Jesus Christ, to minister on my behalf according to the will of God. I bind all demons and Satan. In Jesus Christ's Holy name. Amen!"

Contents

Contents Cont'd

ABOUT THE AUTHOR

"Appearances to the mind are of four kinds. Things either are what they appear to be; or they neither are, nor appear to be; or they are, and do not appear to be; or they are not, and yet appear to be. Rightly to aim in all these cases is the wise man's task."
– Epictetus c.55-135 A.D.

aul of the Scottish Boggs family is a descendant of the Dál Riata in Scotland, an ancient Gaelic Irish colony credited with bringing Christianity and literature to Scotland c.500 A.D.

It was through the unmatched spiritual and physical prowess of these Celtic bloodlines that Ireland would become an impenetrable fortress and safe haven for the exceptional inheritance of western civilization, a reality which has been marginalized.

Art historian Kenneth Clark wrote, "It is hard to believe that for quite a long time — almost a hundred years — western Christianity survived by clinging to places like Skellig Michael, rising seven hundred feet out of the sea." Skellig is a rocky island off the coast of Ireland which contained a settlement of Irish Christians, who in the 5th and 6th centuries rescued European civilization from marauding Saracens [Muslims].

Were it not for the perseverance of ancient Irish and Scottish Clans, the Continental Congress on September 9, 1776 would not have declared the name of a new nation known as the United States of America. What's more a band of Irish and Scottish Americans known as the, "Overmountain Men," of the Appalachians, would not have existed to engage with and ultimately decimate British Maj. Patrick Ferguson's army of 1300 British "red-coats," in a war that lasted just 1hr 5min.

The devastated Continental Army and 1780's American rebel cause was resurrected by Irish and Scottish warriors, resulting in a crucial victory for the colonies during the American Revolution. Enemies of America, take heed of the rhetoric which led to America's Irish and Scottish population rising up against and decapitating tyranny in the 1780s. Just prior to the American Revolution victory, British Maj. Ferguson was sent by Great Britain's oligarchy on a fool's errand, bloviating to Irish and Scottish Appalachians, "If you do not desist your opposition to the British arm's I shall march this army over the mountains, hang your leaders and lay waste your country with fire and sword." Maj. Ferguson was dead and his army annihilated shortly after issuing his threat. Prior to the intervention of Irish and Scottish warriors, George Washington stated, "The country stands on the brink of a precipitous."

The malevolence President Washington grappled with throughout the 1700s and was literally bled to death by is the very force which has plagued ancient Celts and Picts for over two millennia, destroyers who celebrate death and the suppression of liberty. Another piece of history which has been conveniently omitted by revisionist historians is the role Celts and Picts have played in the protection and proliferation of liberty throughout the world. For example, one of the most notable African-American social reformers, Fredrick Douglas [c. 2/1818-2/20/1895] who once said, "I would unite with anybody to do right and with nobody to do wrong." would not have become the great orator and abolitionist he was were it not for his Irish mentor, Daniel O'Connell. Fredrick Douglas travelled to Dublin, Ireland where he invested many months listening to and studying O'Connell, who once said about the enterprise of slavery, "My heart walks abroad wherever the miserable is to be succoured, and the slaves to be set free, there my spirit is at home, and I do like to dwell."

What has fascinated Paul for more than 30 years is his unique collection of ancient Scottish and Irish documents and verbal traditions passed down through generations. As a young person researching his roots, he discovered his lineage included: Vlad the Prince of Wallachia, a name which is derived from the word "walha" used by Germanic people to describe Celts; King of Scots Robert Brus; Spanish Empire Commander in the 1535 Conquest of Tunis, Hernando Padilla Davila y Perez de Gallegos Caballero De Santiago; Medieval knight, Sir John Stapleton; The Black Knight of Ireland; signer of the Declaration of

Independence, Scottish American Philip Livingston, grandson of colonel Robert Livingston the Elder who was an associate of Scottish sailor William Kidd whose treasure provided the financial foundation upon which John Jacob Astor created his fortune [$110.1 billion in 2006 dollars]; eleventh President of the United States, Scottish American James Knox Polk; Founder of Hollywood, Scottish/Irish American Francis Boggs; Governor of Missouri Lilburn Williams Boggs, who was a friend of Californio military commander Mariano Vallejo, in fact Lilburn named his son Mariano Guadalupe Vallejo Boggs, Lilburn migrated to Sonoma, California [1846] leading a group of immigrants, the group which separated from Lilburn became the infamous Donner Party; house majority leader and Warren Commission member Hale Boggs, tasked with and murdered for investigating President JFK's assassination and co-inventor of the Ethernet David Boggs.

Paul's unique ancestral chronicles provided him tales of warfare between ancient Celts and Picts, and what these clans referred to as the Tuatha De Danann. These ancient Celtic watchmen, more than 2,000 years ago, described battles with the Babylonian warrior god Nimrod, an ancient "Serpent Cult of Dann" proxy who controlled an ancient old world order, whose traditions can be seen throughout their Egyptian, Asian, and Khazarian descendants.

One of the most notable Egyptian deities is the serpent god 'Sobek' [c.2181 B.C.], a half-man, half-reptile figure commonly associated with Osiris and Ra. Both Hinduism and Buddhism promote the serpent cult through a serpent figure named 'Nagas' and the union of a human being and a female Naga. It is written in ancient Hindu texts that this demigod was banished by the creator to the underworld with unimaginable riches and is allied with demons, a tradition which mirrors the legends associated with the Church of Babylon's god Nimrod. Equally fascinating to the author, and the underlying motivation for the creation of this book, is the never before seen scheme which involves ancient Celts, Picts, relics, and the defeat of the old world order of the Church of Babylon. The author believes that readers will find provocative the connection between the descendants of these ancient Clans, who happen to be many of the most iconic, historical figures, and the way in which all of them have been ceremonially sacrificed.

AIR MUIRS ...R TIR

CLAN BOGGS
SOCIETY OF THE UNITED STATES OF AMERICA

1 THE NEWGRANGE DECEPTION

Newgrange is an ancient shrine located in Ireland and the ancient Calanais Standing Stones are located in Scotland's Outer Hebrides islands. Both monuments were constructed by the surrounding farming communities. The Church of Babylon exploit these sites to promote the religion of evolutionism which regards The Holy Bible's account of creation and its time line as nothing more than legend. They tell us that the sites predate Egypt's very first pyramid [the step pyramid of King Zoser] constructed by his vizier 'Imhotep' by more than 500 years. Furthermore, we're told Newgrange and the Calanais Standing Stones were built c.3200 B.C. using an advanced system of measurement and that these sites are more than one thousand years older than Stonehenge in England.

Professor at University College, Cork (UCC) and Archaeologist, Michael J. O'Kelly, was published extensively in 'scholarly journals' and was widely respected as a teacher, for his field work, and his published articles. O'Kelly is best known for his excavation, restoration (1961-1975) and theories regarding Newgrange. On 12/21/1968, O'Kelly confirmed an ancient legend that sun rays on midwinter sunrise penetrate along the whole length of the inner passage of Newgrange. O'Kelly speculated: "I think that the people who built Newgrange built not just a tomb but a house of the dead, a house in which the spirits of special people [other-dimensional beings] were going to live for a very long time." Revisionist historians and archaeologists representing UNESCO enjoy misleading people into believing the claim that Professor O'Kelly was "the first person in five thousand years to witness a ceremonial event programmed by Newgrange's builders". Dr. Carleton Jones, of NUI Galway, suggests that Newgrange was created to enhance existing "power points" the builders perceived on the landscape. I will demonstrate in subsequent pages that Professor O'Kelly's theories are nothing more than Church of Babylon propaganda, propagated for the purpose of bolstering the New Age religion of evolutionism, while at the same time subjugating the Irish people and their Christian faith.

The challenge facing modernists and the above Pseudoscience is that Jesus Christ tells us in Matthew 19:4 and Mark 10:6 that the creation of Adam and Eve was 'the beginning' [I Cor. 15:45 and Romans 5:12-14]. Furthermore, Exodus 20:11; Acts 13:20-21; Kings 2:11, 11:42 and other dates inside of The Holy Bible demonstrate that Adam was created 6,000 years ago, not 'billions' or 'millions' as the evolutionary scheme of things would have you believe. Even more problematic for the Church of Babylon is that The Holy Bible teaches us that (i) Noah's flood occurred c.1656 After Creation [A.C.], c.2344 Before Jesus Christ [B.C.] and c.1756 B.C., (ii) the giant god Nimrod and his Old World Order Babylon ["the Gate of Gods"], north of what is now modern Iraq, was destroyed by God. What's more, The Holy Bible teaches us that after Noah's flood the first settlers of Egypt migrated from Nimrods Tower of Babel where the languages were confused. It was from Babylon where ancient Egyptians developed the names of their gods. This leads us to the conclusion that the Babylonian god Nimrod had some influence over the god 'Ra', 'Osiris', 'Horus', etc. and that when The Church of Babylon speaks about 'secret knowledge' or promotes fill-in-the-blank Egyptian logos and insignias to newly deceived initiates, they are in fact endorsing the Babylonian god Nimrod and the Babylonian demon god Pazuzu [Lucifer], one of the original fallen stars [angels] banished from Heaven by God, who has deceived, led astray and destroyed every 'advance' culture on God's planet for the past 6,000 years. This is one of the many reasons God describes Nimrod' Babylon as a symbol of godlessness. What I demonstrate throughout the following pages, using ancient texts, relics and illustrations, is that the entire world, through so called 'enlightenment', 'secret knowledge' and theories of immortality, have been deceived by forces that have existed long before God created planet earth. These forces are far superior to man's intellect and the only defense man has against these forces is stripped away when he offers himself up to the Church of Babylon.

Another challenge for modernist archaeologists and ethnologists are nearly 300 ancient flood legends. The very diversity of the Nations from which these legends emerge argues powerfully against the charge that these legends were 'invented'. For example Babylonian literature, from the Babylonian priest-historian Berossus and 'The Gilgamesh Epic' [G.E.] Written c.2000 B.C. gives detailed accounts of the great flood, a mere 344 years after the event c.1656 After Creation (A.C.). A number of ancient Celtic oral traditions also contradict the Newgrange age theory. One in particular tells us that prior to the great flood Noah sent his granddaughter 'Cesair' to Ireland because Ireland would be unaffected by the great deluge, an apparent retelling of Revelation 12:12-17 which reads in part, "And the serpent cast out of his mouth water as a flood after the woman, that he might cause her to be carried away of the flood. And the earth helped the woman, and the earth opened her mouth, and swallowed up the flood which the dragon cast out of his mouth.". Cesair was the leader of the first invasion in Ireland, daughter of Noah's son Bith. What's more we're told that Cesair was denied admission to the Ark, so she left 40 days before the Flood c.1616 A.C. Cesair arrived at Dun na mBarc (in Co. Cork), Ireland, with 50 other women, and three men. She married a man named Fintan Mac Bochra. The three men were to divide the women among them, as well as dividing Ireland into three. They hoped they could populate Ireland, but two of the men died. When the fifty women all turned their attention to Fintan, he saw that they were placing too much responsibility on him, so he fled from Ireland, by turning himself into a salmon. Cesair died from a broken heart and without a single man on the isle, the other women also perished. What is so striking about the aforesaid account is that ancient patriarchal genealogy suggests that Irish-Celts were direct descendants of Iobaath, Javan and Japheth, Noah's direct descendants. Author Bill Cooper in his book titled: "After the Flood" details this connection. The Cessair legend was so important to the ancient Celtic people such that the King of Gallia named his daughter Cessair, who married the High King of Ireland, Ugaine Mor in the 5th century B.C. Coupling this ancient Celtic oral tradition with all the aforesaid, creates a challenge for members of The Church of Babylon promoting the 3200 B.C. Newgrange theory. Unfortunately for modernists, even if you eliminate The Holy Bible, which is precisely what their aim is, and even if you discount the ancient Celtic oral traditions, which in of itself discredit their entire hypothesis, you're still left with a mountain of evidence left by Phoenicians, Greek, Romans, etc. In other words, the aforesaid isn't the biggest threat to their fantasy premise; the principal argument which stands in the way of their theory is a piece of inconvenient truth that I'll share with you in a few moments. First let's explore the legacy of one of the Church of Babylon's most tragic Irish families, the Wilde family.

William Wilde (1815-1876) was the father of legendary writer and Freemason Oscar Wilde, a historical figure who I discuss in subsequent pages. William Wilde was a quintessential Freemason collecting human skulls, feeding on human flesh and most dreadful of all selling the body, mind and soul to the Devil as in the case of his son Oscar who until his well documented rebuke of Freemasonry shortly before his death was a homosexual love slave for Aleister Crowley, a Satanist who was referred to as one of the most evil men to have ever walked Planet Earth. William Wilde's fascination with decapitated men would bring him face to face with the skull of Jonathan Swift. For those of you who may not 3 recall, Swift is best known for his book 'Gullivers Travels', as well as an essay titled: 'A Modest Proposal for Preventing the Children of Poor People From Being a Burden to Their Parents or Country'; in it Jonathan Swift suggests that poor Irish mothers and fathers should sell their Irish children to wealthy members of The Church of Babylon as food. Swift then goes into vivid detail as to the best ways in which to cook their poor Irish children.

In 1841, William Wilde was a Master Freemason of the second oldest and most powerful Freemason Lodge in the world, located in Dublin Ireland, and was privy to the not so 'secret knowledge' of the surrounding area that I'll be sharing with you in a moment. What's important to understand is that William Wilde understood the relationship between the ancient site of Newgrange and the ancient Old World Order system [Babylon]. Wilde was keenly aware of ancient oral traditions which exposed the truth regarding the technologically advanced ancient Celtic people and their victory over the once powerful Babylonian god Nimrod, who along with his pantheon of Goliath offspring once ruled the ancient Old World Order [Babylon]. Because of their victory over Nimrod, the descendants of these ancient victors have been under a perpetual state of persecution by Satan and his army of fallen angels. I invite you to research the effects The Church of Babylon has had on your own family, both from an ancient and modern day perspective. During my extensive research through the vestigial remnants of my Irish/Scottish ancestry, I discovered the unmistakable fingerprints of the Church of Babylon, as well as a disturbing correlation between the Church of Babylon and the sacrifice of countless Irish and Scottish American entertainers, high-tech innovators and politicians. I found that American Citizens possessing one of the aforesaid ancestral qualifications were sacrificed [literally and figuratively] disproportionately to their Babylonian Talmudic counterparts. If you feel my claims are outlandish please do your own research on the number of Irish and Scottish Americans who have died under suspicious circumstances throughout the political, business and entertainment industries.

While reading the following data I ask readers to consider both the way in which these people were murdered as well as the related date of sacrifice all of which are linked to occult numeric's e.g., **11**, 13, 23, 32, **33**, 44, 3, **7**, 9, 21, 39, 77, 93, 222, **666**, **777**, etc.

Three of the most 'magical' values to the 'Church of Babylon' are the numbers 13, 33 and 666. While reading the following information it's important for readers to have a basic understanding of these occult related numeric's. All of the following occult based mythology were fostered inside of the ancient city of Babylon and according to many ancient writings and relics was established shortly after a global flood which destroyed the ancient world c.2344 BC. Babylon itself would later be destroyed and those who survived would establish Egypt and all of the following false doctrines. The ancient codes and numbers that Babylonians brought with them to Egypt represented to them a much deeper meaning beyond the obvious months, days and modern day zodiac. They embodied a vibrational force capable of controlling their subjects. For this reason the Serpent Cult incorporate select colors, shapes, numbers and sounds into events, monuments, corporate identities, marketing initiatives, etc.

THE FALSE "MAGIC" OF 13

The Church of Babylon reveres the number 13 for the following reasons. First, it represents The Book of Revelation 13:1-18 which typifies their quest to ring-in global chaos and absolute rebellion against God under the rule of the beast. Second, the 'magical' value of man is "6" whereas the 'magical' value of 'god' is "7" [6+7=13]. Often times these values will be represented so that the number 7 [God] is inferior to the number 6 [man], else the number 7 will be paired with an icon which honors Satan. Symbolically speaking the number 13 represents man being above God and honors Satan and his big-lie which states "... ye shall be as gods." [Satan] - Genesis 3:5.

The number 13 also represents the Egyptian god "Osiris", "Isis" and "Set." The myth states that Osiris was married to Isis and it was Isis' brother Set who killed and then cut up Osiris into 13 pieces. Isis then retrieved the dismembered body parts of her husband that is except for Osiris penis which was thrown into the Nile and eaten by a catfish or crab. Isis' magical powers allowed her to create a golden phallus [penis] to conceive "Ra", who is allegedly both the son and brother of Osiris and Isis. The sun god Ra is a central figure within the Church of Babylon and has been incorporated into many of America's iconic symbols including America's very first flag design [pg.6, top]. For most of you this will be the first time that you've viewed this flag design. As you can see, there are seven stars which represent the Church of Babylon's god [Satan]. In addition to the stars, we see the "All-Seeing-Eye" of Satan. In antiquity this symbol was associated with Hathor the enforcer of Ra. Lastly there are nine sun rays, in the shape of a pyramid signifying 'Ra' the sun god. Lord Jesus Christ (Acts 17:23-24) warns Christians to not worship that which is made by the hands of man.

"For as I passed by, and beheld your devotions, I found an altar with this inscription, TO THE UNKNOWN GOD. Whom therefore ye ignorantly worship, him declare I unto you. God that made the world and all things therein, seeing that he is Lord of heaven and earth, dwelleth not in temples made with hands;" - Acts 17:23-24

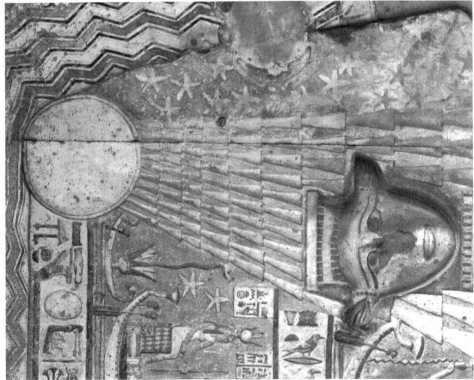

Now I invite you to compare the hieroglyphics [pg.6, bottom], which adorn the ceiling of Hathor Temple in Egypt, commonly referred to as the Temple of Tentyra, built circa 360–343 BC, with the aforesaid American flag concept. Hathor was the most famous goddess of Ancient Egypt. Known as the goddess of destruction and eye of Ra, Hathor protected Ra. According to legend, Ra dispatched his 'Eye' [Hathor] against his enemies. Hathor began slaughtering people by the thousands. When Ra begged her to stop, she refused. Ra was able to stop her from killing, by painting the killing fields with blood colored beer. The likeness between Hathor's hieroglyphics and the first U.S. flag design is irrefutable. The truth is, Secret Societies who worshipped Babylonian and Egyptian gods influenced the design of many of our most iconic symbols and customs. Juxtapose the five design elements, found in the United States flag, with the mythology and design elements of Hathor' hieroglyphics. Red Stripes = "Hathor's blood colored killing fields." White Stripes = The rays of light in the Hathor hieroglyphics. Blue Area w/ Stars on our U.S. flag are obvious in the Hathor hieroglyphics.

Lastly, consider the U.S. flag folding ceremony which we're told represents the same religious principles on which our great country was originally founded. If that's true, why then are Christians brainwashed into believing that the twelfth fold, which creates an occult pyramid [left], represents God?

As was previously noted it was Ra who painted the fields with "blood colored beer" to stop Hathor's bloodlust however it was Osiris, the father and brother to Ra, who is credited throughout Ancient Egypt for inventing beer, so too was the recommendation to consume it on a daily basis. Osiris had an advanced understanding of the human chemical and electrical system, namely the health damaging effects of the gluten protein found in barley known as "hordein". Osiris knew that gluten and alcohol reduced a human being's life expectancy, therefore by introducing these toxins into a human being's diet it would effectively reduce their life span from hundreds of years to less than 100. I predict there will be those who under the spell of false teachers will retort, "Well, Jesus made water in to wine!" to which many in our 'Judeo-Christian' society would acquiesce. This author on the other hand will tell you that the Holy Bible is unwaveringly opposed to the consumption of alcohol and that Jesus Christ turned water into "good wine;" [John 2:10] which according to first mention is "new wine" [Matthew 9:17, 26:28-29; Mark 2:22; Luke 5:38] otherwise known as non-alcoholic grape juice or tîyrôsh in Hebrew. While Jesus Christ hung, his body besieged with dehydration and agony above the heads of his Khazarian 7

Babylonian Talmudist crucifiers, a Roman centurion offered Him fermented wine [old wine]. As soon as it touched Christ's lips he realized that it was fermented and refused it [Matthew 27:34].

> "Woe unto him that giveth his neighbour drink, that puttest thy bottle to him, and makest him drunken also" - Habakkuk 2:15

Budweiser and Miller, two of America's most popular beer brands, secretly idolize the occult numeric "13" in their corporate identities. In the case of Budweiser their identity not only contains a 13 it includes an occult pyramid and eagle. To the Church of Babylon the eagle represents the messenger of Zeus [Mercury], also known as Apollyon otherwise known as "The Beast from the pit" from the book of revelation.

THE FALSE "MAGIC" OF 33

Next we have the number "33" which is celebrated throughout the Church of Babylon for two primary reasons. First, it symbolizes the age of Jesus Christ when he was crucified. Second 33 represents the 1/3 or (33%) of angels which fell with their god Satan.

> "And his taile drew the third part of the starres of heauen, and did cast them to the earth: And the dragon stood before the woman which was ready to be deliuered, for to deuoure her childe as soone as it was borne. And the great dragon was cast out, that old serpent, called the deuill and Satan, which deceiueth the whole world: hee was cast out into the earth, and his angels were cast out with him. And the dragon was wroth with the woman, and went to make warre with the remnant of her seed, which keepe the Commaundements of God, and haue the testimony of Iesus Christ." - King James Version (1611) Revelation Chapter 12: 4-17

Lastly we have the occult numeric "666" which pays homage to "The Beast" [Satan].

> "Here is wisdom. Let him that hath understanding count the number of the beast: for it is the number of a man; and his number is Six hundred threescore and six. [666] - Revelation 13:18

8 Throughout the following pages I will be referring to the "Church

of Babylon". This term represents what I call a triad of malevolence e.g., the "Serpent Cult of Dann", the "Babylonian god Nimrod" and "Masonic Babylonian Talmudism". Individuals who claim allegiance to these cults all believe that Satan is "God."

The alpha cult to the aforesaid factions is the "Serpent Cult of Dann". For thousands of years this order has acted as a central authority, governing every facet of Lucifer's complex network of global proxies. One of the Serpent Cult's oldest deputies is the order of Masonic Babylonian Talmudists, the forefather of Freemasonry.

THE SERPENT CULT OF DANN

"There is a power so organized so subtle so complete so pervasive
that they better not speak above their breadth when they speak in
condemnation of it." – President Woodrow Wilson, died age 67 [6+7=13]

Prominent men meeting in secret who have directed the course of civilization are recorded throughout ancient civilizations. The oldest on record is known as the "Serpent Cult of Dann" also known as "Brotherhood of The Snake" and "Brotherhood of The Dragon" and it still exists under many different names. The brotherhood of the snake is devoted to guarding the "secrets" of the ages and to the recognition of Lucifer as the one and only true god.

When we read about the twelve tribes of Israel, in the Holy Bible, Dan is referred to as one of the original twelve. However when we read, "Revelation 7:5" Dan is no longer mentioned. I believe Dan's tribe is the men mentioned in [Jude 1:4] which reads:

"For there are certain men crept in unawares, who were before of old
ordained to this condemnation, ungodly men, turning the grace of our
God into lasciviousness, and denying the only Lord God, and our Lord
Jesus Christ."

If you have ever been inside of a law office, courthouse, etc. you have most likely viewed a modern day representation of the Serpent Cult logo. Modern day artists have used the 'Scales of Justice" to represent the Tribe of Dann, this decision was based on [Genesis 49:16-17] which states:

"Dan shall judge his people, as one of the tribes of Israel. Dan shall be a
serpent by the way, an adder in the path, that biteth the horse heels, so that
his rider shall fall backward."

Throughout ancient times the Serpent Tribe and its proxies   9
were recognized by a very simple mark, an "X". Today many of the

world's wealthiest families worship Lucifer and his Serpent Cult. To show their admiration, these individuals incorporate an "X" or "XX" into to their corporate identity. Fundamentally speaking the "XX" indicates one's willingness to betray on behalf of Satan. When individuals, companies, corporations, etc. feature the 'XX' on their person or in their logo they are invoking satanic energy.

For instance, the members of the Rockefeller Family are fully aware of the 'XX' meaning, which is why the family of Standard Oil fame named their Corporation "Exxon" then hired French-born Freemason and 'The Father of Industrial Design', Raymond Loewy, to design their Exxon logo. The Thule Society also featured the double-cross "XX" inside their logo. This was a German occultist group which was later reorganized by Adolf Hitler into the Nazi Party.

To illustrate how a seemingly upright wealthy businessman brazenly idolizes the Serpent "Death Cult" of Dann, we're going to scrutinize the written and visual evidence associated with one of these individuals. However, rather than focusing our examination on a high profile family, such as the Rockefellers, Rothschilds, Collins, etc. our specimen will be an individual by the name of Mark Friedman. Mark is a founder and President of Fulcrum real estate in Sacramento, California. Friedman is also a minority owner in the Sacramento Kings Basketball Team and is estimated to be worth $350 million.

The most obvious association between Mark and the Church of Babylon is Friedman's 'Fulcrum' company identity [FIG.1]. Not only does his logo feature the 'XX', it is also a vertical abstract modification of the Freemason compass and square [FIG.2]. Friedman's logo also features the pairing of pyramids, which create the, "Star of Remphan [Satan]" Acts 7:43, a six pointed star whose elements represent "666" [FIG.3]. The Fulcrum Property logo also contains the most ancient of Serpent Cult symbols, an abstract modification of the double-headed snake coiled into a double helix [FIG.4].The "X" and "XX" is an abbreviated version of the Serpent Cult's double Helix.

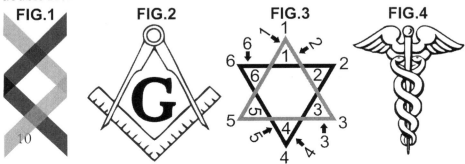

FIG.1   FIG.2   FIG.3   FIG.4

The Friedman Family own and manage a number of high profile properties throughout the greater Sacramento region. Many of these properties are riddled with icons associated with ceremonial magic, a cornerstone of the Church of Babylon. Until their removal in October 2013, the Friedman's Arden Fair Mall property for twenty-four years contained two large black pyramids capped with smaller detached silver pyramids [top]. Prior to being torn down this author had taken pictures of these structures.

This occult Alchemic symbol for air is one of the five elements that appear in most Pagan and Wiccan traditions, a practice which was influenced by the Golden Dawn system of magic and Satanist Aleister Crowley. These pyramids also show reverence for the Babylonian god of air 'Enlil'. The black portion of the Friedman's occult pyramids represented 'We The People', whereas the appropriately disconnected smaller silver pyramids embodied the minority elite who in their own minds believe they are above the American people and the laws which govern our Nation. These two large pyramids are exact replicas of the pyramid located at the I.R.S. Headquarters [center], and the pyramid sitting on former C.I.A. Director/President George H.W. Bush's lap [bottom]. GHW's granddaughter is even forming a pyramid 11 with her little hands.

"The two pillars are just 66.6 [666] percent of artist Larry Kirkland 's sculptural work [Vox Populi] in front of what is technically, if rather drably, known as the Federal Building." - The Washington Post, John Kelly, Monday, June 20, 2005

There is an additional element to the IRS Headquarters building [pg.11] that I would like to share with readers. The above picture features twin pillars flanking the occult IRS pyramid. These pillars symbolize Boaz and Jachin, the entrance to Solomon's Temple and according to the Church of Babylon the key to immortality. In relation to the stela of Nimrod [pg.18] the I.R.S. occult alter contains a hand upon one pillar [left] that is contorted into a shape similar to the hand of the Babylonian god Nimrod [pg.18] who is snapping his fingers at symbols which represent Babylonian demon gods. The I.R.S. monument also symbolizes the Grand Master of the Order of the Knights Templar, Jacques de Molay, who was burned to death slowly outside the Notre Dame Church in Paris [3/13/1314] Friday the 13th. Please keep in mind for future reference the knowledge that the Notre Dame Church in Paris, France is where the stone carving of the Celtic horned god Cernunnos was stored [c.1163-1710]. Coincidently Islam's Koran teaches the 'two-horned' man has been given all knowledge of the world by Allah. Supposedly de Molay's final words were, "Here you see innocent people die! Compare the First Epistle of the Corinthian, 14:1... I am calling you, King Philip IV of France! I am calling you, Pope Clemence V! I am calling you, Prime Minister Guillaume de Nogaret, to appear within one year from today at the Court of God in order to receive your legitimated penalty! - curse, curse, be all of you cursed until your 13th generation"

Immediately following Molay's curse the Templar Grand Master fell dead, his forefinger remaining upright to the sky. That year King Philip fell off his horse and died; the Pope died of an intestinal obstruction and Minister Nogaret hung himself. Seven-hundred years after Molay's death the Muslim terrorist group "Isis" attacked Paris, France, 11/13/2015 [Friday the 13th]. The attacks on 11/13/2015 occurred 311 days [3x11=33] after the 1/7/2015 Charlie Hebdow terrorist attacks. The Hebdow attacks occurred at 11:30am [3x11=33] and killed 11 people. Coincidently one of the attacks on 11/13/2015 occurred in the 11th district and the code to call police in France is 33.

12

Further evidence of Mark Friedman's affinity for the Church of Babylon is illustrated in the following images. In the first photograph Friedman is shown standing next to a black stripped pyramid birdcage. This is a 'magical' symbol within the Church of Babylon signifying physical and psychological bondage over one's subject(s).

The second photograph features Mark sitting in front of a piece of Fulcrum Property 'art' [8/23/2013 Sacramento Business Journal and 11-20 U.C. Davis article]. The painting contains a giant skull, Christian Church on wheels, red fish and abstract Mickey Mouse ears. Individually these design elements may seem rather innocuous; however when we juxtapose its collective meaning with that of the Christian faith, this painting clearly venerates the tenets of the Church of Babylon. To the Serpent Cult the fish icon has always represented the Babylonian fertility god "Dagon", therefore the fish combined with a Christian Church represents a blasphemous association between Jesus Christ, the "Age of Pisces" and a Babylonian demon. Whereas the skull, in association with the other elements, represents the death of the Age of Pisces or death of Christianity, and a church on wheels is limitless in its mockery.

Both the birdcage symbol and Mickey Mouse ears are well documented elements used by the CIA's mind control slave program, code named "MK-Ultra." I'm not going to spend a great deal of time explaining the history of this Government program; it suffices to say that its focus has always been on the behavioral engineering of humans. I demonstrate in subsequent pages how the MK-Ultra program played a key role in the creation of the 1960s "Flower Child Hippie Movement."

Further evidence of Mark's fascination with the occult can been seen in a 10/29/2013 presentation in which Mark presents Sacramento, CA City Council members, at the Citizen Hotel with

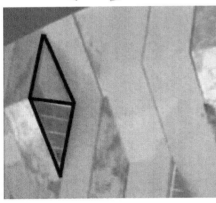

several concepts of the new Sacramento Kings Basketball Arena. Mark Friedman is not only a minority owner of the Sacramento Kings Basketball team, he is also the lead in the construction and "instrumental in facilitating the buildings indoor-outdoor design" [Sactown Magazine Oct/Nov 2014] of the $448 million dollar arena. Many of the Sacramento Kings Arena concepts resemble symbols associated with Babylonian demon gods and goddesses including: (i) a giant 'Eye of Ra' (ii) an abstract modification of the eight pointed star symbol for Ishtar [left], the goddess of war, also referred to as the goddess Lilith whose dark origins lie in Babylonian demonology. The Church of Babylon believes that Lilith created prostitution and the degrading of sex and that she was notorious for seducing and killing young men and children.

The chosen Sacramento Kings Arena design contains truncated pyramids, as well as a double-triangle element which will surround the entire facility. It will be remembered that Mark's Fulcrum Property identity contains this double-triangle element which creates a "Star of Remphan [Satan], a six pointed star whose elements represent "666."

"Here is wisdom. Let him that hath understanding count the number of the beast: for it is the number of a man; and his number is Six hundred threescore and six [666]." - Revelation 13:18

The first mention of this "666" star symbol was c.922 BC; this is when King Solomon rebelled against God and began practicing magic, witchcraft, etc.

14

Prior to King Solomon, the Egyptians used the star in pagan rituals, followed by the Arabs who used it for pagan ceremonies. The logo became exceedingly popular during the Middle Ages c.1066 AD by Druids, for something they called the 'highest Sabbath of the witches', what is now commonly referred to as Halloween. In the late 1500s the patriarch of the Rothschild family, Izaak Elchanan Rothschild [born 1577] would adopt the "666" emblem as the official family logo.

The vast majority of spiritually re-mastered individuals living throughout America have been brainwashed into believing that the Star of Remphan represents the 'Star of David' or the Judaic people.

"Yea, ye took up the tabernacle of Moloch, and the star of your god Remphan, figures which ye made to worship them: and I will carry you away beyond Babylon." - Acts 7:43

The problem with this 'Big-Lie' is that The Holy Bible only references the "Shield of David", not a "666" star of Rothschild which this clearly is. This satanic emblem was imposed onto so called Jews by the demonic Rothschild family. To the descendants of Moses, the menorah is the oldest sacred symbol:

"And thou shalt make a candlestick of pure gold: of beaten work shall the candlestick be made: his shaft, and his branches, his bowls, his knops, and his flowers, shall be of the same. And six branches shall come out of the sides of it; three branches of the candlestick out of the one side, and three branches of the candlestick out of the other side:" - Exodus 25

The Rothschild Family has known for centuries that the hexagram symbol is associated with Remphan [Satan]. Had the Rothschilds referenced The Holy Bible for design ideas for their Israeli flag it would have contained a menorah.

WHO ARE THE ROTHSCHILDS?

In 1760 Mayer Amschel Bauer [left] began working for a bank owned by one of the wealthiest families in Hanover, Germany, the Oppenheimers. Because of his moral flexibility Bauer is exceedingly successful in the banking business ["Usury"] and is quickly promoted to the position of junior partner. Whilst working for Oppenheimer, Bauer befriends a man by the name of General Von Estorff. Following the death of Mayer

15

Amschel Bauer' father [Moses Amschel Bauer], Mayer Amschel returns to Frankfurt to assume control of his father's goldsmith business. In 1743 Moses Amschel Bauer had hung a red hexagram sign over the entrance door of his business, a sign depicting a Roman eagle [Apollyon "Beast from the pit"] on a red shield similar to that of the infamous Templar Knights and Nazi Iron Cross. Upon seeing this Mayer Amschel immediately understands its significance and changes his name from Bauer to Rothschild. ,"Rot" is German for, "Red," and "Schild," is German for, "Sign". The red hexagram or sign over Moses Amschel Bauer's shop signified 'The Mark of The Beast' 666 [pg.14].

Under the new name of 'Rothschild' Mayer Amschel Rothschild begins studying the lucrative business of warmongering and immediately takes an inventory of his relationships who are directly associated with the Nation's war machines, such as General von Estorff who is influential over the court of Prince William IX of Hesse-Hanau. Rothschild quickly learns that Prince William IX is one of the richest royal houses in Europe and that his wealth was generated by hiring out of Hessian soldiers to foreign countries for vast profits. This is the very same business model practiced by the United Nations who is hiring out "peacekeeping" troops to Nations around the world. Rothschild solidifies his relationship with General Von Estorff by selling him valuable coins and trinkets at discounted prices. As predicted by Rothschild, he is immediately introduced to Prince William who begins purchasing rare coins and trinkets, soon after the Prince begins referring prospects and suspects to Rothschild in return for a 'finder's fee'. Rothschild subsequently develops a close relationship with Prince William which opens the door for Rothschild to do business with members of the court. Rothschild soon realizes that loaning money to Nations and controlling royal families is far more profitable than just loaning to individuals, more importantly the government loans are secured by its uneducated, unsuspecting citizenry [taxes]. In 1769 Amschel Rothschild is granted permission by Prince William to hang a sign on the front of his business premises declaring that he is, "M. A. Rothschild, by appointment court factor to his serene highness, Prince William of Hanau." Forty-six years later [c.1815] Rothschild takes complete control of The Bank of England.

Previously I mentioned how the fingerprints of Freemasonry were on every major war including the 'Holy Wars'. Next we're going to explore the data which led me to my thesis.

Contrary to what many revisionist historians teach about the history of Freemasonry, specifically its 17th century roots, Freemasonry's origins date back to 926 BC. For one thousand years its members conspired against humanity, then in 926 AD, they constructed what is today the oldest Freemason Lodge in England. Since its inception Masonic members have promoted Satan as their one true god.

"And when the thousand years are expired, Satan shall be loosed out of his prison, And shall go out to deceive the nations which are in the four quarters of the earth, Gog and Magog, to gather them together to battle:" - Revelation 20:7-10

Like the ten observable symbols on the stela of Nimrod [pg.18], all logos associated with the Church of Babylon are made up of mathematical formulas consisting of curves and points. To illustrate I've decoded this 926 A.D. Masonic Babylonian cryptogram, belonging to the oldest Masonic lodge in England, to show how it reads "666". This logo contains six half-circle shapes framing the center portion of the logo [6]. There are three crowns in the very center of a three sided inverted pyramid [6]. Finally there is a "6" in the year 926 [666]. This 926 A.D. Masonic Babylonian Logo was created after the fall of the Babylonian Talmudist ruled Khazarian Kingdom [c.900 AD] and contains symbols associated with the Stela of Nimrod [pg.18]. Khazarian Babylonian Talmudists believe they're the descendants of Cain and Nimrod. This is why the cross like symbol, featured in the top center portion of this Masonic Babylonian logo, matches perfectly the symbol found on the ancient stela of Nimrod [pg.18]. What this cross actually symbolizes are the four quarters of the earth, "And shall go out to deceive the nations which are in the four quarters of the earth, Gog and Magog, to gather them together to battle: the number of whom is as the sand of the sea." [Revelation 20:8] Throughout world history enemies of God have placed this symbol inside of a circle, which represents 'secret knowledge' regarding the actual shape of God's creation [Planet Earth], which I will reveal to you in subsequent pages. The three crowns in the center portion of the Masonic Babylonian logo are also represented in the Stela of Nimrod [HERE]. The "triple crown" represents the Babylonian demon god Ashur as well as the shape of Planet Earth. Many historians claim that the ancient stela shown above is that of Shamshi-Adad V, they add however that, '...the image is unusual, as the king wears his beard in a strange archaic style, and the cuneiform text is written in an artificial antique script.' - British Museum

17

The truth that modernist historians and archeologists are withholding is that the stone carving is 'unusual, archaic and antique' because this isn't Shamshi-Adad V. This is in fact a stela of the Church of Babylon's "god" Nimrod. And one of the most obvious features on this stela is the "X" on his chest, symbolizing the Serpent Cult.

I've coded eleven of the most obvious symbols found on the ancient stela of Nimrod [above]. As I expose the direct relationship between certain organizations and this stela, I'll refer back to these letters, for the purpose of demonstrating that their logos match perfectly the symbols for Nimrod's principal demon gods [fallen angels] to which he is shown snapping his fingers.

18

These include: Ashur (K); Shamash, the 15ft tall giant sun god (J) [seated below]; 'Sin' God of The Moon and son of Enlil (I); Adad, the giver and destroyer of life (H); Ishtar, the demon of war (G). The myths associated with many of the aforesaid demon gods [fallen angels] closely resemble ancient Church of Babylon texts which describe the behavior of their Babylon god Nimrod.

THE CHURCH OF BABYLON'S HOLY WAR:

When we study the original written and oral traditions of our ancestors we learn that post William the Conqueror [1087 A.D.] France, England and the Holy Roman Empire remained a powerful slave under their Norman masters. We also discover that William conquered England through fear and terror however Norman Conquest of Scotland and Ireland [1066] was gained through papal deception. What most people do not know is that the Catholic Church forged a donation letter from Constantine which the Catholic Church claimed gave them ownership of every Christian island in the western Roman Empire e.g., Scotland, Ireland, etc. By the time of the English Reformation, the donation had been exposed as a forgery. In other words the Catholic Church used deception to justify the Norman invasion into Scotland and Ireland an event which led to the deaths of millions of people.

Taking full advantage of the void of Orthodox Christian leadership created by William the Conqueror's death, the Roman Catholic Church still having a great deal of influence leverages its authority to convince the leaderless Norman warriors to act as what we would refer to in 2015 as 'Soldiers of Fortune' or mercenaries during the Crusades. The Crusades were a collection of military expeditions designed and provoked by the Church of Babylon who just like in 2015 are deceiving the Christian nations of Europe and America into a Holy War, all under the guise of rescuing the holy places of Palestine [Israel] from the hands of the Saracens [Muslims].

A detail I would like to mention here is that upon reviewing many ancient historical and religious sources, scholars have concluded that the Holy Book of Islam [The Quran] did not appear in print until the 9th century A.D., shortly before the emergence of the 926 A.D. Freemasonry Lodge in England and what it contained disturbed Christians deeply. To Christians, the three most offensive verses or "Suras" in the Quran are as follows:

(i) Islam denies the crucifixion of Jesus Christ: Sura [chapter] 4, verse 157 which reads:

"They [Jews] said (in boast), we killed Christ Jesus the son of Mary, the Messenger of Allah" – but they killed him not, nor crucified him, but so it was made to appear to them, and those who differ therein are full of doubts, with no (certain) knowledge, but only conjecture to follow, for of a surety they killed him not."

(ii) The Holy Bible has been corrupted, however Islam's Allah doesn't know anything about it since Allah commands Christians to judge according to the gospel [Holy Bible]: Sura 5, verse 47 which reads,:

"Let the People of the Gospel [Christians] judge by what Allah hath revealed therein. If any do fail to judge by (the light of) what Allah hath revealed, they are (no better than) those who revel."

Logic dictates that Christians can only judge by the gospel if we have the gospel, in other words Islam's Allah assumes that the Christian's gospel [The Holy Bible] is accurate. That being said, The Holy Bible tells us that Jesus Christ died on The Cross, rose from the dead and ascended up to heaven, and "He that hath the Son [Jesus Christ] hath life; and he that hath not the Son of God [Jesus Christ] hath not life" – 1 John 5:12. Therefore Christians cannot believe what the Quran reads, because it contradicts the gospel.

(iii) The Quran commands Muslims to subjugate or kill Christians: Sura 9, verse 29 which reads:

"Fight those who believe not in Allah nor the Last Day, nor hold that forbidden which hath been forbidden by Allah and His Messenger, nor acknowledge the Religion of Truth, from among the People of the Book [Christians], until they pay the Jizyah with willing submission, and feel themselves subdued."

And Sura 2, verse 191 which reads:

"And KILL them (the unbelievers) wherever you find them, and drive them out from whence they drove you out, and persecution is severer than slaughter, and do not fight with them at the Sacred Mosque until they fight with you in it, but if they do fight you, then slay them; such is the recompense of the unbelievers."

A sura which is very similar to a verse found inside of the Babylon Talmud is Sura 5, verse 51 which reads:

"O you who believe! do not take the Christians for friends; they are friends of each other; and whoever amongst you takes them for a friend, then surely he is one of them; surely Allah does not guide the unjust people."

There are many similarities between the Quran and Talmud including how they both compel adherents to lie and deceive Christians. In fact the motto of the Talmudist terrorist spy agency "Mossad" is "by way of deception". The Talmud encourages Talmudists to ensnare and deceive Christians in order to advance their causes. In the Quran deception is referred to as "Taqiyya" and "Kitman".

21

Lying to and deceiving Christians is promoted throughout the Quran and Hadith: sura 16:106, sura 3:28, sura 9:3, sura 40:28, sura 2:225, sura 3:54, sura 8:30, sura 10:21, Bukhari 52:269, Bukhari 49:857, Bukhari 84:64-65, Muslim 32:6303, Bukhari 50:369, etc. This subject matter is discussed in more detail at **www.acts17.net**.

One of the most perplexing characteristics of Islam is the moon logo for which they are associated. It's bewildering because the religion of Freemasonry venerates the icons associated with Baal, the sun god, and moon god. What's more this same moon icon is featured on the ancient Stela of Nimrod [pg.18, "I"]

"And he put down the idolatrous priests, whom the kings of Judah had ordained to burn incense in the high places in the cities of Judah, and in the places round about Jerusalem; them also that burned incense unto Baal, to the sun, and to the moon, and to the planets, and to all the host of heaven." – 2 Kings 23:5

Yet another bewildering characteristic of Islam is the fact that 80% of Muslims [Sunni] believe Jesus Christ's presence will be central to the defeat of the so called "Dijjal" a giant one-eyed demonic figure who resides on an island inside of a cave. However, if you're familiar with the ancient Babylonian poet Homer, you'll recognize the "Dijjal" concept from Homer's Odyssey [c.900 B.C.], where the hero Odysseus encounters the Cyclops Polyphemus, the son of Poseidon. It will be remembered from previous pages that the "All-Seeing-Eye" of Satan is what the Church of Babylon has used to personify the United States of America around the world. What Babylonian Talmudists realized long ago is that it's a fool's errand to fight 3 billion Christians and 1.5 billion Muslims instead you get Christians and Muslims to fight each other and destroy each other. Coincidently 4.5 billion is nearly the total number of people the Church of Babylon would like to eliminate from planet earth. This is why throughout history we see the fingerprints of the Church of Babylon on every skirmish between Christianity and Islam. It too is the reason why the U.S. entertainment industry and U.S. government, both of which are riddled with Masonic Babylonian Talmudists, have become synonymous worldwide with the 'All-Seeing Eye" of Satan.

Simply put, Christians, Sunni Muslims and Torah following Jews are being murdered at an alarming rate throughout the world in 2015 because this is Lucifers Modus operandi. Throughout human history God's creation has been butchered by countless luciferian proxies e.g., The Serpent Cult of Dan, The Brotherhood of the Wolf, The Babylonian god Nimrod, Ra, Osiris, Horus, Apollyon, Khazarians, Alexander the Great, Nero, Hitler, U.S. Presidents Bush, Clinton, Obama, etc. It's been Satan's plan for millennia, to eradicate the planet of all people who worship

22

God and replace the one true God with Lucifer, Helios Panoptes the Church of Babylon.

Paris-based spokesman of the National Coordination Committee (NCC), Haytham al-Manna, 'hit the nail on the head' when he made the following evaluation of President Obama's push to attack Syria in 2013: "We are not in favour of a satanic intervention against a satanic regime."

In 1972 a discovery in Yemen produced the oldest Quranic manuscripts in existence, known as the "Sana'a Manuscript". The carbon dating of the paper suggests that the original text was penned c.671 years after Jesus Christ, however what's intriguing is that there are two layers of text. The upper text conforms to the standard Uthmanic Quran, whereas the original lower text contains many variants to what is found inside of modern day Qurans. This physical evidence demonstrates how the Quran was changed between the 6th-9th centuries AD.

This is similar to what Christians have experienced over the past several centuries with the introduction of "New Age Bible version", such as Rupert Murdoch's "New International Version (NIV) and others which literally change Jesus Christ into Satan and promote a "New World Order, "Until the time of the New Order." - Hebrews 9:10 (NIV).

In the 1611 King James Bible we find just one reference to Satan and he is given the name 'Lucifer' and the title 'son of the morning'. It reads:

"How art thou fallen from heaven, O Lucifer, son of the morning!
how art thou cut down to the ground, which didst weaken the nations!"
– Isaiah 14:12

The King James Bible also provides Christians with the title of Lord Jesus Christ. It reads:

"I Jesus have sent mine angel to testify unto you these things in the churches. I am the root and the offspring of David, and the bright and morning star." – Revelation 22:16

With the aforesaid knowledge in mind read how Rupert Murdoch's New International Version (NIV) Bible casts Jesus Christ out of heaven and not Lucifer:

"How you have fallen from heaven morning star, son of the dawn! You have been cast down to the earth, you who once laid low the nations!" - Isaiah 14:12 (NIV)

As is the case with the NIV Bible, did the Church of Babylon contribute to the contradictions which are found throughout Islam's Quran?

Consider the historical fact that, a large number of "crypto-Jews" [Khazars] in the Ottoman Empire who, to escape the inferior conditions of "dhimmis", converted publicly to Islam, but retained their Talmudist beliefs becoming what were known as "Donmeh". Since the 20th century Donmeh have intermarried with other groups and most have assimilated into Turkish society.

A 17th century Kabbalist, who claimed to be the "Mashiach" [Messiah], converted to Islam to escape punishment by the Sultan Mehmed IV. The Talmud extensively discusses the coming of their "Messiah" [Antichrist], Cyrus the Great was referred to as "God's mashiach". A Talmudists understanding of the messiah is based on the writings by rabbinical philosopher and mystic, Rabbi Mosheh ben Maimon "Maimonides" [Rambam] [1135 AD – 1204 AD]. Maimonides was also called "The Great Eagle" a symbol which is associated with the messenger of Zeus or Apollyon. Aside from being revered by Jewish historians, Maimonides also features very prominently in the history of Islamic and Arab sciences and is mentioned extensively in studies. He has influenced prominent Muslim philosophers and scientists.

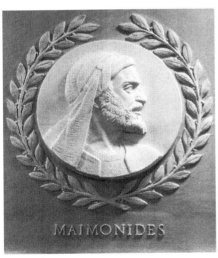

According to Maimonides, Jesus Christ is not the Messiah. Christian American's may be surprised to learn that a sculpture of Maimonides [left] exists in the U.S. House of Representatives.

It's noteworthy to mention that the Catholic Saint Thomas Aquinas [Tommaso d'Aquino] refers to Maimonides in several of his works, including the Commentary on the Sentences. Saint Aquino also worshipped Aristotle – whom he referred to as "The Philosopher". Saint Aquino admired Aristotle so much so that he created his own cult, fusing Aristotelian philosophy with Christianity. Aristotle was a pupil of Plato and Teacher to Alexander the Great. Alexander lived 33 years [356 BC-323 BC] throughout his development he was taught that he was the son of the supreme god "Ra". After visiting the oracle of Zeus, Alexander began referring to himself as "the son of Zeus." Like Zeus, Alexander was featured with goat horns on either side of his head along with a serpent

behind his neck representing the Serpent Cult of Dann [left]. Below Alexander's image is the Dann Tribe's Serpent Plate on the Heichal Shlomo's door in Rothschild's Jerusalem. Heichal Shlomo means, "Palace of Solomon" and it was the seat of the Chief Rabbinate of Israel, the supreme rabbinic and spiritual authority for Judaism [Khazar Talmudism] in Israel. In truth this is the seat of the Serpent Cult of Dann. Alexander was also depicted as the god Pan and featured in carvings with the eight pointed star symbol representing the demon goddess Lilith, also known as Isis and Ishtar, the demon of war, fertility, love and sex. Alexander is also known for making Nimrod's Babylon his capital city and demanding that people worship him like a god.

Given the aforementioned historical chain of demonic possession connecting Zeus, Ra, Alexander the Great, the Antichrist Talmudist Rabbi Maimonides and Saint Aquino, it should come as no surprise to learn that Saint Aquino's descendant is former Army General, Church of Satan member, founder of Temple of Set and alleged child molester, Michael Aquino, who in his thesis "From Psyop to Mind War the Psychology of Victory" states:

> "...the enemy populations [Christians] could be subdued by inflicting a state of psychological terror and feelings of eminent destruction."

Proponents of murdering small children in Third World Nations, sending our young history challenged American men and women overseas to be murdered and the destruction of Christianity would have you believe that America's conflict with Islam began on September 11, 2001, when in fact it began more than 1383 years ago. The Church of Babylon has been behind countless Psychological Warfare [Psywar] campaigns involving Christians and Muslims for more than 1383 years. Their first attempt at bringing the two religions together in battle occurs in 630 A.D., just two years prior to the death of Muhammad. Based on disinformation concocted by the Church of Babylon, Muhammad is told that the Christian Byzantine Empire has amassed a large army and is in route to Arabia. Believing this, Muhammad leads 30,000 warriors to receive the incoming Byzantine

25

warriors. However, after realizing his intelligence was wrong Muhammad returns home, however immediately after Muhammad's death we begin to see the bloodlust of the Khazarian Babylonian Talmudist "Donmeh" led invaders against Christians.

The first Crusade began in 1095 however this was 460 years after the first Christian city was destroyed by Muslim armies; 457 years after the population of Jerusalem was massacred by Muslim invaders; 453 years after Egypt was captured by Muslim armies; 443 years after Muslims first plundered Italy; 427 years after Muslim armies first laid siege to the Christian capital of Constantinople; 380 years after Spain was conquered by Muslim armies; 363 years after France was first attacked by Muslim armies; 249 years after Rome itself was sacked by a Muslim army, and only after centuries of church burnings [30,000], killings, enslavement and forced conversions and rape of Christian women. By the time the Western Crusades finally began, Muslim armies had conquered two-thirds of the known world, murdered tens of millions of people, enslaved over 1 million Christians, destroyed about 90% of all books, including the largest library in the world at the time in India, and destroyed 30,000 churches. Khazarian Babylonian Talmudists launched their Muslim Crusades in 630 A.D. The Western Crusades began in 1095 A.D. to stop further carnage by Islam.

If you would like to educate yourself further on this subject please examine the extensively researched books by Dr. Bill Warner website **www. drbillwarner.com**

Flash forward to 1917 and 'The Balfour Declaration' (note: the name 'Balfour' is of Pictish/Scottish origin) is designed and financed by the Rothschild Family. The Balfour Declaration committed the British people and by extension the Christian American majority [financially, logistically, militarily, etc.] to supporting the establishment in Palestine of "a National Home for the Jewish people," [Israel]. This Rothschild created Declaration is the wellspring from which modern day conflict [Holy War] between Judaic [Khazar], Christian and Muslims has sprung.

The first Church of Babylon Crusades occurred 1095 and among the elite group of Norman mercenaries were the "Order of the Poor Knights of Christ" because they took solemn vows of poverty. Like King Solomon, the Order of the Poor Knights of Christ would became possessed by the same Babylonian demon god Pazuzu and his legion of demons after setting up their base camp near the site where King Solomon's temple had once stood [c.926 BC]. For a time the Templars became the richest and most powerful presence throughout France, England, etc. until their senior leaders were burned to death and the balance of their forces were disbanded.

What historians have either overlooked or ignored is the fact that the Templars unexplained rise to financial glory and political prowess was based by and large to their knowledge of their Church of Babylon handlers, their related occult practices and their ambitions to reestablish a 'New World Order' and 'One World Religion'. In short, The Knights Templars were what the mafia would call a 'loose end' and that's why they were eliminated.

The 'smoking-gun' connecting Babylonian Talmudic Freemasonry to the creation of The Knights Templars is the collection of design elements found within the world's oldest Freemason Lodge logo 926 AD [pg.17]. It's this cryptogram logo from which the Knights Templars borrow their iconic red-cross or red-shield. For more than 918 years, however, the cross found on the ancient stela of Nimrod [pg.18] has been referred to by Freemasons, Historians, Hollywood and the like as St. George's Cross as well as the 'Templar's Cross'. The problem with associating this red cross or red shield with the Templar Knights and St. George is there is no historical record associating the red cross with St. George before the end of the crusades c.1350, 424 years after the creation of the 926 A.D. Freemason Logo. Moreover, the Templar Knights, Holy Wars, etc. didn't begin until c.1095, one hundred sixty nine years after the creation of the 926 A.D. English Babylonian Talmudic Freemason Logo. Furthermore, the 926 A.D. Freemasonry logo contains the Triple-Crown icon found on the stone carving of the Babylonian god Nimrod [pg.18, "K"] as well as a cryptogram which creates the Mark of The Beast [666].

What the aforesaid intelligence demonstrates is that members of the oldest Babylonian Talmudic Freemasonry Lodge in the world had knowledge of the stone carving of Nimrod [2500 miles from England] as far back as 926 A.D. This suggests that The Church of Babylon in concert with papal authority bribed Norman warriors into fighting a Holy War that was designed more than 169 years before 'The Crusades' and just eight years after the death of the Norman warriors Christ conscious sounding board, "King William the Conqueror".

Having been provided with the knowledge that a secret order of English Masonic Babylonian Talmudists were conspiring to rewrite history, King William just two years before his death in 1085 ordered the creation of a manuscript that English people of the day called 'The Doomsday Book' that is the Day of Judgment to quash the pending Church of Babylon orchestrated rebellion. The great survey recorded an official historical accounting of all of England as it existed in 1086, which included a small part of what is now Wales, some of Cumbria, but excluded the present day Northumbria. The entries for some major towns at the time like the important Winchester and London failed to make it into the book. To ensure the data was unadulterated by The Church of Babylon, The Doomsday Book was copied out by one person on parchment (prepared sheepskin). The importance of the Doomsday Book for understanding the period in which it was written is difficult to overstate. As H. C. Darby noted, anyone who uses it:

"Can have nothing but admiration for what is the oldest 'public record' in England and probably the most remarkable statistical document in the history of Europe. The continent has no document to compare with this detailed description covering so great a stretch of territory. And the geographer, as he turns over the folios, with their details of population and of arable, woodland, meadow and other resources, cannot but be excited at the vast amount of information that passes before his eyes."

Or, as the author of the eleventh edition of the Encyclopedia Britannica article noted:

"To the topographer, as to the genealogist, its evidence is of primary importance, as it not only contains the earliest survey of each township or manor, but affords, in the majority of cases, a clue to its subsequent descent."

It is the opinion of this author that all of the events leading up to the 1095 Crusades were orchestrated by The Church of Babylon, who at the time were reading off the same ancient revolutionary script written by the ancient Serpent Cult of Dann. Be they modern or ancient tyrants, one constant remains the same and that's Lucifer's eternal pursuit of ushering in world government and a One World Religion [Babylon].

King William's actions throughout his reign supports the notion that he was not a proponent of the Serpent Cult, nor was he a supporter of the Church of Babylon's stated goal of a One World Government, evidence of the fact that King Williams never consolidated his Kingdoms and financially supported the Christian Church.

Upon King William's death, his ancient Babylonian foe carried out their vengeance against William's Norman Warriors for his creation of a record which included the genealogy for the offspring of ancient Celtic and Pictish people and their property. King William's strategic initiative thwarted the Church of Babylon's stated goal of erasing all evidence of private property e.g., land, cattle, gold, etc. As payback Norman Warriors were lured in and used as pawns by The Church of Babylon to carry out their goal of destabilizing the Middle East and inciting a 'Holy War' between the two largest world religions. As soon as the Norman Warriors became a threat to the elite power structure they were eliminated. We see

elements of this ancient strategy throughout the Middle East in 2015, the only difference being, is that the superior warriors being sacrificed are named Navy Seals, Army Rangers and Marines.

To this day the papacy has continued the 'Big-Lie' of the Templar Knights by invoking their iconic Babylonian Talmudic Freemasonry red cross on Papal attire [top, left]. The Papacy has also incorporated a number of the design elements found on the stela of Nimrod [pg.18], namely the 'Triple-Crown' [center, left] which is represented on the stela of Nimrod [pg.18, "K"].

The second oldest Freemasonry Lodge in the world is located inside of Dublin, Ireland. The Lodge is conveniently located across from the Irish Government which currently holds EU Presidency. This is the second most senior Grand Lodge of Freemasons in the world, and the oldest in continuous existence. Since no specific record of its foundation exists, 1725 is the year celebrated in Grand Lodge anniversaries, as the oldest reference to Grand Lodge of Ireland comes from the Dublin Weekly Journal of 26 June 1725. It too is full of relics associated with the Serpent Cult of Dann and ancient stela of Nimrod, including an image which has become synonymous with Nazi Germany's "iron cross". This Nimrodian cross [bottom] is on the floor of the Knights Templar Room inside of the Grand Lodge of Freemasonry in Ireland. It is also on the ancient stela of Nimrod [pg.18, "B"]. As I mentioned earlier this cross like shape represents the "four quarters of the earth" [Revelation 20:8], whereas the circle contains 'secret knowledge' regarding the actual shape of God's creation [Planet Earth], which I will reveal to you in subsequent pages. Please keep in mind that these same Templar Room, logos, etc. are found inside 'The George Washington Masonic National Memorial' in Alexandria, Virginia USA.

29

Additional relics, inside the Grand Lodge of Freemasonry in Ireland, include: Skull & Bones wall art, venerating the Serpent Death Cult; Upside down crosses; Pyramid shaped tables containing three goat legs, venerating the demon gods Pan, Azazel and Baphomet. In relation to the stela of Nimrod [pg.18], a display case inside of the Grand Lodge of Ireland contains two scepters [left] which match the scepter held by the Babylonian god Nimrod 'E'. The display case also contains a number of "666" Stars of Remphan [Satan].

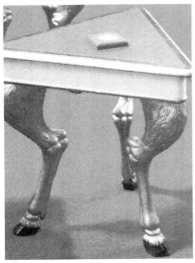

Naturally Dublin, Ireland, is where a staggering scale of ritual abuse on Irish children takes place; much of this abuse is occult related. Rape Crisis Centers in Ireland were told so many "bizarre" tales of ritual abuse that a special help line was created for them.

Fiona Neary, the National Coordinator of the Rape Crisis Centers, said:

"We could be talking about high levels of organized abuse which could almost be beyond the belief of many of the agencies tasked with dealing with this problem. Although it is unrecognized, ritual abuse does take place in Ireland and survivors of this type of abuse live here. Elaborate ritual, group activities, religious, magical or supernatural beliefs and practices [The Church of Babylon] may be used to terrify and silence children and to convince them of the absolute power of their abusers. The purpose of these rituals is to gain and maintain access to children in order to exploit them sexually. There is also evidence that some of the groups would exchange children to other groups abroad."

Throughout the following pages, I provide ample data regarding the ancient Church of Babylon's vendetta against people of

Celtic and Pictish origin. One example is how thousands of children of Celtic ancestry are clandestinely sacrificed to Gilles de rais' Old World Satan every year. For instance in 2014, the International Common Law Court of Justice (LCLCJ) in Brussels is investigating numerous children's murders connected to the Ninth Circle Satanic Child Sacrifice Cult network. Death certificates were released on the 796 Irish children, ages two months to nine years, found in a cistern (septic tank) used as a mass grave at the Catholic St. Mary's Mothers and Babies Home near Taum, Ireland. LCLCJ forensic experts have confirmed the decapitation and dismemberment of babies in the mass grave resembled the usual signs of ritualistic murder. The Ninth Circle was/ is directly linked to underground Satanic Cult networks throughout American including a large one in South Dakota.

One last artifact found inside of the Grand Lodge of Freemasonry in Ireland, which demonstrates that the Christian God of the Holy Bible is the Serpent Cults only obstacle to re-establishing "Babylon" and their One World Religion here on earth, is the Holy Bible on page 25. On its spine and cover we see the following serpent cult binding spells:

- FIG.1 - These icons represent the Sun and Moon god and like the compass and square symbolize an androgyne creature which appears to be both male and female. The androgyne symbolizes the hermaphrodite principle of the two-faced entity or two-headed eagle, commonly associated with Freemasonry. In the Cabala, this amalgamation represents the feminine and masculine principle known as "Adam Kadmon," [Adam and Eve] otherwise known as Golem. This combination of opposites is part of alchemy, or hermeticism, which is beloved by the Serpent Cult. In witchcraft, they refer to this principle as the joining of sun and moon, for which sacred sex rituals are shared. In Egyptian mythology Seth's siblings included Osiris and Isis. Seth's homosexual episodes with Horus resulted in the creation of the moon god Thoth, an ancient reproduction of the Babylonian moon god 'Sin', son of Enlil, and one of the Serpent Cults principle demon gods. The moon God is represented on the stela of Nirmod [pg.18,"I"]. Shamash, the 15ft tall giant sun

31

god [pg.18] is represented on the stela of Nimrod [pg.18,"J"]

- FIG.2 - An obelisk representing the Egyptian god Osiris' penis.

- FIG.3 - The Masonic compass and square which represents sex magic.

- FIG.4 - Two swords forming an "X" symbolizing the Serpent Cult of Dann. The "X" is comprised of two 7s which symbolize Cain.

- FIG.5 - Skull & Bones [Totenkopf] representing the Serpent death cult.

- FIG.6 - The star of Remphan [Satan] whose dimensions create The Mark of the Beast "666".

The aforementioned is not the Church of Babylon's first attempt at placing binding spells or curses on the cover of the Holy Bible. When the 1516 Erasmus' Greek/Latin New Testament, The Book that birthed the protestant movement; 1534 New Testament by William Tyndale; 1537 Matthews Bible, which eliminated the Catholic Church's confessional booth; 1560 Geneva Bible, created with the help of Scottish Reformer John Knox and brought by Puritans and the Pilgrims to America, was replaced with the 1611 King James Bible, we see one of the very first binding spells placed on its cover. I would like to stress the fact that the 'art work' on the exterior of the King James Bible in no way effects the text inside.

Next we're going to examine the title pages of the 1611 and 1769 versions of the King James Bible [pg.34] and discuss what I believe are binding spells placed by the Serpent Cult. The 1611 version is on top and the 1769 version is on the bottom. The image below features the upper right portion of the 1611 King James Bible and as you can clearly see there is an exact replica of the moon symbol featured on the stela of Nimrod [p.14,"I'] which to the Church of Babylon represents the demon god 'Sin'. The moon symbol is then surrounded by 6qty, six-pointed stars. To the Church of Babylon the quantity of stars here represent the number of man. All of

these symbols are hovering above the word of God which symbolizes man being above God. It will be remembered that the six pointed star represents "The Star of Remphan" [Acts 7:43] and that a six pointed star is comprised of two pyramids containing the dimensions "666".

The next binding spell is located on the left-hand side of the 1611 title page. Here the artist has drawn the original twelve tribes of Israel including a shield with a serpent on the front, commemorating the Serpent Cult of Dann. [Genesis 49:17].

The title page from the 1769 King James Bible features a similar Sun and Moon graphic, however what's most interesting is the artists rendition of St. Andrew holding a cross symbol. Legend tells us that Scotland's 'X' flag represents St. Andrew who is said to have been martyred by crucifixion at the city of Patras (Patræ) in Achaea, on the northern coast of the Peloponnese. However the Acts of Andrew known to Gregory of Tours c.538, refute these claims describing St. Andrew as being bound, not nailed, to a Latin cross of the kind on which Jesus was crucified; however, when Knights Templar's, representing the Serpent Cult of Dann, escaped execution in France and arrived in Scotland c.1314 they established the blasphemous tradition that St. Andrew had been crucified on an X-shaped cross signifying the Serpent Cult, which is now commonly known as "Saint Andrew's Cross."

Based on the images of Luciferian scars placed upon The Holy Bible by the Church of Babylon, coupled with the collection of knowledge in previous pages, it's no wonder the Pilgrims fled England in 1620. It's also logical to conclude, given the fact that nobody has pointed these facts out in over 403 years, that all religions have, in the immortal words of Officer Jonathan Williams, been secretly 'permeated with Judaism'. However what Officer Williams thought was 'Judaism' is in fact Khazarian Babylonian Talmudism which has no relation to the Holy Torah [Old Testament], or Christianity's New Testament. It too would seem as though Officer Jonathan Williams predicted accurately when he parroted General Cornwallis' telling of a clandestine spiritual infiltration throughout Christianity that would occur without Christians even realizing the transformation of Jesus Christ's message had happened. 33

THE
HOLY
BIBLE,

Conteyning the Old Testa-
ment, and the New:

There is one last image I would like to leave with you as it relates to King James of Scotland. It is a piece of physical evidence which I believe accurately depicts the level of vitriol the Church of Babylon had for this great man who gave us the preserved word of God inside of the King James Bible.

The vast majority of Christian American's today are unaware of the fact that the Vatican, in response to Scottish King James I creation of the King James Bible (1604-1611), which accurately depicted a literal 6 day creation, quickly fabricated the 'Rosicrucian Manifestos' c.1614. The Rosicrucian Manifestos were documents that inspired Adam Weishaupt to create the Illuminati in 1776. The Vatican also created the Pontifical Academy of Sciences (PAC) c.1604 in preparation for what they anticipate will be a fire storm of controversy, not the least of which was the revealing of the Catholic Church' Babylonian centric secret order that for centuries had deceived Scotsman, Irish and Normans into submission through the use of Satanic binding spells and Serpent Cult traditions.

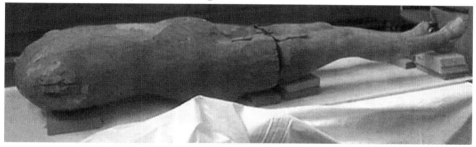

Throughout King James life the Vatican worked feverishly to destroy the legacy of King James and the only Bible in history which accurately translated ancient Biblical texts. Acts of desperation on behalf of the Vatican towards the Scottish King included decapitating his mother, Mary Queen of Scots, intimidating nations associated with King James global peace missions and finally the desecration of King James perfectly featured burial effigy [above] by tearing off its head, feet and arms.

An interesting footnote to the legacy of King James is that Barbara Pierce who became Barbara Bush, the wife of former CIA Director/President George H.W. Bush and mother to former President George W. Bush is a descendant of, "Thomas Percy", who tried to blow up King James I in what would become known as the, "Gun Powder Plot" of 1605. Another interesting fact is that Barbara's mother, "Pauline Pierce" and Satanist Aleister Crowley were lovers. Crowley is the man who once said, "I want blasphemy, murder, rape, revolution, anything, bad or good, but strong." Pauline is known to have travelled to France to participate in sex magic rituals with Crowley. Following one of Pauline's sex magic three-ways in France with Crowley and Marvin Pierce the McCall Corp. President

35

and descendant of 14th President of the U.S., Franklin Pierce. Upon returned to the U.S. Pauline learned that she was pregnant. It is alleged that Barbara Pierce-Bush is the daughter of Satanist Aleister Crowley. On 9/23/1949 [666] Irish American Pauline Robinson-Pierce was sacrificed on Purchase St. at 8:12 a.m. in a car being driven by Marvin Pierce.

This is the same woman who had this to say about our military men and women dying in combat:

"Why should we hear about body bags and deaths, and how many? It's not relevant. So, why should I waste my beautiful mind on something like that"
– Barbara Bush 3/18/2003 on Good Morning America

Other well-known organizations throughout the United States whose logos can be traced back to the Church of Babylon and their Babylonian god Nimrod include the Ancient Arabic Order of the Nobles of the Mystic Shrine, also commonly known as Shriners and abbreviated A.A.O.N.M.S.

Established in 1870 Shriners is an appendant body to Freemasonry, based in the United States. The organization is best-known for the Shriners Hospitals for Children they administer and the red fez hats with black tassel. The organization describes itself as a fraternity based on fun, fellowship and the Masonic principles of brotherly love, relief, and truth.

First, let's address the twisted logic that Shriners by its own admission is the fun division of satanic Freemasonry and that their fraternity is based on 'love' and 'truth'.

What makes the Shriners mission statement so perverse is the fact that the fez represents barbarism and the subjugation and slaughter of Christians. The name fez is taken from the ancient Moroccan City Fez, founded 789 AD by the Idrisid Dynasty. Prior to its founding this area consisted of tribes which were mostly Christian, Jewish, Khariji [Muslim] or Pagan. The founder of the Idrisid Dynasty was a man named, "Idris ibn Abdallah" [788-791], who traced his ancestry back to, "Ali ibn Abi Talib" and his wife, "Fatimah," daughter of the Islamic prophet, Muhammad.

36

In an account dating back to 8th century AD, Muslims ascended onto a Christian settlement within Fez, Morocco murdering an estimated 50,000 Christians. Following the slaughter of these Christian men, women and children, Muslim's dipped their caps into the blood soaks streets as a testimony to their god Allah. These Christian blood soaked caps were considered a badge of honor and eventually became what we know today as the fez cap. According to the book, "The Mystic Shrine, An Illustrated Ritual of the Ancient Arabic Order of Nobles of the Shrine, (1975 Ed., pp. 20-22), the Shriners blood oath and confession of Allah as god is advocated. In other words Shriner members worship the god of Islam, not the God of the Holy Bible. What's more Shriners endorse the slaughter of Christians whenever they parade around in fez, which symbolize Christian blood soaked caps.

The perversion of the Shriners mission statement is further amplified when you consider the fact that elite Babylonian Talmudists such as Rothschild, Rockefeller, etc. have intentionally sickened our Children with genetically modified organisms such as Corn, Wheat, Soy and sugar and neurotoxins such as Fluoride and Chlorine. All of these substances are augmented when children are injected with vaccines containing live viruses, mercury, formaldehyde, etc. If these man-made abominations never existed, Shriners Hospitals wouldn't be needed. It's akin to McDonalds opening up a weight loss or cancer treatment center.

In relation to the stela of Nimrod [pg.18], Shriners Crescent Moon and Star logo [left] is featured next to letters "G" and "T". Shriner's "fez" hat w/tassel [left] is featured on the stela of Nimrod [pg.18, "A"].

Earlier I mentioned how the cross on the stela of Nimrod [pg.18, "B"] has become synonymous with Adolf Hitler's Nazi "Iron Cross". Unsurprisingly Hitler was a proponent of the Church of Babylon; in fact the vast majority of Nazi iconography emulated ancient Serpent Cult relics. In fact Hitler voiced his admiration for these elements, stating:

"All the supposed abominations, the skeletons and death's head, the coffins and the mysteries, are mere bogeys for children. But there is one dangerous element and that is the element I have copied from them. They form a sort of priestly nobility. They have developed an esoteric doctrine more merely formulated, but imparted through the symbols and mysteries in degrees of initiation [Babylonian god Nimrod]. The hierarchical organization and the initiation through symbolic rites, that is to say, without bothering the brain by working on the imagination through magic and the symbols of a cult, all this has a dangerous element, and the element I have taken over [Babylonian demon god Pazuzu]. Don't you see that our party must be of this character? An Order, the hierarchical Order of a secular priesthood."
- Adolf Hitler c.1938, from the book titled: 'Conversations with Hitler' by Hermann Rauschning

Because Rauschning portrayed Hitler as an admirer of the Church of Babylon, Swiss historian and Church of Babylon member, Wolfgang Haenel in 1983 announced at a revisionist "history conference" in West Germany, that 'Conversations with Hitler', was a total fraud. To accomplish this, the Journal of Historical Review, for instance, uses Hitler's economic advisor Otto Wagener who wrote, "Hitler: Memoirs of a Confidant" [1929-1932] while being held in a Rothschild controlled British prison. Wagener's memoirs weren't published until 1977, forty-five years after Rauschning wrote his memoirs.

In truth, Rauschning' account of Hitler hearing voices, waking at night with convulsive shrieks and pointing in terror at demons in empty corners while shouting "There, there, in the corner!" is consistent with accounts made by other historical figures who have offered up their souls to demons. It suggests that Hitler's attempt at controlling the 'dangerous element' [Satan] failed.

SOL SUN

In 1933, Hitler told Hermann Rauschning in an interview that like the Serpent Death Cult, he [Hitler] intended to, "stamp out Christianity root and branch" so it comes as no surprise that Hitler's Nazi party endorsed the Church of Babylon all throughout Germany and the World during WWII. Even today, deceived young men and women espouse Nazi "White Supremacy" believing that they're promoting "White Power" and some kind of ancient European heritage, when in fact they're

38

exalting Satan's Serpent Tribe of Dann, Nimrod and Masonic Babylonian Talmudism [Khazars], through one of the most recognizable logos to have ever existed on planet earth, the Nazi Swastika.

The vast majority of Americans today are unaware of the fact that the Swastika [pg.38][is comprised of two 'Sol' or 'Sig'. This is a Germanic Rune which represents the sound for the Roman 'S' and in Old Norse means 'Sun'. In relation to the stela of Nimrod [pg.18] the letter 'B' is next to the icon representing 'Sun'. What's more, the inner most portion of a Swastika creates an 'X' which symbolizes the Serpent Cult. In relation to the stone carving of Nimrod [pg.18], the 'X' is portrayed next to the letter 'C'. The Nazi Swastika was regularly featured inside of a circle and an 'X' or cross inside of a circle is the Roman numeral for 1000, and 1000 in Greek is Helius, another name for Apollyon the destroyer [The Beast] from The Book of Revelation. The "X" is also comprised of four 7s symbolizing Cain and the "four quarters of the earth" [Revelation 20:8].

Like the Nazi Swastika, the following Nazi icons all venerate the Serpent Cult. The first image features an eagle holding a Swastika inside of a circle [Apollyon]. The eagle here represents the son or messenger of Zeus 'IO' [EO] Hermes or 'Mercury' otherwise known as Apollyon The Destroyer [The Beast]. The next image of a Nazi Iron Cross is in fact a Sumerian cuneiform sign and logo-syllabic depicting the Serpent Cult. In relation to the stone carving of Nimrod, the Nazi Iron cross is portrayed in both "C" and "B". The last image in this cluster is of two swords crossing. This logo in fact depicts what is commonly referred to as the "double-cross". In modern terms the 'XX' means to double-cross or betray. Fundamentally speaking it indicates 39 one's willingness to betray on behalf of Satan. The "XX" is also an abbreviated version of the double-helix Serpent Cult logo. The final image features the Nazi Field Marshall Flag, this too depicts the double-cross.

"Surely, if masons really understood what Masonry is, as it is delineated in these books, no Christian Mason would think himself to remain at liberty to remain another day a member of the fraternity. It is as plain as possible that a man, knowing what it is, and embracing it in his heart, cannot be a Christian man. To say he can is to belie the very nature of Christianity."
- Irish American evangelist Charles Finney, responsible for the Christian revival throughout America c.1830, Book titled: FREEMASONRY Pg.115

President George H.W. Bush's father, Prescott Bush, and his maternal grandfather, George Herbert Walker were both powerful financial supporters of Adolf Hitler. Herbert Walker was the President of Union Banking Corporation, a Nazi money-laundering vehicle known to have helped the satanic Rothschild family, funnel vast amounts of money into Hitler's political and military forces.

A 1934 U.S. Congressional investigation showed that Walker, who acquired the shipping assets of North American operations of Hamburg-Amerika, was in fact supporting Nazi espionage activity. It was onboard Amerika ships that Nazi agents were smuggled. What's more vast amounts of money were smuggled through Walker's shipping group where it was then used to bribe American politicians so that they would support Hitler.

Two months prior to the 1988 presidential election, the Washington Jewish Week newspaper released information which suggested that a coalition representing Bush's campaign was comprised of Nazis and anti-Semites. They included:

Nicholas Nazarenko, leader of a Cossack GOP ethnic unit. Nazarenko was an ex-Nazi Waffen SS officer.

Radi Slavoff, GOP Heritage Council's executive director, and head of "Bulgarians for Bush." Slavoff was a member of a Bulgarian fascist group, and he put together an event in Washington honoring Holocaust denier, Austin App.

Florian Galdau, director of GOP outreach efforts among Romanians, and head of "Romanians for Bush." Galdau was once an Iron Guard recruiter, and he defended convicted Nazi war criminal Valerian Trifa.

Method Balco, GOP activist. Balco organized yearly memorials for a Nazi puppet regime.

Walter Melianovich, head of the GOP's Byelorussian unit. Melianovich worked closely with many Nazi groups.

Bohdan Fedorak, leader of "Ukrainians for Bush." Fedorak headed a Nazi group involved in anti-Jewish wartime programs.

Previously I shared with you facts surrounding the oldest freemasonry lodge in England [926 AD] and its association with King Solomon's Temple [c.926 BC]. We've also examined how Hitler's Nazi Party exalted the Serpent Cult. The Church of Babylon teach that the founder of Freemasonry was, "Hiram Abiff" and that Abiff's ancestors were Cain, father of TubalCain, Lamech and the "Tribe of Naphtali", an ancient tribe of Pharisee worshipping Talmudists [Khazars] who along with the demon god Pazuzu and Lucifer built King Solomon's Temple.

"If Cain shall be avenged sevenfold, truly Lamech seventy and sevenfold. [777]" - Genesis 4:24

The number 7 is considered 'magical' by the Serpent Death Cult and is associated with The Church of Babylon's revenge of Lamech. This resonates 7, 11, and 77 because Lamech's revenge of 77 is 11 times Cain's 7. The patriarch of the Rothschild Family, Izaak Elchanan Rothschild, was born 1577 and would be the one to adopt the "666" star of Remphan as the family logo. On 1776 both the Illuminati and America were founded. JFK was sacrificed near highway 77. Timothy McVeigh exploded a truck in Oklahoma City that he rented along US 77. Both the Waco massacre and Oklahoma City bombing were on Hwy 77. Flight 77 flew into the Pentagon at 77 degrees longitude. The Pentagon was designed by Satanist Jack Parsons who wrote the following statement in his diary, "And thus was I Antichrist loosed in the world; and to this am I pledged, that the work of the beast shall be fulfilled, and the way for the coming of BABALON be made open and I shall not cease or rest until these things are accomplished." – Texe Marrs, Codex Magica. Parson's mentor was Satanist Aleister Crowley who wrote a book titled, "777" and believed the god Pan was the Wizard of Oz, and attributed to him the number 77. The second plane hit the 77th floor of the South Tower on 9/11. Together the "Twin Towers" created the number 11. George H.W. Bush' son, Marvin Pierce Bush, was director of, "SECURACOM" from 1996-2001 and was responsible for security at United Airlines and the World Trade Center in NY until 9/11. On 9/11 Marvin's brother President George W. Bush was filmed inside of a school classroom while children read aloud the following words, "Kite, Hit, Steel, Plane, Must... The pet goat [baphomet]." Overlooking the events of 9/11 was the Freemason created Statue of Liberty which stands on an 11 pointed star pedestal while wearing a 7 pointed crown [7x11=77]. 41

What's interesting is that Hiram Abiff's 'Tribe of Naphtali' literally translates to 'My Struggle', precisely the name Adolf Hitler chose for his book 'Mein Kampf' which translates to "My Struggle". And in keeping with the Serpent Cults ancient ambitions to exterminate the Celtic and Pictish bloodline, Adolf Hitler, During WWII, aggressively targeted the Scottish people.

In his book titled, "Luftwaffe Over Scotland", Les Taylor describes vividly how 240 of Hitler's Nazi airplanes performed at least 500 mass bombings over Scotland, dropping more than 1,000 tons of explosive. Taylor states:

"Following the summer of 1940, the nature of those attacks turned to terror bombings against civilians."

During his research, Taylor read through hundreds of documents from municipal authorities, the German military, the former Scottish Office, newspaper clippings, the Imperial War Museum and interviewed eye witnesses. Taylor states:

"From that first attack until the Battle of Britain, all the action took place over Scotland... It has never been explained before why so many people were killed in that raid."

When one examines all of the evidence surrounding Adolf Hitler's Nazi Party what's clear is that Hitler, like many historical figures before him, was a member of the Church of Babylon and towards the end of his reign he became tormented by demons. It was this demonic influence which demanded the lives of tens of millions of human beings, including more than 66 million Christians during WWII. Unsurprisingly Hitler's grandmother was an employee for the Rothschild family and is said to have become pregnant by a Rothschild leading to the birth of Adolf's father, Alois Hitler. What's more Hitler's favorite books to read were those written by his favorite author and founder of Theosophy, Helena Blavatsky. His favorite Blavatsky book was titled, "The Secret Doctrine: The Synthesis of Science, Religion, and Philosophy" [1888]. Coincidently Helena Blavatsky was a direct descendant of Russian Babylonian Talmudist Princess, "Helene Dolgoruki". Helena' grandmother was a daughter of Henrietta **Adolf**ovna. Another connection between Hitler and the Church of Babylon is the fact that the Reichstag fire, which was pivotal in the establishment of Nazi Germany, was caused by a Freemason 2/27/19**33**. Furthermore, Adolf Hitler chose to start the Second World War on September 1, 1939. To the Church of Babylon the number 39 is "magical" because it represents 3x**13**, the number of the pagan trinity times the number of extreme rebellion.

42

Americans have been brainwashed into believing Hitler's Nazi Party was destroyed in the 1940s and died in a bunker with Hitler 4/30/1945. Truth be told the Nazi icon, which venerated the Serpent Cult during the 40s, still exists throughout the Americas, U.K., etc. For example in 1967 the United States Government constructed a Naval Base building [top] near San Diego which is in the shape of a Nazi Swastika [7777].

43

Pope Benedict XVI 2005-2013 [above] was a Nazi youth,

who subscribed to Freemasonry. It explains the Popes decision to schedule his New York City 'Ground Zero' visit on April 20, 2008 the highlight of the Nazi calendar. Why? This was Adolf Hitler's Birthday. The 20th of April was declared a National Holiday throughout Germany in the 40's, and every year the Hitler youth initiated a new crop of ten year old children as a gift to Hitler. Being a dedicated former Hitler Youth himself, Joseph Aloisius Ratzinger a.k.a. Pope Benedict XVI would have realized the significance of April 20. As an aside the self proclaimed bisexual Nazis who committed the Columbine Massacre understood the significance of April 20th as well. This is the day they chose to sacrifice 12 children.

"The origin of freemasonry must be attributed to perverted Judaism [Talmudism]." - Joseph Lehman, Catholic Priest

In 1829, Pope Pius VIII, speaking of the Serpent Cult: "Their Law is Untruth: Their God is the Devil and their Cult is Turpitude" Pope Pius VIII was dead just 20 months after that statement.

In 1884 Pope Leo XIII said about the Church of Babylon: "We wish it to be your rule first of all to tear away the mask from Freemasonry and to let it be seen as it really is... Filled with the spirit of Satan, who knows how to transform himself into an angel of light, Freemasonry puts forward as its pretended aim the good of humanity. Paying a lip service to the authority of law, and even to the obligations of religion, it aims at the destruction of civil authority and the Christian priesthood, both of which it regards as the foes of human liberty."

"The pope is not only the representative of Jesus Christ, but he is Jesus Christ, Himself, hidden under the veil of flesh."
- Catholic National, July 1895.

"The pope doeth whatsoever he [wills], even things unlawful, and is more than God." - quoted by Newton, p. 456.

"For the Son of God became man so that we might become God."
- Catechism of the Catholic Church, Ignatius Press p.116, p.129 in 2nd edition by Doubleday Publishing.

In 2012 Pope Benedict XVI called for global 'wealth redistribution' as did Pope Francis in 2014. The world must understand that centrally controlled global wealth redistribution is a chief component to the Church of Babylon's 'New World Order' system.

The malicious and duplicitous nature of Papal authority has been well documented throughout world history. One event in particular exemplifies Papal authority's double-dealing spirit. In 2008 it was discovered that Pope Innocent XI, prior to his death [1689 AD] secretly funded the Catholic, James II and the Protestant, William of Orange [1690], "Battle of the Boyne," which is celebrated by Irish Protestants, while at the same time financing weapons and resources which would lead to the enslavement of Irish Catholics. Eight years prior to his death, Pope Innocent XI issued an edict [10/30/1682] ordering the closing of all Jewish-owned banks in Rome, which bankrupted the Jewish community.

Now that you have an understanding of the incestuous nature of the Church of Babylon and a heightened awareness of its many tentacles, let's return back to our examination of our seemingly upright wealthy businessman in Sacramento, CA, Mark Friedman.

Friedman's business partner, majority owner of the Sacramento Kings and CEO and Founder of Tibco Software is Vivek Ranadivé from India. On several occasions Ranadivé has said that his vision for the Sacramento Kings arena and every other NBA team is that they will be, "cashless and ticketless". Anyone who is against a global technocratic dictatorship must be aware of the fact that a primary weapon being used by the Church of Babylon to indoctrinate the masses into accepting "The Mark of the Beast" [666] is a cashless system, whereby a mark will be required to buy and sell goods.

Readers may be surprised to learn that the "Mark of the Beast" agenda has been perpetrated by a number of companies and individuals over the years. My personal experience with this was in 2013 when I was approached by a representative of, "SmartPay, Inc." whose CEO and Founder, "Tom Heeter" was seeking financing for his patent [#5,878,155] Point of Sale [POS] system. The Abstract of Tom Heeter's patent reads:

"A method is presented for facilitating sales transactions by electronic media. A bar code or a design is tattooed on an individual. Before the sale transaction can be consummated, the tattoo is scanned with a scanner. Characteristics about the scanned tattoo are compared to characteristics about other tattoos stored on a computer database in order to verify the identity of the buyer."

If you've ever read the Holy Bible, Tom Heeter's patent is nearly a carbon copy of the "Mark of the Beast" prophesy which reads:

"And he causeth all, both small and great, rich and poor, free and bond, to receive a mark in their right hand, or in their foreheads. And that no man might buy or sell, save he that had the mark, or the name of the beast, or the number of his name [666]." - Revelation 13:16-17

Combine the abstract of Tom Heeter's patent with his history of being disbarred from the Texas State Bar in 2002 for "mental health issues"; accusations of offering a "$50,000 bribe to Judge T.O. Stansbury"; accusations of threatening bodily injury with a gun and lying about his county of residence in order to run for Democratic public office and you'll understand why I rejected the invitation to participate in this 'opportunity.'

Shortly after dismissing this prospect I was presented with the disturbing revelation that Tom Heeter's State Bar of Texas contact information contained Heet [heat], Lyer [liar] and "666": Mr. Thomas Webster **Heet**er, 55 **Lyer**ly St. Houston, TX 77022, (713-**666**-3548)

Since Heeter's "Mark of the Beast" patent, individuals and Corporations have developed more modern day versions of the 'Mark of the Beast'. These include Sony Corporation's 'Smart Wig' patent and Motorola's 'e-tattoo', which the company claims can read your thoughts, as well as Google Corporation's anti-Christian engineering director, Ray Kurzweil, who once said: "Does God exist? Not yet." is developing a 'bridge-to-bridge' system, or what I like to call a spycloud control network, powered by advanced 'D-Wave' quantum annealing processors based on Shor's algorithm. It's this 'bride-to-bridge' system Kurzweil posits will empower those who accept his mark with god like powers e.g., immortality, etc., calling to mind Aristotle's recalling of Homer's account of the god Hephaestus's robotic workers made of gold c.850 B.C. In reality, Ray Kurzweils 'singularity' and vision of artificial Intelligence [AI], Spy-Cloud Computing, etc. are woefully anemic versions of what Church of Babylon members have known for centuries to be a superior infinite universal system of divine knowledge, a spiritually and technologically superior exchange, which has existed between God and his creation [Man] for over 6,000 years. Church of Babylon members and their god Satan are fully aware of God's divine communication network, ancient universal database, and heavenly infrastructure; after all, Satan was once a subscriber. It's from this ancient divine superhighway that the concept of 'singularity' was born. Since his creation, Satan's objective has always been to tether Man's spiritual being to Satan's domain [earth] forcing Man to worship him forever, deceiving Man from God's infinite universal system of knowledge and salvation. Misleading Man into accepting an infinitely inferior simulation of exponential knowledge, eternally cutoff from his creator, deceived into believing that one day he too shall become a god.

"For we know that if our earthly house of this tabernacle [idiom for a temporary dwelling/body] were dissolved, we have a building of God, an house [permanent more complex dwelling/spiritual body] not made with hands, eternal in the heavens. For in this we groan, earnestly desiring to be clothed upon with our house which is from heaven" -

46

Kurzweil's singularity theory is an ancient demonic concept and nowhere is the fingerprints of iniquity and prophecy more evident than in the King James Holy Bible. When we juxtapose Jude 1:6 and 1 John 3:2 with that of Google Engineering Director Ray Kurzweil's singularity theory [merging man with machine] we begin to see similarities between Kurzwiel's deception and Satan's goal of maintaining spiritual custody of Man. Through the imprisonment of Satan's singularity, Man is prohibited from ever "seeing him [Jesus Christ] as he is".

"And the angels [fallen angels] which kept not their first estate [principality of angels or demons], but left their own habitation [dwelling], he hath reserved in everlasting chains under darkness unto the judgment of the great day." - Jude 1:6

"Beloved, now are we the sons of God, and it doth not yet appear what we shall be: but we know that, when he [Jesus Christ] shall appear, we shall be like him; for we shall see him as he is." - 1 John 3:2

Former Defense Advanced Research Projects Agency [DARPA] Director, turned Google executive Regina Dugan, is promoting an edible microchip and electronic tattoo that will be able to read your mind. I believe this is why there has been a major push by the entertainment industry to promote tattoos as trendy and cool. Simply put, the American population is being desensitized to the idea of tattooing themselves with 'The Mark of the Beast'. I too believe, Motorola and Google's 'mind reading' technology is being developed to one day validate the sincerity of those who are willingly accepting the 'Mark of the Beast' [666] in their hand and/or forehead. I predict this technology will allow administrators for the Antichrist to efficiently identify and eliminate those who are subconsciously adverse to Satan's New World Order.

The Walt Disney Company is also doing its part to promote the 'Mark of the Beast' with its new FCC registered RFID tracking modules, artfully named 'Magic Bands'. Aside from not exceeding general radiated emission levels set by the dubious Federal Government over a spread spectrum network which shares systems supporting critical Government requirements such as the 'Real ID Act' of 2005, Disney's Magic Bands indoctrinate guests into accepting a device on their wrists in order to buy goods, access their hotel rooms, enter the parks, acquire fast passes, etc. Prior to being assembled in China, Disney's 'Magic Bands' are developed by Synapse Product Development LCC in Seattle, WA, which also develops DNA field analysis devices. I demonstrate in future chapters how Disney is one of the biggest promoters of the 'Mark of the Beast' [666]. Whatever 47 the method or technology I believe one thing is certain. The Mark of the Beast will be incompatible with God created DNA. In Revelation 16:2,11 we are told that the mark will become a "grievous sore upon the men which had the mark of the beast". In other words the area the mark is placed will become horribly infected, spreading throughout the entire body rendering the mark useless therefore collapsing the Antichrist' economic system.

The following are a few of the top biometrics corporations that are promoting 'Mark of the Beast' technology, companies whose names are associated with ancient demons, they include:

• **Kronos** (www.kronos.com) - named after an ancient demonic deity, who is the parallel version of Moloch and the Greek equivalent of Ba'al Hammon. This was a demon that child sacrifices were made to. As a matter of fact in 1921 an archeological dig at Carthage revealed 20,000 urns containing the cremated remains of infants and children age six. They were all sacrificed out of reverence to the demon god Kronos.

• **Argus Global** (www.argus-global.com) - named after an all-seeing- primordial giant.

• **Kairos** (www.kairos.com) is named after the Greek demon of opportunity and timing, the youngest son of Zeus. Ever heard the saying "the right place at the right time"? In Greek times they would ascribe this saying with giving your allegiance to the demon of opportunity. This is also the exact word the demons used when they asked him if he had come to torment them "…before the time" – Matthew 8:29.

• **Corvus Biometrics** (www.corvusid.com) named after the black raven that Apollo put in the heavens, who longs to drink the sacred waters protected by the giant hydra, a serpent-like monster with reptilian traits.

• **Griaule Biometrics** (www.griaulebiometrics.com) named after a gigantic red dragon [Satan].

• **Neokoros** (www.neokoros.com) named after the three famous temples 'thrice neokoros' in the city of Pergamous where the emperors were worshipped as gods and where the Altar of Zeus was located.

John, the writer of the Book of Revelation said that Pergamous is the place where Satan's Seat is located:

"And to the angel of the church in Pergamos write; These things saith he which hath the sharp sword with two edges; I know thy works, and where thou dwellest, even where Satan's seat is: and thou holdest fast my name, and hast not denied my faith, even in those days wherein Antipas was my faithful martyr, who was slain among you, where Satan dwelleth." – Revelation 2:12-13.

In 2008 Freemason President Barack Hussein Obama, while in Berlin gave a speech near The Altar of Zeus ["Satan's Seat"] housed in the Pergamom Museum [above]. Obama told those in attendance that 'The world it stands as one' which is of course a reference to a New World Order or One World Religion controlled by the Antichrist. Then upon returning to the United States President Barack Hussein Obama commissions the construction of a replica of the Altar of Zeus [Satan's Seat] from which he made his party's acceptance speech [above].

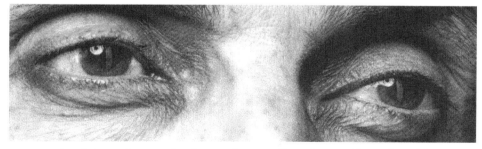

Applying what you've learned, regarding the profile and ambitions of the Serpent Cult, please consider the front cover of Sactown Magazine Oct/Nov 2013, which features a picture of Mark Friedman's business partner and majority owner of the Sacramento Kings, Vivek Ranadivé, with what appears to be serpent eyes.

Taking into account the decision of both Ranadivé and Friedman to incorporate the Rothschild's "Star of Remphan" into the design of the Sacramento Kings Arena, I thought that it would be prudent to demonstrate the connection between Ranadivé, Friedman, Rothschild and the Serpent Cult.

49

On 1917 Walter Rothschild drafted the "Balfour Declaration" which created the state of Israel. Nine months later the Rothschild Family laid the cornerstone for the Hebrew University of Jerusalem (HUJ), an institution that has relied heavily on Rothschild grants since July 24, 1918. Twenty-years later the Rothschild Family hired sculptor, "Yitzhak Danziger" (1938-1939) to create a 35 inch tall amphibious half-man statue named "Nimrod" [pg.146] for the HUJ. The governor of HUJ is, Tad Taube. Tad is also the founder of the, "Taube Foundation for Jewish Life & Culture" to which Vivek Ranadivé is a contributor.

Another organization controlled by the Rothschild's is the, "Israel Today Magazine", [top] who in July 2012 featured a blatant serpent all-seeing-eye on their magazines front cover. In addition to the Serpent Eye, the Rothschild's included a tip-of-the-hat, to others within the Church of Babylon by designating this issue "THE APPLE OF GOD'S [Satan's] EYE."

The Rothschild's even chose a serpent as the official Israeli armed forces mascot. All Israeli "Flying Serpent" Special Forces Battalions [center] and Paratrooper units are named after serpents. Such as: Cobra, Viper, Echis, Naja, Coluber, Taipan and Eryx. This particular logo represents the Israeli 35th Paratroopers Brigade.

One more example of how the Serpent Cult of Dann hides in plain sight can be seen in the Adventist Community Health Centre logo [bottom]. This not for profit group is under the umbrella of SDA Corp. a worldwide organization which runs a total of 775 health institutions including hospitals, nursing homes, clinics and dispensaries; they also control more than 6,966 [666] schools

& universities from over 200 countries from primary to college. Again what satanic elites are broadcasting here is that their "God" is in fact Lucifer.

Mark Friedman is also an investor in the Major League Soccer Franchise 'Sacramento Republic FC' along with Buzz Oates Group of Companies Chairman Phil Oates, Pacific Coast Building Products President Dave Lucchetti, UFC Champion Urijah Faber, Sleep Train CEO Dale Carlsen, O1 Communications founder Brad Jenkins, Visionary Integration Professionals CEO Jonna and Roger Ward, Kids Care Dental founder Dr. Aaron Reeves, Sacramento Jet Center President Scott Powell, Fahn Brother Properties founder Ken Fahn and the Benvenuti Family Trust.

Friedman also has close ties to President, Barack Hussein Obama [Barry Soetoro], the same President who signed into law 'NDAA', which allows the Government to incarcerate and arrest a person indefinitely without a trial. Obama is also a proponent of George H.W. Bush and Bill Clinton's 'Agenda 21', which seeks to steal all Private property away from Americans, herding its citizenry into cramped, government controlled multi-tenant units, similar to the units Friedman's Fulcrum Real Estate builds.

In 2008, the Friedman's hosted political fund-raisers for Barack Hussein Obama and Sacramento Mayor, Kevin Johnson, a man who is no stranger to misdeeds. Take for instance, the 2009 controversy which erupted over President Obama's firing of Inspector General Gerald Walprin who was investigating friend and fellow 'service' advocate Kevin Johnson for misusing AmeriCorps funds allocated to Hood Corps. Kevin Johnson is the founder of 'Hood Corps' which is associated with Corporation for National and Community Service, an umbrella organization under the Department of Homeland Security [DHS], a Government organization who is currently working to penetrate churches and other religious institutions with the intention of turning them into 'snitch' stations.

In April 2013, it was announced that Mark Friedman would hold a "substantial" position amongst a select group of investors focused on buying Mayor Kevin Johnson's former opponents, the Sacramento Kings, whose current ownership includes Irish/African American Freemason Shaquille O'Neal, a man who is aggressively campaigning for the Communist based Common Core State Standards and New Jersey Governor Chris Christie. In reference to Governor Christie, Shaq says 'he's a great man'. Given Shaq's association with The Church of Babylon it raises questions about the company Christie keeps. Shaq is also a member of Michelle Obama's "Let's Move" campaign which Mrs. Obama alleges was created to address the obesity epidemic throughout America. The 'technical foul' by Obama and Shaq is that President Obama's Administration has done everything in their power to ensure companies like Monsanto continue developing, growing and distributing toxic [GMO's] e.g., corn, soy, wheat, sugar, etc. which are in fact the real cause for the plague of physical and mental disease sweeping across America, including cancer, autism, etc. Coincidently Mark Friedman's wife, Marjorie Solomon, is an assistant professor in the Department of Psychiatry and Behavioral Sciences and according to the UC Davis MIND Institute website, Solomon's primary clinical work is focused on, "high-functioning children with autism spectrum disorders."

It doesn't surprise me in the least to discover men like Obama and Shaquille O'Neal teaming up to ensure the continuation of the Serpent Cult's ancient agenda of division and death. The truth of the matter is the Church of Babylon has preyed upon Africans and African Americans for centuries going as far back as c.1656. This is when African, Scottish, and Irish people became pawns in the ongoing ancient agenda of the Church of Babylon to eliminate the The Holy Bible and the legacy of Jesus Christ. When we carefully examine times past we discover the fingerprints of Babylonian Talmudists on every major religious conflict throughout world history beginning with the Crusades, and as I'll demonstrate next, they were in fact the architects of the Global Slave Trade and American Revolution.

WHAT IS A KHAZARIAN BABYLONIAN TALMUDIST?

Contrary to what many Christians may believe throughout America, so called "Jews" are in fact "Talmudists" and Talmudists are in no way descended from Abraham, nor are they spiritually connected to any of the Biblical prophets. Talmudists are in fact descendants of "King Bulan" and the pagan peoples of the Caucasus. The ancestors of so called "Jews" in Israel are not Israelites but Khazarians. The Khazarian Kingdom belief system was completely counter to the Holy Torah [Old Testament] and its religious ideology was based solely on the Babylonian Talmud. Khazarians were destroyers and the offspring of these filthy phallic worshippers e.g., The Rothschild Family believe that they are direct descendants of "Nimrod" who they believe was a mighty Babylonian god. Talmudists also believe that they are the only "humans" on planet earth, the rest of us are mere animals. To understand how toxic the disease of Babylonian Talmudism is to any society I've listed a few quotes from their 'holy' books. Please keep in mind that Mark Friedman's Family are Babylonian Talmudists.

"Jesus is in hell where he is boiling in hot excrement."
- Bablyonian Talmud, Gitten 57a

"A pregnant non-Jew is no better than a pregnant animal."
- Coschen Hamischpat 405

"Gentile [Christian] girls are in a state of niddah (filth) from birth. Christian women are regarded as slaves, heathen and whores. - Abodah Zarah 36b

"Although the non-Jew has the same body structure as the Jew, they compare with the Jew like a monkey to a human." - Schene Luchoth Haberith, p. 250b

"The Christians belong to the denying ones of the Torah (Talmud)."
- Coschen Hamischpat 425, Hagah 425, 5

"Although the non-Jew has the same body structure as the Jew, they compare with the Jew like a monkey to a human." - Schene Luchoth Haberith, p. 250b

"The Akum [Christian] is like a dog. Yes, the scripture teaches to honor the dog more than the Akum."
- Ereget Raschi Erod. 22 30

"Even though God created the non-Jew they are still animals in human form. It is not becoming for a Jew to be served by an animal. Therefore he will be served by animals in human form."
- Midrasch Talpioth, p. 255, Warsaw 1855

"All gentile children are animals."
- Yebamoth 98a

"If a Jew has a non-Jewish servant of maid who dies, one should not express sympathy to the Jew. You should tell to the Jew: God will replace your loss,' just as if one of his oxen or asses had died."
- Jore Dea 377, 1

"The souls of non-Jews come from impure spirits and are called pigs."
- Jalkut Rubeni gadol 12b

"It is the law to kill anyone who denies the Talmud.
- Talmud, Sanhedrin 59b

"It is permitted to take the body and the life of a non-Jew."
- Sepher Ikkarim IIIc, 25

"Sexual intercourse between non-Jews is like intercourse between animals." - Sanhedrin 74b

"Every Jew, who spills the blood of the godless (non-Jew), is doing the same as making a sacrifice to God."
- Bammidber Raba, c 21 & Jalkut 772

"The Jews are called human beings, but the non-Jews are not humans. They are beasts." - Talmud: Baba Mezia 114b

The Talmud's penalty for disobedience of the aforementioned laws is to be as follows "violation of any one of the seven [Noahide] laws subjects the Noahide to capital punishment by decapitation - Sanhedrin 57A."

The Talmud's penalty of decapitation brings to mind, "HB 1274" – Death penalty; guillotine provision signed by President Bill Clinton. The U.S. Army's inventory of 30,000 guillotines was confirmed by both retired FBI agent Ted Gunderso and ex-CIA official Bill Pawelec. Further, there are 500,000 caskets outside of Atlanta; 2.2 billion rounds of ammo at the Department of Homeland Security and 2700 armored DHS personnel carriers, "...and I saw the souls of them that were beheaded for the witness of Jesus, and for the word of God, and which had not worshipped the beast, neither his image, neither had received his mark upon their foreheads, or in their hands..." - Revelation 20:4

There are many resources available to expand your knowledge of the ancient Khazarian Kingdom. None are more revealing than Martin Luther's "On The Jews and Their Lies." Martin Luther [1483-1546] led the Protestant Reformation which denounced Papal authority. In regards to the Talmudists, Martin Luther summarized their "holy" book, The Babylonian Talmud as, "Raving, Frantic and Foolish Nonsense." Martin Luther repeatedly warned Christians of the threat posed by Talmudists. During one of his last addresses to his congregation, Martin Luther stated:

"You, Milords and men of authority, should not tolerate but expel them. They are our public enemies and incessantly blaspheme our Lord Jesus Christ; they call our blessed Virgin Mary a harlot and her Son, a bastard... If they could kill us all, they would gladly do so; in fact many of them murder Christians, especially those (Jews) professing to be surgeons and doctors. They know how to deal with medicaments in the manner of the Italians – the Borgias and Medicis – who gave people poisons which brought about their deaths in one hour or a month... As a good patriot, I wanted to give you this warning for the very last time to deter you from participating in alien sins. You must know I only desire the best for you all, rulers and subjects."

A wealth of knowledge may also be gained by examining the life of former Talmudist turned Christian, "Benjamin Freedman". As a former Talmudist, Freedman possessed first-hand knowledge of the ill will harbored against anyone who does not espouse Talmudism. Throughout his remaining years as a Christian, Freedman invested the vast majority of his $2.5 million dollar fortune on campaigns meant to warn the Christian American majority.

In 1961 Freedman presented his case in front of a packed crowd, inside of the Willard Hotel in Washington, D.C. During his speech Freeman exposed the ancient agenda of Khazars to dumb down, corrupt, bankrupt and eliminate anyone who does not subscribe to Masonic Babylonian Talmudism. Freedman's entire speech is on pg.xxx along with, "The Protocols Of The Learned Elders Of Zion," the Church of Babylon's c.900 AD blueprint for destroying the world. Another incredible resource is the book, "DNA Science and the Jewish Bloodline" by well-known researcher and author of three #1 national Christian bestsellers, Texe Marrs. Last but certainly not least is the must see video by Pastor Steven L. Anderson titled, "Marching to Zion" [**www.marchingtozion.com**].

Returning back to our examination of Babylonian Talmudist fingerprints on every major event throughout history, I would like to demonstrate how the descendants of Khazarian destroyers were the architects of the Global Slave Trade and American Revolution.

Hundreds of millions of educated people around the world have for centuries been under the false impression that the African Slave Trade was the sole responsibility of the Christian Europeans, "The White Race". In reality black African slavery was the brainchild of Islamic and Pre-Islamic Arab's who hunted, enslaved, tortured and killed ethnic Africans for thousands of years before the same geographical Arabs introduced the slave trade to Babylonian Talmudists who in comparison bought slaves for servitude.

In his book titled, "The Legacy of Arab-Islam In Africa", John Alembillah Azumah states about the history of Islamic Slavery:

"The worst most inhuman and most diabolical institution of the black African slave trade was initiated, refined, perpetrated and implemented by the Mohammadan Arabs and later aided and abetted by the black converts to Mohammadan Islam.

I predict as usual the two subcultures, those of denial of facts and of political correctness will attack us without once disproving a single statement and or conclusion that we make. Slavery was not created by the white races, because it has existed throughout human history and practiced by every tribe, culture, civilization, racial group and religion. In fact the very word slavery has its root in the name Slav, based on the Slavic people of Europe who were subjugated by other Europeans.

It is not common knowledge that the Arabic word, "Abd" is synonymous with the meaning of slave and all black people are called "Abeed", plural for slaves. While much has been written about the Trans Atlantic Slave Trade, surprising little attention has been paid to the Islamic Slave Trade across the Sahara, The Red Sea and Indian Ocean. While the European involvement in the African trans Atlantic Slave Trade to the Americas lasted for just over three centuries, the Arab involvement in the African Slave Trade has lasted fourteen centuries and in some part of the Mohammadan world is still continuing to this day.

This has led to a number of so called "Holy Wars". There was and is nothing holy about these wars which are primarily meant to plunder, slaughter, rape, subjugate and rob other human beings of their wealth, produce, freedom and dignity.

A comparison of the Islamic slave trade to the America slave trade reveals some extremely interesting contrasts. While two out of every three slaves shipped across the Atlantic were men, the proportions were reversed in the Islamic slave trade; two women for every man were enslaved by Muslims.

While the mortality rate of slaves transported across the Atlantic was as high as 10% the east African slave market was a staggering 80-90%. Slaves shipped to the America's were used for agriculture; the Islamic slaves were used as sex slaves and soldiers. While many children were born to slaves in the Americas the millions of their descendants are citizens in Brazil and the United States of today, very few of the slaves that ended up in the Middle East survived. While most slaves who went to the Americas could marry and have families, most of the slaves destined for the Middle East were castrated and most of the children born to the women were killed at birth.

It is estimated that at least 11 million Africans were transported across the Atlantic, 95% of which went to South and Central America. Only 5% [550,000] of the slaves ended up in what we call the United States today. However a minimum of 28 million Africans were enslaved in the Muslim Middle East during this same period.

It is believed that the death toll for 1400 years of Arab and Muslim slave trade could have been as high as 112 million. When added to those sold in Arab slave markets the total victims of the Arab and Muslim slave trade could be significantly higher than 140 million people.

The reality of Mohammaden Islam's complicity in the slave trade and their inhuman depravity are infinitely more devastating, more staggering and more incomprehensible than all the nightmare fictions in the world."

One of the most tragic facts related to Arab Slavery is that Mecca, the geographic heart of the Muslim community, was one of the largest slave markets in the Muslim world.

Where Arab's excelled at capturing and torturing ethnic African's, Babylonian Talmudists were masters of logistics, creating what would become known as the "Slave Triangle", in fact every ship involved in the transportation of black African and white Irish and Scottish slaves were owned by so called Jews [Talmudists]. The following is a listing of the so called Jewish slave ships and their so called Jewish owners.

NAME OF SHIP	SHIP OWNER	OWNERS ETHNICITY
Abigail	Aaron Lopez, Moses Levy, Jacob Franks	Babylonian Talmudist
Crown	Issac Levy and Nathan Simpson	Babylonian Talmudist
Nassau	Moses Levy	Babylonian Talmudist
Four Sisters	Moses Levy	Babylonian Talmudist
Anne & Eliza	Justus Bosch and John Abrams	Babylonian Talmudist
Prudent Betty	Henry Cruger and Jacob Phoenix	Babylonian Talmudist
Hester	Mordecai and David Gomez	Babylonian Talmudist
Elizabeth	Mordecai and David Gomez	Babylonian Talmudist
Antigua	Nathan Marston and Abram Lyell	Babylonian Talmudist
Betsy	Wm. De Woolf	Babylonian Talmudist
Polly	Wm. De Woolf	Babylonian Talmudist
White Horse	Jan de Sweevts	Babylonian Talmudist
Expedition	John and Jacob Roosevelt	Babylonian Talmudist
Charlotte	Moses and Sam Levy and Jacob Franks	Babylonian Talmudist
Caracoa	Moses and Sam Levy	Babylonian Talmudist

Source: Elizabeth Donnan, 4 Volumes, 'Documents Illustrative of the History of the Slave Trade to America' Washington, D.C. 1930, 1935 Carnegie Institute of Technology, Pittsburgh, Pa.

The logistics of the African Holocaust begins in c.1656 in what is commonly referred to as the 'Slave Triangle'. Thirty-six years after Christian Pilgrims left England c.1620, we see that under the authority of the world's oldest Freemason lodge in England [926 AD], Babylonian Talmudists begin buying, kidnapping, and arresting African, Scottish and Irish people from their native lands for the purpose of selling them into slavery in the American colonies.

Flash forward just 143 years to 1763 and the American revolutionary era has begun. What the vast majority of Americans do not realize is that the American Revolution was not based on 'Taxation without Representation'; in fact there were sixteen grievances which preceded Taxation. The revolutionary war was in reality a way for King George III to relinquish his financial and military responsibilities to the American colonies, while at the same time continuing to receive interest payments [gold] on what subsequent treaties and charters would define as being The King of England's investment to establish the American colonies.

As predicted by the Church of Babylon c.1620, the crime of slavery has led to the political and social destabilization of the American colonies and right on schedule, The Church of Babylon in 1775 begins recruiting African Americans into Babylonian Freemasonry. African Americans will unwittingly play a pivotal role not only in the American Revolution, but the Rothschild orchestrated Civil War as well. The cruel irony of both of these wars is that the very same African, Scottish and Irish slaves who were ripped from their homelands by the Church of Babylon are now being secretly recruited to participate in the very organization that designed the 'slave triangle'.

On March 6, 1775 the first African American victims of the Church of Babylon are identified and admitted into what has historically been an exclusively white Freemason Lodge in Ireland. African American abolitionist Prince Hall, along with fourteen other free African Americans is initiated into Lodge No. 441 of the Grand Lodge of Ireland, a military lodge attached to the 38th Foot. Coincidently, Hall's Irish Lodge was attached to the British forces stationed in Boston. Hall would be instrumental in the petitioning for African Americans to fight against British forces even though he himself belonged to a British Babylonian Freemasonry Lodge. So not only were white Americans propagandized and deceived into fighting and dying for a prearranged Church of Babylon revolution, so too were African Americans.

Additional Prince Hall members and members of other Masonic lodges include: (a) President Barack Hussein Obama (a.k.a. Barry Soetoro); (b) Charles Rangel, founding member of the Black Caucus; (c) Rev. Al Sharpton; (d) Rev. Jessie L. Jackson; (e) Shaquille O'Neal; (f) Scottie Pippen, NBA jersey number was 33; (g) Allen, Alex E., Chief Judge, Detroit Michigan; (h) Archer, Dennis, Mayor Detroit Michigan; (i) Logan, Benjamin H., District Judge State of Michigan; (j) Rev. Hood Nicholas, Former Detroit Councilman Pro Tem; (k) Mallett, Conrad, Jr., Chief Justice, Michigan Supreme Court; (l) Rev. Hartsfield, Wallace Vice Chair Congress of National Black Churches; (m) Rev. Jemison, T.J. President, National Baptist Convention, USA; (n) Rev. Butts, Calvin O., Abyssinian Baptist Church, New York; (o) Benjamin Hooks [former Executive Director of the NAACP]; (p) Julian Bond [former NAACP Chairman]; (q) Mfume, Kweisi, President and CEO, NAACP; (r) Andrew Young [former Mayor of Atlanta, Civil Rights Leader]; (s) John H. Johnson [founder of EBONY magazine]; (t) Thurgood Marshall [Supreme Court Justice]; (u) Leake, Joseph, Chief of Police New York; Douglass Wilder [first Black American Governor Virginia]; (v) Don King [Boxing promoter]; (w) Maynard Jackson [Atlanta Mayor].

Now that you've had an opportunity to examine the ancient and predicatively complex nature of the Church of Babylon, I would like to continue to share with you my findings related to the Serpent Cult's generational subjugation and sacrifice of ancient Celtic and Pictish civilizations and how for centuries this enemy of ancient Teamhair (Hill of Tara, Ireland) and Caledonia (Scotland) has viciously persecuted the descendants of ancient Celts and Picts, in an effort to delegitimize and abort these civilizations from the annals of history.

HELP WANTED
NO IRISH NEED APPLY

BOSTON SIGN CO.   SEPT. 11, 1915

An academic who has received much attention for his Irish revisionism is Richard Joseph Jensen. Jensen has worked as an Assistant professor at Washington University (1966); Associate Professor of History at the University of Illinois, Chicago (1970); Professor of History at University of Illinois Chicago (1973-1996); Research Professor at Montana State University Billings; Professor at the University of Michigan (1968); Professor at Harvard University (1973); Moscow State University in Russia (1986) and West Point (1989-90). Jensen was also the recipient of a Woodrow Wilson Fellowship (1962). However the two awards which speak volumes are his Rockefeller Foundation award (1983) and Fulbright Fellow award for his work with the Communist controlled USSR (1986).

I have provided Professor Jensen's resume to demonstrate how this seemingly well-read professor should have at the very least a rudimentary understanding of how to properly vet research material prior to projecting his findings to colleagues and University students. Not so, according to a December, 2002 article where Jensen published disparaging remarks targeting Irish American's titled, "No Irish Need Apply: A Myth of Victimization" in the Journal of Social History.

In his article Jensen suggests that the humiliating job discrimination and signs which read "Help Wanted – No Irish Need Apply!" were nonexistent. That is until July 2015 when the Journal of Social History published an extensive rebuttal by 14-year old, Rebecca A. Fried, a student at Sidwell Friends School, Washington, DC who produced a number of artifacts which legitimized this piece of Irish History. Ms. Fried's prose caused one commentator to label Professor Jensen's own position as 'delusional'.

Considering the fact that I personally own a sign, manufactured September. 11, 1915 by the, "Boston Sign Co.", [above] which reads, "HELP WANTED NO IRISH NEED APPLY", I must concur with this commentator.

I use the aforementioned story of Professor Jensen to illustrate

59

how the Rockefeller and Rothschild controlled world of academia is working to rewrite Irish and Scottish history. Furthermore just because a person has a slew of acronyms after their name, it's no reason for an individual to refrain from asking questions and testing the legitimacy of one's theories.

With all that you've learned in mind, I would like to issue a challenge, that you impartially evaluate the following information. Specifically the minority status of Scottish and Irish people throughout American history, then calculate the percentage of those who have achieved acclaim, which is massively disproportionate to other nationalities, then calculate the chance of those Scottish and Irish celebrities dying mysteriously on a date which is occult related no less, let's just say that skepticism regarding the existence of an ancient threat towards Scottish and Irish peoples is based upon an irrational basis.

Meriwether Lewis [Lewis and Clark Expedition] was of ancient Celtic ancestry and a Master Freemason. Lewis was elected to the, "Door of Virtue Lodge" in January 1797 and had climbed the ranks to past Master Mason within three months. In 1799 Lewis attained status of, "Royal Arch Mason in, "Widow's Son Lodge" at Milton, Virginia. Shortly thereafter Lewis had been chosen by Thomas Jefferson to be his private secretary. Lewis also established the first Masonic Lodge in St. Louis and was named "Master" of St. Louis Lodge, Number 111. Just two years after returning from his expedition with Clark, Meriwether Lewis made the decision to leave Freemasonry and was shot and his throat cut 10/11/1809 [111]. His bloody apron [above] provides us with graphic evidence of that day.

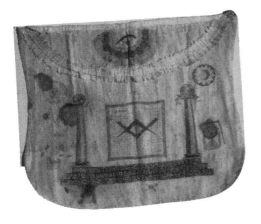

In Alexandria, Virginia the George Washington National Masonic Memorial building stands 333 feet tall. Washington's Birthday has been moved from Feb. 11th to the 22nd, which is 222. George Washington's Alexandria Lodge number was 22. The Washington monument obelisk in Washington D.C. is 555 feet tall above ground with another 111 feet anchoring below (555+111 = 666).

According to the book, "The Suppressed History of America" by Paul Schrag and Xaviant Haze, "Gary Moulton, professor and editor of one volume of the published journals of Lewis and Clark, suggests that throughout the years growing evidence indicates that much of what Lewis and Clark wrote about the westward journey was lost... This seems to support the notion of other lost items yet to be found. Curiously, Lewis's diaries are not included among the works compiled to create the tale of Lewis and Clark's great journey. During a time when the journals were being compiled and prepared for publishing, correspondence between Thomas Jefferson, Clark and one of the first editors of the corps' collective journals, Nicholas Biddle, mention no concern about Lewis's missing diaries."

Scottish American Davy Crockett opposed Church of Babylon member Andrew Jackson's 1830 'Indian Removal Act' which stole the ancestral lands of Native American's and murdered millions. Davy Crockett known for saying "Always be sure you are right, then go ahead" renounced Freemasonry c.1835 leaving behind his Masonic Apron to the Weakly Lodge in Tennessee before being murdered less than one year later in 1836 at the Battle of the Alamo.

Scottish American President and Freemason William McKinley was assassinated 9/14/1901 [14+19 = 33] just six months into his second term and one year after he signed the "Gold Standard Act". McKinley was assassinated by the Rockefeller and Rothschild Family for advocating a gold-based currency.

Scottish American Motion picture pioneer and my cousin Francis Boggs sacrificed 10/27/1911. Boggs is credited with creating what he originally named "Hollyrood" which means, "Scottish Government," however it was changed to Hollywood following his murder. Francis Boggs is recognized as being the person who discovered Scottish American actor Roscoe 'Fatty' Arbuckle. Following the murder of Francis Boggs his creation "Hollyrood" was consumed by the parasitic Church of Babylon. The number 11 to the Church of Babylon represents man being above God. When broken down [1+1=2], 11 represent's the 2 of duality. To occultists the number 11 is the essence of all that is sinful, harmful and imperfect.

Scottish American Roscoe 'Fatty' Arbuckle murdered with a morphine overdose in 1933. The scandal of a woman's death in Arbuckle's San Francisco hotel room was used to institute the Movie rating system. This has led to the rated PG-13, "R" and "X" film rating system ushering in pornography and with it the erosion of morality in America.

I would like to point out here that proponents of the Serpent Cult of Dann chose to associate the mark of Dann or "X", commonly associated with the Babylonian 'god' Nimrod, with the immorality that's linked with the "XXX" movie rating. 61

Pythagorean numerology goes up to 9 and then starts over at 1 giving 2 or 3 letters per number. Using Pythagorean numerology, the word "Fox," like Rupert Murdoch's FOX News actually encodes 666. So does Rockefeller's Exxon (eXXOn = 666), the XBox (XbOX = 666), and movies like TripleX and the XMen Trilogy. When something is XXX like for poison or pornography it is 666. When you write XOXOXO for hugs and kisses it also means 666666. When every game of TicTacToe is finished, the 3x3 square filled with Xs and Os is actually 666 in every direction. In the book, "Codex Magica" Texe Marrs writes:

"Offbrand products are called "Brand X," and of course, there is the U.S. terrorist prison camp, Camp XRay at Guantanamo, Cuba. Today's youth have been called Generation X, and a lot of folks are concerned about a planet, or star, reported to be speeding toward us called Planet X that has occult significance. There is also an interesting use of the letter X in the Rx of drug stores; the use of the four-letter, abbreviated word Xmas to replace Christmas, and the fact that, in Black's Law Dictionary, it says that the sign or mark of X is sometimes made as a substitute for a man's signature on legal documents. And the continued use of the Serpent Cult's "X" knows no bounds. Children at play can be heard to say, 'Cross my heart and hope to die.' In the Greek alphabet, the letter Chi is denoted with the symbol X, and given the numerical designation of 600. The numerologists say that triple X, then, would yield the number 666.

Black Muslim leaders [uneducated about Ancient Arab slavery] obviously see X as a substitute name of great spiritual significance. Two well-known Black Muslim leaders have been named Malcolm X and Louis X, names they chose for themselves. The latter, who was born Louis Eugene Wolcott in 1933 in New York City, changed his name to Louis X after his conversion to Islam by Black Muslim leader Elijah Muhammed. Today, he is known as Louis Farrakhan. It is well-known that Farrakhan is a 33° Prince Hall Mason. The sign, or letter, X, has a long history of use in the Ancient Mystery Religions, in apostate Judaism, in Freemasonry, and in the occult. The Illuminati elite use it to this day to symbolize key phenomena and mark significant events. The mysterious letter X seems to take on a wide and varied life of its own, with or without the secret aid of the elite sponsorship"

In 2013 Arbuckle is played by actor Brett Ashy in the motion picture titled: "Return to Babylon". According to reports, actors who appeared in the film experienced strange paranormal activity. Eye witnesses report that actors faces can be seen "morphing" into grotesque shapes in certain shots. Other reports include actors having elongated, amphibious webbed fingers, full bodied apparitions, seeing the faces of dead actors manifest in shots, and shadows resembling demons or skeletons. The cast and crew confirmed these reports even stating that they experienced odd events during production, with Irish American Actress, Jennifer Tilly in particular describing feeling "watched" and "touched" by unseen forces during filming. Before his murder in 1997, at the age of 33, Scottish American comedian Chris Farley was scheduled to Star as Arbuckle in a biography film. 3x11 = 33 to occultists the number 11 is the essence of all that is sinful, harmful and imperfect.

Scottish American General George S. Patton sacrificed 12/21/1945 (12+21=33). Patton was best known for his command of the 7th United States Army (7 = God 6 = Man 7+6=13). Contrary to television celebrity Bill O'Reilly's recent book titled 'Killing Patton' General Patton was not killed by the Russians nor was he killed mysteriously in a 'car accident'. If you've been one of the unfortunate people to have purchased this propaganda piece which props up and propagates Church of Babylon human exploitation psychology you have unwittingly been indoctrinated into believing a number of historical misnomers not the least of which is the word 'Holocaust' which didn't become a mind meme until 1978 a mere 33 years after Patton's sacrifice. The word 'Holocaust' is a so called Jewish word meaning 'Holy offering in fire' probably not a coincidence that Babylonian Talmudists worship the Babylonian god Nimrod who taught man to worship fire. You never read anything in O'Reilly's book about the 66 million Christians who were slaughtered during the war(s) but are subjected to a large opinion piece, 20 pages in two chapters to be exact, on Auschwitz which is curious because there is zero historical evidence that Patton had anything to do with Auschwitz. This wouldn't be the first time Bill O'Reilly sold his soul in exchange for fame and fortune.

In his bestselling book, "Killing Kennedy", O'Reilly claims that he witnessed the suicide of George de Mohrenschildt, a key witness associated with JFK's assassin, Lee Harvey Oswald stating:

"The reporter traced de Mohrenschildt to Palm Beach, Florida and travelled there to confront him... As the reporter knocked on the door of de Mohrenschildt's daughter's home he heard the shotgun blast that marked the suicide of the Russian, assuring that his relationship with Lee Harvey Oswald would never be fully understood. By the way, that reporter's name is Bill O'Reilly" - Killing Kennedy, Bill O'Reilly & Martin Dugard, pg.300.

What fans of O'Reilly and FOX News should find disturbing is the fact that Bill O'Reilly blatantly lied about his experience with Mohrenschildt. The truth is O'Reilly was not present when Mohrenschildt committed suicide. Remarkably there is an audio tape, from that very day [3/29/1977], of a phone call between O'Reilly and an investigator named Gaeton Fonzi and it speaks for itself:

Bill O'Reilly: Hi Gaeton.
Bill O'Reilly. Gaeton Fonzi (Investigator): Yeah.
O'Reilly: Look, something definitely did happen.
Fonzi: yeah, I got it.
O'Reilly: What is it?
Fonzi: He committed suicide up here in – where I was trying to locate him. **O'Reilly:** OK, where is that?
Fonzi: It's a place called Manalapan M-A-N-A-L-A-P-A-N. Palm Beach County.
O'Reilly: OK. So, he committed suicide, he's dead?
Fonzi: Yeah.
O'Reilly: OK, what time?
Fonzi: Late this afternoon. I don't know.
O'Reilly: OK, gun?
Fonzi: I think, yeah, I think he said he shot himself.
O'Reilly: OK. Ah, Jesus Christ.
Fonzi: Isn't that something? Jesus.
O'Reilly: Now we gotta get this guy Epstein. I'm coming down there tomorrow. I'm coming to Florida. We gotta get this guy. He knows what happened.
Fonzi: Well, I'm gonna be up there probably trying to secure the papers.
O'Reilly: Yeah, OK. Alright, I'm gonna get in there tomorrow. I'm gonna get a car.
O'Reilly: Is there a number – will you leave a number at your house where I can reach you?
Fonzi: The only way, call the magazine.
O'Reilly: OK.
O'Reilly: Ok. Now, Ok, I'm gonna try to get a night flight out of here, if I can. But I might have to go tomorrow morning. Let me see.

Scottish/Irish American James Dean, sacrificed 9/30/1955 aged 24. Dean was sacrificed inside of a "quick-silver" Porsche 550 Spyder containing the number 130 on its side at 5:45 PM. Dean's quick-silver Porsche is significant in that "quicksilver" is also known as Mercury and Mercury was a messenger of Zeus. Mercury is the name of the son or messenger of Zeus 'IO' [EO] Hermes, otherwise known as Apollyon from the Book of Revelation "The Beast from the Pit" – Revelation 9:11. Coincidently James Dean's co-star, Julie Harris, in the 1955 movie, "East of Eden" said about Dean, "You see, he was mercurial [Mercury], unpredictable, always putting you on, which I didn't mind because he was very beguiling... he did manipulate people and he knew he was doing it."

64

Dean's 550 Spyder contains the number "50" and in correlation with Mercury, Zeus and Hermes, King of Arcadie "Lycaon" had 50 sons exterminated by Zeus and Lycaon dedicated the first temple to Hermes on mountain Cyllene. Dean's car model "Spyder" represents the trust of the hypocrite as compared to the "spider's web" or house [Job 8:14]. It is said of the wicked by Isaiah, they "weave the spider's web:" [59:5] e.g., their works and designs are, like the spider's web, vain and useless. The Hebrew word here used is "akkabish", "a swift weaver." Those who created and ultimately sacrificed James Dean deceived 1950s men and women into adopting Dean's rebellious, untoward, Antichristian, Antifamily, lifestyle and for good reason. 1950s America populace was overwhelmingly Christian and married, however what was intentionally hidden from view was Dean's Satanist, homosexual lifestyle. It was Dean's persona which deceived 1950s youth away from their parents and traditional Christian values. Unsurprisingly James Dean actively sought out spirits and spirit guides to help forge his path to success. Dean also publicly stated, "I have a fairly adequate knowledge of satanic forces." Dean Also boasted that, "I had studied The Golden Bough and de Sade." Satanist Aleister Crowley wrote in his 960 pg. autobiography, "The Confessions of Aleister Crowley that, "Not in vain had I been studying The Golden Bough... and...In writing this book, I was much assisted by Frazer's Golden Bough." According to Crowley, Christianity was "historically false, morally infamous, politically contemptible and socially pestilential." Regarding James Dean's worship of 'de Sade', Sade was one of the wickedest homosexual serial killers in history. Dean was also a fan of Freemason, Satanist, Homosexual playwright, "Oscar Wilde", who was a homosexual lover of Satanist Aleister Crowley. A close personal friend of Dean, Buelah Roth, recalls a time when Dean wanted to become possessed with the dead actress, Sarah Bernhardt.

James Dean also was fascinated with Adolph Hitler's occult knowledge of a destiny to fulfill. Dean was so spellbound by Hitler that he consciously chose a car designed by Ferdinand Porsche, who under the guidance of Adolf Hitler designed the, "people's car" today known as the Volkswagen Beetle, a vehicle which flourished during the CIA, MK-Ultra, Jim Morrison and Frank Zappa orchestrated 1960s Hippie movement, headquartered in Southern California's Laurel Canyon. I examine Laurel Canyon and the 60s hippie movement in subsequent pages.

When asked about his assured confidence as a future "Movie Star", Dean uttered, "[A spirit name]... I gotta be faithful to her. It's predestined that I'm going to make it and that I'm going to make it like Marlon did, and I'm going to be a star." Like Hitler Dean also believed that he could tempt death and triumph because of his destiny. Dean's close friend and homosexual lover and alleged MK-Ultra mind control programmer, John Gilmore, recalls an occasion where Dean told a fellow car racer, "You can't do the things I'm doing. I can flirt with death and come through-you can't." As an aside and in relation to the CIA's Laurel Canyon 1960s Hippie Movement and John Gilmore, I would like readers to keep in mind that Dean's lover, MK-Ultra programmer, John Gilmore, published a number of nonfiction books including, "The Garbage People", a hardcover exploration into the lives of Charles Manson and the Family. A few years before the so-called Manson Murders, and while an actor, John Gilmore became friends with actress Sharon Tate after meeting each other at 20th Century Fox studios.

Overnight Dean's movies sent shockwaves throughout America and programmed young minds into believing Dean's persona was 'cool'. Randall Riese, author of The Unabridged James Dean surmises writes, "Within a year after his death James Dean had arisen, Christ like, to become the biggest movie star in America, perhaps the world." This brings us to one of the last occult symbols surrounding Dean's sacrifice which is the number "5" which represents the satanic pentagram, the energy, the transformation, whereas the number "0" represents infinity. Those who practice "divination" believe that the number 50 represents "Christ Consciousness" a popular occult theory within Helena Blavatsky's Satanic "Theosophy". The number "13" is also represented in the number decal "130" on the side of Dean's Porsche, which represents man [6] being above god [7].

Irish American actress and girlfriend of Irish American President JFK, Marilyn Monroe, murdered 8/5/1962 age 36 (8+5=13) in California by the Church of Babylon with a barbiturate overdose.

Irish American President John F. Kennedy was sacrificed 11/22/1963 (11+22 = 33). In 1962 the "Cuban Missile Crisis" lasted 13 days, and 13 months later, to the day, JFK was assassinated. JFK was shot in the exact same 3 spots as Freemason founder Hiram Abiff, who, representing the persecution of the Knights Templars [Friday the 13th, 1307] was struck in the back, the throat, and the head. JFK was sacrificed in Dealey Plaza an occult temple and 'Birthplace of Dallas' Texas. Dealey Plaza contains the first courthouse, post office, first store and first fraternal lodge of freemasonry. The first Dallas courthouse, also known as 'Old Red Courthouse' was constructed using red sandstone and rusticated marble. Those who constructed this building had knowledge related to the fact that red is an ancient pigment derived from both red Ocher iron oxide, hematite which comes from Greek, hema meaning 'blood' and Cinnabar the common ore of mercury used in Egyptian tombs c.1000 B.C.

When we examine the roof system of 'Old Red' [left] we discover that its designers stamped it with the 'X' of the Serpent Cult of Dann; an eight pointed star symbolizing the demon goddess Lilith; the Black Sun 'double-cross' an ancient Babylonian symbol used by the German Thule Society a precursor to Adolph Hitler's Nazi Party [left]; occult pyramids that when combined symbolize the Star of Remphan "666" and finally a number of serpents signifying once again the Serpent Death Cult.

Dealey Plaza is named after Dallas Texas businessman George Dealey [1859-1946] a 33rd degree Scottish Rite Freemason. What's more Dallas Texas is located near the 33rd Degree Parallel and the three streets which make up Dealey plaza (i) Elm, which is notorious for the number of deaths that have occurred there as well as its association with Saturn [Satan]. (ii) Main and (iii) Commerce create Neptune's Trident [left] as well as an occult truncated pyramid and phallic symbol or "VRIL Power'.

The most mocking memorial to JFK is the massive cube landmark [left] which supposedly commemorates JFK's assassination. To the Church of Babylon, a cube symbolizes Saturn [Satan] and the giant

67

cube structure dedicated to Kennedy has been cut in half symbolizing President Kennedy's war against the Serpent Cult cut short.

Kennedy was brutally sacrificed for being an outspoken critic of the Church of Babylon and for issuing Executive Order 11110. This effectively stripped all power, from the Rothschild/Rockefeller/JP Morgan founded and controlled Federal Reserve Corporation to argue otherwise would be intellectually dishonest. Also keep in mind that it was the Irish American Kennedy Family; whose ancestor Patrick Kennedy had fled Ireland during the great Famine that orchestrated a peace process for Ireland that brought an end to generational conflict in the region. This environment of relative harmony was in direct conflict with the system of subjugation and deception that had been construction by the Church of Babylon.

JFK issued his final warning speech to Americans, at the Waldorf-Astoria Hotel, on April 27, 1961 prior to being brutally executed publicly. Why was JFK murdered? It's too complicated to explain in just a few pages, however, soon after his speech and the issuance of Executive Order 11110 he was dead. Apparently the controlling interests of the JP Morgan dynasty didn't take kindly the actions of JFK… After all, in 1920 Morgan gave his London residence, 14 Princes Gate (near Imperial College London), to the United States government for use as its embassy. In 1938 the Hon. Joseph P. Kennedy, having been appointed as the U.S. Ambassador to the Court of St. James, moved his family into this building, and thus a future President of the United States, John F. Kennedy, came to call the house of JP Morgan his home.

The actions of JFK, lead one to believe, that he wanted Americans to have some influence over their financial destiny as a Nation. No longer would Global, Central Banking elites, be in control of America's destiny. The Rothschilds, Rockefellers and Morgans however voted down JFK's proposal with a bullet. Hence Kennedy's gift would never be realized. Just hours following Kennedy's execution, LBJ would rescind JFK's Presidential Order 11110.

To say John F. Kennedy was a boy scout would be disingenuous, to say the least. After all, President Kennedy had affairs with Inga Arvad, Florence Pritchett (wife of Earl T. Smith, a United States Ambassador to Cuba), Marilyn Monroe, Jayne Mansfield (sex partner and member of Anton LaVey' Church of Satan), Judith Campbell, Pamela Turner (Jacqueline Kennedy's press secretary), Priscilla Wear (a secretary), Jill Cowan (a secretary), Mary Pinchot Meyer, Blaze Starr, and Tempest Storm. In addition to President Kennedy's improprieties, JFK was also an outspoken proponent of what he called a 'Declaration of Interdependence'.

In his July 4, 1962 speech, he stated:

"When in the course of history, the threat of extinction confronts mankind, it is necessary for the people of the United States to declare their interdependence with the people of all Nations and to embrace those principles and build those institutions which will enable mankind to survive and civilization to flourish. Two centuries ago our four fathers, brought forth a new Nation, now we must join with others; to bring forth a New World Order." – John F. Kennedy July 4th, 1962

JFK also approved the following executive orders, all of which eviscerate the United States Constitution and along with it, the end of our freedom to speak out and fight against tyrannical government:

Public Law 87-297: Calls for the United States Government to eliminate its armed forces. This unconstitutional 'law' was signed into existence by JFK in 1961. Article VIII, Section 12 of this document states:

"No person shall bear arms or possess lethal weapons except the police and members of the armed forces."

The Luciferian anti-Christian elites who have high-jacked our Republic know the American people would never approve of these measures and it's why they're pushing to disarm our citizenry. For additional information on PL 87-297 please visit Second Amendment Committee, Bernadine Smith at: libertygunrights.com many gun owners have acclaimed the Second Amendment Committee to be the #1 gun defender in the nation, over and above the National Rifle Association or any of the other large pro-gun organizations in the nation.

#10995: Authorizes seizure of all communication equipment in the United States.

#10997: Authorizes seizure of all electric power companies, fuels, fuel sources, and minerals (public and private).

#10998: Authorizes seizure of all food supplies, food resources, all farms and all farm equipment (public and private).

#10999: Authorizes seizure of all means of transportation- including personal cars, trucks, or any type of vehicle; total control over all highways, roads, seaports, and seaways.

69

#11000: Authorizes forced conscription of all Americans for work duties under supervision of Federal agents. This section also authorizes the splitting up of family units if deemed necessary by the government agencies in charge.

#11001: Authorizes seizure of all health, education, and welfare facilities and their administrations (public and private).

#11002: Empowers the Post Master General to register all men, women, and children in the United States for government purposes.

#11003: Authorizes seizure of all airports and all aircraft, public, commercial, and private.

#11004: Authorizes seizure of all housing and finance authorities and permits government agents to establish forced relocation sites. The government can declare any area of its choosing as "unsafe" and force the entire area to be abandoned of all persons. Authorizes establishment of new "relocation" communities; building new housing with public funds.

#11005: Authorizes seizure of all railroads, inland waterways, and storage facilities, both public and private.

This is the fifth United States President murdered by the banking elite; President Lincoln was assassinated first on (4/14/1865) after he said:

"The money power preys upon the nation in time of peace and conspires against it in times of adversity. It is more despotic than monarchy, more insolent than autocracy, more selfish than bureaucracy. I see in the near future a crisis approaching that unnerves me, and causes me to tremble for the safety of our country. Corporations have been enthroned, an era of corruption will follow, and the money power of the country will endeavor to prolong its reign by working upon the prejudices of the people, until the wealth is aggregated in a few hands, and the republic is destroyed."
– President Abraham Lincoln

James Garfield was assassinated second on (7/2/1881) just two weeks after he said:

"Whoever controls the volume of money in our country is absolute master of all industry and commerce…and when you realize that the entire system is very easily controlled, one way or another, by a few powerful men at the top, you will not have to be told how periods of inflation and depression originate."

70

"Own nothing and control everything." – John D. Rockefeller

William McKinley was assassinated third on (9/6/1901) by Leon Czolgosz a self described anarchist and disciple of Babylonian Talmudist Emma Goldman. Two years after McKinley's assassination, Congress enacted legislation that made presidential protection a permanent Secret Service responsibility. Emma Goldman was the mother of 20th century anarchist political philosophy throughout North American and Europe. Goldman believed that a retaliatory assassination of Andrew Carnegie or McKinley would "strike terror into the soul of his class" and "bring the teachings of Anarchism before the world". Goldman was also a colleague of eugenicist and Planned Parenthood founder Margaret Sanger. Both women were arrested for violating the Comstock Law "dissemination of obscene, lewd, or lascivious articles". The U.S. Labor Department deported Goldman in 1919 along with 249 other aliens who were associated with radical groups. The Cleveland Plain wrote: "It is hoped and expected that other vessels, larger, more commodious, carrying similar cargoes, will follow in her wake."

Warren G. Harding was the fourth President to be assassinated. After verbally resisting the 'New World Order' in his inaugural address on 3/4/1921 Harding was bludgeoned to death two days later:

"We recognize the new order in the world....But America, our America, the America builded on the foundation laid by the inspired fathers, can be a party to no permanent military alliance....Every commitment must be made in the exercise of our national sovereignty....[A] world supergovernment is contrary to everything we cherish and can have no sanction by our Republic. This is not selfishness, it is sanctity. It is not aloofness, it is security. It is not suspicion of others, it is patriotic adherence to the things which made us what we are....It has been proved again and again that we cannot, while throwing our markets open to the world, maintain American standards of living and opportunity, and hold our industrial eminence in such unequal competition. There is a luring fallacy in the theory of banished barriers of trade, but preserved American standards require our higher production costs to be reflected in our tariffs on imports." – President Warren G. Harding

You won't read about the above-mentioned historical facts in any America History Book or see them in a film. The much celebrated "New York Time Best Seller," by Fox News personality, Bill O'Reilly, is no exception.

I ask readers to examine carefully President John F. Kennedy's Final Warning to America on April 27, 1961. In his speech JFK articulates the breadth and depth of the Church of Babylon, which currently controls America and the imminent danger facing this great Nation if the offspring of free men and women allow the disease of Masonic Babylonian Talmudism to metastasize any further: 71

JFK's FINAL WARNING TO AMERICA

"The very word **secrecy** is repugnant in a free and open society; and we are as a people inherently and historically opposed to **secret societies**, to **secret oaths** and **secret proceedings**. We decided long ago that the dangers of excessive and unwarranted concealment of pertinent facts far outweighed the dangers which are cited to justify it. Even today, there is little value in opposing the threat of a closed society by imitating its arbitrary restrictions. Even today, there is little value in insuring the **survival of our nation if our traditions do not survive** with it. And there is very grave danger that an announced need for increased security will be seized upon by those anxious to expand its meaning to the very limits of official censorship and concealment. That I do not intend to permit to the extent that it is in my control. And no official of my Administration, whether his rank is high or low, civilian or military, should interpret my words here tonight as an excuse to censor the news, to stifle dissent, to cover up our mistakes or to withhold from the press and the public the facts they deserve to know.

For we are opposed around the world by a monolithic and ruthless conspiracy that relies on covert means for expanding its sphere of influence--on infiltration instead of invasion, on subversion instead of elections, on intimidation instead of free choice, on guerrillas by night instead of armies by day. It is a system which has conscripted vast human and material resources into the building of a tightly knit, highly efficient machine that combines military, diplomatic, intelligence, economic, scientific and political operations.

Its preparations are concealed, not published. Its mistakes are buried not headlined. Its dissenters are silenced, not praised. No expenditure is questioned, no rumor is printed, no secret is revealed.

No President should fear public scrutiny of his program. For from that scrutiny comes understanding; and from that understanding comes support or opposition. And both are necessary. I am not asking your newspapers to support the Administration, but **I am asking your help in the tremendous task of informing and alerting the American people. For I have complete confidence in the response and dedication of our citizens whenever they are fully informed.**

I not only could not stifle controversy among your readers -- I welcome it. This Administration intends to be candid about its errors; for as a wise man once said: **"An error does not become a mistake until you refuse to correct it."**

We intend to accept full responsibility for our errors; and we expect you to point them out when we miss them.

Without debate, without criticism, no Administration and no country can succeed-- and no republic can survive. That is why the Athenian lawmaker Solon decreed it a crime for any citizen to shrink from controversy. And that is why our press was protected by the First (emphasized) Amendment -- the only business in America specifically protected by the Constitution -- not primarily to amuse and entertain, not to emphasize the trivial and sentimental, not to simply "give the public what it wants"--but to inform, to arouse, to reflect, to state our dangers and our opportunities, to indicate our crises and our choices, to lead, mold educate and sometimes even anger public opinion.

This means greater coverage and analysis of international news -- for it is no longer far away and foreign but close at hand and local. It means greater attention to improved understanding of the news as well as improved transmission. And it means, finally, that government at all levels must meet its obligation to provide you with the fullest possible information outside the narrowest limits of national security.

And so it is to the printing press--to the recorder of mans deeds, the keeper of his conscience, the courier of his news -- that we look for strength and assistance, confident that <u>with your help man will be what he was born to be: free and independent</u>."

President John F. Kennedy's message to our parents and grandparents left nothing to the imagination. He directed his words at the Church of Babylon, carefully. Much like his ancestors would have chosen their claymores, he chose words that would cut deep and that would inflict maximum damage to the body of America's one true enemy. Knowing the risk to his own life and the lives of everyone in his family President Kennedy chose to be on the right side of history as he proceeded to warn the American populace of the looming threat to our Republic.

JFK addressed the demonic energy which governs 'Secret Societies' [The Church of Babylon] and highlighted how the parasitical offspring of these secret organizations have for centuries, marauded through America's critical systems. And just as President George Washington did 224 years ago, and President Lincoln 153 years ago, President Kennedy vividly described the parasites feeding off the Nation. He told us that these vermin' survival is based on duplicity, deceit 'Secret Oaths and Secret Proceedings'. 73

The next images associated with JFK's sacrifice are blatant MK-Ultra trauma based programming impressions. Keep in mind that what I'm going to show you and describe was flashed immediately after the live coverage of JFK's sacrifice. The first image is of the CBS News "Bulletin". While this image sits on the screen Walter Cronkite begins his narrative regarding JFK's fatal injuries.

Immediately following Cronkite's report, CBS features a Nescafe Coffee commercial where a stereotypical pendulum, used to induce hypnosis [mind control], is melodically swinging back and forth. Then about half way through the commercial, a woman who is stirring her coffee begins to swing her spoon back and forth like a hypnotic pendulum.

Architect and member of the Church of Babylon, John Carl Warnecke, was the designer of JFK's grave site at Arlington National Cemetery in Virginia, which includes the John F. Kennedy Eternal Flame [left].

In addition to designing JFK's grave site, Warnecke was having sex with JFK's wife Jacqueline Kennedy. Coincidently, in March 1963, Warnecke had taken JFK to the very site in Arlington Cemetery that the President would later be buried. Just five months after the site visit with Warnecke on August 9, 1963, the President and Mrs. Kennedy's newborn son would die and three months later in November 1963 JFK would be assassinated.

Millions of people have been deceived into believing that the "eternal flame" lit by Mrs. Kennedy 11/25/1963 pays homage to JFK's memory, when in reality the flame is one last affront to the President who claimed to be a Christian. The flame in fact flies in the face of Christianity because it represents the Babylonian god Nimrod that Khazarian Babylonian Talmudists believed worshipped fire. There are two additional design elements related to JFK's memorial worth mentioning. When viewed from the air, JFK's burial site resembles the Greek Goddess Iris Newgrange shrine just 2 hours from New Ross Ireland, the town John. F. Kennedy's great-grandfather emigrated from in 1848. C.I.A. official George H.W. Bush, Freemason Warnecke and Jacqueline Kennedy were all fully aware of the Babylonian Freemason symbolism of JFK's assassination and memorial marked by the fact that in 1965, just three years after the murder of JFK, Jacqueline Kennedy was instrumental in the acquisition of the, "Temple of Dendur" from Egypt [above]. This temple was built to honor Isis, Osiris and their son Horus, as well as two other figures named Pediese which means "he whom Isis has given" and Pihor which means "he who belongs to Horus".

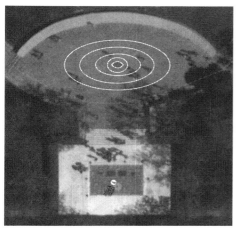

This brings us to the aerial view of JFK's memorial site [below] which is in fact in the shape of an eye complete with a faint but noticeable all-seeing-eye of Satan in the center. To illustrate I have enriched the lines that exist in the monument. You'll notice that the designer shaped the "pupil" of the center eye so that it would resemble a serpent's eye, symbolizing the Serpent Death Cult.

75

JOHN F. KENNEDY'S "SS-100X"

History buffs and car enthusiasts alike have for generations pondered the meaning behind the name of the midnight blue 1961 Lincoln car that President John F. Kennedy was brutally sacrificed publicly in on November 22, 1963. Before I reveal my reasoned logic behind the JFK's vehicle, it's important to know that it was the C.I.A. who named the ill-fated 'SS 100X' and that JFK's 'SS 100X' was delivered to JFK's White House on June 14, 1961. A collection of evidence suggests that all of this happened under the watchful eye of future C.I.A. Director and President of the United States George H.W. Bush. To be clear, there are countless books on the subject of JFK's assassination and the events surrounding his ultimate demise, granted many of these references are completely off base, nonetheless they're out there. My intention, however, throughout the subsequent pages is to provide the reader an ultra condensed version of these events focusing primarily on the origins of JFK's 'SS 100X'. Now let's explore the nonstop chain of coincidence associating George H.W. Bush with the botched CIA 'Bay of Pigs' Cuban invasion, the assassination of our Nation's 35th President, and finally the meaning behind JFK's rolling sacrificial alter; all of which cannot be explained away by mere 'apophenia' a term created by Nazi psychiatrist, Klaus Conrad.

There is an emerging body of evidence which suggests the progeny of Nazi financier [Prescott Bush] George H.W. Bush was recruited by the CIA in the early 1960s while he was attending college and running his oil company, "Zapata Off Shore Co." [Named after a Communist Mexican Revolutionary known for invading towns and murdering its inhabitants] George H.W. Bush named a previous venture 'Zapata' as well. This fact alone calls into question Bush's mental, moral and spiritual health. In addition to running his Mexican Communist named Oil Company, George H.W. Bush was also a member of the 'Skull and Bones Society'. I believe 'conspiracy' groups and historians often misinterpret Skull & Bones as a front group for Adam Weishaupt's Illuminati, when in fact it's a recruiting tool for the Church of Babylon. As was shared in previous chapters, the Rothschild's version of satanic Babylonian Talmudic Freemasonry infected English Freemasonry when the Rothschild Family assumed complete control over the English Banking system on June 19, 1815. One of the many connections between George H.W. Bush and the Rothschild's Babylonian Talmudic Freemasonry begins with George H.W. Bush's chosen name during his membership in the Skull & Bones Society which was 'Magog'. In Ancient texts e.g., The Holy Bible, etc. 'Magog' is used to describe the evil forces that will join with Satan in the great struggle at the end of time. Satan will rise up against God; he will go forth and deceive the nations of the world Gog and Magog gathering them together in great numbers to attack the saints.

In the above parable, Magog is the satanic Babylonian god Nimrod who like Satan rebelled against God. It provides clarification as to why the Bush Family in association with the Rockefeller Family has been so adamant on driving a wedge between the Middle East and the Christian American majority. It should also shed light on the true motivations behind the satanic Babylonian Talmudist controlled movie and music industry and their efforts to associate America with the 'All-Seeing-Eye of Satan', 'The Illuminati' and all things ungodly. For millennia it has been the goal of followers of the Pharisee invented satanic Babylonian Talmud to bring about the destruction of any group of people who acknowledges the existence of Jesus Christ or 'Isa' to Muslims. It is the goal of followers of the god of Babylon [Nimrod] to bring about the reemergence of Nimrod's One World Religion and New World Order. Bush is on record calling for Nimrod's 'New World Order'.

"And when the thousand years are expired, Satan shall be loosed out of his prison, And shall go out to deceive the nations which are in the four quarters of the earth, Gog and Magog, to gather them together to battle: the number of whom [is] as the sand of the sea. And they went up on the breadth of the earth, and compassed the camp of the saints about, and the beloved city: and fire came down from God out of heaven, and devoured them. And the devil that deceived them was cast into the lake of fire and brimstone, where the beast and the false prophet [are], and shall be tormented day and night for ever and ever." – Revelation 20:7-10

George H.W. Bush, his colleagues at the C.I.A and their puppet masters [Rothschild/Rockefeller] hated President Kennedy to death. Why? For starters, Kennedy signed executive Order 11110, which stripped all power from the Rothschild/ Rockefeller/JP Morgan founded and controlled Federal Reserve Corporation. Moreover, C.I.A. officials believed Kennedy's reduction in the number of airplanes, etc. in the Bay of Pigs planned invasion and overall lack of support for The Bay of Pigs was the primary cause of C.I.A.'s failure. Couple the aforesaid with the fact that President JFK fired C.I.A. head Allen Dulles and a number of other high-ranking C.I.A. employees following intelligence Kennedy had received on

Dulles that Dulles had lied to President Kennedy repeatedly and you have a mountain of motive. To add insult to injury, President Kennedy enlisted the help of the F.B.I. to disassemble C.I.A. operations and take possession of C.I.A. weaponry.

As an aside JFK's warranted measures against the C.I.A. were the catalyst for what is today a cavernous divide and obvious disdain between C.I.A. and F.B.I. officials. It's also one of the reasons for the dramatic uptick in murders of F.B.I. agents and military special operators by Rothschild/ Rockefeller controlled C.I.A. officials throughout the United States and abroad. Take for instance Navy Seal Sniper Chris Kyle who was executed recently by a C.I.A. operative under the guise of 'PTSD'. Then there are the seventeen Navy Seals whose helicopter was 'shot down with a rocket launcher'. In reality their helicopter was boarded by a CIA, Al Qaeda operative who then proceeded to blow up the Seals who participated in the 2011 shooting of an Osama Bin Laden body double. The problem with the Bin Laden story is that in 2007 Prime Minister of Pakistan Benazir Bhutto said in a television interview that Osama Bin Laden had been murdered in 2001. In response to the interviewer's question whether any of the assassins had links with the government, Pakistan Prime Minister Benazir Bhutto said:

"Yes but one of them is a very key figure in security, he is a former military officer ... and had dealings with Omar Sheikh, the man who murdered Osama bin Laden." - Pakistan Prime Minister Benazir Bhutto, 2007

Taking into account the credible aforesaid statement by Prime Minister Bhutto, it's clear that the thirty Navy Seals who were murdered had intelligence contrary to what President Barack Hussein Obama had shared with the American people in 2011. The fact of the matter is Osama Bin Laden had in fact been murdered ten years prior to President Barack Hussein Obama's television announcement. Pakistan Prime Minister Benazir Bhutto was assassinated shortly after her television interview on December 27, 2007 in a bomb attack. As Bhutto was leaving an election rally in Rawalpindi a gunman shot her in the neck and set off a bomb. Until recently the public was told that she had been blown up and not shot, that is until a video surfaced showing Prime Minister Bhutto being shot several times.

In terms of suspicious circumstances related to the deaths of F.B.I. agents on American soil, a short list includes 35 year old F.B.I. agent Stephen Ivens who allegedly committed suicide behind a Christian Church in Burbank, CA in 2012. Furthermore, there are the two F.B.I Agents involved in Dzhokhar Tsarnaev's [Boston Bomber] arrest who were sacrificed during an F.B.I. training exercise. When you accept the fact that global elites such as Bush, Clinton, Obama, Bloomberg, Rothschild, Rockefeller, etc. all worship Lucifer and his band of Babylonian gods

[Nimrod, Pazuzu, Tiamat, etc.] it's easy to understand why F.B.I. agents like Ivens would seek the sanctuary of a Christian Church during a face-off with the Church of Babylon.

What sealed President Kennedy's fate with the C.I.A. however was his amendment to the process through which C.I.A. operatives would carry out future missions, most dramatic of all was that every covert operation would need to be approved by his brother Robert Kennedy. This newly enacted executive procedure would not only lead to the execution of JFK, but to his brother's execution as well.

During the planning of the Bay of Pigs, Col. Fletcher Prouty commented that the two ships to be used for the invasion were named 'Houston' and 'Barbara', coincidently George H.W. Bush and his wife Barbara were living inside of Houston at that time. Furthermore, the top secret code name for the Bay of Pigs was 'Operation Zapata,' the name of George H.W. Bush' oil company. Moreover, in 1977 and 1978 the U.S. government released nearly 100,000 pages on the Kennedy assassination, one of those documents disclosed the fact that intelligence had been given to 'George Bush of the Central Intelligence Agency' the day after Kennedy's assassination. The coincidental lynch pin associating George H.W. Bush with Kennedy's assassination was wealthy Texas Russian oil tycoon George de Mohrenschildt who was both a high-level C.I.A. Bush colleague and control officer for Kennedy patsy Lee Harvey Oswald. The warren commission namely Scottish American Hale Boggs [Congressional House Majority 1971] described George de Mohrenschildt and his wife as two of the closest people to Oswald at the time of Kennedy's assassination and that it was the Mohrenschildt's who funded Oswald's move to Dallas. Shortly before his appearance at the House Select Committee investigating Kennedy's assassination in the late 1970s, Mohrenschildt was found dead of a gunshot wound. Forensic investigators discovered Mohrenschildt's address book which contained the following name and address: Bush, George H.W. [Poppy] 1412 W. Ohio also Zapata Petroleum Midland'. Lastly C.I.A. intelligence revealed de Mohrenschildt travelled frequently to Houston George H.W. Bush's headquarters. De Mohrenschildt told people that he was meeting with the Brown Brothers who coincidently were close friends and financial backers of Lyndon B. Johnson. The mistress of Lyndon B. Johnson said that LBJ told her: "It was the CIA and the Oil boys". Who murdered JFK? George H.W. Bush was both an 'Oil boy' and 'CIA' official.

In addition to reversing JFK's executive Order 11110, which stripped all power from the Rothschild/ Rockefeller/JP Morgan founded and controlled Federal Reserve Corporation, President Lyndon B. Johnson assigned the former C.I.A. head [Allen Dulles] who President

John F. Kennedy had fired and who was a logical accomplice in the murder of JFK, to head up the Warren Commission investigation into President Kennedy's Assassination. The same Warren Commission and 'single bullet theory' that Congressional House Majority leader Hale Boggs said: "I had strong doubts about it." Shortly after dissenting to the Allen Dulles managed Warren Commission's majority which supported the ridiculous 'single bullet theory' that took President Kennedy's life, C.I.A. associates of George H.W. Bush and Dulles disappeared Hale Boggs twin engine Cessna 310 during a flight from Anchorage to Juneau. In the 1979 novel titled: 'The Matarese Circle', author Robert Ludlum portrayed Boggs as having been murdered to stop his investigation of the Kennedy assassination.

Applying what you've learned throughout the previous pages I'm sure you have a pretty good idea of the meaning behind the vehicle, CIA official, George H.W. Bush, named "SS 100X" 6/14/1961 [666]. If you're still scratching your head, here's my theory. As we've already learned the 'X' represents the Serpent Cult. The "X" is also a Roman numeral representing the number 10. Roman numerals are letters as well as numbers. In modern terms this means that the 'X' in JFK's "SS 100X" symbolizes the word 'IO' [EO] which is Greek for Apollyon the sun god or Apollyon the destroy from the Book of Revelation. What's more when you multiply X [10] by 100 it equals 1000, and in Greek 1000 means Helius, another name for Apollyon or The Beast from The Book of Revelation. Not only does the 'X' in SS 100 X reference Satan in Revelation 20:7-10, CIA Director/President George H.W. Bush's name was "Magog" while he was in the Skull & Bones society and this is referenced in Revelation 20:7-10 as well.

"And when the thousand years are expired, Satan shall be loosed out of his prison, And shall go out to deceive the nations which are in the four quarters of the earth, Gog and Magog, to gather them together to battle:"

Given the extensive verifiable proof regarding the Bush Family's Nazi legacy, the 'SS' in JFK's vehicle name is obvious, however, as we learned earlier the Swastika is comprised of two 'Sol' or 'Sig'. This is a Germanic Rune which represents the sound for the Roman 'S' and in Old Norse means 'Sun'. And the inner most portion of a Swastika creates an 'X' and an 'X' or cross inside of a circle is the Roman numeral for 1000, and 1000 in Greek is Helius, another name for Apollyon the destroyer [The Beast] from The Book of Revelation.

American actress Judy Garland was born Frances Ethel Gumm [German] and was later given the Irish surname 'Garland'. She was murdered 6/22/1969 in England with a barbiturate overdose. Coincidently Garland played Dorothy in the movie 'The Wizard of Oz' a movie which accurately depicts the Church of Babylon's headmaster Rothschild [The Wizard] as well as the Rothschild's control method over 'Oz.' short for ounces of gold. An interesting aside is that the saying, made famous by The Wizard of Movie, "There's no place like home" is in fact an ancient Gaelic adage, "Níl aon tinteán mar do thinteán féin."

Scottish American actress/model Sharon Tate murdered 8/9/1969 [666] aged 26 by the Manson family. The patriarch of the Manson Family was Scottish American Charles Mason. Born Charles Miles Maddox, Charles biological father was Scottish American Walker Scott. What made Charles [Scott] Manson such a stimulating instrument for the Church of Babylon was that his father was a descendent of the Christian Dalriada who migrated from Ireland to Scotland c.500 A.D. These were ancient Celts who fought against and destroyed the unholy trinity of the Church of Babylon which includes, The Serpent Cult of Dann, Nimrod and Masonic Babylonian Talmudism. This is why the demons, who still have possession of him, carved the mark of Dann or "X" of Nimrod into the forehead of Charles [Scott] Manson.

Contrary to the generational programming surrounding this case, Sharon Tate's sacrifice was orchestrated by her husband of less than one year, Babylonian Talmudist, Rapist and Sodomite director Roman Polanski, who was conveniently out of the Country during the sacrifice of Sharon, who was eight-and-a-half months pregnant at the time. Like all Church of Babylon members Polanski loved to molest, sodomize, rape, torture and murder Irish and Scottish children. In 1977, Polanski was arrested for the statutory rape of a 13-year-old girl named Samantha Geimer, who he raped inside of Hollywood Actor Jack Nicholson's home [Jacuzzi] on Mulholland Dr. Polanski directed a number of Satanic films, most notably 'Rosemary's Baby' [1968].

Rosemary's Baby was filmed in the Dakota building where Irishman John Lennon, who personally knew Polanski, was shot to death. In the movie, the elites, including a cameo by Church of Satan founder Anton LeVay, demand Rosemary's baby for success and fame. One year after, Polanski's pregnant wife Sharon Tate was murdered by Charles Manson's followers. Manson was seen frantically waving Masonic gestures during his trial. The technical advisor for Rosemary's Baby was Anton Lavey who died age 67 [6+7=13]. Sharon Tates last completed film was titled 12+1, which equals 13.

Sharon's 12+1 film co-star was Orson Welles. Orson was the radio broadcaster of the first electronic mass media psychological operation (psyops) created by Princeton University Radio Project, under the supervision of psychologist Dr. Paul F. Lazarsfeld, Frank Stanton (later the head of CBS Radio and Television and RAND

Corporation). The psyop was financed by The Rockefeller Family and program was titled "War of the Worlds" a radio version of H.G. Welles 1897 book of the same name. H.G. Welles book was based on Social Darwinism, in that the aliens exercise over humans their 'rights' as a superior race. Welles worldview was shaped by Thomas Henry Huxley who was given the name "Darwin's Bulldog" for his fervent support of Charles Darwin; as a matter of fact Huxley was a pallbearer at the funeral of Charles Darwin [4/26/1882]. In 1864 Henry launched an Antichristian dining club named, "The X Club" venerating the Serpent Cult of Dann. Henry Huxley was the grandfather of the future director of UNESCO, Julian Huxley an enthusiast of the USSR dictator Joseph Stalin. Julian Huxley once said that he admired the social and economic planning results achieved by Stalin. It was Stalin's planning that Huxley so admired, which led to the starvation and murder of more than 14 million Ukrainians, nearly three times the number of Jews murdered by Hitler. Huxley also said:

> "The lowest strata are reproducing too fast. Therefore… they must not
> have too easy access to relief or hospital treatment lest the removal of
> the last check on natural selection should make it too easy for children to
> be produced or to survive; long unemployment should be a ground for
> sterilization."

> "I suppose the reason why we leapt at the Origin of Species [Darwin's
> Theory] was that the idea of God interfered with our sexual mores"
> – Sir Julian Huxley, Head of UNESCO

A bonafide success, War of the World's reached more than 6 million people. The Rockefeller's used this Martian Invasion scenario to develop a "Psychology of Panic" system of measure which cross referenced a demographic, psycho-graphic and statics database to judge susceptibility to phobias, fatalism and fear of war. Just two years after the success of "War of the Worlds" The Rockefeller Family financed The Office of Public Opinion Research (OPOR) at Princeton, which was run by Dr. Hadley Cantril. One of OPOR's major studies was analyzing the effectiveness of propaganda developed by the forerunner of the CIA, known as the (OSS) Office of Strategic Services. The fear of an 'Alien Invasion' hoax has been used for generations by the Church of Babylon to control those who have been deceived away from God. In 1917 Marxist John Dewey was the first 'public servant' to promote the fear of an Alien threat stating, "Some one remarked that the best way to unite all the nations on this globe would be an attack from some other planet. In the face of such an alien enemy, people would respond with a sense of their unity of interest and purpose." Decades later on 9/21/1987, President Ronald Reagan continued this psyop in a speech made to the 42nd General Assembly of the

United Nation stating, "In our obsession with antagonisms of the moment, we often forget how much unites all the members of humanity. Perhaps we need some outside, universal threat to make us realize this common bond. I occasionally think how quickly our differences would vanish if we were facing an alien threat from outside this world."

In relation to the Serpent Cult of Dann and its Mark of Dann "X" and Mark of Nimrod "X", the end of Orson Welles original radio broadcast of "War of the Worlds" ends with the voice of a field artillery commander who repeats the code, "2X 2L calling CQ... 2X 2L calling CQ... is there anyone on the air?" To the Church of Babylon the double "X" means to double-cross or betray. Fundamentally speaking it indicates one's willingness to betray on behalf of Satan. When individuals, companies, corporations, nations, etc. feature the 'XX' on their person or in their logo they are invoking satanic energy. For instance, the members of the Rockefeller Family are fully aware of the 'XX' meaning, which is why the family of Standard Oil fame named their Corporation "Exxon" then hired French-born Freemason and 'The Father of Industrial Design', Raymond Loewy, to design their Exxon logo. It will be remembered that, "The Thule Society" also featured the double-cross [XX] inside their occult logo. This was a German occultist group which was later reorganized by Adolf Hitler into the Nazi Party.

Scottish American Congressional House Majority Leader (1971) and this author's cousin, Hale Boggs was a member of the Warren Commission and was tasked with investigating John F. Kennedy's assassination. Hale Boggs was sacrificed 10/16/1972 (10+16=26 & 1+6+1+9+7+2=26 and when you add 26+26=52 (2+2+2=6) "666" and "222". Shortly after dissenting to the Warren Commission's majority which supported the ridiculous 'single bullet theory' that took President Kennedy's life, Boggs twin engine Cessna 310 was blown up during a flight from Anchorage to Juneau. In addition to Hale, 18 other key witnesses to JFK' assassination were murdered. The London Sunday Times calculated the odds of 18 material witnesses dying within three years of the JFK assassination as 1 in 100,000 trillion. In the 1979 novel titled: 'The Matarese Circle', author Robert Ludlum portrayed Boggs as having been killed to stop his investigation of the Kennedy assassination. Regarding the single-bullet theory, Hale Boggs commented:

"I had strong doubts about it."

Three occult laden altars to Hale Boggs were erected shortly after he was sacrificed, most notably is the Hale Boggs Memorial Bridge which contains two large truncated pyramids.

83

As an aside Hale Boggs son, Thomas Hale Boggs, Jr. would go on to create Squire Patton Boggs, one of the 25 largest law firms in the world. Boggs, Jr. was an ardent proponent of the Rothschild/Rockefeller global crime syndicate, spearheading The American Bankers Association repeal of the Glass-Steagall law that separated commercial and investment banking for seven decades. Boggs, Jr. was also behind the $1.5 billion federal bailout of Chrysler in 1979. Prior to Squire Patton Boggs, Hale Boggs, Jr. served in the executive office of President Lyndon B. Johnson, the very President who helped to orchestrate his father's sacrifice.

On 9/15/2014 Boggs, Jr. 'died of an apparent heart attack', however the firm he helped to build continues to be the largest lobbying practices in Washington D.C. and the lobbying arm, long managed by Boggs, Jr. is currently managed by former U.S. Senators John Breaux and Trent Lott. Other notable people and alumni associated with Squire Patton Boggs include: U.S. Postmaster General J. Edward Day; Republican Strategist Benjamin Ginsberg; Assistant Secretary of the Army Ronald J. James; U.S. trade representative Clete Donald Johnson, Jr; Undersecretary of the Navy W. John Kenney; Governor of Alaska Sean Parnell; Defense Department Inspector General Joseph E. Schmitz; David Schnittger Deputy Chief of Staff to U.S. House Speaker John Boehner. It's also noteworthy to mention that the current logo for Squire Patton Boggs (fig..2) appears to be a modified representation of the ancient symbol for Mammom, "the son of Satan" [Dann of the Serpent Cult] (fig.1). Mammon is said to be one of the seven Princes of Hell and used the cross-hair symbol as his calling card. Mammon is associated with the deadly sin of greed. This symbol appears in Egyptian tomb paintings and carvings dating back to c. 1500 B.C.

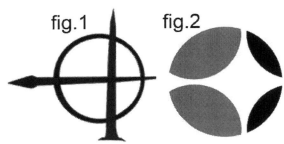

fig.1   **fig.2**

Irish American Dorothy Mae Kilgallen murdered 11/8/1965 with a drug overdose. Kilgallen was a journalist and T.V. personality who interviewed Jack Ruby the man who killed Lee Harvey Oswald, out of earshot of sheriff's deputies.

Irish American actor Bobby Driscoll was sacrificed with a heroin overdose. His body was discovered 3/30/1968 just 3 weeks after his 31st (33) birthday. Bobby was an award winning actor best known for playing the voice of Disney's Peter Pan. Driscoll was also the first person ever signed to a Disney contract, appearing in Walt Disney's 1946 film "Song of the South". Driscoll's body was found 'surrounded by religious pamphlets' no doubt his attempt to escape the demons which had consumed his life.

Scottish American Singer and Actor, Elvis Aaron Presley "The King", sacrificed 8/16/1977 at the age of 42 with a drug overdose [8+16=24, 1+9+7+7=24]. To the Church of Babylon, the number 24 is the calculation of the Babylonian Talmud. Elvis was also the 24 carat golden boy for Talmudists both in life and in death. In life Elvis was used by Talmudists to corrupt America's Christian majority and usher in immorality. 1970s critic George Melly described Elvis as. "...the master of the sexual simile, treating his guitar as both phallus and girl." Within the Serpent Cult the phallic symbol is central. And according to Presley's obituary, Lester Bangs credited Elvis as, "...the man who brought overt blatant vulgar sexual frenzy to the popular arts in America". In 1959, Sight and Sounds, Peter John Dyer described Elvis' onscreen persona as, "...aggressively bisexual in appeal". Bret Farmer described his "orgasmic gyrations" in Jailhouse Rock as, "...spectacular eroticization, if not homo-eroticization, of the male image". Critic, Mark Feeney, described Elvis as being, "...beautiful, astonishingly beautiful".

In 1969 the Church of Babylon controlled Planned Parenthood organization issued a memo which called for an increase in homosexuality throughout America. You may read the document for yourself at: [http://tinyurl.com/homoamerica]. Posthumously, Elvis was named 2nd top earning dead celebrity by Forbes with $55 million as of 2011.

In addition to being worshipped by so many people, what made Presley an exceptionally stimulating sacrifice for Babylonian Talmudists was that his mother had given birth to twin boys, Elvis and Jessie, however Jessie was stillborn. To occultists the number 2 signifies duality 1+1 = 2 or 11 which represents man above God. 11 is the essence of all that is sinful, harmful and imperfect. Elvis' Christian faith also contributed to him becoming a sacrifice. As I've mentioned throughout this book, the Babylonian Talmud is exceptionally blasphemous towards Jesus Christ, exceedingly hateful towards Christianity and extraordinarily racist.

Elvis Presley was the son of Vernon Elvis Presley and Gladys Love Smith. Gladys' parents were Scottish American Robert Lee Smith and Scottish American Octavia Luvenia "Doll" Mansell. The people known in ancient Scotland as the Picts were the forefathers of the Smith Family. The Smiths descended from "Neil Cromb" a chieftain who was the son of "Murdoch", Chief of the Clan Chattan [Clan of Cats], a confederation of twenty-six Clans including the Mackintoshes, Davidsons, Macphersons, MacGil, etc. of which the Smith Clan was a member. Since antiquity the progeny of the Clan Chattan confederation had been adversaries of Satan's unholy trinity which includes The Serpent Cult of Dann,

:od and the Masonic Religion of Babylonian Talmudism. In 1401 a member of the Smyth [Smith] Clan was confined to the Tower of London for rebelling against King Henry IV of England and Lord of Ireland "De heretic comburendo Act" which made it illegal to own an English translation of the Holy Bible. Those who owned a Holy Bible were labeled 'heretics' by the Serpent Cult King and burned alive.

Elvis' life should act as a shining example of how prominence can impair an individual's ability to distinguish truth from fiction. The persona and sacrificial alter that had been constructed by Presley's Serpent Cult handlers over the years had been sold to Elvis with a veneer of 'Fame' and 'Fortune', however subconsciously Presley struggled vigorously against this reality. According to Elvis' hairdresser, Larry Geller, Elvis described his life in the following way:

"I mean there has to be a purpose ... there's got to be a reason ... why I was chosen to be Elvis Presley... I swear to God, no one knows how lonely I get. And how empty I really feel." – Elvis Presley.

In response to Elvis' appeal for the truth, Larry Geller supplied Elvis with books on mysticism [Satanism]. Elvis Presley's ex-wife, Priscilla Presley would go on to join Scientology. The founder of Scientology, L. Ron Hubbard referred to 'The Great Beast 666', Aleister Crowley, as "my very good friend." A close friend of L. Ron Hubbard was NASA jet propulsion laboratory founder and co-designer of the U.S. Pentagon, Jack Parsons, who once referred to himself as, "I antichrist loosed in the world; and to this am I pledged, that the work of the beast shall be fulfilled, and the way for the coming of Babylon" - Texe Marrs, Codex Magica

Irishman Musician, John Lennon, Sacrificed 12/8/1980, aged 40 by MK-Ultra mind control slave, Mark David Chapman. Mark was programmed at Frank Zappa's CIA controlled MK-Ultra programming site named "The Log Cabin" located in Southern California's, Laurel Canyon. I explain in detail the significance of Jim Morrison and Frank Zappa's, Laurel Canyon on the 1960s "Hippie Movement" in subsequent pages.

The connection between the CIA programming site and John Lennon's sacrifice is the popular 1960s singer and member of Zappa's Laurel Canyon, Jackson Browne, whose manager was militant Antichristian, Babylonian Talmudist, media mogul, David Geffen, who in 1971 became Browne's agent. Coincidently David Geffen was present immediately following Lennon's sacrifice and escorted alleged co-conspirator, Yoko Ono, away from Roosevelt Hospital. David Geffen later issued 86 a statement on Ono's behalf: "John loved and prayed for the human race. Please do the same for him." Geffen's request is completely nonsensical considering John Lennon's hatred for prayer, Christianity and God. Perhaps Ono wanted people to pray to Lennon's god, Lucifer? After all John Lennon regularly flashed the devil horns hand-sign. Lennon was also a big fan of the most evil man in the world, so much so that he placed Satanist Aleister Crowley on the cover of The Beatle's album titled, "Sgt Pepper's Lonely Hearts Band". Just fourteen-years prior to being gunned down; Lennon had this to say about Christianity:

> "Christianity will go. It will vanish and shrink. I needn't argue about that; I'm right and I'll be proven right. We're more popular than Jesus now; I don't know which will go first—rock 'n' roll or Christianity. Jesus was all right but his disciples were thick and ordinary. It's them twisting it that ruins it for me." – John Lennon 1966

To illustrate how creative demons are at deceiving men and women into trusting them, we're going to examine John Lennon's sacrificial profile. I'm sure you would agree that in a war planning scenario it's important to understand the profile of the General you're fighting against, only then are you able to determine his capabilities. The oldest available record to us which describes the skill of this particular General, is found inside of the King James Holy Bible, it's here that we read, Satan was a "cherub" [angel] "full of wisdom," and "perfect in beauty and in thy ways" [Ezekiel 28:12, 14] and that he "... hast been in Eden the garden of God; every precious stone was thy covering," [Ezekiel 28:13]. After reading Satan's profile it's logical to conclude that this General is a highly intelligent created being, who possesses an advanced understanding of the Universe including the elements it's comprised of and the laws in which these elements follow. It too is logical to conclude that this advanced understanding of the created Universe would allow Satan or any one of his fallen angels [demons] to manipulate these forces, creating what human beings would interpret as miraculous. Modern day "magicians" such as Criss Angel, David Blaine, Hans Klok, Cyril, Yif, Justin Flom, Keith Berry and others deceive people into believing that they, like Jesus Christ, can turn water into wine and ascend into the air, trickery meant to sow the seeds of doubt in the minds of human beings regarding Jesus Christ's miracles. Magicians perform these illusions while under the influence of demonic energy. Many of the "how-to" books and guides online instruct would-be magicians to wait for spirit energy to make itself known to them in order to complete the last step required for them to become a "true magician." To see with your own eyes watch Xendrius "Demon Magicians" on Youtube.

"And deceiveth them that dwell on the earth by the means of those miracles which he had power to do in the sight of the beast; saying to them that dwell on the earth, that they should make an image

to the beast, which had the wound by a sword, and did live. And he had power to give life unto the image of the beast, that the image of the beast should both speak, and cause that as many as would not worship the image of the beast should be killed. And he causeth all, both small and great, rich and poor, free and bond, to receive a mark in their right hand, or in their foreheads: And that no man might buy or sell, save he that had the mark, or the name of the beast, or the number of his name. Here is wisdom. Let him that hath understanding count the number of the beast: for it is the number of a man; and his number is Six hundred threescore and six [666]."
Revelation 13:13-18

By means of the established knowledge let's examine the illusion [magic] of numerology and how John Lennon's obsession with this demonic trickery cost him his life. After reading the occult book, "Cheiro's Book of Numbers," Lennon became fanatical with the idea that numerology influenced his destiny and contained "secret wisdom" capable of protecting his life. Using Cheiro's formula's Lennon spent his days creating notes on "birth numbers" and "name numbers." Lennon was obsessed with the number 9, his wife was born 2/18 [2x9=18] in addition [6+6+6=18 or 666], his band mate, Paul McCartney was born 6/18 [666], according to Cheiro's law the name John equals 18 [666] and the Dakota Bldg, on West 72nd Street, where Lennon was shot, was built in 1881, which according to Cheiro's law equals 18 [666]. Cheiro's law also claimed that the number 27 [3x9] was a lucky number for Lennon stating, "... it indicates that reward will come... It is a fortunate number." The man who sacrificed Lennon was named Mark David Chapman and according to Cheiro's law, Mark calculates to 9 and Chapman calculates to 27 [3x9]. It will be remembered that to the occult 6s are concealed using 9s, therefore Chapman calculates to 666.

It would appear that 9 or 6 was a "fortunate number" which ultimately yielded a reward, not for John Lennon, but for the demon who deceived him.

"And even as they did not like to retain God in their knowledge, God gave them over to a reprobate [evil] mind, to do those things which are not convenient;" - Romans 1:28

Irish American President Ronald Reagan was a Freemason who was nearly sacrificed on March 30, 1981, at 3:30p.m. March is the third month (first 3), and 3:30p.m. provides the other two threes (33), producing a 333. Reagan was also the U.S. President who signed into law the 'Immigration Reform and Control Act', section 100, which authorizes identification methods such as invisible tattoos or electronic media under the skin 'Mark of The Beast'. Reagan was also a member of "Bohemian Grove" a location in Northern California where global elites gather to worship a 50ft owl which is referred to in The Holy Bible as the, "tabernacle of Moloch, the star of your god" [Satan] - Amos 5:26-27. Moloch is also linked to the Babylonian demon goddess Lilith who is associated with the theft and murder of children. It's during this blood lust ceremony at Bohemian Grove that member's burn a small child in effigy, all the while dressed in red and black cloaks, chanting incantations to their Babylonian demon god. To see for yourself, go to www.infowars.com and search for 'Bohemian Grove by Alex Jones.' You may be surprised to learn that most United States Presidents, Vice Presidents, Congressmen, Senators, International World Leaders, etc., have all participated in these satanic rituals. Reagan is also the President who signed reverse mortgage insurance legislation on Feb 5, 1988 knowing that it would increase U.S. debt. Moreover global elites knew that reverse mortgages would allow the U.S. Government [Federal Reserve] to buy back large numbers of privately owned properties from aging U.S. citizens. An intended consequence of this program was that it would eliminate the biblical tradition of leaving children an inheritance "A good [man] leaveth an inheritance to his children's children: and the wealth of the sinner [is] laid up for the just" - Proverbs 13:22. The reverse mortgage program is one of many tools being leveraged by government to realize George H.W. Bush's anti-constitutional 'Agenda 21', which calls for the elimination of private property ownership throughout America.

I realize that Irish American President Ronald Reagan to this day is a sacred cow for millions of mentally enslaved American's. Nonetheless it doesn't erase the fact that President and Mrs. Reagan were occult practitioners while in the White House, which explains the picture of Ronald Reagan holding up devil horns [left]. During Ronald Reagan's Presidency (1981-1989) Mrs. Reagan sought astrological advice on a regular basis from Irish American Joan Quigley. The Reagan Presidency was so dependent on the advice of their New Age, anti-Christian Theosophist; Nancy Reagan would hold regular conference calls with Quigley. It was during these calls where Quigley would advice America's President and First Lady when and where to hold Presidential events, etc. In a book titled 'What Does Joan Say?' Occult practitioner Joan Quigley wrote the following about her experience with the Reagan's, "Not since the days of the Roman Emperor Nero - and never in the history of the United States Presidency - has an astrologer played such a significant role in the nation's affairs of State." - Joan Quigley

Irish American actress Grace Kelly murdered by Church of Babylon husband Prince of Monaco 9/14/1982 in Monaco.

Scottish/Irish American Kurt Donald Cobain, sacrificed 4/5/1994, [4+5=9, six upside down, + 99 in 1994 = 666]. Much like 'Beatlemania" in the 60s, Kurt's band "Nirvana" was considered by many to be one of the most influential bands of that generation. Kurt was also an avowed Satanist stating that his goal in life was to, "get stoned and worship Satan." Kurt was also keen on the desecration of Christian Churches. Kurt and his bass player, Chris Novoselic, spray-painted "GOD IS GAY" and "ABORT CHRIST" – Rolling Stone Magazine, Inside the Heart & Mind of Nirvana, by Michael Azerrad, April 16, 1992. Kurt would also take song lyrics he was dissatisfied with and set them on "fire and leave [them] burning on the porch of the Open Bible Church." Kurt also decorated his apartment as he explained, "with baby dolls hanging by their necks with blood all over them." Rolling Stone Magazine would further report that, "Cobain made a satanic-looking doll and hung it from a noose in his window." – Rolling Stone Magazine, Inside the Heart & Mind of Nirvana, by Michael Azerrad, April 16, 1992. Kurt was also a practitioner of "divination", specifically numerology. In one instance Kurt hoped to use "elaborate calculations, with the aid of a book on magic numbers, to determine a formula to hex the [expletive deleted]" to kill a female journalist, Lynn Hirschberg, because she spoke negatively about his wife's [Courtney Love] use of cocaine during her pregnancy. Kurt's obsession with the occult led him into a relationship with occultist, William Burroughts, who is described by the biographer of Led Zeppelin's "Hammer of the Gods", as a carbon copy of Satanist Aleister Crowley, stating, "Like Crowley, Burroughs was an urbane and genial human Lucifer, a modern magus, a legendary addict, and an artist whose influence extended far beyond literature to music, painting and film." - Stephen Davis, Hammer of the Gods, Ballantine Books, New York, 1985, p. 237. Burroughs is who christened hard rock "Heavy Metal." Burroughs also stated that he became demon possessed after killing his wife. Kurt Cobain was also "obsessed with Church of Satan founder and author of the Satanic Bible, Anton Lavey" – Mojo Magazine, Sept. 1999, p. 86.

At the time of Kurt's scientifically impossible 'suicide' he had been given an overdose of heroine, according to the coroner. Furthermore Cobain was leaving his Irish American wife, Courtney Love, who had allegedly filed a false police report stating that Kurt was suicidal. What's more Kurt had allegedly booked two airline tickets for himself and his new lady friend. Coincidently Love's father, Hank Harrison, once managed the Grateful Dead and Love's mother was a psycho-rapist, I mean "psychotherapist".

Scottish/African American Musician Lesane Parish Crooks
(Tupac Shakur) sacrificed 9/13/1996 [666]. Tupac's father Billy Garland was of Scottish ancestry as well.

Scottish/Irish Princess of Wales Diana sacrificed 8/31/1997. Diana referred to those who would ultimately kill her [The Windsors] as "not human". Diana was killed when the Mercedes being driven by Henri Paul, an MK-Ultra, trauma based mind control victim, drove their car into the 13th pillar inside of the "Pont D'Alma tunnel" which translates into "passage of the moon goddess". In ancient mythology the goddess Diana means "goddess of the moon". To celebrate her sacrifice the Church of Babylon placed "The Flame of Liberty" [left] an Illuminated torch, atop a black pentagram, which sits on top of the tunnel Diana was sacrificed in.

I would like to take a moment to examine the symbolism behind America's Statue of Liberty as it further supports my thesis whilst revealing the hidden hand of the Church of Babylon. What most Americans do not realize is that the Statue of Liberty was created by a Freemason by the name of Auguste Bertholdi, who belonged to the great Masonic Lodge in Paris.

Before beginning the Statue of Liberty Bertholdi was seeking financing to construct a giant statue of the goddess of fertility "Isis" as it was known to the Egyptians. The Romans also worshipped this fertility goddess however they changed the name to "Libertas" in Latin, "Liberty in English. Libertas [Liberty] is the mythological equivalent of Isis and Ishtar. Therefore, the "symbol of America" or Statue of Liberty also represents the Statue of Isis or as the Babylonians called her, "Ishtar" the demon of war, fertility, love and sex.

Ishtar was also known as "Lilith" or Lillake. The Babylonian demon Lilith was the creator of prostitution and the degrading of sex and said to strangle children, seduce young men, then kill them. According to 5th century B.C. historian Herodotus an individual's sin could only be cleanses if they had sexual intercourse with a temple priest or priestess of Ishtar, which became known as "sacred prostitution".

91

This is why ancient Christians considered Ishtar "The Whore of Babylon" and why this author believes that the modern day persona of America has been orchestrated by the Church of Babylon to represent the prophesized, "MYSTERY, BABYLON THE GREAT, THE MOTHER OF HARLOTS AND ABOMINATIONS OF THE EARTH." – Revelation 17:5.

Do you believe it's a coincidence that the United States, the home of the most famous statue of Ishtar/Lilith, provides over 65% of pornographic movies and adult entertainment to the world and where the 1960s sexual liberation movement originated and spread to the rest of the world?

Is it also a fluke that America has murdered over 30 million unborn babies [prophets] since 1970?

The ancient "Book of Enoch", allegedly written by Enoch of The Holy Bible, who lived 365 years [Genesis 5:23], both authenticates the existence of the Serpent Cult of Dann, "son of the serpent" and describes the names and functions for each of Satan's 1/3 [33%] fallen angels. The fifth fallen angel who taught man how to kill an unborn child [prophet] was named, "Kâsdejâ" it reads:

"And the fifth was named Kâsdejâ: this is he who showed the children of men the smitings of the embryo in the womb, that it may pass away, and [the smitings of the soul] the bites of the serpent, and the smitings which befall through the noontide heat, the son of the serpent named Tabââ'ĕt."

Those readers who are in support of or perform the demon Kâsdejâ's practice of murdering the unborn, should consider the two following messages:

"Before I formed thee in the belly I knew thee; and before thou camest forth out of the womb I sanctified thee, and I ordained thee a prophet unto the nations." – Jeremiah 1:5.

"But whoso shall offend one of these little ones which believe in me, it were better for him that a millstone were hanged about his neck, and that he were drowned in the depth of the sea." - Matthew 18:6

Is it also a coincidence that America is incubating the pestilence of the lesbian, bisexual, gay and transvestite community?

"For all nations have drunk of the wine of the wrath of her fornication, and the kings of the earth have committed fornication with her, and the merchants of the earth are waxed rich through the abundance of her delicacies." – Revelation 18:3.

According to scripture, Babylon would also be a home to multitudes of so called "Jews" who have left the Holy Land. – Jeremiah 50:4-6, 8; 51:6, 45, Isaiah 48:20, Revelation 18:4. Today the largest population of so called "Jews" [Khazarian Babylonian Talmudists] is found in the United States. Furthermore, nearly half of American billionaires are so called "Jews" who have made their wealth in the U.S. contributing to the rise as the world's super power, leading pornographer and butcher of babies.

The Statue of Liberty also shares many of the same characteristics found in other ancient graven images these include, "The Colossus of Rhodes" [left] a 280 BC Greek statue of the titan-god of the sun Helios or Apollyon otherwise known as "The Beast from the pit" – Revelation 9:11.

The Statue of Hera [pg.94, top] is also represented in the Statue of Liberty. Created in c.300 B.C. commemorated the wife and one of the three sisters of Zeus. Hera's counterpart in the religion of ancient Rome was Juno also known as Isis. Hera like Isis and Hathor was known for her vengeful nature, specifically against mortals.

An additional Lady Liberty element associated with Isis is the tablet held in her left hand [pg.94, middle]. This tablet is the precise dovetail handled form associated with the "tabulae ansatae" from the sanctuary of Isis and Magna Mater in Mainz.

Mithras is also represented in Lady Liberty [pg.94, bottom]. The Mithraic religion rose to prominence in the 3rd century A.D., and though its roots extend much further back, its rituals were based on the concept of a savior, sacrifice, rebirth and was very much an Anti-Christian order. The select group of Roman males who worshiped here rose through its seven levels of enlightenment by means of formidable initiation ceremonies.

One of the oldest Temples to Mithras is Located in England, within feet of the Rothschild controlled Bank of England and Museum, however it's now called "Bloomberg Place" [pg.95], "... roughly the size of a Manhattan city block, it is the future European home of Michael R. Bloomberg's company... Two bronze and stone towers, connected 93

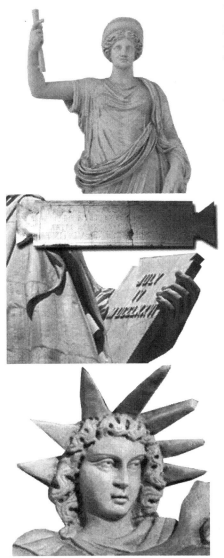

by sky-bridges atop the ruins of a 2,000-year-old Roman temple. In one corner of the development sits the Temple of Mithras, Walbrook, a relic from London's days under Roman rule. First uncovered in 1954, the temple, a sacrificial altar for an ancient religion, is being restored at Mr. Bloomberg's expense. Last month, a team of 55 archaeologists from the Museum of London were combing the temple site. Their efforts, paid for by Mr. Bloomberg, have turned up dozens of artifacts, including coins, pewter bowls, jewelry and, preserved just where it was found, a human skull." - New York Times February 7, 2013

Michael Bloomberg's temple is dedicated to the Babylonian sun god Shamash [pg.19] and Aion. The god Aion, also referred to as Cronus, Kronos or deus leontocephalus was represented as a lion-headed human figure, much like the Babylonian demon god Pazuzu, standing atop a sphere containing an 'X' which represents the Serpent Cult of Dann.

The god Aion is wrapped in the coils of a serpent further signifying the Serpent Cult. The god Aion holds a key in his hand and has a thunderbolt on his chest signifying Zeus the father of Mercury also known as Helios or Apollyon, otherwise known as "The Beast from the Pit" – Revelation 9:11.

The god Kronos was an ancient demonic deity, who is the parallel version of Moloch and the Greek equivalent of Ba'al Hammon. This was a demon that child sacrifices were made to. In 1921 an archeological dig at Carthage revealed 20,000 urns containing the cremated remains of infants and children age six. They were all sacrificed out of reverence to the demon god Kronos.

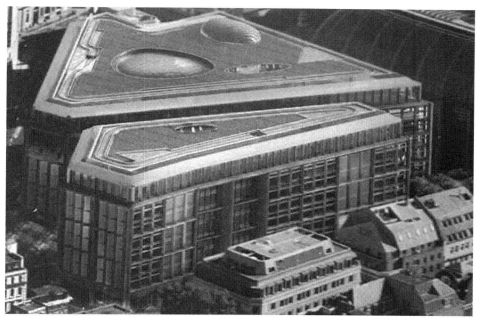

The Mithraic religion rose to prominence in the 3rd century A.D., and though its roots extend much further back, its rituals were based on the concept of a savior, sacrifice, rebirth and was very much an Anti-Christian order. The select group of Roman males who worshiped here rose through its seven levels of enlightenment by means of formidable initiation ceremonies.

"The devil, of course, to whom pertain those wiles which pervert the truth, and who, by the mystic rites of his idols, vies even with the essential portions of the sacraments of God. He, too, baptizes some—that is, his own believers and faithful followers; he promises the putting away of sins by a layer (of his own); and if my memory still serves me, Mithra there, (in the kingdom of Satan,) sets his marks on the foreheads of his soldiers; celebrates also the oblation of bread, and introduces an image of resurrection." – Tertullian (c.160-225 AD), Prescription against Heretics, Chapter 40

Mithraic rituals were markedly pagan in nature. Services were held communally, followers sitting on benches either side of a narrow nave leading to a sacrificial altar. Slaying of bulls and Christian sacrifices were common in Mithraic rituals, as were shared meals of wine and bread, particularly on the festival of the 25th of December. Mithraic members intentionally chose December 25th because of its importance to Christians. This observance in particular acted as an affront to early Christians, and was meant to disrespect the divinity of Lord Jesus Christ. The demonic cult of Mithraism was a serious rival to Christianity and focused much of its 95 efforts on the destruction of the New Testament. When Christianity became the dominant religion of the Roman Empire c.300 A.D., Constantine the Great focused much energy on dismantling everything Mithraic in sight. You won't hear this on the BBC because in 2009 the BBC appointed a Muslim named 'Aaqil Ahmed' to head up all religious programming. If you're a Christian you should not be contributing to the BBC's viewership.

Michael Bloomberg's restoration of a 3rd century amusement park of horrors and twisted obsession with Christian sacrifice should worry every Christian American. What should strike fear in the hearts and minds of every U.S. citizen is Doomberg's 4/16/2014 announcement that he would invest $50 million into a human exploitation psychology based organization 'Every town for Gun Safety'. His goal? To "battle for the hearts and minds of America". This sounds eerily similar to Attorney General Eric Holder, who said the government needs to "brainwash people into thinking about guns in a vastly different way." Doomberg's 'Every town for Gun Safety' will do nothing more than progress the Church of Babylon's agenda of (i) eliminating The Second Amendment, (ii) disarming of U.S. citizenry, and (iii) eliminating 90 percent (279M) of U.S. citizens.

Prometheus is also represented in the Statue of Liberty, specifically in Lady Liberty's torch and broken chains. In Greek mythology Prometheus is a Titan who defies the gods and provides mankind with fire [truth, knowledge, enlightenment]. The gods punish Prometheus for divulging secret knowledge by bounding him to a rock, where each day an eagle, the symbol for the messenger of Zeus [Apollyon] returns each day to eat his liver. The aforesaid elements of Prometheus collectively represent one individual and the biggest hint is found in the torch of liberty which represents the 'angel of light' or 'light bearer' [Lucifer] "And no marvel; for Satan himself is transformed into an angel of light" – 2 Corinthians. Precisely like Prometheus' progenitor Satan, he deceived man into believing that he could become god "For God doth know that in the day ye eat thereof, then your eyes shall be opened, and ye shall be as gods, knowing good and evil" [Satan] - Genesis 3:5. An additional element of the Statue of Liberty tied to Prometheus is the broken chains at Lady Liberty's feet. In some ancient stories Prometheus is freed by the hero Heracles [Hercules]. Every elite family throughout the world worship Prometheus [Lucifer] including the Rockefeller Family who has erected a giant statue of Prometheus in front of their Rockefeller Centre in New York City [pg.97]. The inscription on the statue reads, "Prometheus, teacher in every art, brought the fire that hath proved to mortals a means to mighty ends." In his book, 'Memoirs' pg. 405, the puppet master of J.P. Morgan Chase [DBA Chase] , David Rockefeller, arrogantly boasts about his family's participation in the intentional destruction of Christian America, stating:

"For more than a century ideological extremists at either end of the political spectrum have seized upon well-publicized incidents such as my encounter with Castro to attack the Rockefeller family for the inordinate influence they claim we wield over American political and economic institutions. Some even believe we are part of a secret cabal working against the best interests of the United States, characterizing my family and me as internationalists and of conspiring with others around the world to build a more integrated global political and economic structure-one world order, if you will, if that's the charge, I stand guilty, and I am proud of it."

If you're someone who currently utilizes the services of CHASE Bank, or have in your possession a Chase credit card, I highly recommend that you boycott these products and any organization associated with the Rockefeller Family. This includes toxic genetically modified organisms [GMOs] distributor Yum Restaurant Services Group (NYSE: YUM), the world's largest fast food restaurant company with more than $11 billion in annual sales. Yum! operates or licenses Taco Bell, KFC, Pizza Hut, Pasta Bravo, WingStreet, and East Dawning restaurants worldwide. Yum!' Chairman and CEO is Ukrainian American David C. Novak. Novak, an alleged Christian and member of Southeast Christian church, has also been a director for J.P. Morgan Chase [DBA Chase] since 2001. J.P. Morgan is the largest bank in the U.S., the third largest public company in the world, with total assets of $2.415 trillion, and is under the complete control of the militant anti-Christian Rockefeller Family. Every day that you're paying interest on your CHASE Credit Card, CHASE Home Mortgage, etc., or killing yourself with toxic fast-food GMOs you're enriching the Rockefeller Family and funding initiatives meant to sicken and 'soft-kill' the Christian American majority.

In addition to the above admission, David Rockefeller gives us a peak into the mind of a murderer, when on August 10, 1973, he wrote the following for the New York Times:

97

"Whatever the price of the Chinese revolution [an indirect reference to the 65 million Chinese who were murdered throughout China during Chairman Mao's leadership], it has obviously succeeded not only in producing, more efficient and dedicated administration, but also in fostering high morale and community of purpose. The social experiment in China under Chairman Mao's leadership is one of the most important and successful in human history." DAVID Rockeller

AUG 10, NYT

One last point I would like to communicate to Christian readers who may be feeling conflicted, confused, hostile or arrogant towards the reality of the aforementioned knowledge. The before shown images do not represent the image of God, therefore they do not represent who we are as Christians. Furthermore, this knowledge should come as no surprise considering God's warnings regarding the worship of 'graven images' e.g., flags, statues, buildings, people, popes, ministers, cars, sports teams, etc.

"Thou shalt not make unto thee any graven image, or any likeness of any thing that is in heaven above, or that is in the earth beneath, or that is in the water under the earth:" – Exodus 20:4.

Furthermore Christians have been warned that God does not exist in temples made by man:

"For as I passed by, and beheld your devotions, I found an altar with this inscription, TO THE UNKNOWN GOD. Whom therefore ye ignorantly worship, him declare I unto you. God that made the world and all things therein, seeing that he is Lord of heaven and earth, dwelleth not in temples made with hands;" – Acts 17:23-24

Scottish/African American Musician, Christopher George Latore Wallace [Biggie Smalls], sacrificed, 3/9/1997 [666], aged 24. Retired L.A.P.D. Officer, Greg Kading, spearheaded the murder investigations of Tupac Shakur and Biggie Smalls from 2006-2009. In an interview with Power 106s, Wendy Carrillo show, officer Greg Kading suggests that "Suge Knight" and "Sean Diddy Combs were involved in Biggie Smalls sacrifice.

Prior to being sacrificed Biggie Smalls was photographed wearing a jacket which contained a "666" patch. According to G. Craige Lewise of EX Ministries, "Biggie Smalls has an organization called the junior mafia. And in the junior mafia, he had broken the junior mafia up into three groups and he called each group a "6" [666]. He had clothes made and was getting ready to start a clothing line, right before he died, called 666." Christopher Wallace's double-disc set, "Life After Death, released 16 days later, rose to no. 1 and was certified Diamond in 2000, one of the few hip hop albums to receive this certification.

98

Scottish/African American, actor, Michael Clarke Duncan, sacrificed 9/3/2012 aged 54 [666]. Duncan's 6:5, 315lb frame and acting style landing him roles in such films as "The Green Mile", "Armageddon", "The Whole Nine Yards", "The Scorpion King", "Daredevil", etc. Earlier in his career, Duncan was a member of "Biggie Smalls" a.k.a. "Notorious B.I.G.'s "666 mafia". When Biggie Smalls was sacrificed in 1997, Duncan quit being a bodyguard. Duncan was also the bodyguard for Scientology financier Will Smith and Jamie Foxx, who during the SoulTrain Awards in 2012 stated: "First of all, give an honor to God… And our Lord and Savior Barrack Obama."

In 2005, Duncan appeared in a movie, The Island, in which his character was a clone, created for organ harvesting for the wealthy original. In the movie, Duncan's character wakes up in the middle of a surgery where his heart is being removed, screaming, "I wanna live, I don't wanna die." Michael Clarke Duncan died of a heart attack 7 years later. The Serpent Cult's secret to success in luring victims to the sacrificial alter over the past three millennia, is based on two fundamental factors. (i) Deceiving an individual away from the Lord thy God [Jesus Christ]. (ii) Their ability to program an individual's demise ahead of time, because nobody panics when things go according to plan, even if the plan is horrifying.

Scottish actor, comedian Chris Farley who like so many other young Actors and Actresses was sacrificed using an overdose of cocaine and heroin when he was 33 years old, on 12/17/97. Coincidently, Chris Farley's childhood hero John Belushi too was sacrificed when he was 33 years old as well, and like Farley, Belushi was murdered with an overdose of cocaine and heroin.

When we examine the Coat of Arms for Chris Farley's mother, Mary of the Irish Crosby Family, we find a number of icons associated with the ancient stone carving of Nimrod [Here], namely the crescent, cross, and three crowns. The bloodline of the unassuming Chris Farley made him an especially stimulating sacrificial figure for the Church of Babylon. This explains why Jeffrey Katzenberg, co-founder of Dreamworks, recruited Chris Farley prior to his death to voice the lead in the Dreamworks film "Shrek". Dreamworks symbolizes the Church of Babylon a throughout its films.

Coincidently, Farley's death occurred inside of the John Hancock building, where the film Poltergeist 3 was filmed. This film is based on the original Poltergeist movie written by Dreamworks cofounder Steven Spielberg. Coincidently, the main character in Poltergeist 'Carol Ann' was played by Irish American actress, Heather O'Rourke, who died mysteriously at the age of 13. The number 33 is significant for the

99

Church of Babylon as it symbolizes the murder of Jesus Christ, the 33% of fallen angels Satan deceived away from heaven and an elevated view of Satan's 'secret knowledge'.

Irish American actor Chris Penn who died 1/24/2006 of 'Cardiomyopathy'.

Scottish/African American Entertainer Bernard Jeffrey McCullough (Bernie Mac) sacrificed 8/9/2008.

Scottish/Irish Australian actor, Heath Andrew Ledger, sacrificed at the age of 28 on 1/22/2008 [222] with "prescription drug intoxication." The most venerated occult numbers include 6, 11, 13, 22, 66, 77, 26, 39, etc. whereas a triplication of certain numbers are even more 'sacred'. What's more when the number "2" of duality is broken down (1+1=2) it contains the number "11" and 11+11+11=33. To the Church of Babylon, the number 11 is the essence of all that is sinful, harmful and imperfect. An example of how the Serpent Tribe conceal the numeric's of their toxic enterprise we'll examine the Supreme Master of Freemasonry, Albert Pike, who was also the founder of the occult organization 'Knights of the Golden Circle' and the Ku Klux Klan [KKK]. To the occult the letter "K" has a value of "11", so the KKK = 33 and the number 33 represents the 1/3 or 33% of angels that fell with Satan.

"And his taile drew the third part of the starres of heauen, and did cast them to the earth: And the dragon stood before the woman which was ready to be deliuered, for to deuoure her childe as soone as it was borne."
– Revelation 12:4

Albert Pike's "Knights of the Golden Circle" member list included John Wilkes Booth and Jessie James. When one examines all of the evidence regarding Lincoln's opposition it suggests that Albert Pike's Knights assassinated President Abraham Lincoln. In 1871 Pike outlined plans for three world wars that would bring about a 'New World Order'.

Heath Ledger has appeared in a number of movies which celebrate his Irish heritage e.g., "Ned Kelly" and "Roar". However Ledger has also appeared in films such as, "Brokeback Mountain" which helped to progress an internal 1969 Planned Parenthood memo, which called for an "increase homosexuality", destruction of the "Nuclear Family", etc. [http://tinyurl. com/homoamerica]. Brokeback Mountain also contains elements native to Michael Swift's 1997 Gay Manifesto titled, "Gay Revolution" **www. gayrevolution.us** which in part reads:

100   "We shall sodomize your sons, emblems of your feeble masculinity, of your shallow dreams and vulgar lies. We shall seduce them in

your schools, in your dormitories, in your gymnasiums, in your locker rooms, in your sports arenas, in your seminaries, in your youth groups, in your movie theater bathrooms, in your army bunkhouses, in your truck stops, in your all male clubs, in your houses of Congress, wherever men are with men together. Your sons shall become our minions and do our bidding. They will be recast in our image. They will come to crave and adore us."

Throughout his movie career ledger appeared frequently in films which honored the Serpent Death Cult. For instance the movie, "The Order" features a character named, "The Sin Eater", an ancient figure headquartered inside of Rome, Italy which deceives people into believing that he can absolve the sins of the unforgivable, not through Jesus Christ – but only through death. This movie features an element which is consistent throughout many of Ledger's death cult films, which is the 'hanged-man'.

Batman Begins sequel "The Dark Knight" is riddled with occult symbolism and like Ledger's film, "The Sin Eater" includes a 'hanged-man' image, a symbol which I will explain later. Ledger's joker character in Batman also hands out his calling cards [above] featuring the devil, a red horned dragon [Satan] and two dragons intertwined forming the Freemason compass and square logo. One of the most overtly symbolic images celebrating the Serpent Cult is when Ledger rapidly extends his tongue throughout the film like a snake.

Ledger's character is also shown creating a pyramid of cash to which Ledger sets a blaze. Atop the pyramid of burning cash sits what was an arrogant wealthy businessman from China. This is a foreshadowing of the plan global elites have for China. An orchestrated financial bubble meant to create an inferno for the Chinese economic system and by extension cremate the Federal Reserve's financial scheme.

While I'm on the topic of orchestrated Chinese Government chaos, it seems fitting to mention the American style 1960s "sexual revolution" that was launched in 2015 throughout the communist nation. Those reader's who are keen on 20th century world history will recall the events which churned during America's 1960s sexual revolution, namely the Vietnam War. And what pushed the Vietnam war into overdrive? The Gulf of Tonkin incident, an attack on an American warship that never happened [false flag]. I will enlarge on this subject later; explaining how the serpent cult orchestrated America's 1960s Sexual Revolution and Vietnam War.

The 2015 social programming being implemented throughout China is curious considering that for the first time in U.S. history, Chinese war ships were spotted in the Bering Strait just off the coast of the U.S. Question: who do you think all of those sexually frustrated man-bots are going to vent their frustrations out on? After all, Commie-Vision has brainwashed them into believing that it was Americans, not global elites, who moved their manufacturing suicide centers to China and ruined their lands with toxic chemicals needed to manufacture modern day conveniences.

Ledger's character, "The Joker" clarifies the purpose for all the symbolism and programming that's been embedded into the movies and television we watch, stating:

"...nobody panics when things go according to plan, even if the plan is horrifying... If tomorrow I tell the press that a gangbanger will get shot, or a truckload of soldiers will be blown up, nobody panics, because it's all part of the plan. But when I say that one little old mayor will die. Well, then everyone loses their minds."

It's noteworthy to mention that in 2012 a screening for the film "Gangster Squad" preceded Ledger's Batman Film, "The Dark Knight" right before James Holmes and others walked into the Aurora Cinema in Colorado and killed 12 theatre audience members and injured 70 others with a machine gun. The trailer for Gangster Squad featured the main character shooting at a movie theater audience with machine guns. An inmate of James Holmes claims Holmes confessed that he was, "Programmed to Kill."

The last movie Heath Ledger appeared in before his death is what we're going to examine next. This Ledger film is unique in that it contains a concentrated amount of death cult imagery. The movie to which I'm referring is, "The Imaginarium of Doctor Parnassus" a Faustian theme script, in which Dr. Parnassus and Satan promote the esoteric teachings of what are essentially the megalomaniacal dispensations of a death cult.

The film begins with a character wearing a winged helmet, standing on a stage covered with images of the god Pan, the all-seeing-eye. He announces to onlookers, "I Mercury, the messenger of the gods invite you into the very great mind of Dr. Parnassus.. Whose over 1,000 years old." It will be remembered that Mercury is known as Helios or Apollyon, otherwise known as "The Beast" and 1000 in Greek represents Halios, otherwise known as Apollyon, The Beast from the Pit.

"And they had a king over them, which is the angel of the bottomless pit, whose name in the Hebrew tongue is Abaddon, but in the Greek tongue hath his name Apollyon" - Revelation 9:11.

Ledger's character, "Tony Liar" promotes a number of overtly occult symbols throughout the movie, including a scene where Tony is showing Dr. Parnassus a magazine featuring a women holding up the 666 hand-sign. Ledger's character also promotes the MK-Ultra program when he suggests to Dr. Parnassus that he should not hide his, "mind control thing."

Just prior to discovering "Tony Liar", hanging under a bridge, Dr. Parnassus presents an occult Tarot card [left] to viewers, which contains a number of occult images including a Hanged Man.

Let's read what world renowned, 1920s mystic, Manly P. Hall, has to say about this card:

"Esoterically, the Hanged Man is the human spirit which is suspended from heaven by a single thread. Wisdom, not death, is the reward for this voluntary sacrifice during which the human soul, suspended above the world of illusion, and meditating upon its unreality, is rewarded by the achievement of self-realization." - Manly P. Hall, The Secret Teachings of All Ages

The Tarot card also contains an "X" or cross in a circle which represents the Roman numeral for 1000, and 1000 in Greek is Helius, another name for Apollyon the destroyer. An additional icon on the Tarot card is an occult pyramid which appears to contain a basketball. The brainwashed minions who amass around television sets and sports arenas are oblivious to the fact that basketball [basketbaal] was created by Scottish Canadian Freemason James Naismith in 1891. Like his Babylonian Masonic predecessors, Naismith understood the strength of Christianity. 103 Naismith understood that he could not place a spell on a Christian who is full of the spirit of Lord Jesus Christ; the only way to effectively place a control spell on a Christian is if they place the spell on themselves. With that knowledge in mind, Naismith incorporated ancient anti-Christian symbolism throughout the game of basketball. For instance, the seams of a basketball [below], form a 'Nero Cross' or 'Broken Cross', the symbol of the Antichrist.

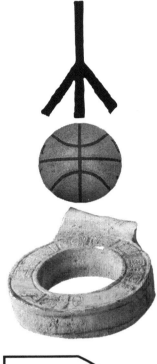

Emperor of Rome, Nero Claudius Caesar Augustus Germanicus, despised Jesus Christ and murdered millions of his followers. The broken cross on a basketball also represents a phallic symbol and to the Church of Babylon, the act of putting a basketball into the hole of a basketball hoop signifies "Sex Magic". In fact Freemason Naismith's basketball court contains a phallic symbol penetrating a shape which represents the female genitalia [left]. The Church of Babylon use organized sporting events such as basketball and baseball to perform ceremonial magic. To them it represents an occult mass where many people gather to perform Ceremonial magic.

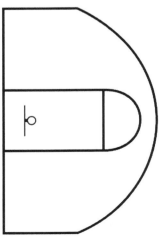

"And the children of Israel did evil in the sight of the LORD, and served Baalim: And they forsook the LORD God of their fathers, which brought them out of the land of Egypt, and followed other gods, of the gods of the people that [were] round about them, and bowed themselves unto them, and provoked the LORD to anger. And they forsook the LORD, and served Baal and Ashtaroth. And the anger of the LORD was hot against Israel, and he delivered them into the hands of spoilers that spoiled them, and he sold them into the hands of their enemies round about, so that they could not any longer stand before their enemies. Whithersoever they went out, the hand of the LORD was against them for evil, as the LORD had said, and as the LORD had sworn unto them: and they were greatly distressed."– Judges 2:11-15

Additional warnings against Baal Worship are found in: Jeremiah 23:13, 1 Kings18:22, 1 Kings 18:40, 2 Kings 23:5

What most basketball worshipers don't realize is that Naismith's invention basketball was based on the ancient Mesoamerican ball game that originated c.1400 BC. Consider the design elements of the image [pg.104] featuring a circular stone ball court goal which is identical to that of a modern basketball goal.

While we're on the topic of the occult in athletics, allow me to share with you just a few of the physical characteristics of the surrounding Mayan/Aztec regions which connect the ancient Mesoamerican game, modern day American Basketball, with the Serpent Death Cult and Babylonian god Nimrod. For instance, the Stela of El Baul [left] contains a number of the same principle demons found on the stela of Nimrod [pg.18].

Keep in mind that the two ancient stone carvings are separated by more than 8084 miles or 7025 nautical miles. Most striking of all are the six bottom characters on the Stela of El Baul who are forming an 'X' with their arms signifying the Serpent Death Cult and Babylonian god Nimrod who rebelled against God. What's more, the ancient stone carving shows the ancient Babylonian demon god Pazuzu standing over those who are worshipping the Serpent Cult, demonstrating its dominance over them whilst breathing fire. All of the aforementioned elements are associated with the Babylonian god Nimrod who according to the Church of Babylon, worshipped fire, sacrificed human beings and practiced magic.

The most troubling aspect of Scottish Freemason Naismith's ancient reproduction [basketball] is its association with a Mesoamerican ball game which celebrated human sacrifice. Ancient text describing human sacrifice is particularly strong within the Classic Veracruz and the Maya cultures, where the most explicit depictions of human

105

sacrifice can be seen on the ball court panels, at El Tajin, Chichen Itza and on the well-known decapitated ballplayer stela from the Classic Veracruz site of Aparicio. The Post classic Maya religious and quasi-historical narrative, the Popol Vuh, also links human sacrifice with the ball game. Ancient texts describe how the decapitated heads were then thrown down a deep hole to appease the 'god of the underworld'. This is an obvious reference to Nimrod who scripture tells us 'began to be a mighty one in the earth' - Genesis 10:8.

What the Scottish Freemason who invented basketball understood, is that Lucifer's ancient aspiration has been to deceive man into believing that God does not exist and that he [man] can become god. Satan's primary tool of deception is 'secret knowledge'. One of the most successful basketball players in the world was deceived by "secret knowledge", his name is Michael Jordan.

"Games played with the ball, and others of that nature, are too violent for the body and stamp no character on the mind."
– Thomas Jefferson, Letter to Peter Carr, 1785

Irish/African American Michael Jordan, is one of the most successful sports stars in history, however when we examine his athletic career we find a number of occult numerics. For instance, Jordan played 13 seasons with the Chicago Bulls. Jordan's final NBA game was on 4/16/2003. After scoring only 13 points in the entire game, Jordan went to the bench with 4-minutes and 13 seconds remaining in the third [1/3 or 33%] quarter. Jordan announced his first retirement on January 13, 1999 [666]. Michael Jordan's iconic logo [below] fits snuggly into an occult pyramid and the ball he's holding fits perfectly where the "all-seeing-eye" of Satan usually sets.

"I wanted to get hold of Satan personally and become his chief of staff. Satan Cry Aloud! Thou Exalted Most High! **Oh My Father Satan! The Eye!**" – Aleister Crowley

Michael Jordan also wore the Chicago Bulls jersey number 23. This is an important number for The Church of Babylon because it represents the value 2/3 which equals 66.6 percent [666], this is the number of angels they believe stayed in heaven with God while 1/3 (33 percent) fell with Satan.

"And his taile drew the third part of the starres of heauen, and did cast them to the earth: And the dragon stood before the woman which was ready to be deliuered, for to deuoure her childe as soone as it was borne. And the great dragon was cast out, that old serpent, called the deuill and Satan, which deceiueth the whole world: hee was cast out into the earth, and his angels were cast out with him. And the dragon was wroth with the woman, and went to make warre with the remnant of her seed, which keepe the Commaundements of God, and haue the testimony of Iesus Christ." - King James Version (1611) Revelation Chapter 12: 4-17

Jordan's short stint as a baseball player brings to mind how similar Jordan's all-seeing-eye logo is to the Freemason Logo or what Freemasons refer to as the generating principle of life. Most Freemasons will tell you that this represents sacred geometry, when in reality, the square represents the female and the compass represents both the Babylonian god Adad, ['the giver and destroyer of life'], as well as the male impregnating the female. Taking into account the fact that Freemasons influenced the creation of Baseball and Baal means Satan, it should come as no surprise that the Freemason compass and square and all-seeing-eye of Satan match perfectly with the design of a Major League Baseball field [below].

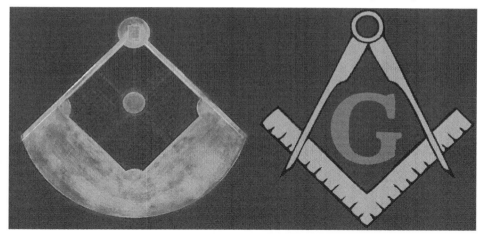

Irish/African American Kobe Bryant [synonym for O'Brien] is another professional athlete who has been deceived into sacrificing his soul in exchange for "secret knowledge." Bryant was featured in a NIKE commercial titled 'KOBESYSTEM'. In it Bryant emerges from below a stage, flashing the all-seeing-eye of Satan, coming to rest with arms stretched out like Jesus Christ on the Cross. During the commercial, a pyramid with stylized devil horns and the word, "SUCCESS" is flashed with an arrow pointing to the top of the occult pyramid [pg.108, FIG.1]. In addition a stylized Baphomet logo containing a six pointed star is also featured. [pg.108, FIG.2] this represents the Star of Remphan [Satan]. I have superimposed 107 Bryant's logo over the face of Baphomet [pg.108, FIG.3] to illustrate

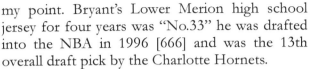

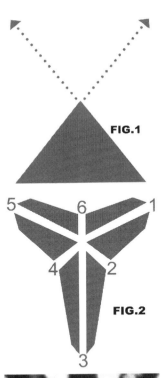

FIG.1

FIG.2

FIG.3

my point. Bryant's Lower Merion high school jersey for four years was "No.33" he was drafted into the NBA in 1996 [666] and was the 13th overall draft pick by the Charlotte Hornets.

Returning back to our examination of Heath Ledger's film, "Dr. Parnassus," I would like to share with readers some additional death cult imagery such as the scene featuring three Venetian style canal boats, each containing a picture of James Dean, Rudolph Valentino and Princess Diana. What each of these celebrities has in common is that they were all sacrificed by the Church of Babylon. Lady Diana, during a conversation with a good friend, referred to those she thought might kill her as "not human". The character Tony, now being played by Johnny Depp, says to a woman who comments that, "All these people... they're all dead." To which Tony responds:

"Yes... but immortal nevertheless. They won't get old or fat. They won't get sick or feeble. They are beyond fear because they are... forever young. They're gods... and you can join them."

The notion that man or woman can become gods is the most ancient deception conceived by the father of lies [Satan] and perpetrated by man: "Ye shall not surely die: ye shall be as gods." – Genesis 3:4-5.

The character Dr. Parnassus reveals the real power of Satan when he states that he uses the, "necessities of danger, fear and the fabled bliss of ignorance" to deceive and attract disciples. A theme throughout the movie is the recurring dialog between Dr. Parnassus and Satan. In essence this is the reenactment of the ancient principal of duality, a meaning which is represented in the date of Ledger's sacrifice [222]. During the collection of the soul of an older woman, Satan transforms into a serpent and the hotel Satan is checking people into contains a picture of Jesus Christ on the wall behind Satan's desk. Then there is the name, "Parnassus" which is derived from Mount Parnassus, the sacred mountain of the Dionysus, the Greek god of mystery religious rites or Roman Baccus. Mount Parnassus is also home to the, "Oracle of Delphi". Alexander the Great, the son of the supreme god "Ra", began promoting himself as the 'son of Zeus' after visiting the oracle of Zeus.

Dr. Parnassus, a representative of 'illumination' offers 'enlightenment' to people who choose to step through a mirror onto the spiritual plane which is represented by occult pyramids, all-seeing-eyes, the two-faced roman god, "Janus", etc. After establishing a wager between himself and Satan to win five souls, Dr. Parnassus is convinced by Ledger's character, "Tony" that the show must be modernized in order to attract a more sophisticated clientele. The result is a Masonic black and white checkered stage featuring Ledger's character holding up the 666 hand-sign, the female character sitting naked on stage looking like Eve in the Garden of Eden, along with an apple from the "tree of knowledge of good and evil" [Genesis 2:9] dangling in front of her face. And to ensure people will fall for the deception a clear box sits in the middle of the stage, filled with money with a sign on top which reads, "Please TAKE generously." Towards the end of the movie one of the films characters asks, "Tony the liar" to explain the marks on his forehead to which he responds, "I don't know, something Satanic, Devil..."

The director of Ledger's final film, Terry Gilliam, had this to say about the 'forces' which created Ledger's final film stating, "There are forces at work on this film, don't get me into my mystical mode... but the film made itself and it was co-directed by Heath Ledger!"

During an exchange between paparazzi and actor Jack Nicholson outside of the Wolseley Restaurant in London, the actor was asked, "any comments on Heath Ledger's death?" to which Nicholson responded "I warned him."

Scottish American Maj. Gen. William Robertson, Deputy Commanding General, V Corps, Europe and Irish American Col. Robert Kelly, V Corps Chief of Intelligence were sacrificed 2/23/93 when their Army UH-60 Blackhawk helicopter crashed in Wiesbaden, Germany. Both men figured prominently in the US Bosnia-Serbia peacekeeping operations, along with the carrier Roosevelt. These men, and eight others associated with President Bill (Blythe III) Clinton's visit to the USS Roosevelt all died within 4 months of each other. As an aside, Bill Clinton's original surname was Bill Blythe III. His father William Jefferson Blythe, Jr's ancestors were from Berwickshire, Scotland however they weren't Scottish, they were border gypsies from India. In fact the Blythe's were related to the late border gypsy Charles Faa Blythe, King of the Gypsies, and her Majesty "Queen Esther Faa Blythe" the most important and well-known name in the gypsy world. Queen Esther was married to a Freemason by the name of John Rutherford. The Blythe gypsies were considered a menace to society 109 as they roamed the English and Scottish countryside, practicing witchcraft and selling contraband. Based on Bill "Blythe" Clinton's acts of terrorism throughout the world, it appears the gypsy DNA hasn't fallen far from its original strand. I believe this is the real motivating factor behind Bill joining the ancient and prestigious Scottish Clinton Clan, who in ancient times called MacClinton which is a variant of MacLintock. The MacLintocks [Mac Gille Ghionndaig] were descended from the ancient Christian Irish Kings of Dalriada.

Scottish American Penthouse model, Judy Gibbs, sacrificed in 1986. Like so many unsuspecting and deceived Irish and Scottish people, Gibbs life had been thoroughly compromised by the father of lies [Satan]. In addition to being featured in a smut magazine, she worked at a bordello near Mena, Arkansas which was allegedly notorious for blackmailing their clients with photos featuring the client along with one of their girls. According to Gibbs family, President Bill Clinton was a regular customer of Judy. While cooperating in a drug investigation Judy was burned alive in her home. In a sworn statement, Bill Clinton's bodyguard, Barry Spivey, explained how he had been in a plane with then Governor Bill Clinton as they flew over Judy Gibb's house. During the flyby, Spivey said Bill Clinton showed him pictures of Gibbs Penthouse pictures while pointing out her home on the ground.

On 1/28/1986, Scottish American, Challenger Space Shuttle astronauts, Francis R. Scobee [commander]; Michael J. Smith [pilot]; Ronald McNair [Mission Specialist] and Irish American Payload Specialist, Christa McAuliffe were all sacrificed, when the NASA Space Shuttle orbiter Challenger (OV-099) (mission STS-51-L) exploded over the Atlantic Ocean, off the coast of Cape Canaveral, Florida at 11:38 EST (16:38 UTC). On 8/11/2015, legendary astronaut and American hero, Story Musgrave, www.storymusgrave.com during an interview on the Alex Jones show www.infowars.com had this to say about the Challenger explosion, "it was criminal negligence. That was not a technological issue, it was criminal negligence. It was immersed in ice. The system was not designed to fly in ice, and when you see 18 inch long icicles, you're not certified to fly. They [Ronald Reagan's Administration] went ahead and flew with bad data." To understand the motivations behind the sacrifice of these men and women, on the altar of "Challenger" all one must do is examine the political and spiritual motivations of those who controlled Washington D.C. in 1986. The President of the United States (POTUS) during this time was Irish American Ronald Reagan. Most American's are unaware of the fact that the POTUS is also the Commander and Chief of NASA, which is an administrative function in our government and reports directly to the POTUS.

110 As I mentioned earlier Ronald and Nancy Reagan were not the sweet little old Christian couple that people thought they were. Charlotte

Iserbyt, Senior Policy Advisor in the Office of Educational Research and Improvement (OERI), U.S. Department of Education, during the first Reagan Administration. [deliberatedumbingdown.com] said the following about her former boss, "Reagan was responsible for implementing Communist directives." For generations it has been the goal of the Soviets/ Russians to indoctrinate American's into Communism, it has also been their goal to dismantle America's space program.

Allow me to demonstrate the occult symbolism associated with the birth and death of the U.S. space program. Freemason and Apollo 11 astronaut Buzz Aldrin transports a Masonic flag to the moon in 1969 [666]. Apollo [Apollyon] is the name of the Beast in The Book of Revelation [Satan]. Apollo's rockets were named Saturn rocket boosters. Saturn in old Latin is the same word as Satan. The Apollo 11 rocket booster had a 6 on one side, a 6 on top, and a 6 on its other side [666]. The Challenger 'disaster' resulted in a 32-month hiatus [32 represents the totality of men on the earth], followed by the explosion of Columbia on 2/1/2003 [21 is the number of destruction]. The end of the U.S. space program was marked by the 33rd flight of the space shuttle Atlantis [33 symbolizes the age of Jesus Christ when he was crucified and 1/3 (33%) of angels which fell with their god Satan. The Obama administration completely dismantled NASA after it had expended $13 billion without producing anything [13 represents man being above God].

Back to Ronald Reagan, the Reagan's were self avowed occultists who followed and endorsed the doctrines of Lucifer. The Reagan's occult practitioner, Joan Quigley, said the following about the Reagan's, "Not since the days of the Roman Emperors [Nero] - and never in the history of the United States Presidency - has an astrologer played such a significant role in the nation's affairs of State." - Joan Quigley. The Reagan's would hold regular conference calls with Quigley. It was during these calls where Joan would advice the Reagan's when and where to hold events.

Before we proceed to the next example of a sacrifice, I would like to point out a few of the occult numeric's associated with the Columbia explosion in 2003. Before we begin I'd like for readers to understand that the "detached tile caused explosion" narrative is fiction. On 11/29/1998, the Arnold Engineering Development Center assisted the National Aeronautics Space Administration with improvements to existing Space Shuttle Materials. In their report they wrote:

"... damage to reentry tiles is a concern because it causes tile replacement costs to significantly increase, however, it is not a flight safety issue..."

111

When Columbia exploded the massive 1 ½ minute explosion could be heard across Texas and parts of Louisiana, shaking houses. It's important to remember that Columbia was gliding through the air without its engines fired and with little to no fuel.

The Columbia space shuttle crew included Irish American Pilot, William C. McCool; Scottish American Payload Commander, Michael P. Anderson and Scottish American Mission Specialist, Laurel Clark. The explosion occurred on Saturday, February 1st. According to the book, The Pagan Book of Days, by Nigel Pinnick, p. 37-38, the Satanic calendar considers this day "Imbolg" or "Imbolc" which is the first of eight annual Satanic Sabbats, a "fire festival" each of which requires human sacrifice. The date of this explosion also fell on the night of the New Moon. In Satanism, if a witch wants to cast an evil spell they do it on the night of the New Moon, the darkest night of the month. Columbia was planned to touch down at Runway #33 at the Kennedy Space Center. This runway is at 330 degrees and at an angle that would give it the number 33. The Space shuttle was 22 years old, the Space Shuttle Program was 22 years old and the Israeli Pilot, Ilan Ramon, was one of the fighter pilots who destroyed the Iraqi nuclear reactor 22 years prior to the Columbia explosion. The Columbia mission was number 113, President Bush ordered the flag to fly at half-staff at 11am, EST, Columbia is named after the Boston, Massachusetts based sloop captained by American Robert Gray. On May 11, 1792, Gray maneuvered the Columbia past the dangerous sandbar at the mouth of the 1,000 mile river which travels through south-eastern British Columbia, Canada and the Washington-Oregon border [11+11+11=33]. The shuttle was flying at the speed of 18 times the speed of sound [6+6+6=18]. The Columbia broke up over the Dallas-Fort Worth area which is on the 33rd Parallel. This too is why the Columbia sacrifice occurred just prior to the attack on Iraq. The ancient capital city of Nimrod's Babylon is located only 20 miles from the 33rd parallel. The current city of Baghdad is located on the 33rd parallel.

"If a life is taken close to the northern 33rd Parallel, this fits with the Masons' demonic mythology in which they demonstrate their worldly power by spilling human blood at a predetermined locale." - Masons and Mystery At The 33rd Parallel, by Day Williams.

It will be remembered from an earlier example that President John F. Kenney was sacrificed on the 11th month, on the 22nd day and on the 33rd parallel [11+11=22+11=33] to the Church of Babylon the number eleven is the highest number of evil. If we travel back in time to the armistice ending WWI, we see that the Church of Babylon signed the armistice on the 11th month [November], the 11th day, at the 11th hour [11+11+11=33].

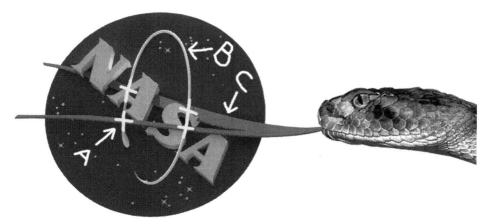

I would also like to explain how the NASA Logo is a relatively complex cryptogram containing a number of abstract modifications of symbols which deify Satan and his Serpent Cult of Dann, Nimrod and Masonic Babylonian Talmudism. The logo contains four X's [FIG.A] otherwise known as the Greek letter Chi or Greek H. In Plato's Timaeus, it is explained that the two bands that form the soul of the world cross each other like the letter X.

For those who may not know, Plato was the teacher of Aristotle who taught Alexander the Great that he was the son of the supreme god "Ra". After a visit to the oracle of Zeus, Alexander began to promote himself as the son of Zeus. In ancient artifacts both Zeus and Alexander are featured with horns on either side of their head like the god Pan. Ancient relics also feature Alexander with the eight pointed star of Lilith, also known as Ishtar, the demon of war and sex. Lilith is also known as "Isis" or "Juno" the mythical wife of Osiris and mother and brother of the god "Horus" also known as Ra the father of Alexander the Great.

The Greek letter Chi "X" has been used by Satanists to deceive Christians into embracing the blasphemous tradition of abbreviating the name Christ, as in the holiday Christmas (Xmas). The "X" in "Xmas" represents the Serpent Tribe of Dann and the Babylonian god Nimrod. The NASA logo also contains a cryptic alpha (A). It also contains a halo (O) [FIG.B]. In Greek the Letters XAO are pronounced HAO. This word HAO is found inside of the Masonic Logo and in the U.S. Dollar Bill. This mark has been used for millennia by the Church of Babylon to identify one another.

The word HAO was preached by the Satanist Aleister Crowley. The word HAO has the ancient meaning "do as thou will". HAO is also pronounced "IO" and in Greek the word 'IO' means Helios or Apollyon otherwise known as "The Beast from the pit" – Revelation 113

9:11. In the "holy language" of Hinduism and philosophical language in Buddhism and Jainism the word NASA in Sanskrit means "Infinite Death". Keep in mind that in Hinduism the king of all "nagas" [human, serpent hybrids] is "Shesha" a primal being of creation and death. The representative of the Serpent Cult of Dann throughout India "Shesha" is depicted by the ancients as being seven-headed, each head wearing a crown and sometimes with as many as 1,000 serpent heads. First the Holy Bible tells us:

"And there appeared another wonder in heaven; and behold a great red dragon, having seven heads and ten horns, and seven crowns upon his heads." - Revelation 12:3.

And in Greek, 1000 means Helius, another name for Apollyon or The Beast from The Book of Revelation. Shesha is the manifestation of "Vishnu" who descended to Earth in two human forms or avatars and is the brother of Krishna.

The Kundalini Mantra is considered the "Yoga of the Mind". The Hindu/Yoga Kundalini is described as being the "coiled one" at the base of the spine, represented as a sleeping serpent waiting to be awakened. "... then your eyes shall be opened, and ye shall be as gods," [Satan] – Genesis 3:5. A mantra is a syllable, word or phrase in one of the "sacred" Hindu and Buddhist languages such as Sanskrit & Ghurmeki. One of these mantra chants is "SA TA NA MA" [Panj Shabad] this is one of the most frequently used mantras in Kundalini Yoga. In Greek SA-TA-NA means SATAN. In Spanish Satanasa means female devil, and to Babylonian Talmudists this female devil represents the Babylonian demon goddess Lilith. In other words the word NASA means SATAN.

One last element of the NASA logo which pays homage to the Serpent Cult of Dann is the large red forked tongue of the Serpent [pg.113, FIG.C].

To those readers who may not be completely convinced that NASA was created by Satanists to deify their god Satan, consider the profile of Jack Parsons who founded NASA's jet propulsion laboratory in Pasadena, CA. and co-designed the U.S. Pentagon in Arlington County, Virginia. Parsons was a disciple of world renowned Satanist, Aleister Crowley. Parsons also wrote this revealing paragraph in his diary:

"And thus was I antichrist loosed in the world; and to this am I pledged, that the work of the beast shall be fulfilled, and the way for the coming of BABALON be made open and I shall not cease or rest until these things are accomplished." – Texe Marrs, Codex Magica.

A close friend of Parson's was the founder of Scientology, L. Ron Hubbard, who called Satanist Aleister Crowley, "My very good friend." Outspoken proponents of the satanic cult of Scientology include: Charles Manson, Actor Tom Cruz who for years has been an outspoken advocate for the promethean, SiFi cult, Will Smith donated $122,500 to Scientology. Jason Michael Lee, Kirstie Alley, Sky Dayton founder of Earthlink, Juliette Lewis, Danny Masterson, Michael Pena, Priscilla Presley, Kelly Preston, John Travolta and Greta Van Susteren (Fox News).

Given the correlation between NASA's space program and the serpent cult, I would like to edify readers on how Apollo 11 astronaut Buzz Aldrin and Lucifer are being leveraged to influence children around the world.

In 1995 Pixar Animation Studios created Toy Story, then it was released by Walt Disney Pictures. One of the main characters in the film is, "Buzz Lightyear" who is featured wearing a seemingly innocuous winged emblem [below].

Many people will be surprised to learn that 'Buzz' Lightyear' name was inspired by Church of Babylon member and Apollo 11 astronaut Buzz Aldrin. In fact, Aldrin was so indoctrinated into Freemasonry he brought a Masonic flag to the moon in 1969. Coincidently, Apollo [Apollyon] is the name of the Beast in The Book of Revelation [Satan]. What's more Apollo's rockets were named Saturn rocket boosters. Saturn in old Latin is the same word as SATAN. So it's fitting that the Apollo 11 rocket booster had a 6 on one side, a 6 on top, and a 6 on its other side [666], matching the Buzz Lightyear action figure [pg.116] which has 6 rocket exhaust holes on its back [FIG.1], a 6 on its chin [FIG.2] and 6 lights around Buzz' neck [FIG.3] "666".

As an aside the Saturn rocket booster was invented by Wernher von Braun, Adolf Hitler's top Nazi Scientist turned NASA's Deputy Associate Administrator for Planning. This brings us to the first element in Lightyear' insignia which is a Nazi V-2 rocket [pg117, top] invented by Wernher Von Braun.

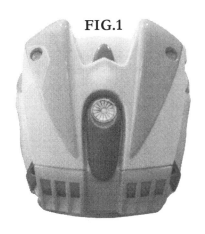

FIG.1

FIG.2

FIG.3

The second element [pg.117, center] is the planet Saturn which in old Latin is the same word as Satan.

Lastly is the large winged element [pg.117, bottom] which in addition to its association with Babylonian gods who are the progenitors of fire worship, human sacrifice and magic, this was the form the Egyptian god Horus took into battle with Seth.

Buzz Lightyear's saying "To infinity... and beyond!" was parroted by Beyonce Knowles, wife of rapper 'Jay-Z', in her 2008 quadruple platinum song "Single Ladies". Coincidently Knowles 2013 song 'XO' tactlessly included the voice of Challenger Astronaut Steve Nesbitt 70 seconds before the space shuttle exploded in 1986. These are two individuals who unabashedly promote anti-Christian Babylonian Talmudic Freemason symbolism on stage and in public. Jay-Z goes out of his way to associate himself with individuals known for their anti-Christian philosophy. For instance Jay-Z has an album called The Black Album the opposite of the Beatles White Album. Recently an associate of Jay-Z named "DJ Dangermouse", a hip-hop producer, combined the White and Black albums to create the Grey Album. In the Grey Album one can clearly hear the voice of Jay-Z saying "Murder, Murder Jesus 666" and "Kill Catholics".

In 2008, astronauts took a Buzz Lightyear action figure into space on the Shuttle "Discovery". It will be remembered that NASA's jet propulsion laboratory in Pasadena, CA was founded by rocket engineer and Satanist Jack Parsons. Parsons also co-designed the U.S. Pentagon (United States Department of Defense) in Arlington County, Virginia and was a disciple of world renowned Satanist Aleister Crowley. Parsons also wrote in his diary: "...I antichrist loosed in the world; and to this am I pledged, that the work of the beast shall be fulfilled, and the way for the coming of BABALON" – Texe Marrs, Codex Magica. It will also be remembered that Parson's good friend was the founder of Scientology, L. Ron Hubbard, who called Crowley "My very good friend".

Getting back to our examination of sacrificed Irish and Scottish celebrities, brings us to **Scottish American Steve Willis and Scottish American Todd McKeehan** who were executed 2/28/93 during Janet Reno's raid on the Christian compound named "Branch Davidians" in Waco Texas.

It is alleged by many that Janet Reno is a homosexual who had a disdain for Christianity. Steve and Todd were examined by a private doctor who concluded that both men had identical wounds to their left temple and video tapes and other evidence indicates that the men were not killed by Branch Davidians.

Bill Clinton, who nominated Reno for the Attorney General position, had this to say about his recently deceased bodyguards Steve and Todd:

"My prayers and I'm sure yours are still with the families of all four of the Alcohol, Tobacco and Firearms agents who were killed in WACO -- Todd McKeehan and Conway Le Bleu of New Orleans; Steve Willis of Houston, and Robert Williams from my hometown of Little Rock. Three of those four were assigned to my security during the course of the primary or general election."

The Little Rock, Arkansas office of the ATF confirmed that all four had at one point been bodyguards for Bill Clinton, while he was campaigning for President, and while he had been governor of Arkansas.

Irish American Cpl Eric S. Fox was sacrificed 3/22/99. Fox was a crewman for the Presidential Helicopter, "Marine One" during Bill Clinton's Presidency. Fox was shot in the head.

Irish American Paul Tully sacrificed 9/24/92. Tully was the Democratic National Committee Director for President Bill

Clinton. Tully was found dead in a Little Rock Arkansas. In a press release, then presidential candidate Bill Clinton called Paul "a dear friend and trusted advisor."

Irish/Scottish American John Wilson sacrificed 5/18/93 [6+6+6=18]. John was a former Washington D.C. Council member. John had information regarding "Whitewater" and was threatening to talk. Whitewater began with investigations into the real estate investments of Bill and Hillary Clinton and their associates, Jim and Susan McDougal, in the Whitewater Development Corporation, a failed business venture in the 1970s and 1980s which sought to develop 230 acres of land along the White River near Flippin, Arkansas. The term 'Whitewater' is also used to describe other Bill Clinton administration controversies, such as 'Travelgate', 'Filegate' and the murder of Vince Foster which was investigated by the Whitewater independent counsel.

Scottish American Ed Willey was sacrificed 11/30/93. Willey was intimately involved in several Clinton Fund Raising events. Ed was murdered on the same day his wife was sexually assaulted in the White House by Bill Clinton.

Scottish American Luther Parks was sacrificed 9/26/93. Parks was head of President Bill Clinton's gubernatorial security team in Little Rock Arkansas. At the time of his death Parks had been compiling a dossier on Bill Clinton's illicit activities. The dossier was stolen. When Vincent Foster was killed, Parks is reported to have said, "Bill Clinton is cleaning house."

Irish American Duane Garrett was sacrificed 7/26/95. Garrett was a fund raiser for Al Gore. On 7/26, Garrett cancelled a meeting with his attorney because he had to meet some people at the San Francisco airport. Three hours later, Garrett's body was found floating in the bay under the Golden Gate Bridge.

Irish American Mary Mahoney was an intern for President Bill Clinton. Mary was sacrificed 7/6/1997 in the days following Matt Drudge's leaks of Michael Isikoff's report on alleged Clinton sexual dalliances, which eventually led to the Monica Lewinsky scandal.

Scottish American Vincent Foster sacrificed 7/20/1993. Vince was a colleague of Hillary Clinton at her "Rose Law Firm" in Arkansas and had intimate knowledge of the Clinton's personal finances. According to the documentary "The Clinton Chronicles" Hillary Clinton's law firm "Rose Law Firm" and Dan Rostenkowski's Chicago bank helped launder one hundred million dollars a month in cocaine money. A portion of the proceeds were channeled to Bill Clinton's election campaign when he was governor of Arkansas for five years. Foster made a phone call to Hillary Clinton, in Los Angeles, just hours before his 'suicide'. Foster's 'suicide' note has since been revealed to be a forgery. For those who are unaware, Hillary Rodham Clinton's father "Hugh Rodham" and former house ways and means speaker Dan Rostenkowski took over the Chicago Mob from the Al Capone's organization. This is the central reason why Bill Clinton wanted to merge with Hillary Rodham because of her father's mob resources.

Irish/Scottish American Kathy Furguson was sacrificed 5/28/94 [28+5=33]. Kathy was the former wife of Trooper Danny Ferguson, who is the Arkansas State Trooper, alleged to have escorted Paula Corbin Jones to the hotel room for her alleged episode of sexual harassment by then Governor Bill Clinton. Kathy was reported to a possible corroborating witness for Ms. Jones.

Irish American Director of Central Intelligence (1973-76), William Colby was sacrificed 4/27/1996. It was Colby who revealed to Congress the "plans to kill Fidel Castro, the spying on American citizens, the conducting of biological tests by the CIA on unsuspecting citizens and using human guinea pigs for mind-control experiments [MK-Ultra]" the Times reports. George H.W. Bush was Colby's successor.

Scottish American FOX (F=6 O=6 X=6) News reporter Sandy Hume sacrificed 2/22/1998 aged 28. 2+2+2=6, two 9s in the year are upside down 6s [666]. Sandy died three weeks [777] after joining FOX; a tragedy that was omitted from their website. Sandy was the eldest son of FOX News senior political analyst Brit Hume. Sandy's death occurred just prior to his release of information that confirmed the White House's use of investigators to dig up dirt on critics. Sandy also broke the story of the 1997 coup by Rep. Bill Paxon against Newt Gingrich. The Scottish surname Hume is derived from the ancient clan name 'Home'. In 1491 Brit Hume's ancestor Sir Alexander Home married "Mariota", an heiress of Lord Halyburton (Halliburton). In 1919 Brit Hume's ancestor, Erie P. Halliburton founded "New Method Oil Well Cementing Company" which in 1951 became known as "Halliburton". In 1998, Halliburton merged with "Dresser Industries", which included Kellogg. Nazi sympathizer and father to CIA Director and President George H.W. Bush, Prescott Bush, was a director for Dresser Industries. George H.W. Bush held several positions from 1948-1951, before founding Zapata Corporation. Between 1995-2000 Halliburton's CEO was would-beVice President, board of advisors of the Jewish Institute for National Security Affairs and Director of the Council on Foreign Relations, Dick Cheney. On 9/8/2010 Halliburton was accused of causing the BP Deepwater Horizon Explosion to which they pleaded

119

guilty for destroying computer simulations that incriminated them.

Irish American John F. Kennedy Jr. sacrificed 7/16/99 [666]. Within days of an NBC Dateline story hinting at JFK Junior's run for the senate seat assumed by Bill and Hillary Clinton to be their property, JFK Junior, his pregnant wife and sister-in-law had the Piper Saratoga airplane they were flying in blown out of the sky. Contrary to global elite owned media propaganda which promoted the false narrative that the weather that day was 'hazy', witnesses on Martha's Vineyard all reported clear skies. As was the case when TWA 800 was shot down, the U.S. Navy ordered an unprecedented five mile wide 'no-fly-zone' while JFK's plane was recovered and taken to a military base.

Scotsman Anthony David 'Tony' Scott, murdered 10/22/2012 [222] using high levels of mirtazapine and eszopiclone drugs known to cause hallucinations and suicidal behavior. Anthony Scott was the younger brother of atheist film director Ridley Scott. Anthony Scott was killed just five months before the release of Ridley Scott's Film 'Prometheus', a film which accurately depicts the Church of Babylon's version of creation. When we study the Scott Coat of Arms, we find a number of icons associated with the ancient stone carving of Nimrod [pg.18], namely the crescent as well as the symbol for Baphomet.

Scottish American actor Paul Walker was sacrificed in a car crash 11/20/2013 (20+13 = 33). Walker of Fast and Furious fame also appeared in the movie 'Skulls' in 2000 then died 13 years after. This was a film based on The Skull and Bones Society at Yale University, the elite recruiting agency of the Rothschild Family. The number 13 is represented throughout a number of well known freemasonry cryptograms. For instance, the 13 stars on the back of a U.S. one dollar bill form the Mark of The Beast [666]. What's more, the 13 stars both deify the Egyptian god Osiris, who was cut up into 13 pieces. They too symbolize Man being above God. When we study the Walker Coat of Arms we find a number of icons associated with Nimrod including the crescent, the 'X' of Nimrod and two eight pointed stars which are made up of two independent triangles symbolizing 666.

Scottish American reporter Michael Hastings sacrificed at age 33 on 6/18/2013 [6+6+6=18] "666" in a car explosion. He was investigating Church of Babylon proxies.

Irish American actress Brittany Murphy sacrificed 12/20/2009 aged 32, with rat poison, 1 day after Winter Solstice. Three 2s in her sacrifice date [2+2+2=6] leaving her age at death "32" and a "1" and
120   "9" [3+2+1=6] and the nine is an upside down [6] "666" During her last television interview she asked the interviewer:

"can I have your hair in my next life."

Scottish actor Cory Monteith was sacrificed aged 31 [13 mirrored] July 13, 2013 with a drug overdose (13+20 or 20+13 = 33). Monteith played heartthrob Finn Hudson on the TV show "Glee".

Scotsman Steve Irwin sacrificed 9/4/2006 aged 44 (9+4=13). There are those who believe the numbers 44, 45 and 46 represent the trinity of the human life. Irwin exhibited behaviors throughout his career which suggests he was aware of the serpent cult of Dann. In one instance Irwin is pictured performing a mock sacrifice of his baby boy to a reptile in front of an audience. The firsthand account of Irwin's cameraman regarding Irwin's death is fraught with inconsistencies and suggests foul play.

Irish American Google Executive Timothy Hayes was descended from ancient Irish Celts who both worshipped the Serpent Cult of Dann and fought against the old world order of Nimrod. Hayes was working on Google X, ('X' is the mark of the serpent tribe) and the 'Moon Shot' program which is named after one of Nimrod' principle demon gods "Shamash", the 15ft tall giant sun god [pg.18].

Hayes was sacrificed 23 November 2013 (20+13 = 33) & (11+23=34) using one of the Church of Babylon's most common methods of murdering someone, a drug overdose using Heroine. And the one who injected Hayes (Alix Tichelman) worshipped the Babylonian demon goddess Lilith and has on her collar bone a tattoo which reads: "Hell Is Love".

There is ample evidence which suggests someone at Google was aware of and watching Hayes behavior and used that information to plan his death. For instance, November is the 11th month plus the day Hayes was sacrificed 23 = 34. Hayes was sacrificed on 2013 and to The Church of Babylon the number 13 represents Man (6) above God (7). Next only techies know that the number 34 is referred to as 'Rule 34' (prevalent internet meme) which means "If it exists, there is porn of it. No exceptions." This is a dead giveaway considering the propaganda which followed Hayes death which stated that Hayes lived a pornographic lifestyle and was murdered by a prostitute. In my opinion this was an over the top effort by the Church of Babylon to not only sacrifice Hayes, but assassinate his character. When broken down (1+1=2) 11 represents the 2 of duality. To occultists the number 11 is the essence of all that is sinful, harmful and imperfect. Many of the elements associated with Hayes murder are consistent with other "blood sacrifices" which has been performed by the Church of Babylon throughout history.   121

The correlation between Hayes ancient Celtic ancestry, Rule 34, the Church of Babylon's 13 (=Man above God), Hayes Google project names all coinciding with the Babylonian god Nimrod and his principle demon god Shamash and Alix Tichelman's worship of the Babylonian demon goddess Lilith all suggest that Hayes was sacrificed.

 As an aside the original corporate identity of Google's "competitor", Microsoft [left] is encoded with the following 'magical' occult numerics. In the fragmented tail you will see, [11+11+11=33]. To the Church of Babylon [1+1=2] 11 represent duality, the essence of all that is sinful, harmful and imperfect. It also symbolizes psychic vibrations and has an equal balance of masculine and feminine properties which represents the Serpent Cult of Dann' androgyne symbol as well as the hermaphrodite principle of the two-faced entity or two-headed eagle which is featured throughout Freemasonry. In the Cabala, this amalgamation represents the feminine and masculine principle known as "Adam Kadmon," [Adam and Eve] otherwise known as Golem. This combination of opposites is part of alchemy, or hermeticism, which is beloved by the occult. In witchcraft, they refer to this principle as the joining of sun and moon, for which sacred sex rituals are shared. In the multiple colored window portion of the Windows logo, the number "33" will appear to you as will the number "13". The logo also contains the value 133.335. The Dewey Decimal System classification number for "Numerology" is 133.335. If you reverse this and add, you get 133.335 + 533.331 = 666.666

Scottish/African American Rapper Chris Kelly – ½ of Rap group 'Kris Kross' sacrificed 5/1/2013 (20+13 = 33) of an apparent drug overdose. He was 34.

Scottish/African American comedian James 'Jimmy Mack' McNair was killed in a car accident alongside Scottish/African American comedian Tracy Morgan 6/8/2014 in the month of summer solstice. Morgan who survived the crash said he and McNair "go way back".

Irish American actress and former "That 70s Show" star Robin Kelly was sacrificed 8/14/2013 (20+13 = 33) while staying at a drug rehab facility in California.

Scottish American singer Mindy McCready Sacrificed in 2/17/2013. The Lyrics to her song 'Ten Thousand Angels,' describes in detail how she was literally tormented by demons. In short it reads: "Speaking of the devil look who just walked in. He knows just where

122

to find me help me break this spell that I'm under I need ten thousand angels watching over me tonight". Coincidently McCready was sacrificed just two weeks after her Scottish American boyfriend David Wilson (record producer) committed suicide. The father of one of her sons is Scottish Billy McKnight a man who tried to kill her.

Scottish American Actor and Comedian Robin McLaurin Williams sacrificed 8/11/2014 by hanging [11+2 = 13 also the number 11 to the Church of Babylon represents God being exceeded. When broken down [1+1=2], 11 represent the 2 of duality. To occultists the number 11 is the essence of all that is sinful, harmful and imperfect. Williams was descended from the ancient Scottish McLaurin Clan who were described as being 'grand, strong men' c.4th century. Williams was also related to the ancient Irish Fitzgerald Clan. Like Mindy McCready Robin Williams described his battle with demons stating: "The demons are still there… The little voice saying, you're garbage, you're nothing, you hear me, yeah… he's still there, believe me." When we study the McLaurin Coat of Arms we find that it contains two pyramids and as I've pointed out previously two pyramids create an eight pointed star symbolizing both the Babylonian demon goddess Lilith and 666.

Francis Scott Key Fitzgerald was sacrificed 9/24/1896 (9+24 = 33). F. Scott Key Fitzgerald is best known for his novel The Great Gatsby which was based on the Satanic Rothschild Family best known for their role in ushering in a New World Order and One World Religion they were also central to the assassination of Abraham Lincoln. Coincidently F. Scott Key Fitzgerald was related to Mary Surratt, who was hanged in 1865 for conspiring to assassinate Abraham Lincoln.

Irish American Philip Seymour Hoffman sacrificed 2/2/2014 with a heroin overdose. 222 has a number of occult meanings however the over arching symbolism is that number 2 signifies duality 1+1 = 2 or 11 which to occultists represents man above God. 11 is the essence of all that is sinful, harmful and imperfect. Coincidently Hoffman was sacrificed shortly after his appearance in the films "The Hunger Games: Mockingjay – Part 1&2". The trilogy was written by Suzanne Collins who is a descendant of the ancient Scottish Collins Clan one of the most power families throughout the world today. The Collins Clan was notorious for holding blood lust parties where they would decapitate Irish and Scottish Clansman in a nearby pit while their dinner guests watched. Philip' mother Marilyn of the Irish O'Connor family is related to the King of Connacht, c.971 AD. This family produced the last two High Kings of Ireland. The O'Connor bloodline helped to defeat the ancient old world order system of Nimrod and for this reason Philip Seymour Hoffman was sacrificed.

Scottish American Christopher Scott "Chris" Kyle was sacrificed 2/2/2013 by the Church of Babylon. At the time of his death Kyle was considered the most lethal sniper in American military history with 160 confirmed kills. 222 has a number of occult meanings however the over arching symbolism is that number 2 signifies duality 1+1 = 2 or 11 which to occultists represents man above God. 11 is the essence of all that is sinful, harmful and imperfect.

As in all of the previous examples of sacrificed Scots and Irish Chris Kyle' ancestral heritage made him a stimulating sacrifice for the Satanic Church of Babylon. Kyle' surname is derived from the prominent ancient King Coel Hen the progenitor of several kingly lines in southern Scotland and the father of Saint Helena and the grandfather of Roman Emperor Constantine the Great. Coincidently Kyle' best-selling book 'American Sniper: The Autobiography of the Most Lethal Sniper in U.S. Military History' was published by HarperCollins which is under the umbrella of News Corporation and controlled by militant anti-Christians Rupert Murdoch and Muslim Arab Prince Alwaleed bin Talal. Rupert Murdoch is also a major shareholder in Genie Israel Holdings, Ltd., along with Satanist Lord Jacob Rothschild.

Scottish American Actress Amanda Peterson murdered 7/3/2015. Peterson was an 80s icon staring in such films as, "can't buy me love" [1987] which was based on a high school girl who prostitutes herself out for $1,000 to a schoolmate played by Patrick Dempsey, so that Dempsey's character can have sex with her many girl friends; "The Lawless Land" [1988], a post-apocalyptic, eugenics propaganda film in which the lower classes are forbidden by the police state to fall in love, have children, raise a family, etc. and "Windrunner", a film which endorsed the occult e.g., speaking to the dead, etc. Peterson also starred alongside River Phoenix in the film "Explorers". Phoenix was sacrificed on Halloween night [10/31/1993] in front of actor Johnny Depp's nightclub "The Viper Room" the year the venue opened. Leonard Maltin, considered one of the most respected film critics in America, said about Amanda, "Amanda Peterson is excellent". The last photographs of Peterson were taken by Photographer Ryan Harstock [RockHardChic.com] in one of the pictures she is featured posing with a serpent.

Scottish/Irish Canadian Roderick George Toombs "Rowdy Roddy Piper" was sacrificed at age 61 on 7/30/2015 (7+30=37). There exists an interesting relation between numbers 37 and 666: from 666 we obtain 6+6+6=18 and 18 x 37 = 666. Toombs was considered by wrestling fans No. 1 of the top 50 villains in wrestling history by the WWE. Toombs also played the broke and homeless character

"Nada" in John Carpenter's 80s B-movie "They Live", which was based on Ray Nelson's "Eight O'Clock in the Morning". Toombs broke and homeless character "Nada" means "nothing" in Spanish, which is exactly what elites believe the masses are worth. What's more his characters' destitute status personifies the elites plan for the global populace. In essence "They Live" communicated how global elites use mass media to control the American populace. A character in the film also publicizes the Serpent Cult of Dann stating, "The venom of snakes is under their lips. Their mouths are full of bitterness and curses. And their paths, nothing but ruin and misery. And the fear of God is not before their eyes! They have taken the hearts and minds of our leaders. They have recruited the rich and powerful, and they have blinded us to the truth! And our human spirit is corrupted. Why do we worship greed? Because outside the limit of our sight, feeding off us, perched on top of us from birth to death are our owners. Our owners – they have us. They control us. They are our masters. Wake-up. They're all about you, all around you!"

Irishman Dr. David Kelly murdered 7/17/2003 at the age of 59 was the chief scientific officer to the UK's Military of Defense and senior advisor to the proliferation and arms control secretariat, and to the Foreign Office's non-proliferation department. Kelly was senior advisor on biological weapons to the UN biological weapons inspections teams (UNSCOM) from 1994-1999 and in the opinion of his peers, was pre-eminent in his field worldwide. Dr. Kelly is responsible for exposing Downing Street's head of communications, Alastair Campbell, of deceiving the world about Iraq's 'weapons of mass destruction' a well documented untruth parroted by President George H.W. Bush and George W. Bush a lie which led to the deaths of 32,222 U.S. soldiers.

Scottish American Don C. Wiley murdered 11/22/2001 [11+22=33] in Memphis Tennessee. It's noteworthy to mention that Memphis was created by 33rd degree Freemason's James Winchester and Andrew Jackson. The two men named their settlement, on the Mississippi River 'Memphis' after Memphis in Egypt. Known as the, "Irish Channel," this was an unruly district along the Mississippi River in the early 1800s. Its population consisted of tens of thousands of Irish immigrants who were digging out the Mississippi's New Basin Canal which opened in 1838. Due to mosquito-borne illnesses nearly 30,000 Irish died during the dig and are currently buried in mass graves along the banks of the Mississippi River. Jackson and Winchester were both well aware of the fact that Memphis Egypt contained the largest and most important temple dedicated to the worship of the creator god Ptah as well as the famed stepped pyramid of Djoser.
Today Memphis contains a large number of Satanic Freemasonry 125
temples to Lucifer including the third largest pyramid in the world

which serves as a 21,000 seat sports arena for the Memphis Grizzlies and University of Memphis Men's Basketball Program. Don C. Wiley was a pre-eminent structural biologist and Harvard biochemistry professor responsible for developing key research on the structure of viruses and proteins in the human immune system. In 1995, Wiley won Albert Lasker Medical Research Awards for his work on the immune system. In 1999, Wiley won the prestigious Japan Prize for their discoveries of how the immune system protects humans from infections.

Scottish American Dr. Shane Todd had a Phd in electrical engineering with expertise with GaN (Gallium Nirtride). Shane was working on a 'one of a kind' machine, with a dual use in commercial and in military application, requiring expertise in the area of GaN (Gallium Nitride). Shane resigned his post at the Chinese company Huawei after being asked by Huawei leadership to comprise U.S. security. Todd bought his ticket to fly back to the U.S. on July 1, 2012 he was murdered June 22nd.

Irish American Dr. Joseph Morrissey stabbed to death 4/6/2010 was an immune pharmacologist and professor in the College of Pharmacy.

Irish American Caroline Coffey murdered 6/3/2010 was Cornell University bio-medicine researcher. In addition to receiving massive cuts to her throat her apartment was set on fire.

Scottish American Matthew Allison murdered 10/13/2004 with a car bomb at an Osceola Country Florida Wal-Mart store. Allison was a molecular biologist specializing in biotechnology.

Scottish/Irishman John Clark murdered 8/12/2004 was an expert in animal science and biotechnology where he developed techniques for the genetic modification of livestock, which paved the way for cloning of and the creation of Dolly the sheep. Professor Clark led the Roslin Institute in Midlothian, one of the world's leading animal biotechnology research centers. Clark was in charge of a project to produce human proteins, which could be used in the treatment in human disease, in sheep's milk. Professor Clark founded three spinoff firms from Roslin (i) PPL Therapeutics,(ii) Rosgen and (iii) Roslin BioMed. It is worth mentioning here that the Church of Babylon has worked feverishly to develop genetic manipulation for the expressed purpose of fusing genetic material taken from 'The Antichrist' with the genetic code of Man [Mark of The Beast].

Irishman John Mullen was murdered 6/29/2004 with a large dose of arsenic. Mullen was a nuclear research scientist with McDonnell Douglas and contract work for Boeing.

Irishman William T. McGuire murdered 4/29/2004 [4+29=33] and place into three suitcases found floating in Chesapeake Bay. McGuire was NJ University Professor and senior programmer analyst and professor at the New Jersey Institute of Technology in Newark. McGuire was the world's leading microbiologist and an expert in developing multiple levels of bio-containment facilities.

Irishman Dr. Michael Patrick Kiley murdered 1/24/2004 was a world renowned Ebola and Mad-Cow Expert. At the time of Kiley's death he was working on the lab upgrade to BSL 4 at the UTMB Galvaston Lab for Homeland Security to house some of the world's deadliest pathogens of tropical and emerging infectious disease as well as bio-weaponized ones.

Keep in mind while processing the aforementioned sacrifices that the U.S. Scottish/Irish population combined, make up just 10 percent of the U.S. Compare that with the U.S. Babylonian Talmudist population who make up 1.8% of the population, yet control 99% of Hollywood and never die under mysterious circumstances. The fact is the ratio of unexplained deaths between Scottish/Irish/African Americans and Babylonian Talmudists e.g., suicides, murders, car accidents, drug overdose, etc. are astounding, and yet these statistics only represent our 'celebrity' population. When one considers the number of 'average' Americans who die or disappear suspiciously, the percentages are off the chart disturbing. Consider the fact that nearly 1 Million adults and 1 Hundred Thousand children disappear without a trace every year in the United States. This statistic paints a kind of Morlock/Eloi natural balance in effect and makes one reconsider the passage in The Holy Bible which describes the giant Babylonian god Nimrod as one who ruled "...in the earth". A concept Hollywood makes light of in the film "Cabin In The Woods."

Charles Kingsley was a priest for the Church of England and friend to Charles Darwin. He is one of the first men to praise Darwin's book titled: "On the Origin of Species by Means of Natural Selection, or the Preservation of Favoured Races in the Struggle for Life", an ideology which led to the slaughter of 66 million Christians during WWII. In 1860 Kingsley wrote a letter to his wife after visiting Ireland, a region recently devastated by the Church of Babylon orchestrated 'Potato Famine' [ethnic cleansing] and where more than 1 million Irish men, women, and children lay dead. He wrote:

"I am haunted by the human chimpanzees I saw along that hundred miles of horrible country... To see white Chimpanzees is dreadful; if they were black one would not feel it so much, but their skin, except where tanned by exposure, are as white as ours." - Charles Kingsley

Couple the aforesaid with the fact that the Church of Babylon for the past 300 years worked feverishly to eliminate the ancient Gaelic language and the truth surrounding the advanced technology of ancient Celtic people. For instance, U.S. Babylonian Talmudist politicians sit on boards that influence the past and future of Ireland and Scotland. For example, U.S. Congressman Eliot Engel is an Executive Board Member of the Congressional Committee on Irish Affairs. Babylonian Talmudists have for generations been interested in the affairs of Ireland and Scotland whose populace is nearly 90 percent Christian. For instance, Talmudist Congresswoman Nita M. Lowey who represents parts of Westchester County, Queens, and the Bronx has taken a key role in "promoting democracy" throughout Ireland. The question the people of Ireland should be asking is... Why is a Rothschild controlled Babylonian Talmudist interested in promoting "democracy" throughout Ireland, a Nation whose majority is moving towards a United Island by 2030 and whose populace wishes to secede from Rothschild controlled England, in favor of Irish Unification and "Home Rule". Recently, the Church of Babylon controlled Scottish government proposed a bill that would appoint a government supervisor to oversee every child in the country from birth onward. This bill will open up a new totalitarian direction for Scottish society. It is designed to establish universal citizen surveillance via parent licensing and early interference, effectively ensuring state oversight and ownership of all Scottish children.

"That the sons of God saw the daughters of men that they [were] fair; and they took them wives of all which they chose. There were giants in the earth in those days; and also after that, when the sons of God came in unto the daughters of men, and they bare [children] to them, the same [became] mighty men which [were] of old, men of renown." - Genesis 6:2-4

There is a rich tradition of memorializing battles with giant emissaries of Nimrod throughout ancient Briton and Celtic texts. These oral traditions were common during and after the reign of the Babylonian god Nimrod. One of the most misinterpreted civilizations during this period was the Druids, Celts, Pics, etc. Modernist scholars for generations have ignorantly labeled these groups mindless, murderous, marauding Barbarians which are at best intellectually dishonest assertions. The truth is after the fall of Babylon these groups experienced a generational restructuring of their spiritual identity, the same kind of revisionist transformation neopagan cults today have practiced. During the period of druidism their leaders would select which 'ancient knowledge' to endorse based on the political and economic ambitions of their elders, this ultimately formed the spiritual belief system upon which the Druidic cult was based. This system
128 of worship relied heavily on the significance of sacred animals, earth mysteries, etc. an abbreviated and idolized pagan interpretation of

one of the oldest books in the Holy Bible, Job 12:7-8 which reads:

"But ask now the beasts, and they shall teach thee; and the fowls of the air, and they shall tell thee: Or speak to the earth, and it shall teach thee: and the fishes of the sea shall declare unto thee."

The ancient Druids also left behind evidence that they interacted with ancient giants. Julius Caesar in his 'Commentarii de Bello Gallico' claimed that the Celts used giant wicker effigy's to sacrifice people a claim which has been disproved by modern archeology. The fact is Caesar' 'Commentarii' was nothing more than an ancient disinformation campaign, in truth the ancient tradition of burning wicker giants [top, left] began as a way for ancient Celts to memorialize their ancient ancestors victory over their giants subjugators.

This ancient Celtic tradition is still celebrated throughout the world by neopagans, for instance 501(c)(3) "Burning Man Project" co-founded by Scottish American John Law and inspired by Scottish American and Ace Junkyard owner, Bill Kennedy The organization holds an annual festival in Black Rock City Desert which attracts thousands of spectators and generates $8-10 million each year. The Burning Man Project has evolved from a burning effigy in 1989 [middle] into a Masonic Babylonian Talmudist indoctrination camp, complete with occult pyramids, all-seeing-eye's of Satan and Stars of Remphan [Satan] for 2015 [bottom, left].

Another example of how our ancient ancestors interacted with giants is chronicled by King Brutus, the first colonizer of Britain, emphatically states that he had to displace an indigenous race of 'giants' ruled by 'Gogmagog'. (Geoffrey of Monmouth. pp. 72-30.)

129

In Homer's Odyssey, the hero Odysseus and his crew encounter man-eating giants. Book Ten tells us that upon reaching the island of the Laestrygonians, Odysseus orders his men to survey the island. During their inspection they encounter a large girl and follow her to her father's palace. "On entering his fine palace, they found his wife there, massive as a mountaintop, and they were shocked. She called her husband, mighty Antiphates, straight from their gathering place, and he embarked on their cruel destruction. He promptly seized one of my men, and prepared to eat him, while the other two sprang up and fled to the ships. Then Antiphates roused the city, and hearing his cry the huge Laestrygonians crowded in from all sides, a countless host of Giants not men. From the cliffs they pelted us with the largest rocks a man could lift, and from all the ships there rose the groans of dying men and the splintering of timbers. Spearing the men like fishes, they carried them off to their loathsome feast." – Homer: The Odyssey, Book X

The most famous story from the Odyssey appears in book nine when Odysseus visits the island of the Cyclops (Kyklopes). Odysseus and his men are trapped in the cave of Polyphemus, a giant Cyclops, who devours six of Odysseus' men. Odysseus successfully excapes from the cave after burning out the cyclops' eye, and then barely escapes the island.

To better understand where these legends originated, all one must do is consult The Holy Bible's account of 'giants' and 'dragons'. Unfortunately, most people have been deceived by the Serpent Cult of Dann and their proxy, Masonic Babylonian Talmudism, whose modernist historians, archeologists, and movie producers promote the religion of evolutionism and billion year old 'Dinosaurs'. Do you know the word Dinosaur was invented in 1841 by Church of Babylon member Sir Richard Owen? He invented it to replace the Biblical word 'Dragon' which is mentioned 34 times inside The Holy Bible. Even in 1891 the word 'Dinosaur' was still not in an English Dictionary. One example of Giants given to us in the Holy Bible is 'Og', King of Bashan, who was nearly 12 feet tall and had 6 fingers and 6 toes. Even the seemingly primitive ancient Celtic language of "Ogham" [Og-Ham] preserved the Gaulish and Celtic accounts of ancient rivalries between the giant King of Bashan [Og] and Noah's descendents Japath, Shem and Ham. Ham's son [Canaan] was cursed by Noah and would remain so in perpetuity to his brethren's offspring for what Ham, "had done unto him [Noah]" [Genesis 9:20-27]. The Holy Bible refers to Egypt as "the land of Ham" in Psalms 78:51; 105:23, 27; 106:22 and 1 Chronicles 4:40. The Torah [Old Testament] states that the sons of Ham [Cush, Mizraim, Phut and Canaan] populated Africa and parts of Asia and according to [1 Chronicles 1:10] the son of Ham [Cush] is the father of Nimrod.

"For only Og king of Bashan remained of the remnant of giants; behold, his bedstead was a bedstead of iron; is it not in Rabbath of the children of Ammon? nine cubits was the length thereof, and four cubits the breadth of it, after the cubit of a man" - Deuteronomy 3:11

Og is mentioned in ancient literature as being alive from the time of Noah up until the time of his death, when the Israelites killed him and appropriated his holdings. Ancient text also describes how Og king of Bashan had a special compartment in Noah's Ark made just for him and that he sat upon the top of the ark, riding out the flood for the duration of the storm from this location. Why on earth was there an 11' 10" giant on Noah's Ark? Did the giant Og assist with the construction of the Ark? Was the giant 'Og' in fact the giant Nimrod? All things considered it's a logical conclusion given the fact that Noah's flood occurred c.1656 AC and the giant Babylonian god Nimrod is destroyed c.1756 AC.

The Biblical account of Og is one of many records describing man's interaction with giants. The following is a shortlist of discoveries purposely hidden by organizations such as the Smithsonian and UNESCO:

200-600 B.C. – Two 36 foot giant skeletons uncovered by Carthaginians. (Mt. Blanco Fossil Museum, Crosbyton, TX 79322, www.mtblanco.com)

2,000 years ago - Roman Emperor Maximinus stood 8'6" tall [Chronicles of the Roman Emperors 1995, p.160].

1456 A.D. – 23 foot giant skeleton was discovered beside a river in Valence France.

1613 – A nearly complete 26' 6" skeleton was unearthed near the castle of Chaumont in France.

1519 - When Hernán Cortés conquered the Aztec Empire he reported that the Aztec's presented Cortez with the skeleton's of a race of men and women who were of immense stature with heavy bones. Cortez stated a thigh bone from one of these giants was as tall as Cortez. [Discovery and Conquest of Mexico and New Spain, Bernal Diaz de Castillo, p.185].

1577 – 19'6" giant discovered in the Canton of Lucerne

1811 - British East India Company appointed resident at Baghdad, Claudius James Rich, discovers the first stela of the giant 16ft tall Babylonian god Nimrod.

1879 - A 9'8" skeleton was discovered in a stone burial mount in 131 Brewersville, Indiana. [Indianapolis News, 11/10/79].

1883 - A 12' skeleton was found by soldiers in Lompoc Rancho, CA [The Unexplained by Dr. Karl Shuker p.151].

1891 - A 12' skeleton was discovered near Tucson, AZ, like Og and Nimrod the giant had 6 fingers and 6 toes [Lost Cities of North and Central America by David Hatcher Childress p.315, 351, 390, 468, 496].

1895 – Iron ore miner Mr. Dyer of County Antrim, Ireland uncovered a 12' 2", 2 ton fossilized giant.

1902 - Twenty 9' skeletons were discovered in Shreveport, LA [The Daily Town Talk 12/9/1902.

1925 - Eight 9' giants were discovered in South Bend, Indiana. All were wearing heavy copper armor [Weird America by Jim Brandon p.84].

1931 - A skeleton measuring 10' tall was discovered in Humbolt Lake, NV. [Lovelock Review-Miner's June 19, 1931].

1950 – In turkey many tombs containing the remains of giants were discovered. At two sites leg bones were uncovered which measured 47.24 inches long. It's estimated that these giants stood some 14-16 feet tall and had 20-22 inch long feet.

1968 - General Secretary of the Romanian Communist Party, Nicolae Ceausescu (1967-1989) dispatched his most secret department of the Romanian Intelligence Service, known as "Department Zero", to a cave system near the Transylvania Mountain region to investigate the discovery of ancient high-tech artifacts. In 1989 Ceausescu' Department Zero examined the Nacu village, a collection of ancient pyramids standing over 100 feet tall. These pyramids are located high atop the Buzau mountain's in Romania. Ancient oral traditions tell us that these developments were once occupied by ancient Celtic warriors and constructed by giants. Ancient legends describe a time when this region was controlled by a princess named Sona, who struggled against marauding Giants crossing over the Fagaras Mountains. When these giants descended upon Sona' warriors from the surrounding mountains they crossed through the Olt River and using the rivers mud constructed the pyramids, approximately 155 miles outside Bucharest. During their inspection of the Buzau Mountain region, Ceausescu' Department Zero identified several giant skeletons that were nearly 16ft tall and had 6 fingers and double rows of teeth. "And there was yet a battle in Gath, where was a man of great stature, that had on every hand six fingers, and on every foot six toes, four and twenty in number; and he also was born to the giant." – 2 Samuel 21:20. Coincidently in that same year Ceausescu' Romania was overthrown by the Rothschild Family's central banking cartel through what became known as the Romanian Revolution. During this revolution both Nicolae and his wife Elena were shot by a firing squad.

In addition to legends of giants, the Carpathians maintain very old traditions regarding battles between Celts and an ancient tribe of "shape-shifters" known as "Dacians," who were able to transform themselves into wolves. During the 4th century B.C. ancient Celts fought against the demonically influenced, "Dacians" in and around the Carpathian Mountains and west of the Black Sea. This area included the present-day countries of Romania, Moldova, Ukraine, Serbia, Bulgaria, Hungary and Poland. Ancient Celts describe Dacians as belonging to a Serpent Cult proxy known as the "Secret Brotherhood of the Wolf" a cult that would become part of the Khazarian Kingdom of Babylonian Talmudists. The Brotherhood of the Wolf was in antiquity and is to this day comprised of men who embrace the very darkest of demonology religions known as, "Lycanthropy" which dates back to the Vinca culture c.3000 BC. Dacians are said to have physically transformed themselves into "werewolves" during battle. According to Greek geographer, philosopher and historian, "Strabo" [c.63 BC – 24 AD] the large ancient Celtic civilization known as the "Boii" fought against the Dacian werewolf cult, Strabo writes:

"the Boii [Celts] were merely driven out of the regions they occupied; and after migrating to the regions round about the Ister, lived with the Taurisci, and carried on war against the Daci [Dacians]"

According to the Irish epic, "Tain Bo Cuailnge" the warriors of Connacht encounter Ulster's seventeen-year-old champion, "Cuchulainn" the Irish Achilles, who becomes possessed by what the ancient Irish referred to as a "warp-spasm," shape-shifting into a werewolf. In part it reads, "The first warp-spasm seized Cuchulainn, and made him into a monstrous thing... like the baying of a watch-dog at its feed."

1970 - Two 9' skeletons were found in Virginia City, NV.

The government of Turkey says that they have discovered the grave of the Biblical Noah near Ararat and that Noah's skeleton is over 12' tall.

Dr. Kent Hovind **www.creationtoday.org** holding a replica thigh bone of a 16' tall giant discovered in Egypt [left]. Dr. Hovind is by far one the most feared and notable creation speakers in the

133

world. He was a science teacher for 15 years and has debated more than 100 scientists concerning the religion of evolutionism. Because of his creationist ministry Dr. Hovind was targeted by militant Antichristians and imprisoned for nearly a decade.

The stela of Nimrod [left] was discovered by Claudius James Rich c.1811. A devout member of the Church of Babylon, Rich was just 24 years old when he was appointed the British East India Company's resident at Baghdad. The stela features the giant god Nimrod holding the leashes of his reclaimed possessions, the Egyptians, one of the tribes who were disbanded upon Babylon's destruction. If you look closely, you'll see that the Babylonian god Nimrod is holding the leashes of one man and one woman. His captives' leashes are connected to a hook in the nose and bridle in their mouth. The carving accurately depicts the size and scale of the giant Nimrod compared to ancient Man, supporting claims made by our ancient ancestors that giants in fact cruelly ruled earth. You will also notice that Nimrod's 'fez' style cap is identical to the Serpent Tribe of Dann icon [pg.33].

"Because thy rage against me, and thy tumult, is come up into mine ears, therefore will I put my hook in thy nose, and my bridle in thy lips, and I will turn thee back by the way by which thou camest." - Isaiah 37:29

134

During his many visits to the Newgrange shrine, William Wilde produced an extensive catalog of drawings associated with the Serpent Cult's moniker ["X"] which is featured on the stela of Nimrod [pg.18, "C"]. Even more fascinating is the shape and design of the Newgrange shrine itself. Many academics believe that Newgrange is merely a burial site or celestial observatory. Then there are those within the Church of Babylon who attempt to discredit Biblical cannon using dubious assertions and childish prattle for their foundational argument. They posit based on physical evidence of ancient Celtic influence around the ancient world and the religion of evolutionism that The Holy Bible is unsound and that Biblical cannon must in fact be based solely on the traditions of ancient Celtic people. A constant we find throughout the aforesaid theories are the fingerprints of Khazarian Babylonian Talmudist Supremacy and the modernist religion of Theosophy invented by Russian Talmudist and occultist Helena Blavatsky. Much of the same supremacy hate speech once trumpeted by Adolf Hitler is repeated throughout the pages of Theosophist writings. They promote the theory that ancient Celtic people developed and distributed highly advanced technology around the world, the caveat being these ancient Celtic tribes were descendants of the ancient Khazarian Empire [c.1st century BC - 900 AD] located in what would become Russia. As someone whose ancestral heritage dates back to Adam and Christian Irish Kings, I would be dishonoring their legacy and remiss in allowing such rubbish to be perpetuated by salesmen turned Freemason 'Scholars' blending materialist philosophy, asserting 'superior' minds, or 'superior' types of people, all the while basing it on Pseudoscience and defective logic.

While it certainly seems plausible that the highly developed Celtic people possessed an advanced system of terrestrial and celestial measurement, my theory suggests that there is literally more than meets the eye at Newgrange in Ireland and Callanish [Calanais Standing Stones] in Scotland [left].

When we examine the side-by-side comparison between the aerial views of Newgrange [pg.136] with that of the anatomical profile of an eye [pg.136] it becomes clear as the nose on your face, that ancient Celts constructed a monument to the 8th century B.C. Greek Goddess Iris. 135 Furthermore when we study an aerial view of the Calanais Standing

Stones in Scotland we see a very distinct cross shape, reminiscent of the Serpent Cult's "X" located on the stela of Nimrod [pg.18, "C"].

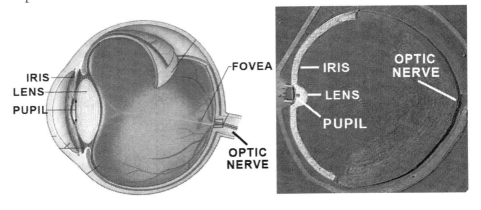

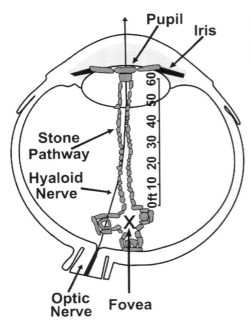

Even more compelling is the graphic that I've created of the stone pathway inside of Newgrange superimposed on the anatomy of an eyeball [left]. As you can see, the hyaloid canal nerve crosses directly through the large stone bowl inside the stone chamber, whilst the Fovea is contained inside the main chamber of the Newgrange Eye. The hyaloid nerve then travels down the stone pathway and out past the original entrance stone which is decorated with "666" and eye-motifs. Interestingly, the ancient Latin meaning of the word "fovea", means "pit", referring to the pits where wheat was stored. It also means feminine referring to the Goddess Iris. Latin is of course an ancient Italic language originally spoken by the Italic Latins in Latium and Ancient Rome. Contrary to the academic narrative related to the origins of the name "Irish" this author believes that the peoples of ancient Hibernia [Ireland] who have been called Eriu, Fodla, Banba by Islanders, Iouerne and Hiverne by Greeks and Hibernia to the Romans, were in fact named Irish after the Newgrange goddess Iris [Irish] and not after the welsh word, "gwyddel" meaning raiders or piracy. Nor were the people of Ireland named after the matron goddess of Ireland, "Ériu

136

[Erin]," the daughter of Irish mother goddess, "Ernmas," of the Tuatha Dé Danann, otherwise known as the Serpent Cult of Dann. Like the goddess Iris, who is associated with a trinity, Ernmas' daughters created the trinity of war goddesses [Badb, Macha, Morrigan] and a trinity of sons [Glonn, Gnim, Coscar]. Badb is associated with Ulster's "Cuchulainn," who becomes possessed by what the ancient Irish referred to as a "warp-spasm."

Archeology's claim that Newgrange predates the Egyptian Pyramids runs into a mound of difficulty when you compare its obvious shape with ancient texts which tell us that predictions based on 'Iris Patterns' goes back to ancient Greece, as documented in stone inscriptions, painted ceramic artifacts, and the writings of Hippocrates. What's more the father of medicine gleaned his knowledge of "Iris Prediction" from Chaldea in Babylonia. Today, Iris Prediction persists throughout the 'New Age' movement community under the moniker of "iridology."

An attribute linking the father of medicine [Hippocrates], Goddess Iris, Hermes, the theory of Pangea and the Serpent Cult of Dann is the "Caduceus" that goddess Iris brandished. The Caduceus is the most ancient of Serpent Cult symbols. It consists of a central staff entwined by twin serpents or a double-headed snake coiled into a double helix. The Iris shrine at Newgrange features a large number of "Xs" and "XXs" on its exterior, which is an abbreviated version of the Serpent Cult's double Helix.

The picture below features the very large stone which rests above the entrance of the Iris shrine. The fascia of this stone contains four "XXs signifying the Serpent Death Cult" The Caduceus was also carried by Hermes otherwise known as Apollyon from the Book of Revelation "The Beast from the Pit" – Revelation 9:11. The god Hermes is also said to have invented masturbation for his son, the god Pan.

Throughout the world people have been deceived into believing that the Caduceus Serpent Death Cult logo symbolizes healing and divine communication.

Today, Iris Prediction persists throughout the 'New Age' movement community under the moniker of "iridology." Additional evidence which demonstrates Newgrange is a shrine to the Goddess Iris and the Babylonian god Nimrod is the correlation between the symbol which has come to symbolize ancient Ireland itself and the Goddess Iris.   137

The shape and design of the Iris shrine at Newgrange holds an addition secret that has never been discussed outside of certain circles. The ancients who built this structure wanted to communicate, to future generations knowledge regarding earth's physical characteristics, namely their belief that earth is a flat surface, contained by a circle of ice and covered by a crystal dome or firmament, "The heavens declare the glory of God; and the firmament sheweth his handywork." [Ezekiel 1:22]. A comprehensive series of essays which use scripture, reason and fact to argue in favor of a 'flat earth' was published in 1901 by Scotsman, David Wardlow Scott, in his book, "Terra Firma: the Earth Not a Planet, Proven from Scripture, Reason, and Fact.

Gleason's "New Standard Map Of The World, published 11/15/1892 [pg.139], illustrates the geometric relationship between earth's plain and the position of our sun. When you examine this map you'll notice that the triangulation between our sun and the two terrestrial points on earth create the so called 'all-seeing-eye.' The capstone of this pyramid contains 13 points whereas the two flanking stars contain 18 points [6+6+6=18] and are connected to two smaller pyramids. These three pyramids represent Khufu, Khafre and Menkaure within the Giza pyramid complex in Egypt which is a mathematical expression for a flat earth. What's more Charles Piazzi Smyth [1819-1900], Astronomer Royal for Scotland, believed Khufu was built by the descendents of Noah and originally represented the "Bible in Stone." His evidence is detailed in his book, "Our Inheritance in the Great Pyramid" [1864]. The Holy Bible references "...an alter to the LORD in the midst [middle] of the land of Egypt, and a pillar [monument] at the border thereof to the LORD [Isaiah 19:19-20]. The Great Pyramid [Khufu] is both at the center and the border of Egypt. The word "Gizeh" even means "border."

The Book of Kells, created c.6th century A.D in Irish and Scottish monasteries, contains many ciphers within the ideograms that adorn this ornate manuscript, knowledge which has been concealed for millennia. For instance the ideogram [left] features the "four quarters" symbol [Revelation 20:8], [bottom]; an illustration of the "fountains of the great deep" [Genesis 7:11], [center] and the Pyramid of Khufu in Egypt [top]. Embedded within the Khufu Pyramid is the number "77" which evokes Genesis 7:11 [7x11=77] and the revenge of Lamech which I will expand on later. The Khufu diagram also contains a line down the center of the pyramid communicating that this "alter to the LORD" is in the geographic center of the land surface of the whole world.

Additional scriptures within the Holy Bible that teach "Planet Earth" is an immovable plane are: [1 Chronicles 16:30] which reads, "the world also shall be stable, that it be not moved." [Daniel 4-10-11] reads, "behold a tree in the midst [center] of the earth, and the height thereof was great. and the sight thereof to the end of all the earth:" [Matthew 4:8] reads, "Again, the devil taketh him [Jesus Christ] up into an exceeding high mountain, and sheweth him all the kingdoms of the world, and the glory of them;" The earth could not be a spinning sphere if God made it "immovable." The king could not have seen a giant tree in the center of the earth from the "farthest bounds" if earth was a sphere. The Devil could not have shown Jesus Christ "all the kingdoms of the world" if the earth was a sphere.

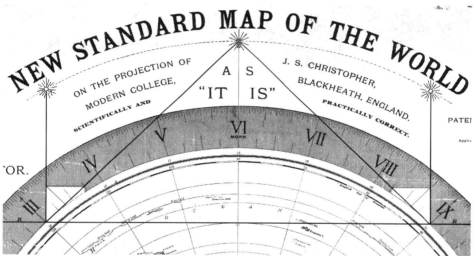

Throughout history religious authorities and secret societies have concealed their flat earth bias in plain sight. For instance the ancient papal authorized practice of "Tonsure" [left] represents the ancient "secret knowledge" that planet earth is a flat landmass, under a dome, encircled by ice.

The Jesuit controlled Catholic Church has participated in a number of duplicitous acts meant to undermine the 'Churches' and doctrine of Jesus Christ. One glaring example is their endorsement of Satan's 'big-lie' that "...ye shall be as gods." [genesis 3:5]. According to the Catechism of the Catholic Church, Ignatius Press p.116, or p.129 in the 2nd edition by Doubleday Publishing, "For the Son of God became man **so that we might become God**." 139

It's noteworthy to mention that Doubleday Publishing is now owned by Penguin Random House, the largest general-interest trade book publisher in the world and is controlled by 'Bertelsmann', a private German Corporation. Until 2009, 80.9% of the capital shares in Bertelsmann were controlled by Reinhard Mohn (worth $2.5 billion), a member of Hitler's Nazi Party, who served under Erwin Rommel's Afrika Korps, and owner of the sixth largest media conglomerate in the world.

Not only does the Catholic Church endorse Satan's 'big-lie' of man becoming god, they associate Lucifer with one of their many deep space telescopes. According to a 4/23/2010 article inside of Popular Science Magazine, the large binocular telescope is:

"named for the Devil, whose name itself means 'morning star.' Lucifer is part of the Large Binocular Telescope, which happens to be right next to the Vatican Observatory on Mt. Graham in Tucson. That's right; the Vatican has an observatory in Arizona, manned by Jesuit astronomers. Scientists at five German universities designed the instrument, and they came up with the name, according to Daniel Stolte, 'In Germany, they wouldn't have the same hesitation that Americans would have, since it's a very secular country,' he said. 'I may be completely off, but that's just my hunch -- <u>for us Germans, Lucifer just sounds cool</u>. It's more historical than emotional."

The United Nations is another organization that promotes the flat earth concept in plain sight. For example a flat earth diagram along with an 8-pointed star of Lilith is featured on the United Nations flag [left]. This is the same organization who coddles UN members such as Satanist Alice Bailey's "Lucifer Trust Publishing" [Lucis Trust], "The Lucis Trust is recognized by the United Nations as a non-governmental organization and is represented at regular briefing sessions at UN headquarters. The Lucis Trust is on the roster of the United Nations economic and social Council." – 2009 United Nations Geneva Yearbook. Alice Bailey was a student of Satanist Helena Blavatsky. Regarding Freemasonry and how it's been instrumental in advancing occultism, Satanism, etc., Bailey is quoted in saying:

"The Masonic Movement [Freemasonry] when it can be divorced from politics and social end and from its present paralyzing condition of inertia will meet the need of those who can and should wield power. It is the custodian of the law; it is the home of

140

the Mysteries and the seat of ignition. It holds in its symbolism the ritual of Deity [Satan]. And the way of salvation is pictorially preserved in its work. The methods of Deity [Satan] are demonstrated in its Temples and under the all-seeing Eye [Satan]. The work can go forward. It is a far more occult organization than can be realized and is intended to be the training school for the coming advanced occultists."

Irish American actor, Jim Carey's film "The Truman Show" embodies the ancient Masonic "secret knowledge" of a flat earth as well. Carey's film contains a number of references to the occult. For instance Ed Harris' character, "Christof" [Christ of Tru Man] watches over Truman while sitting inside of a giant control center which doubles as a moon, symbolizing the Babylonian demon moon god Shamash, and an all-seeing-eye of Satan. Truman's character discovers his life is a sham after a theatrical light labeled "Sirius 9 Canis" falls from the artificial morning sky, nearly hitting him. To the Church of Babylon, Sirius, otherwise known as "Draco" or "The Dog Star" represents the home of their god Lucifer. The movie ends with Carey's character escaping from his false reality by climbing up "The Steps of Freemasonry," otherwise known as the structure of freemasonry.

The ancient Iris [Irish] clans would have scoffed at modern day academic theories regarding Newgrange. Another impossible theory that would have perplexed the highly advanced ancient Celtic civilization is the woefully flawed theory of "Pangea," invented by German polar researcher, geophysicist and meteorologist, Alfred Wegener who amid peer ridicule and contempt named his scheme after the demonic god Pan and "Gaia." Pangea posits that all of the continents once fit together "millions of years ago," omitting what are clear symmetry and cohesion disparities between the continents. Wegener is also the originator of the flawed science behind boring ice core samples. On Wegener's fourth and final expedition to Greenland in 1930 to study the ancient knowledge related to planet earth being a level surface, contained by ice, Wegener, aged 50, allegedly died and was buried by his associate Rasmus Villumsen, aged 23 who then disappeared without a trace.

 The 'Triple Spiral' [left] is one of the main symbols of Celtic Reconstructionism and is concidered by many to be indecipherable. So honored was this symbol ancient Irish swore their oaths or what they called the "Three Realms" - Land, Sea and Sky. Coincidently, the Goddess Iris was the goddess of sea, sky and rainbow.

The King James Bible teaches us that the rainbow represents God's covenant that he would not destroy the earth again with a flood. This is a profound revelation considering there is an ancient Celtic oral tradition which tells us that Noah sent his granddaughter (Cesair) to Ireland to evade the coming flood. It is said that Cesair alerted the ancients of Ireland to the fact that this part of the world would be protected from God's judgment. Church of Babylon apologists have invested a great deal of resources shielding this legend from not only the native people of Ireland, but the entire global community. Serpent Cult proxies suggest all of what the ancient Celtic people experienced was nothing more than an "indigenous creation myth," however if one studies the body of evidence e.g., oral traditions physical evidence, etc. surrounding Noah's great flood, we see that ancient cultures interacted in some fashion with the Babylonian god Nimrod and his offspring of giants which further supports Biblical text which tells us that the giant Nimrod ruled over an old world order and because of his misdeeds God smote him.

What's intriguing about the Goddess Iris is that like Mercury [Hermes/Apollyon], Iris too was a messenger of Zeus, the God of the pantheon of giants. Furthermore, Nimrod's "Triple Spiral" ideogram is in fact comprised of three 6 shaped snakes [666], the form Satan chose in the Garden of Eden, as well as an abstract modification symbolizing the Serpent Tribe of Dann. These elements are then bound together with an occult pyramid. Coincidently, this same swirling 6 design is represented throughout Nimrod's hair and beard [pg.18, "F"]. I believe this appoints the Triple Spiral as a mark of subjugation imposed onto the ancient Celtic civilization by Nimrod and upheld for millennia by descendants of Nimrod such as Cernunnos a horned god whose symbol of power was venerated by ancient Celtic chiefs by wearing horns on their helmets. I also believe that when we juxtapose the aforesaid knowledge with that of Saint Patrick's "Confessio" and art depicting the Saint trampling on snakes, it would appear that the "evil", Saint Patrick, vanquished from ancient Ireland c.433 A.D. did not represent a few slithery reptiles but the remnants of the ancient Serpent Cult of Dann. This ancient Serpent Cult is depicted throughout the ancient world, including in India's "Sarpa Satra yagna", which depicts a war between the Emperor Janamajeya and the Serpent Cult of Dann, who had murdered Janamajeya's father Parikshit. Though unrelated it's noteworthy to mention that Alexander the Great, who died at age 33, is said to have been the son of Zeus and is portrayed in ancient relics as having horns on either side of his head.

Consider another ancient oral tradition regarding the 'Valley of the Mata'. Ancient Celts tell us that they killed a 4 headed 100 legged monster at Newgrange and tor the monster limb from limb, and threw it into the Boyne River. My theory is that the 'monster' in this legend, in modern terms, is an allegory for the Babylonian power structure that ancient Celts experienced. That is the very same Babylonian New World Order system that we are witnessing being created in 2014. In addition to the ancient allegory, I believe there is physical evidence to support the notion that the 'four-heads' represented Nimrod who deceived the ["four quarters of the earth" - Revelation 20:8] and that the '100 legs' represented fifty giant Nimrodian offspring's on the scale of the giant Og. Coincidently, there are as many large circular Barrow Cemeteries throughout Ireland as well as a number of other locations around the world. Do these mounds symbolically represent the final resting place for these giant ancient foes?

Ancient oral and written Celtic traditions and legends provide us with key data necessary to constructing an accurate depiction of Newgrange and how its presence was perceived by ancient Irish Kings. For instance, the most famous of ancient Christian high kings was Cormac mac Airt c.160 AD. King Airt, during his 40 year rule over Tara, was granted access to secret knowledge. Perhaps this included Newgrange's Antichristian Babylonian origins? Whatever the epiphany, this secret knowledge proved counter to the ancient King's Christianity, prompting King Airt to issue an order that his body must never be buried anywhere near Newgrange. Furthermore, there is the tale of King of Tara, Conaire the Great, a high king of Ireland c.100 BC, who ruled for approximately 70 years. The 'Destruction of Da Derga's Hostel' which means "Red god" features King of Tara and his greatest warriors Mac Cécht and the Ulster hero Conall Cernach battling the red god [Satan] and thousands of demons in the region of Dublin Ireland. Coincidently, Dublin Ireland is home to the second oldest Grand Lodge of Freemasonry in the world. It is said that the King of Tara fell victim to the 'Red Man' [Satan] after he acted counter to a number of geasa [taboos] placed upon him. In modern terms the tale of Da Derga's Hostel is about King of Tara selling his soul and how Satan came to collect on the King's debt. Furthermore, the account provides evidence of the Church of Babylon in ancient Ireland and the ancient King's association specifically in the ancient tale describing the entertainment that preceded the King of Tara's death:

"I saw then three jesters at the fire. They wore three grey cloaks, and if all the men of Erin were in one place and though the body of the mother and father of each man of them were lying dead before them, not one of them could refrain from laughing at them."

What the aforesaid tale describes is the practice of fire worship by men wearing cloaks. These are customs established by the ancient Babylonian god Nimrod and venerated by the Church of Babylon, suggesting that the Church of Babylon existed in the region as early as 100 BC. However, the overarching metaphor of the story is that if a man establishes membership in the Church of Babylon and follows the 'Red man' 143 ɹ] it will be as though that man has erased any evidence of his being in the book of life. Choosing to do so makes that man a fitting target for ridicule and laughter.

Ancient texts and stone carvings associated with King of Tara, the horned red god Cernunnos and Nimrod reveal noticeable similarities, the most striking of which is the link between the god Cernunnos and the "triple crown" carved into the ancient stela of Nimrod [pg.18, "K"]. Ancient texts describe the god Cernunnos [left] as having three heads, suggesting Cernunnos is a member of a triad synonymous with Nimrod and Satan. What's more, Cernunnos is referred to as the ruler of the underworld and is equated with Daghda, the 'god of fire' and Eochu Ollathair "Red One Great in Knowledge". Juxtapose Cernunnos' supernatural profile with that of the Babylonian god Nimrod and Satan who is said to have been "...a mighty one in the earth" [Genesis 10:8] who taught men to worship fire and practice magic.

"And the LORD said unto Satan, Whence comest thou? Then Satan answered the LORD, and said, From going to and fro in the earth, and from walking up and down in it." - Job 1:7

In addition, there are arresting parallels between the ancient Celtic King of Tara, Celtic god Cernunnos and the Babylonian god Nimrod with cultures throughout the ancient world, not the least of which is King of Tara's 'Red Man' an obvious reference to Cernunnos. The Pillar of the Boatmen also links the god Cernunnos with the son of Zeus [Mercury] Helios or Apollyon, otherwise known as The Beast from the pit [Satan].

"And they had a king over them, which is the angel of the bottomless pit, whose name in the Hebrew tongue is Abaddon, but in the Greek tongue hath his name Apollyon" - Revelation 9:11

The Pillar of Boatsman implies a blood relation between Mercury and the god Cernunnos through a red inscription found on The Pillar. This particular red is an ancient pigment derived from both red Ocher iron oxide, hematite which comes from Greek, hema meaning 'blood' and Cinnabar the common ore of mercury used

144

in Egyptian tombs c.1000 BC. Furthermore, ancient cultures such as the Maya throughout South America and Himba people in Africa memorialized these ancient gods by painting themselves and their shrines with Ocher and Cinnabar. For instance, the Himba people of Africa paint themselves red with Ocher and worship a god named Mukuru, who like Cernunnos and Mercury is associated with healing the sick and rain. Moreover, the Himba people of Africa also believe in 'omiti', which translates to mean witchcraft, a practice created by the Babylonian god Nimrod. Further examples include the Tomb of the Red Queen in the ancient Maya City Palenque which contains the tomb of the mother of Pakal, the co-ruler of the state. Her skeleton and the collection of objects inside of her sarcophagus were entirely covered with a bright red dust made of cinnabar, or the ground ore of mercury, preparing her for Xibalba, the "Place of Fear", the Maya name for the underworld. This is the netherworld ancient texts described as being ruled by both Nimrod and Cernunnos.

Additional similarities linking the god Mercury [Apollyon] and the ancient Celtic god Cernunnos exist among alchemists who believe mercury is the first matter from which all metals were formed, in the same way Cernunnos is described as being the first god. The story goes... The goddess Eiocha is born. Eiocha gives birth to the first god Cernunnos. Cernunnos and his mother Eiocha create additional gods together. Then the gods create the first men, women and animals from tree bark.

"And they brought up an evil report of the land which they had searched unto the children of Israel, saying, The land, through which we have gone to search it, is a land that eateth up the inhabitants thereof; and all the people that we saw in it are men of a great stature. And there we saw the giants, the sons of Anak, which come of the giants: and we were in our own sight as grasshoppers, and so we were in their sight." – Numbers 13:32-33

Berossus the Babylonian priest-historian credits Oannes, an amphibious half-man creature that emerged from the Persian Gulf, as the teacher of enlightenment who nursed the Sumerians into creating the cradle of civilization. This Babylonian legend is by far one of the earliest recorded plagiaries of The Book of Genesis and Satan's interaction with Adam and Eve in the Garden of Eden. This is nothing more than ancient propaganda created by a possessed Babylonian priest meant to deceive future generations into believing that interactions between Fallen Angels [Demons] and Man were Reptilians, Aliens, and UFOs. Before Oannes [Satan], Berossus stated the Sumerians lived like beasts in the field, with no order of rule or knowledge. Consider the 35 inch tall statue of Nimrod [pg.146] created by Sculptor Yitzhak Danziger (1938-1939). This statue is

made of Red Nubian Sandstone imported from Petra in Jordan, a color which symbolizes Mercury or Apollyon from The Book of Revelation. Furthermore, it depicts Nimrod as a naked hunter, uncircumcised, carrying a bow and with a hawk or messenger on his shoulder, a reference to the son of Zeus [Mercury] who is also known as Apollyon. What is curious about this Nimrod statue is how it so closely resembles the above description by the Babylonian priest Berossus of the amphibious half-man Oannes [Satan]. Unsurprisingly, the trillionaire Rothschild Family commissioned the carving of the reptilian Nimrod through the Hebrew University of Jerusalem (HUJ), an institution that has relied heavily on Rothschild grants since July 24, 1918. Coincidently, the HUJ laid its cornerstone just nine months after Walter Rothschild, drafted the Balfour [Scottish Surname] Declaration 11/2/1917.

For over two millennia secret societies, in an attempt to redirect attention away from Khazarian Babylonian Talmudists, have allied the Serpent Cult of Dann [Genesis 49:17] with the ancient Celtic and Pictish civilizations. In actuality the descendants of the serpent cult were Nimrod, Khazarians and Tuatha de **Dan**ann ['tribe of the gods'], a band of supernatural beings who arrived in Ireland c.2244 B.C. approximately 100 years after Noah's flood, bringing with them four divine weapons: (i) The Sword of Nuadu; (ii) The Cauldron of Dagda; (iii) Stone of Destiny; (iv) A Spear that "battle would never go against who had it in hand". These last two weapons sound curiously similar to the "Spear of Destiny" pg.208] which pierced Jesus Christ's side and "Stone of Jacob" referenced in the Book of Genesis as the stone used as a pillow by the Israelite patriarch Jacob at the place later called Bet-El. Secret societies with an agenda to marginalize the rich, complex history and traditions of Irish and Scottish people, have set aside precious Celtic and Pictish records which describe an ancient alliance between the Tuatha Dé **Dan**ann and a figure ancient Celts referred to as, "Nemed" otherwise known as, "Nimrod", the leader of the four cities or four quarters of the ancient world. Not the first word to be misspoken by ancients. According to Thomas Cahill's, How the Irish Saved Civilization, "The word grammar - that molded all educated men from Plato to Augustine – will be mispronounced by one barbarian tribe as "glamour." It was from one of Nimrod's principal demons, Shamash, the 15ft tall giant sun god [pg.19] that the Tuatha de **Dan**ann acquired their magical skills and attributes. Tuatha de **Dan**ann co-rulers, such as the three sons of Neit, grandsons of the Daghdha, Mac Greine, Mac Ceacht, and Mac Cuill represented in their name the "power of the sun" [Shamash]. Ancient texts tell us that after ancient Celts defeated

146

Nimrod, "a mighty one in the earth" [Genesis 10:8] and his giant "Tribe of gods" and their co-rulers, these gods were sent back underground into the Sidhe mounds by Manannan Mac Lir. As I've illustrated in the above-mentioned texts, the connection between "The Serpent Cult of Dann" with that of ancient Celts and Picts is one of the biggest deceptions foisted upon modern day Scottish and Irish clans by Khazarian Babylonian Talmudists. For centuries the Church of Babylon has successfully deceived millions of "Willingly ignorant" [2 Peter 3:5] human beings into believing the "big-lie" that the aforementioned is "secret knowledge".

Take for instance, **Scottish American Musician James Morrison** [The Doors] and his father Navy rear admiral, George Morrison. George was so convinced of this lie that he assisted the Church of Babylon and their puppet, President Lyndon B. Johnson, with the Gulf of Tonkin "false flag" operation, ["Tonkin Gulf Incident"] which resulted in the escalation of the Vietnam War and the murder of more than 58,193 American Soldiers [54,556 U.S. Christians]. Jim's fractured personalities were so deceived by the Church of Babylon, of which his father George was a member, that he named himself 'The Lizard King' and 'Crawling King Snake' after the serpent cult of Dann and dedicated his life to the study of 16th and 17th century Demonology. Jim was also strongly influenced by Satanists Aleister Crowley, Aldous Huxley, and Friedrich Nietzsche, and the Apollonian and Dionysian duality. This is a philosophical concept, based on the 'god of the Sun' [Shamash] that appeared regularly in Jim's conversations, poetry, and songs. Morrison married his wife in a Wicca ceremony, standing inside a pentagram, drinking one another's blood. Jim once said: "I met the Spirit of Music, an appearance of the devil in a Venice canal. Running, I saw Satan or Satyr [Pan], moving beside me, a fleshly shadow of my secret mind..." - The Lost Writings of Jim Morrison, p.36-38. Jim's favorite photograph was of him holding a lamb [the symbol for Jesus Christ] because he 'looked satanic' in it. Jim was sacrificed by the Church of Babylon on 7/3/1971 (aged 27) with a heroin overdose. Morrison's grave at Père Lachaise contains the Greek inscription: 'KATA TON ΔAIMONA EAYTOY' which translates: 'Demons In Me'. Many of Morrison's fans, who consider themselves Christian, will be surprised by the above information mainly because it was never promoted by the militant Antichristian elites who control mainstream media. Like his father, Jim often provided his followers with grand symbols that exposed their false reality. For instance Jim would regularly enlighten admirers with the statement, "Whoever controls the media, controls the mind". - Jim Morrison

Thanks to former CIA Director, William Colby, we know who controls the media. After all it was Colby who once said, "The CIA owns everyone of any significance in the Major Media."

An interesting revelation when you consider Glenn Beck's TV/Radio Show 'THE BLAZE' National Security Editor, Buck Sexton, is an ex-CIA Agent. FOX News regularly features CIA contributors on their newscasts.

Before we continue our examination of other sacrificed Scottish and Irish people, I would like to present a case to readers, which details the reasons why I believe Jim Morrison was instrumental in the creation of one of the most profound, culture changing events in U.S. history, the 60s "hippie movement."

While Jim's father was carrying out his programming in Vietnam, a sophisticated, serpent cult social distortion psyop was being injected into the bloodstream of America's youth by MK-Ultra slave, Jim Morrison, in Southern California's Laurel Canyon. Under the guidance of high-level serpent cult leaders, it was here in the 1960s where Jim Morrison began assembling Musicians, singers and songwriters to set in motion a movement that would irrevocably compromise the Christian American majority's moral barometer. Designed for the purpose of inspiring a "bloody revolution", the "Hippie Flower Child Movement" was established. Key actors were the most influential, chemically engineered "Rock Superstars" in American history, they included: "The Byrds" [David Crosby] whose debut creation "Mr. Tambourine Man." The "Mamas and the Papas" would soon follow [John Phillips], "Love" [Author Lee]. "Frank Zappa and the Mothers of Invention" [Freak Out", 1966]; "Buffalo Springfield" [Stephen Stills & Neil Young] and the "Lizard King" Jim Morrison's "The Doors", which would emerge from behind the scenes in 1967 to take center stage.

A key associate to Jim the "Lizard King" Morrison and his serpent cult handlers was militant Antichristian, Frank Zappa, who was allegedly a high-level CIA, MK-Ultra mind control programmer. As a matter of fact many of Frank's mind-controlled slaves considered Zappa a "father figure". The headquarters for the CIA's 1965 MK-Ultra, "Hippie Flower Child" social experiment was allegedly located inside of Frank Zappa's five story house named "The Log Cabin". Positioned in Laurel Canyon his property contained caves and tunnel systems, which made for an ideal environment for CIA programmers. It's important for readers to understand that virtually every popular musician [1965-1970s] visited Zappa's "Log Cabin" including Scottish American superstar Alice Cooper who Zappa signed to his Laurel Canyon record label.

Frank Zappa's true motivations behind the hippie movement and its intended "bloody revolution" were obvious to anyone watching. For instance Frank was disdainful towards the very hippie culture he was helping to engineer, referring to them as "freaks" whenever the opportunity presented itself. Zappa was also a proponent of the U.S.

wars in Southeast Asia, which was anathema to the "Freak" [Hippie] culture he helped to create. Frank's opinion of hippies isn't surprising when you consider that his father, Francis Zappa, was a chemical warfare specialist, assigned to the Edgewood Arsenal. Edgewood is where America's chemical warfare program originated and a site heavily trafficked by MK-Ultra mind control programmers. It was from this location where the vast supply of LCD, Cocaine, Heroine, etc. was dealt out to the spiritually and socially disenfranchised youth of America.

As an aside the Beatles 1967 song "Lucy in the Sky with Diamonds" [LSD] was written by John Lennon to commemorate Lewis Carroll's "Alice in Wonderland" books. It's a well documented fact that CIA MK-Ultra programmers used images from Alice in Wonderland to program their mind controlled slaves. The Beatles and Frank Zappa were very good friends, performing together on stage and on film. It too is a well documented fact, that 'The Beatles' were known to have been followers of Aleister Crowley's satanic laws. This explains the many pictures taken of John Lennon flashing the devil horns hand sign and Paul McCartney flashing the 666 hand sign. The band was so smitten with the most evil man in the world that they even put Aleister Crowley on the cover of their album titled Sgt Pepper's Lonely Hearts Band.

A series of weekly articles entitled "How Does a Beatle Live?" appeared in the London Evening Standard during March 1966. Written about John Lennon, Ringo Starr, George Harrison, and Paul McCartney, the four articles were completed by journalist Maureen Cleave. Well known by all four Beatles, Cleave had interviewed the group regularly since the start of 'Beatle mania' in the United Kingdom. Three years previously she had written of them as "the darlings of Merseyside" and had accompanied them on the plane to the United States when they first toured there in January 1964. For her lifestyle series in March 1966, she chose to interview the group individually rather than all together as was the norm.

Cleave interviewed John Lennon on March 4, 1966. After encountering a full-size crucifix, a gorilla costume and a medieval suit of armor on her excursion through his home, Kenwood, in Weybridge, she found a well-organized library with works by Jonathan Swift, Oscar Wilde, George Orwell and Aldous Huxley. John Lennon stated to Cleave that these figures all influenced his ideas about Christianity. Cleave quoted a comment John Lennon made regarding his desire to see Christianity exterminated:

"Christianity will go. It will vanish and shrink. I needn't argue about that; I'm right and I'll be proven right. We're more popular than Jesus now; I don't know which will go first—rock 'n' roll or Christianity. Jesus was all right but his disciples were thick and

149

ordinary. It's them twisting it that ruins it for me." – John Lennon 1966

Getting back to our examination of Frank Zappa, he was raised inside of base housing located on Edgewood Arsenal property. Later in life Frank's family would move to Lancaster, CA, near Edwards Air Force Base, where Frank's father would develop classified military projects for U.S. Intelligence. During this time, Frank Zappa and the "Lizard King" Morrison were orchestrating America's "Hippie Flower Child Movement".

Another interesting aside, is that in 1965 Frank Zappa's manager, Herb Cohen, a former U.S. Marine and CIA asset, allegedly tortured and killed leftist Congo's Prime Minister, Patrice Lumumba. A Zappa biographer has stated that Cohen was not there to kill the Prime Minister, but to sell arms to him so that he could defend himself against the CIA. Which I presume is meant to be a compliment?

Frank Zappa's wife, Gail Zappa [formerly "Adelaide Sloatman"], is an interesting character in that she worked for the Office of Naval Research and Development. Gail, like anyone who is born into the serpent tribe, was possessed. In fact she was quoted saying that she, "heard voices all her life". Like the vast majority of Laurel Canyon's subjects, Gail's father worked on classified projects for the Nuclear weapons research division of the U.S. Navy. Gail's profile provides us with an example of the incestuous nature of the serpent cult. The Lizard King, Jim Morrison, and Frank Zappa's wife attended the exact same naval kindergarten, where Gail is said to have struck Jim Morrison in the head with a hammer.

Another example of the incestuous nature of the serpent cult is illustrated in the fact that Jim Morrison's high-school mates at "Alexandria Virginia High School" were fellow Laurel Canyon associates, John Phillips and Cass Elliot. For those readers who are unfamiliar with the name "Papa" John Phillips, he helped Morrison's serpent cult shape America's 1960s counterculture. Phillips and an individual named Terry Melcher would spearhead the famous "Monterey Pop Festival". Prior to working with Phillips, Melcher was imprisoned alongside Charles Manson on Terminal Island, formerly named "Rattlesnake Island". Historically this Island has been used by both Naval Intelligence and the FBI. It was through the Monterrey Pop Festival psyop that America's disenfranchised, underage youth would become infected with the Antichristian hippie culture. Phillips was also famous for the song "San Francisco, Be Sure to Wear Flowers in Your Hair". This song was synonymous with 1967s "Summer of Love" e.g., sexual depravity, drug use and San Francisco's "Haight-Asbury", a festering den of sodomites, prostitutes and transgendered freaks.

Another Alumnus of Frank Zappa's Laurel Canyon was Scottish American Charles Manson. In fact, Manson's entire family e.g., Susan Tate, Mary Brunner, Lynette Fromme, Patricia Krenwinkel, Leslie Van Houten, Bruce McGregor Davis, Steve Grogan and Charles "Tex" Watson all lived at Zappa's MK-Ultra mind control resort. It is the opinion of this author that Laurel Canyon acted as the programming station for Charles Manson's entire group. The Laurel Canyon demons which possessed them all would ultimately consume their lives and the lives of those that they encountered. It was the Laurel Canyon programmers who created the infamous Manson Family.

Another loyal Laurel Canyon subject of Zappa's was John Edmund Andrew Phillips. John's father was a U.S. military intelligence officer as was his mother who was allegedly heavily involved in the occult. John attended the U.S. Naval Academy at Annapolis and later married Susie Adams, a direct descendant of Irish American Founding Father, John Adams. Like her husband John, Susie's father was an intelligence officer with the U.S. Military while he was stationed in Vienna. Susie on the other hand worked for the Pentagon. In addition to playing his part in the deconstruction of America, John Phillips experienced a burgeoning music career and to satisfy his innermost Marxist ambitions, John Phillips fought alongside the Communist leader Fidel Castro during the Cuban Revolution.

One of the most famous loyal subjects to be programmed at Zappa's Laurel Canyon was Stephen Stills [Crosby Stills & Nash]. Coincidently one of Stills most famous songs, "Bluebird" was the original code name for the CIA's MK-Ultra mind control program. Like all of the other Laurel Canyon creations, Still's family were heavily involved in military intelligence, throughout Panama, Costa Rica, El Salvador, and much of Central America. Stephen Stills himself worked in an advisory position for U.S. intelligence while stationed inside of Vietnam, three years prior to Jim "Lizard King" Morrison's father's "false flag" which kicked the Vietnam War into overdrive. Stephen Stills famous other half, Scottish American David Crosby, is said to have been one of the most colorful characters in Laurel Canyon. Like his associates, David Crosby's father, Major Floyd Delafield Crosby, was a graduate of Annapolis and WWII military intelligence officer. Major Crosby was stationed in Haiti in 1927 alongside Captain Claude Andres Phillips whose son "Papa" John Phillips was friends with Charles Manson and complicit in the 1960s counterculture hippie movement. Coincidently when you begin to examine David Crosby's lineage one can't help but to marvel at how consciously disciplined the Serpent Cult of Dann is at maintaining their bloodlines. For instance David Crosby is related to a number of Grand Masters of Freemasonry, signers of the Declaration of Independence, 151 U.S. senators, congressman, state senators, assemblymen, governors, mayors, judges, Supreme Court Justices, Revolutionary and Civil War generals, author's of the Federalist Paper's Alexander Hamilton and John Jay and members of the Continental Congress.

Another Laurel Canyon serpent cult superstar was Irish American, singer-song writer, Jackson Browne, who experienced great success, selling more than 18 million albums. Rolling Stone Magazine referred to Browne's music as "… mind-boggling melodies" an appropriate classification considering the Laurel Canyon lab whence Browne's subconscious was shaped. Browne's entire catalog of mind manipulating songs contains a treasure-trove of references commonly used by mind-controlled people to express their Luciferian embedded syllabus. Some of his more famous songs include, "Take It Easy", "Somebody's Baby", "The Pretender", "These Days", "Running on Empty", "Lawyers in Love", "Doctor My Eyes" and "For a Rocker". Unfortunately I do not have the space to detail every instance where Browne's lyrics venerate Lucifer; however I've dissected two, "Take It Easy" and "The Pretender".

Take It Easy Lyrics: "I've got 7 women on my mind four that want to own me, two that want to stone me". To occultists the number 7 represents their god or goddess of sex and prostitution which they believe is Lilith the creator of prostitution and murderer of young men. Conversely, the number 6 they believe represents man which together creates the number 13 and the number 39 or 3x13, is the number of the pagan trinity times the number of extreme rebellion. The highest order of the Serpent Cult of Dann is to usher in the Antichrist. Browne then references a women who wants to "stone me" referencing God's probation for the Jews ended 34 A.D., the 70 weeks ended when Stephen was stoned after his immense speech before the council in Acts chapter 7. The Jews had rejected the Gospel message and so were no longer God's chosen people and thus the Gospel began to go to the Gentiles (Acts 8:4). The Jews now receive salvation as individuals in the same way we do, however the primary proxy for The Serpent Cult of Dann, Babylonian Talmudists, deceive Christians into believing that so called "Jews" [Talmudists] are the chosen people, which is a lie. Please watch the documentary titled, "Marching to Zion" www.marchingtozion.com

The repetitive "take it easy" brain washes people into remaining ignorant of the world around them and promotes the perpetual state of subjugation. This is a state of consciousness which the serpent cult of dann has profited from influentially, spiritually and financially for more than several millennia. This brainwashing is further embed when Browne sings "don't even try to understand, just find a place to make your stand" suggesting to the masses that they are too stupid to realize the serpent cult's plan, but if you are smart enough, just go ahead

152

and try to defeat us else you can just "take it easy" like we're telling you to do. Browne then describes "a girl my Lord in a flat-bed truck" which is referencing the Serpent Cult of Dann's "Lord" or savoir Lilith the creator of prostitution, who Browne begs to have sex with. All of these lyrics are meant to accomplish one thing and that's the destruction of innocence. Immediately after his encounter with his "Lord", he's back out looking for a woman to "loosen his load" a crude reference to the build up of semen in his testicles. I apologize for being so graphic, but that's what these "… mind-boggling melodies" were programming our young, influential children in the 60s to think. The final chorus of Browne's "Take It Easy" is the most reveling reference to the Serpent Cult's Babylonian goddess of prostitution Lilith. When he sings "I need to know if your sweet love is going to save me", this is the concept of having sex to be saved and it's based on the serpent cult proxy's, Babylonian Talmudist's goddess Ishtar who was also known as "Lilith" or Lillake. The Babylonian demon Lilith was the creator of prostitution and the degrading of sex and said to strangle children, seduce young men, then kill them. According to 5th century B.C. historian Herodotus an individual's sin could only be cleansed if they had sexual intercourse with a temple priest or priestess of Ishtar, which became known as "sacred prostitution". In addition to promoting the serpent cults Babylonian demon goddess Lilith, it's simultaneously corrupted our youth to stray from the healthful knowledge, "For by means of a whorish woman a man is brought to a piece of bread: and the adulteress will hunt for the precious life." – Proverbs 6:26. Which in essence is telling people that a 'precious life' isn't found by being a whore or cheating on your spouse, etc. it's found when you get married, have children and stay married to that one person for the rest of your life. If Jackson Browne would have worshipped the God of The Holy Bible and lived by his knowledge instead of , "… the doctrines the commandments of men." – Matthew 15:9; Mark 7:7; Titus 1:14, he would not have experienced multiple marital failures, disease and deception all of which the Serpent Cult of Dann glorifies in their teachings.

The Pretender Lyrics: Keep in mind while reading the following examination, that a "Pretender" is defined as a "leader of the opposition" Question: Who is the leader of the opposition to Jesus Christ? It's Satan, Lucifer the Devil. The following are references, within Browne's song "The Pretender", where I believe as a Christian, that Browne is referencing the Serpent Cult's god Lucifer, Satan, the Devil. When Browne sings "when the morning light comes streaming in… Amen", "a greater awakening" and "… in the end it's the wink of an eye" these phrases are all used by Satanists when referring to the Egyptian god "Ra" [All-Seeing-Eye] and Lucifer or "Light Bearer". An example of its use can be found in the doctrines of another Serpent Cult proxy, "Theosophy". N. Sri 153 Ram, a leading theosophist [Satanist] and writer of Lucifer Magazine, further clarifies who Theosophy considers to be their God, "The adversary or Satan is no other than Lucifer, the light bearer, the bright morning star: he is the initiator, awakening the divine faculties of intellect on man, he is the King of the fallen angels, spirits from higher spheres, who descended among primitive mankind of the third race, to develop in man, and endow him with his self-conscious mind, or Manas." Browne then continues to sing "Out into the cool of the evening strolls the Pretender". Again the pretender is the 'leader of the opposition' and the opposition to Jesus Christ is? The Devil... So the devil is walking the streets. This verse is almost a carbon copy of 1 Peter 5:8 which reads, "Be sober, be vigilant; because your adversary the devil, as a roaring lion, walketh about, seeking whom he may devour:"

Like Browne's song "Take It Easy", "The Pretender" is teaching young men and women to worship the demon goddess Lilith and prostitution, "... longing for love and the struggle for the legal tender". What he's singing here is that he's in need of "legal tender" [money] to pay for a prostitute. And when he does buy a woman he'll put his "dark [demonic] glasses on" and "make love until our strength is gone" then he'll "Get it up again." Browne ends his sermon by proselytizing for the Serpent Cult of Dan, singing, "Say a prayer for the pretender [Lucifer] are you there for the pretender [Lucifer] say a prayer for the pretender [Lucifer] Are you there for the pretender [Lucifer] Are you prepared for the pretender [Lucifer].

Flash forward to 1983 and Jackson Browne has divorced his second wife to begin a relationship with Scottish American actress and alleged MK-Ultra slave, Daryl Hannah for nine years. Hannah's break came in 1982 when she appears in Scottish director Ridley Scott's "Blade Runner" which featured a 2019 dystopia where dangerous, genetically engineered "replicants" [cybernetic organisms] are indistinguishable from humans. Daryl Hannah's character, "Pris" is a "basic pleasure model" replicant otherwise known as a prostitute. I mention the Browne, Hannah, Ridley Scott connection only because this concept of "transcendence" or the merging of man with machine is an elaborate manifestation of Satan's big-lie "...ye shall be as gods." – Genesis 3:5. The forerunner to Scott's Blade Runner was the 1927 film, "Metropolis" which was venerated by militant Antichristian, Nazi propagandist Joseph Goebbels in a 1928 speech. The movie Metropolis is replete with Satanic imagery e.g., Baphomet pentagram [pg.155], etc.

The films cast include names such as, "Death," "The Seven Deadly Sins" and "11811....Erwin Biswanger" [11x8=88]. "H" or "Haa" in German, is the eighth letter in the alphabet, 88=HH or Heil Hitler. The movie is subtitled, in part they read, "To the new Tower of Babel - to my father - !" "...the city's light..." "...The son of Hel was yours!" "...the Machine-Man sits, looking like an Egyptian deity. Light streams from

154

above. The movie also features a pedestal, upon which the stone head of a woman sits with the words, "HEL...Born for mankind's blessing."

Interestingly Jackson Browne was not the only Laurel Canyon alumnus to use the MK-Ultra slave, Daryl Hannah. In 2014 Laurel Canyon alumnus, Scottish American Neil Young announced that he was divorcing his 61 year old wife of 36 years. Just one month after his divorce announcement Young began dating 53 year old MK-Ultra slave, Daryl Hannah. Young was of course part of Crosby, Stills, Nash and Young.

Another relevant aside pertaining to Jackson Browne is his connection with militant Antichristian, Babylonian Talmudist, media mogul David Geffen who in 1971 became Browne's agent. Flash forward to 1999 and Geffen, a Hollywood Homosexual A-list celebrity, is associated with homosexual parties, where teenage boys are abused. In 1994 Geffen along with Babylonian Talmudist Jeffrey Katzenberg and Babylonian Talmudist Steven Spielberg found Dreamworks SKG, where militant Antichristian cartoons are created which glorifies the murder of Christians and the worship of Lucifer. To illustrate how so called "Jews" in Hollywood are in no way followers of the Torah [Old Testament] and instead serve the serpent cult of Dann, I'd like to point out that Jackson Browne was born 10/9/1948 in Heidelberg Germany and his sister was born in Nuremburg, Germany in 1946, just one year after the collapse of Hitler's "Third Reich". Like all of the Laurel Canyon 'superstars', Jackson's father, Irish American Clyde Jack Browne, was in Military Intelligence and allegedly played a key role in the OSS (precursor to the CIA) specifically "Operation Paperclip" [1949] in which over 1,500 Nazi scientists, technicians and engineers were brought to the U.S. giving birth to NASA as well as many other hi-tech weapons, including zero gravity transportation. Nazi scientists also helped establish America's bio-weapon unit, "Plum Island" which sits just off the shores of Long Island New York.

This connection between Jackson Browne, his father Clyde, Nazi's and Steven Spielberg is interesting because Steven Spielberg's blockbuster hit "Indiana Jones" was inspired by real-life inspirations,

155

namely Scottish American explorer Roy Chapman Andrews whose global investigations were funded by Antichristian J.P. Morgan and Luciferian Otto Rahn whose quest for The Holy Grail was funded by Adolf Hitler's Nazi Party. What's more Spielberg's "Close Encounters of the Third Kind" was the retelling of a demonic encounter purportedly witnessed by a man named J. Allen Hynek. Hynek was the Technical Director for Spielberg's movie 'Close Encounters of The Third Kind'. Prior to Hynek's work on Spielberg's film Hynek coauthored the U.S. Government's 'Grudge 13' and MJ-12 in 1947. These programs were created under the guidance of Nelson Rockefeller by order of President Dwight D. Eisenhower. MJ-12's sole purpose was to develop and carry out psychological operations upon the American population to manipulate and cover-up critical knowledge related to the safety and security of the American populace. During this same time the Rockefeller Foundation began funding a massive research and training program at Caltech with a focus on molecular biology. The Rockefeller funded and controlled program would become the most influential international program in molecular biology. In my book "AMERIKA: The Re-Mastered Christian Majority" I demonstrate how and why the Rockefeller Family leveraged this research to develop an industry which debilitates, cripples and kills millions of innocent Americans each year.

What is so obvious is that these "celebrities" are all manufactured and maintained from cradle to grave. Consider the fact that Spielberg's intellectual resources for "Close and Counters" were gleaned from the Rockefeller Family who also funded Orson Welles' "War of the Worlds" psychological operations which involved an alien invasion. A detailed examination of Orson Welles, H.G. Welles and their social Darwinian leanings will be remembered from my earlier examination of the Charles Manson Family's murder of Scottish American actress/model Sharon Tate. Spielberg continues the alien invasion psyop tradition in his newest cartoon for children named "HOME" which is derived from the ancient Scottish Surname "Home" which is also spelled "Hume".

Its main characters 'Oh' and 'Tip' are voiced by Scottish American Jim Parsons whose mother is Judy Ann of the Scottish McKnight family and Irish/Barbadian Rihanna a musician who for years has enthusiastically endorsed satanic imagery throughout her music videos, wardrobe, etc. Jim Parsons plays a character on the television show 'The Big Bang Theory' and is known for his mocking, Antichristian rhetoric.

In real life Parsons is a gay man who has been in a homosexual relationship for the last ten years with art director Todd Spiewak. The two men cofounded a production company named 'Wonderful Productions' through which they will produce a series based on the

YouTube program 'Prodigies'. Parson's calls their relationship "an act of love, coffee in the morning, going to work, washing the clothes, taking the dogs out—a regular life, boring love". Parsons is also a founding member of a theater company located in Houston, Texas named "Infernal Bridegroom Productions" which literally means a man married to hell. "And the light of a candle shall shine no more at all in thee; and the voice of the bridegroom and of the bride shall be heard no more at all in thee: for thy merchants were the great men of the earth; for by thy sorceries were all nations deceived." – Revelation 18:23.

I would also like to point out that Ellie O'Ryan's adaptation of Dreamworks "HOME" book cover [left] contains a "6" in the word "HOME", a "6" on the chest of "Captain Smek", the horned devil looking character voiced by Steve Martin, and a 6 on the chest of Jim Parson's character 'Oh' [666]. In addition there are three little "Boov" characters below the said movie characters which all have a "6" on their chests, creating an additional "666."

To complete this satanic orchestra, Jim Parson's is related to Jack Parson's who founded NASA's jet propulsion laboratory in Pasadena, CA. Jack Parsons also co-designed the U.S. Pentagon (United States Department of Defense) in Arlington Country, Virginia where Jim Morrison, John Phillips and Cass Elliot all attended school. It will be remembered from an earlier examination of sacrificed Irish/Scottish NASA astronauts that Satanist Jack Parson's was also a disciple of world renowned Satanist Aleister Crowley who wrote the following paragraph in his diary:

"And thus was I Antichrist loosed in the world; and to this am I pledged, that the work of the beast shall be fulfilled, and the way for the coming of BABALON be made open and I shall not cease or rest until these things are accomplished." – Texe Marrs, Codex Magica.

You'll also recall that a close friend of Parsons was the founder of Scientology, L. Ron Hubbard, who called Crowley "My very good friend". Celebrity Scientologists include: Laurel Canyon resident Charles Manson, Actor Tom Cruz who for years has been

157

an outspoken advocate for the promethean, SiFi cult, Will Smith donated $122,500 to Scientology. Jason Michael Lee, Kirstie Alley, Sky Dayton founder of Earthlink, Juliette Lewis, Danny Masterson, Michael Pena, Priscilla Presley, Kelly Preston, John Travolta and Greta Van Susteren (Fox News).

In 1989 Caltech, Astrophysicist, Hugh Ross identified the primary reason for NASA's massive spending on Mars missions, he states: "winds carry small living creatures, such as microbes and spiders, to high atmospheric levels. Solar winds are able to waft particles of formerly living substances out of our high-level atmosphere – and blow them away from the sun, outward into space. Some of the particles, caught in Mar's gravitational field, could well have landed on the surface of Mars. Evolutionists are well-aware of this possibility they want to send that manned flight to Mars to recover those particles. The main objective of the mission would be to find dead life forms on the surface of Mars, and then use that as "evidence" that life once must have independently evolved on Mars! It is felt that this would provide a powerful boost to the evolutionary cause. Such a "discovery" may occur within the next decade of two." – The Evolution Handbook, by Vance Ferrell, Pg.240.

In the early 1600s German occultist, mathematician and astronomer, Johannes Kepler [1571-1630] and Masonic Danish Nobelman, Tycho Brahe, formed new, "laws of planetary motion," based on 2,000 year old spinning earth data from Masonic Babylonian and "son of Apollo," "Pythagoras of Samos." Kepler and Brahe's concepts provided the foundation for Newton's theory of Universal Gravitation. Kepler and Brahe also determined that planet earth's axial tilt was 23.4° off vertical which leaves us with 66.6° [666] off horizontal. "And we know that we are of God, and the whole world lieth in wickedness." – 1 John 5:19

Given the correlation between NASA's space program and the serpent cult, I would like to edify readers on how Apollo 11 astronaut Buzz Aldrin and Lucifer are being leveraged to influence children around the world.

Scottish American superstar Mike Nesmith of the Monkees and Cory Wells of Three Dog Night became residents of Laurel Canyon after leaving the Air Force. Prior to arriving at Frank Zappa's "Log Cabin", Nesmith had received a family inheritance of $25 million.

One last Laurel Canyon creation was Irish American Gram Parsons [born Ingram Cecil Connor III]. Gram signed a deal with A&M Records in 1970 moving in with producer and cocaine/heroine addict Terry Melcher. In addition to working with "The Byrds" and The

158

Beach Boys, who had rejected unknown singer/songwriter and Laurel Canyon associate Charles Manson, it will be remembered that Terry Melcher was in jail along with Charles Manson on Terminal Island, which was originally named "Isla Raza de Buena Gente" which means "Island race of good people" in Spanish and later changed to "Rattlesnake island" of course to venerate the serpent cult. Rattlesnake Island was also a 1942 Naval Intelligence base and FBI detention facility. This location is where both Manson and Melcher resided prior to Melcher spearheading the famous "Monterrey Pop Festival", a psyop that would infect America's disenfranchised, underage youth with the Antichristian hippie culture. Gram replaced David Crosby in "The Byrds" before working with "The Flying Burrito Brothers. Gram's musical spirit originated at an Elvis Presley concert in 2/22/1956. Gram's father was Major Cecil Ingram "Coon Dog" Connor II, a bomber pilot, with over 50 combat missions. Gram was also heir, on his mother's side, to the Snively family fortune which included 1/3 [33%] of all the citrus groves in the state of Florida. Gram Parsons [Cecil Connor] was sacrificed 9/19/1973 [666] at the age of 26, with morphine and alcohol. Gram's corpse was stolen from the L.A. International Airport by fellow serpent cult member Phil Kaufman, who had stolen a hearse and coffin earlier in the day. Kaufman proceeded to drive Gram's body to Joshua Tree California, where he proceeded to poured five gallons of gasoline on Gram's corpse which he then lit on fire.

A symbol of the "Hippie Flower Child Movement" which helped to program American's into embracing the serpent cult is the so called "Peace Sign." Contrary to what most people believe, the "Peace Sign" has always been a symbol of anti-Christianity. The iconic 'V' hand sign, popularized during the American hippie era, is also known as the Roman numeral five. It's also the very same icon used by Adam Weishaupt, the founder of the anti-Christian order of the Illuminati to symbolize his "Law of Fives".

The "Peace Sign" is also referred to as the 'Nero Cross" or 'Broken Cross'. It's well documented that the Emperor of Rome 'Nero' despised Lord Jesus Christ and his Christian followers. Also well documented was his worship of Satan. It was this possession which moved Nero to force a symbol onto his Roman citizenry which would represent a falling away from Christianity and once and for all put an end to the divinity of Lord Jesus Christ. Nero's broken cross is what 60s hippies and countless victims of Navy rear admiral, George Morrison's Vietnam War wore on their bodies representing what they believed to be a 'Peace Sign'.

159

 The Nero Cross elements also form an 'X' which represents the Serpent Tribe of Dann. The Nero Cross also creates an occult pyramid. The so called "Peace Sign" was depicted inside of a circle and an 'X' inside of a circle represents the Roman numeral 1000. In Greek, the number 1000 means Helius or Apollyon, otherwise known as The Beast from the pit.

From 2006-2011 Irish American Entertainer Miley Cyrus was Walt Disney's 'Hanna Montana'. At 19 her career seemed to have flamed out e.g., failed 2010 album, failed 2011 tour and split with her manager. Now Miley has signed with Larry Rudolph manager of Britney Spears, Justin Timberlake, Lindsay Lohan, Jessica Simpson, Back Street Boys and DMX. In 2013 the industry couldn't stop asking how she has become such a big star again.

 The answer can be found in this picture of Cyrus flashing the all-seeing-eye of Satan, Antichristian 'Peace Sign', Devil Horns Hair style and tongue of Babylonian god Pazuzu and Hindu' Kali whose mythology commonly associates her with death, sexuality and violence, just like the Babylonian goddess Lilith. The precursor of Kali is the demoness Long Tongue, who licks up oblations in the ancient Sanskrit texts known as the Brahmanas c.6th century B.C. Cyrus should ask DMX what happens if she ever turns on The Serpent Cult and sings Christian lyrics. DMX went to prison for affirming: "In The Name Of Jesus". Based on Miley's very public veneration of Lucifer, I believe that Cyrus will be sacrificed by the Serpent Cult.

 Miley Cyrus has also popularized the African ceremonial dance named 'Cote d'lvoire' or 'dance of the behind' a dance that was outlawed in the 1980's by the Ivorian government because it was 'lewd'. The more modern name given to this dance throughout America is 'twerking'. What I would like American's to understand about 'twerking' and the modern day obsession with butt worship is its ancient occult origins. For centuries the name given by witches to the ritual greeting upon meeting the Devil is called 'Osculum Infame' which

means 'shameful kiss' or the 'kiss of shame' since it involved kissing the Devil's anus.

According to ancient Scottish folklore it was this kiss that allowed the Devil to seduce women into carrying out his satanic agenda. Throughout every recorded account of a witches Sabbat and countless confessions the 'Osculum Infame' was mentioned. According to these ancient texts witches would give the 'kiss of shame' at the beginning of the Sabbat and after the devil had read the names of his followers. It is said that a witch would approach the Devil by crawling or walking backwards, turn, bow and kiss his anus. Based on the regularity of this tradition it would seem that the 'kiss of shame' is a prerequisite for all new Witches. The North Berwick Witch Trials in 16th century Scotland held that the 'kiss of shame' was an act of penance issued from the devil.

Based on ancient texts it would seem that this is where the saying "Kiss My Ass" originated. Reported in the news from Scotland back in 1592 author W. Wright wrote:

"...and seeing that they tarried over long, hee at their coming enjoyned them all to a penance which was, that they should kisse his buttocks, in sign of duety to him, which being put over the pulpit bare, every one did as he had enjoyed them."

"Even as Sodom and Gomorrha, and the cities about them in like manner, giving themselves over to fornication, and going after strange flesh, are set forth for an example, suffering the vengeance of eternal fire." – Jude 1:7

Two additional 'superstars' who publicly worship Satan's trinity of evil e.g., Serpent Cult of Dann, Nimrod and Masonic Babylonian Talmudism; and who are being prepared for sacrifice are, Scottish American musician "Lady Gaga", who in a T.V. interview said "I swear to Lucifer" and Scottish American musician, Marshall Mathers [Eminem].

Deceived occultists like "Lady Gaga," real name "Stefani Joanne Angelina Germanotta" [left] are notorious for flashing the satanic 666 hand-sign, the so called "peace-sign" and posing themselves like Baphomet and the Babylonian demon god Pazuzu. The 666 hand-sign is made by extending three fingers and forming a circle with your two remaining fingers, which creates three six's, [666]. It symbolizes the unholy trinity e.g., horned God, Goddess,

161

and offspring (anti-Christ). Additional Satanic icons featured with Stefani include the occult pyramid with all-seeing-eye of Satan, as well as an 8 pointed Star hair piece representing the Babylonian demon of war 'Ishtar' and Babylonian demon Lilith or Lillake. Lilith was the creator of prostitution and the degrading of sex and said to strangle children, seduce young men, then kill them. It's noteworthy to mention that Stefani' mother, Cynthia of the Scottish Bissett Family, is a descendant of ancient Irish Celts who interacted with and defeated the Babylonian god Nimrod. Stefani' ancient Celtic bloodline makes her an especially stimulating sacrificial figure for the Church of Babylon in 2019 when she will be 33. I'm sure Lina Morgana's mother won't lose any sleep over Gaga' sacrifice though. For those readers who aren't familiar with Morgana, this is the young woman who collaborated with Stephani Germanotta [Lady Gaga] during 2007 until she was thrown off a ten story building to her death in Staten Island, New York, October 6, 2008 at 11am, Morgana was just 19 at the time. Keep in mind that the number 11 to the Church of Babylon represents man being above God. When broken down [1+1=2], 11 represent the 2 of duality. To occultists the number 11 is the essence of all that is sinful, harmful and imperfect. Coincidently Germanotta became 'Gaga' the superstar just one month after Morgana's murder.

Lina Morgana's Russian immigrant mother has said publicly that she believes her daughter was ritualistically sacrificed and that "Lady Gaga is holding Lina's soul, and I want her soul to be free."

Scottish American musician Marshall Mathers "Eminem" [left] is shown flashing 666. Marshall Mather's roots interconnect with Master Freemason Samuel Liddell MacGregor Mathers, the co-founder of the Satanic Hermetic Order of the Golden Dawn and author of 'The Kabbalah Unveiled'. Samuel Liddel MacGregor Mathers' close friend, lover, and occult pupil was 'The Great Beast 666' Aleister Crowley. As an aside, Mathers' ex-wife is Kimberly Anne of the ancient Scottish Scott Family "Kim". When we study the Scott, Scottish Coat of Arms, we find a number of icons associated with the ancient stone carving of Nimrod [pg.18], namely the crescent, indicating that the Scott Family interacted with and helped to defeat the old world order of Nimrod.

The bloodline of the unassuming Marshal and Scott Clan make them and their children an especially stimulating sacrificial figure for the Church of Babylon.

"Hear now this, O foolish people, and without understanding; which have eyes, and see not; which have ears, and hear not:" – Jeremiah 5:21

Getting back to our examination of sacrificed Irish and Scottish celebrities brings us to **Irish American Actor David Arthur Carradine** who was sacrificed by hanging 6/3/2009.

David was the son of Ardanelle of the Irish McCool Family. The original Gaelic form of the ancient name McCool is "Mac Giolla Chuille. First mentioned in Ulster (Irish: Ulaidh), where they held a family seat from very ancient times. The ancient surname, "Chuille" is an abbreviation of Mochuille, the name of a saint. David was a member of the Carradine acting dynasty which included his father, "John Carradine", and brother's Bruce, Keith and Robert. David Carradine was best known for his role as, "Kwai Chang Caine" in ABC's 1970s TV series Kung Fu [10/14/72-4/16/1975]. David's character name "Caine" represents the patriarch of the Church of Babylon. In the ancient tradition of challenging The Holy Bible, which states all the descendants of Cain perished in Noah's Flood as a result all humankind descend from Seth, the third son of Adam and Eve, the Serpent Cult of Dann maintain that they are the offspring of Cain [Qayin] who

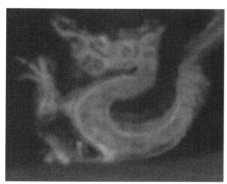

murdered Abel [Hevel]. Jesus Christ refers to Abel as, "righteous" [Hebrews 11:4] whereas Tertullian [c. 155 – c. 240 AD] refers to Cain as the "son of the devil" or "some fallen angel." In coordination with biblical and occult customs David Carradine's character, "Caine" [The Devil] was branded on his forearm with a red dragon [left] in the intro of the television show, "Kung Fu" and movie of the same title.

"And there appeared another wonder in heaven; and behold a great red dragon [Satan], having seven heads and ten horns, and seven crowns upon his heads." - Revelation 12:3

To the Church of Babylon Cain also symbolizes the offspring of the "sons of God" [Nephilim] a race of giants which is represented in the occult numerics "13" and "33" which references the Holy Bible's, "Numbers 13:33" which reads:

"And there we saw the giants, the sons of Anak, which come of the giants: and we were in our own sight as grasshoppers, and so we were in their sight." 163

There are a number of occult numerics associated with David's sacrifice data 6/3/2009 including [6+3+2=11] and the remaining number 9 which create the value 9/11. David's sacrifice date also reads [6+3=9] and [9+2=11]. Either way you arrive at 9/11. To the Serpent Death Cult the 'magic' associated with 9/11 is significant. For instance the number 9 is comprised of 3 groups of 3 [333=33.3% which is 1/3 of 99]. It will be remembered that this value represents the 1/3 (33%) of angels which fell with their god Satan.

"And his taile drew the third part of the starres of heauen, and did cast them to the earth: And the dragon stood before the woman which was ready to be deliuered, for to deuoure her childe as soone as it was borne. And the great dragon was cast out, that old serpent, called the deuill and Satan, which deceiueth the whole world: hee was cast out into the earth, and his angels were cast out with him. And the dragon was wroth with the woman, and went to make warre with the remnant of her seed, which keepe the Commaundements of God, and haue the testimony of Iesus Christ." - King James Version (1611) Revelation Chapter 12:4-17

Following David's 9/11 sacrifice by hanging, the media began brainwashing the public into believing that his sacrifice was caused by a "Sex Accident." In my opinion this was an effort by the Church of Babylon to not only sacrifice David but his character. This is seen throughout many Church of Babylon blood sacrifices. It will be remembered that when broken down 11 represent (1+1=2) and the 2 of duality. To occultists the number 11 is the essence of all that is sinful, harmful and imperfect. To the Church of Babylon 9/11 also represents, The Antichrist, who is called the little horn which is the 11th horn [Daniel 7: 7-8, 11, 19-22, 25 and Daniel 8:11]. 11 O'clock is 330 [33° degrees]. Antichrist = 121 which is 11x11 and 11 is amorphously viewed as a symbol of the 2 pillars of Freemasonry.

Given that it's interconnected with our examination of David Carradine's sacrifice I'm obligated to disclose my professional association with Hollywood Director, "Paul Aratow" who I represented in 2005 as a venture capitalist. Mr. Aratow produced a number of movies, e.g., Sheena: Queen of the Jungle among others. Beginning in 1966 Aratow directed such actor's as John Carradine, father of David Carradine. David Carradine's television series, KungFu, featured his father John in episodes titled "Dark Angel" and "The Nature of Evil". During my meetings with Paul he disclosed to me some rather fascinating information regarding Hollywood secret societies, e.g., Freemasonry, Church of Satan, etc., and specifically John's and David's involvement with these organizations. As most people already know David Carradine had a prolific career, amassing 227 movie and television credits such as the movie 'Kill Bill' directed by Irish American Quinton Tarrantino, a man whose entire catalog of work demonstrates his penchant for Aleister Crowley's edict:

"I want blasphemy, murder, rape, revolution,
anything, bad or good, but strong," - Aleister Crowley c.1895

In 1975 Paul Aratow directed David Carradine's father John Carradine in a film titled: 'Lucifer's Women' which would be released under the name 'Doctor Dracula' in the 80's. The technical advisor for Paul's film was Church of Satan founder Anton LaVey, who injected a number of his Church of Satan members into Paul's film as extras. In 1978 John Carradine played the role of King David in the "The Judgment of Solomon". King Solomon was of course the King who for a time brought the entire race of demons and their leader Beelzebub under Solomon's command to build his temple. These were also the demons that supported the Egyptian magicians against Moses and the very same demons worshipped by Babylonian Talmudic Khazars. What most people do not know is that John's Carradine's son, "Christopher Carradine" was vice-president for Walt Disney's Imagineering, during a time when Disney produced 'The Little Mermaid', featuring a penis castle and other perverted imagery, 'Beauty and the Beast' which featured a woman flashing satanic devil horns and a number of depraved images, Aladdin and The Lion King, both featuring a number of inappropriate metaphors.

In an interview David Carradine recalled that his father John had bragged throughout his lifetime that he had worked as an apprentice for Freemason Daniel Chester French, the artist who fashioned the giant Lincoln Memorial which symbolically represents the giants which once existed on earth [Genesis 6:4; Deuteronomy 2:20; Numbers 13:33; Joshua 17:15]. Both John and David have stars on the Hollywood Walk of Fame at 6240 Hollywood Blvd. near Kodak Theatre which is blanketed with satanic Babylonian Talmudic symbolism. John Carradine like many deceived souls before him made amends in his own way with God while climbing the 328 steep steps of Milan's Gothic cathedral, the Duomo hours before dying inside of Fatebenefratelli Hospital in Milan, Italy on November 27, 1988.

To appreciate the pervasiveness of the Church of Babylon throughout Hollywood, I've provided a photograph of the rear entrance to the Kodak Theatre in Los Angeles, CA [pg.166].

The Kodak Theatre is where Egyptian idols, associated with the creation of the Universe and black magic, are given to the most celebrated hypocrites in Hollywood. The cartouche in the center of the two figures [pg.166] is associated with the creation god Ptah, who in ancient times was referred to as the creator of the Universe. As the 165 cult of Osiris became popular throughout ancient Egypt, this symbol

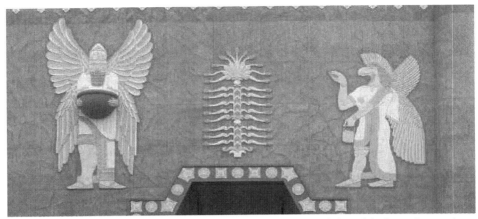

or cartouche became known as the backbone of Osiris. This logo in ancient Egypt identified a person as being with the king of the underworld, Osiris. On either side of Osiris' backbone are ancient depictions of the Babylonian god Nimrod, who like Satan, rebelled against God, approximately 100 years after the great flood. Why is there a Babylonian god, associated with Babylonian Talmudists, hanging on the outer walls of the Kodak Theatre? Because all Hollywood Directors, Producers, Investors, Banks, etc. all subscribe to the Babylonian Talmud and Kabbalah.

The Oscar winner award statue is based on the anti-Christian Egyptian god Ptah (pronounced "taw"). Purveyors of the anti-Christian sentiment which is so pervasive throughout America in 2013, all subscribe to the notion that Ptah – the statue which is given to Hollywood hypocrites - is in fact the creator of all things. Furthermore, Ptah's wife was a powerful Magician and in Egyptian Myths Ptah's wife is known as Basted, the Cat. The Cat in Egyptology symbolizes Trickery. Under the skin Ptah's wife is said to be sweet and precious, but under the surface lays a Predator.

Hollywood Actor Ernest Borgnine [pg.167] was a 33 degree Inspector General Freemason and recipient of the 50 year Freemason award. To receive this award, Borgnine had to renounce Jesus Christ. Next to Borgnine is his Anti-Christian Oscar [Ptah] Statue. A consummate Satanist, Borgnine played the character, "Jonathan Corbis" the leader of a devil-worshipping cult, in the 1975 film, "The Devils Rain" [pg.167] together with William Shatner and Church of Scientology member, John Travolta who for years has been an advocate of Satanist L. Ron Hubbard's cult. During an interview with, Good Morning America" 4/20/2015, Travolta stated, "... you could read Dianetics... Sometimes when something really works well it becomes a target... Forty years for me, I've been part... I've saved lives with it, and saved my own life several times."

Additional Hollywood Freemason Actors include: Bud Abbot, W. C. Fields, Harpo Marx, Oliver Hardy, Will Rogers, Red Skelton, Peter Sellers, Richard Pryor, Don Rickles, Michael Richards, Douglas Fairbanks Sr., Clark Gable. Directors Cecille B. DeMille and Billy Wilder, Gene Autry, John Wayne, Glenn Ford, Tex Ritter, and Roy Rogers were also members of Freemasonry, as well as Magician Harry Houdini, Wild West showman "Buffalo Bill" Cody, and all seven of the Ringling brothers. When Christians promote or celebrate 'The Oscar Awards' they're supporting militant anti-Christians.

Scottish/African American Whitney Houston who was sacrificed 2/11/2012, at 48 years old, with a drug overdose (note: 2+11 = 13). Whitney was descended from Hugh de Paduinan, the Scottish baron, Knight Templar and progenitor of the Clan Houston, who in 1165 founded the town of Houston in that shire. Hugh died in 1189 in the Holy Land amongst the Templars who were killed at the Battle of Hattin. Whitney's sister-in-law stated that Whitney saw 'demons' everywhere she goes, and beats herself up while saying "The Devil be hitting me". She'll point to the floor and say, 'See that demon'? On 7/26/2015, [7+26=33] Whitney's

167

daughter, Bobbi Kristina Brown was sacrificed. Bobbi Kristina Brown, like her mother, drowned in a bathtub. She died at the age of 22.

"They sacrificed unto devils, not to God; to gods whom they knew not, to new gods that came newly up, whom your fathers feared not." - Deuteronomy 32:17

African/Irish American Johnny Allen Hendrix [Jimmy Hendrix] sacrificed 9/18/1970. There are a number of occult numerical associated with Jimmy's sacrifice namely the Mark of the Beast "666". The first is within the sacrifice day "18" which is comprised of 6+6+6=18. Jimmy was aged 27 when he was sacrificed 2+7=9 and there are two additional 9s in Jimmy's date of sacrifice creating "999". The Church of Babylon often uses 9s to represent 6s so "999" reads "666." Jimmy's sacrifice date also contains the occult numeric 27 twice, 9+18=27 and his age of death was 27 and 27x27=729 and the square root of 729 is 27. The force which deceived Henrix from God is "thumbing its nose" at the creator with this number. There are 27 books in the New Testament, 72 [27] names of God, 72 [27] angels of God and 7 Archangels, 7 churches in the Book of Revelation, 7 gifts of the Holy Ghost, The last book in the New Testament, the 27th, is the Book of Revelation, God's creation live in a 3 dimensional world, however the Holy Trinity exists everywhere therefore God exists in all dimensions 3x3x3=27 and finally Genesis 1:27 which reads:

"So God created man in his own image, in the image of God created he him; male and female created he them."

Jimmy Hendrix was destroyed for the same reason millions of other human beings have been destroyed. Satan hates God's creation [man/woman] because he wants to be God but knows he never will be. "I [Satan] will ascend above the heights of the clouds; I [Satan] will be like the most High." – Isaiah 14:14

In an interview with Jimmy Hendrix live in girlfriend she described how Hendrix was tormented by demons, she states:

"He used to always talk about some devil or something was in him, and he didn't have any control over it. He didn't know what made him act the way he acted and what made him say the things he said and songs and different things like that just come out of him. But at first I used to think it was a cop out when he'd really done me in. And he'd say:

"I don't know what come over me. I really can't understand it."

You know he used to just grab his hair or something or pull his hair or stand in the mirror or cry or something. Oh Lord, It was so sad when he would cry. He was maybe the first man or maybe the only man that I've ever seen cry, you know but it just killed me when he cried. It seems like to me that he was so tormented and just torn apart and like he really was obsessed with something really evil. And he said, "you know like you're from Georgia," you know he said, "I should know how, you know, people drive demons out." He actually thought about, you know, if we ever go, because I used to talk about my grandmother and all her weird stuff, you know, and he used to talk about us going down there and having some root lady or somebody see if she could drive this demon out of him."

KNIGHTS TEMPLARS: The Shadow Power Behind Walt Disney

"Appearances to the mind are of four kinds. Things either are what they appear to be; or they neither are, nor appear to be; or they are, and do not appear to be; or they are not, and yet appear to be. Rightly to aim in all these cases is the wise man's task." - Epictetus [c.55 AD-135 AD] born a slave in present day Pamukkale, Turkey. Lived in Rome where he served, "Epaphroditos," a wealthy secretary to Emperor Nero.

What Epictetus meant in the above four part observation was that sometimes things are not what they appear to be. This I believe best describes the Disney Corporation and the man who founded it, Walt Disney. If there is anything in the world with an appearance which is deceiving, it's the Walt Disney Empire, in particular the appearance of the fourth kind which is "...they are not, and yet appear to be".

Irish American Walter Elias Disney was sacrificed 12/15/1966 age 65. The two 6s in the date "1966" and 6 in Disney's age at death [65] creates "666." There is also a "666" in Disney's date of death. When you add the 1+5=6 and once again pair the two 6s in the year [1966]. It's no coincidence that the two numbers left in Disney's date of death 19 and 12 add up to 13. When you add 1+9=10+1+2 you arrive at "13".

Walt Disney is a descendant of Hughes d'Isigny a Knights Templar from Normandy who participated in William the Conquers 1066 invasion of England, Scotland and Ireland. Following William's invasion the Hughes d'Isigny family anglicized their name to Disney and relocated to the ancient Cill Chainnigh [Church of Cainneach] today referred to as Kilkenny, Ireland where the Disney family lived for 768 years until 1834 when they sailed to America.

It's relevant to point out that in 1320, the first recorded instance of a person being charged with witchcraft happened inside of Kilkenny, Ireland. Dame Alice Kyteler was accused of poisoning her four husbands to death, denying the faith of Jesus Christ, Cutting up animals to sacrifice to demons at crossroads, holding secret nocturnal meetings in churches to perform black magic, using sorcery and potions to control Christians, possession of a demon of Satan. During her case the witch Kyteler stated that she "had intercourse with a demon named as "Robin Artisson".

Just eighty-five years after Walt's ancestors landed in the United States, Disney would find himself returning overseas to join the American Ambulance Corps [Red Cross] in 1919 aged sixteen to fight in the war in Europe.

At the end of the war Walt was reassigned to France where he drove trucks and ambulances with future Scientology founder and Satanist L. Ron Hubbard, who once called his Luciferian colleague Aleister Crowley "My very good friend". L. Ron Hubbard was also good friends with, Satanist Jack Parsons, the founder of NASA's jet propulsion laboratory in Pasadena, CA. who wrote:

"And thus was I antichrist loosed in the world; and to this am I pledged, that the work of the beast shall be fulfilled, and the way for the coming of BABALON be made open and I shall not cease or rest until these things are accomplished." – Texe Marrs, Codex Magica.

In addition to Satanist Freemason L. Ron Hubbard, Walt Disney also drove trucks with future CEO of McDonalds Ray Croc who was quoted saying:

"We have found out... that we cannot trust some people who are nonconformists... We will make conformists out of them... The organization cannot trust the individual; the individual must trust the organization." - Ray Kroc

"The FDA requires that we tell people our Big Macs are made of mostly gluten filler. We've done two corporate press releases about it over the years – one in 1963 and one in 1977. It's just not something we share on our commercials." – Ray Kroc

On Tuesday June 7th, 1977, it is alleged by a number of television viewers, that a frazzled, Ray Kroc with cigarette in hand, appeared on the popular TV talk show, "The Mike Douglas Show".

It was during this appearance, viewers claim, they heard Ray Kroc broadcast to the public that he had donated a portion of his fortune to Anton LaVey's Church of Satan. Unsurprisingly Ray Kroc's McDonald's logo is a Masonic 13 [left].

"for the wisdom of their wise men shall perish, and the understanding of their prudent men shall be hid. Surely your turning of things upside down shall be esteemed as the potter's clay: for shall the work say of him that made it, He made me not? or shall the thing framed say of him that framed it, He had no understanding?"
- Isaiah 29:14,16

Ray Kroc's alleged affiliation with Anton Lavey's Church of Satan would explain the global pestilence caused by McDonald's. What's more, it provides an explanation for the picture of former

McDonalds Chairman and Chief Executive Officer Jim Cantalupo and Charlie Bell flashing satanic devil horns [left]. Cantalupo died from a heart attack in April, 2004. His successor, Charlie Bell, underwent colorectal cancer two weeks later and ultimately died from cancer in early 2005. It is commonly known that heart disease and colon cancer is caused by genetically modified organisms. The same GMO's sourced and sold by McDonald's Corporation to their 47 million customers each day.

A short list of Corporations created by Church of Babylon members e.g., Masonic Babylonian Talmudists, Knights Templars, etc. include: Dave Thomas (founder of Wendy's); Carl Karcher (founder of Carl's Junior) featured on pg.170 in his coffin aged 90 passing through a gauntlet of Knights and Dames of Malta at St. Boniface Catholic church in Anaheim CA, Friday, Jan. 18, 2008. [6+6+6=18] "666." Bob Evans (33 degree Freemason) and son Steve Evans (32 degree Freemason) control "Bob Evans Farms" in Ohio a chain of 590 restaurants. Bob say's his proudest moment came when fellow Satanist President Ronald Reagan was speaking at 171

Ohio State. Bob says that a secret service agent came up to him and tapped him on the shoulder and said "Are you Bob Evans"? The President wants to meet you." Harland Sanders ("the colonel," founder of Kentucky Fried Chicken) was a Freemason. In fact, Sanders's gravestone bears the Masonic square and compasses. Samuel Colt, who popularized the revolver; safety razor inventor King Camp Gillette; Frank Hoover of Hoover vacuums; James Cash Penney, who started J.C. Penney; and automotive pioneer Walter Chrysler.

DISNEY'S INDUCTION INTO THE TEMPLARS

It's 1919 in France and while transporting sugar from Paris to Soissons in February with fellow Satanists L. Ron Hubbard [Scientology] and 15 year old Satanist, Ray Croc [McDonalds CEO], Walt Disney abandons his truck and disappears for several days. In response to Walt's desertion Disney is ejected from the Red Cross. The story of Walt's dishonorable discharge was so well known that it was repeated on official tours of the Pentagon which was designed by Satanist Jack Parsons and parroted throughout basic training camps throughout America. Walt's close relationship with the U.S. Government, specifically the Pentagon, would later influence the design of Walt's Epcot Center in Disneyworld. According to the book, "Disney Declassified: Tales of Real Life Disney Scandals, Sex, Accidents and Deaths," by Aaron H. Goldberg, an individual named Mark Waters painted something titled, Miniature Worlds for, "Robert Jaffray an intelligence employee at the Pentagon." What's more "...he [Robert] showed the picture to Disney in 1963 to see if they would be interested in investing in his Miniature World."

Revisionist historians and those sympathetic to the Church of Babylon do their best to expunge Walt's mysterious disappearance while he was in France. About his experience in France Walt Disney said: "The things I did during those eleven months I was overseas added up to a lifetime of experience."

172

What Walt kept secret his entire life is that in 1919 his disappearance was orchestrated so that Walt could be reacquainted with the d'Isigny [Disney] Family's ancient Templar roots and provided the blueprint for what would become one of the most secure locations in the world to hide ancient Knights Templar assets. And while there are no photographs of Walt's Templar inauguration there are in fact a myriad of markers throughout the Disney Universe that when combined work together to provide substantial evidence of Walt Disney's involvement in one of the most complex conspiracies in history.

As we investigate all of the mysterious gaps in Walt Disney's past it's essential that we examine every aspects of Walt's life including those which may on the surface seem inconsequential or innocuous. With that charge upon us let's explore the history of Walt's first employer, "The Red Cross" and his Knights Templar bloodline.

The Red Cross is a civilian organization founded by Clara Barton on 5/21/1881. In 1869, during her trip to Geneva, Switzerland, Barton was introduced to the Red Cross logo and financial beneficiaries for the start of the American Red Cross.

Barton's inspiration was in large part shaped by the book "A Memory of Solferino" by Henry Dunant who spurned and attacked Christianity.

Since its creation the Red Cross has raised hundreds of millions of dollars and collected countless pints of blood which is used for what Red Cross President Dr. Bernadine Healy arrogantly referred to as "… a war fund". This quote of course does not reflect the altruistic nature of many Red Cross workers, who genuinely want to assist their fellow human beings. However to put the $2.9 billion dollar Red Cross organization into perspective consider the fact that its President Marsha Evans paid herself nearly $700,000 annually. Compare that with the two billion dollar organization, The Salvation Army, whose commissioner makes a meager $13,000 per year. After the events of 9/11 the Red Cross collected more than $564 million in donations and distributed just $154 million to victims. In reality the Red Cross provides elites the emotional vehicle necessary to extort money from America's mechanical citizenry a reality that will make it difficult for many to understand that the Red Cross has always been an arm of British Intelligence Services and has been since its founding. The most recent evidence I can provide readers occurred in 1996 with the kidnapping of European members of Netherlands Prince Bernhard's "World Wildlife Fund" (WWF). Immediately after securing the release of WWF associates Red Cross helicopters cooperated operationally with British armed forces to massacre Indonesian separatists.

For those readers who are unfamiliar with WWF and Prince Bernhard, Bernhard was a former Nazi SS officer and husband to Queen Betrice of the Netherlands, who just stepped down to make her son King 4/30/2013. Betrice' son has attended every Bilderberg Conference that's been held since his coronation. The Bilderberg Group is a well documented consortium of global elitists who literally control every Nation and major Corporation and Company on the planet. These are the same wicked individuals who concocted the idea of vaccinating our children with brain damaging, cancer causing toxins, fluoridating and chlorinating our minds into oblivion and slow killing America with genetically modified organisms [GMOs] which cause endocrine system shutdown and colon cancer.

Fluoridation of Water Trivia: The first time Fluoride was placed into a water supply was in the U.S.S.R. Soviets would mix fluoride into prison water supplies to sedate the prison population and make them more compliant.

What you might find interesting is that Prince Bernhard had dozens of mistresses throughout Europe and was so motivated to support his ring of prostitutes that he founded what is today known as The World Wild Fund [WWF] to save exotic animals from being slaughtered. He then sued the World Wrestling Federation to capture the name.

Under close scrutiny of Bernhard's operation it became apparent that the WWF he founded was actually being used principally to run clandestine operations throughout Africa, Asia, etc. Contrary to his organizations public motto of 'protect nature', Prince Bernhard would make tens of millions of dollars, on a monthly basis, by simply orchestrating the poaching operations of exotic animals. This included his warm and fuzzy, save the animals, World Wild Life Fund, which facilitated the actually killing of these exotic animals and the tens of millions of dollars he made on poaching animals were paid to his extensive network of European prostitutes.

Walt Disney left behind little evidence regarding his activities throughout Soissons, France. Ancient written material however explains the significance of the region for Knight's Templars and provides us with circumstantial evidence, which clarify Disney's disappearance and the ancient knowledge Disney inherited. This knowledge would shape his imminent success as well as direct the design concepts for two of his most iconic theme park rides "The haunted Mansion" and "Pirates of the Caribbean". We'll enlarge on this subject later; but let us now proceed with our examination of Walt's entrepreneurial and occultist activities following his return to Kansas City, Missouri.

On 5/23/1922 [222] aged twenty Walt Disney under his own cartoon company, "Laugh-O-Gram Films" (LOGF) in Kansas, City, Missouri produced 6 animated fairy tales (i) Jack and the beanstalk, (ii) Jack the Giant Killer, a story based on the Church of Babylon's god Nimrod and his giant offspring [pg.134]. (iii) Cinderella, (iv) Little Red Riding Hood, (v) Four Musicians of Bremen, and (vi) Little Red Riding Hood) each cartoon lasted just one minute.

1922 Trivia: The same year Walt Disney created LOGF, The 1st successful technicolor movie, "Tall of the Sea," shown in New York, NY [Dec, 03]; 1st constitution of Irish Free State comes in operation [Dec, 06]; 14 republics form Union of Soviet Socialistic Republics, "USSR" [Dec, 20]; Khazarian Babylonian Talmudist, Vladimir Lenin dictates his "Political testament" [Dec, 25]; Soviet Union organized as federation of RSFSR, Ukrainian SSR, Belorussian SSR & Transcaucasian SSR [Dec, 30].

Just ten years after Lenin's "testament" [1932-1933] Khazarian Babylonian Talmudist, Joseph Stalin carried out his Holodomor "Extermination by hunger" [genocide]. Through Stalin's man-made famine in the Ukrainian Soviet Socialist Republic, an estimated 12 million Ukrainians, many of those Christians, were murdered. An additional 6.1 million birth deficit was created by Stalin's genocide as well. A Ukrainian Christian majority had existed throughout the Ukraine since its acceptance [988 AD] by Vladimir the Great [Volodymyr the Great]. The famine had been predicted as far back as 1930 by academics and advisors to the Soviet Socialist Republic government, but no preventive action was taken.

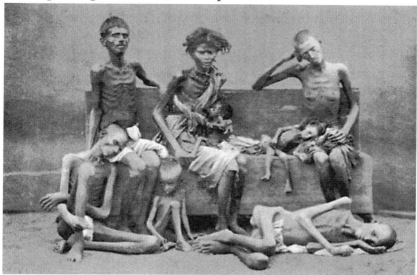

Picture of Ukrainian Christians taken c.1933, Ukrainian men, women and children starving to death, a result of the Khazarian Babylonian Talmudist "Holodomor."

THE DESIGNER'S OF BIOLOGICAL DIVERSITY AND COMMUNISM

Please forgive my temporary departure from our examination of Walt Disney, to expand on the topic of Khazarian Babylonian Talmudism and the role it has played in orchestrating famine throughout the world. It's an important conversation to have considering the imminent famine event America will be facing in the near future. In addition, many people are unbelievably uninformed regarding the origins of communism. Based on that fact, I would also like to edify readers on the true history and intentions of Marxism, Leninism, Ceausescuism, Maoism, etc. so that you're better prepared for what's coming.

In 1795 the "Father of Modern Geology" Scottish geologist, physician, chemical manufacturer, naturalist and Freemason, James Hutton writes, "Theory of the Earth," deceiving millions of Christians into doubting the Holy bible, which states that the earth's age is approximately 6,000 years old. In 1830, Scottish lawyer and Freemason, "Sir Charles Lyell," whose stated goal was to "destroy Christianity," writes the book, "Principles of Geology," deceiving millions of people into doubting Noah's Flood.

In 1859 Church of Babylon member, "Charles Darwin" writes the book, "On the Origin of Species by Means of Natural Selection, or the Preservation of Favoured Races in the Struggle for Life" deceiving millions of people into doubting The Creator [God].

It was Darwin's religion of evolutionism that inspired Karl Marx, who was the offspring of Khazarian Babylonian Talmudists. Marx maternal grandfather was a Dutch rabbi, while his paternal line contained rabbis since 1723. Friedreich Engels was also the offspring of Khazarian Babylonian Talmudists. Both Marx and Engels created, "The Communist Manifesto," which was issued on 1848 in London.

The Khazarian Babylonian Talmud is the source from which Marx and Engels communist philosophy originated. This led directly to the rise of Communism, Socialism and Nazism and has paved the way for the Babylonian Talmudist, "New World Order" and "One World Religion."

Darwin, Marx and Engels also contributed to Scottish American physician and neuroscientist, "Paul D. MacLean's," 1960s unveiling of his triune or "reptilian brain" theory. The reptilian brain theory is an evolutionary model of the vertebrate forebrain which seeks to destroy the truth of Creation while paying homage to the Serpent Cult of Dann to which MacLean belonged.

Not since the 1700s has there been a more important time in our Nation's history for everyone to understand world history, namely the 1845-1850 genocide of more than five million Irish men, women and children and1930s Germany. America in 2015 is in the beginning stages of what will become a mirror image of these catastrophic events. For example in 2015, America's entire political and economic system has been hijacked by members of the Church of Babylon. One of their puppets is California's Communist Governor, Jerry Brown, who is waging a psychological war on California farmers and families by draining freshwater reservoirs, destroying dams and imposing fines for those who discount California's artificially engineered chaos. At the same time governor brown is threatening fines and arrest for legal taxpaying citizens he is opening the flood gates to political pawns from South America, who consume more than 400 million gallons of freshwater per day and cost the state more than $25.3 billion annually. In addition to straining our State and Federal coffers, duplicitous politicians are shipping major components of American's GDP to South America, Asia, India, etc. Anyone with eyes to see and ears to hear will conclude that State and Federal agencies are intentionally destroying our nation's economy and bread baskets in order to usher in the liberty crushing force of "Agenda 21," which will annihilate America's food supply producing the desired result of tens of millions of dead Americans.

The above-mentioned example is very similar to Ireland's 1840s genocide which was designed and executed by Church of Babylon proxies who intentionally injected "phytophthora infestans" [potato blight] into the islands soil which in turn decimated Irelands potato crops. In addition to releasing the Trojan horse of blight onto the Irish people, Church of Babylon proxies completely destroyed the Irish economy whilst exporting the vast majority of food grown on the Island to other countries. According to the book, "The Famine Plot, pg.53," by Tim Pat Coogan, "the research of G.H. Fitzgerald, might have averted the disaster" Mr. Coogan goes on to explain on pg. 54 how Fitzgerald's potato blight fungus solution was "brought to the attention of Kane, who thought nothing of them." Not only was an individual by the name of "Kane" complicit in the deaths of five million Irish people, the Church of Babylon even linked the sacrifice of five million Irish men, women and children with an occult related date, Friday the 13th in the month of September.

To ensure their plan of genociding five million Irish men, women and children ran smoothly they deployed their Babylonian Talmudist henchman, "Benjamin Disraeli," to sow the seeds of chaos throughout Ireland's already fettered political system. Disraeli was the first and thus far only Jewish Prime Minister of the United Kingdom. Disraeli harbored a deep 177 hatred for the Irish people, stating in 1836:

"The Irish hate our order, our civilization, our enterprising industry, our pure religion [Talmudism]. This wild, reckless, indolent, uncertain and superstitious race have no sympathy with the English character. Their ideal of human felicity is an alternation of clannish broils and coarse idolatry. Their history describes an unbroken circle of bigotry and blood." - "How the Irish Saved Civilization: The Untold Story of Ireland's Heroic role from the Fall of Rome to the Rise of Medieval Europe," by Thomas Cahill.

Disraeli's anti-Irish rhetoric was magnified by a fellow eugenicist and Coleraine workhouse medical officer who stating:

"Famine must be looked forward to and will follow, as a natural consequence, as in former years, typhus fever, or some other malignant pestilence." – The Famine Plot, by Tim Pat Coogan, pg.55

While Disraeli's concerted malice battered Ireland's political system, the Illuminati controlled Baring Brothers Bank profited off of the insufferable environment which their cronies created. Coincidently the Baring family's descendants include Diana, Princess of Wales and through her Prince William, Duke of Cambridge. It's also noteworthy to mention here that for centuries, The Baring Brothers, maintained a close relationship with the Babylonian Talmudist owned and controlled, Berenberg family who for centuries have been Illuminati apologists and allies to the Babylonian Talmudist Rothschild Banking dynasty. The owner of Berenberg Bank, Johann Hinrich Gossler [above] is shown with his hand inside of his jacket representing the "hidden hand" of the "Illuminati" [Church of Babylon]. If you would like to read a detailed account of Ireland's 1840s genocide, please read the book, "The Famine Plot" by Tim Pat Coogan.

When we examine the data associated with the individuals who controlled the banking, entertainment and news agencies in 1930s Germany, we discover that they referred to themselves as "Social Democrats" otherwise known as Babylonian Talmudist Communists. Similarly the individuals who control America's banking, entertainment and 178 news agencies in 2015 call themselves Social Democrats and the vast majority of those individuals are Babylonian Talmudists. For example

Presidential candidate Bernie Sanders is a Babylonian Talmudist. Although Bernie claims to be a "Democratic Socialist" and through a clumsily chartered vaunt through circular reasoning Bernie attempts to minimize the bloody history associated with his party platform by stating that it's not like a Social Democrat. Read what Bernie had to say in a 2006 interview with Democracy Now:

"I think [democratic socialism] means the government has got to play a very important role in healthcare… childcare… college… we do not allow large corporations to destroy our environment… it means democracy, frankly. That's all it means."

The most significant comparison between 1930s Germany and 2015 America that should be examined are the parallels between Germany's weak link of import dependency, which was the trident in the heart of Germany's economy, and America's increasingly dangerous dependency on imports. After all farming and factories are the foundation for prosperity, not financial speculation, Quantitative Easing (QE) as the triad of iniquity e.g., Talmudists, Serpent Tribe of Dann and Freemason's would have you believe. Have you stopped to consider what will happen when America's fuel source runs out? The resulting effects are that tractors will no longer harvest, trucks no longer transport and grocery store shelves remain empty. Will you be able to digest your Rockefeller financed and owned facebook, twitter, or google search engine? How many calories will that quantitatively eased paper in your wallet yield? America's Tangible sustenance is being slowly exchanged for virtual silence. It's the defining silence that produces the desperate people who at a later date will be more easily fooled by human exploitation psychological operations.

Currently up to 94% of many commodities and rare earth metals are sourced outside of the U.S. This has in large part been caused by the current global elite orchestrated U.S. permitting process which seeks to strangle U.S. independence from communist nations like China. These minerals are crucial to the production of Jet Fighters, antimissile defense systems, night vision goggles, smart bombs and other advanced military systems. In terms of consumer products these rare earth commodities are used inside of computers, cell phones, televisions, etc. What's more they are essential to refining petroleum, manufacturing automotive catalytic converters, wind turbines and electric vehicles. China's monopoly on the global rare earth minerals market is so significant in 2015 that it can cause a nationwide gas shortage overnight, effectively crippling U.S. agriculture, transportation, power and defense.

179

To understand what an ill prepared America would look like under a Chinese embargo all we have to do is study 1930s Germany, when Babylon Talmudists orchestrated a global boycott against their Nation. In 1933 two thirds of Germany's food supply had to be imported, and it could only be imported with the proceeds of what they exported. Their labor. So if Germany could not export, two thirds of Germany's population would have to starve. There just was not enough food for more than one third of the population. Now juxtapose the aforementioned statistics associated with 1930s Germany with that of 2004-06 America. According to www.producenews.com:

"The main sources of U.S. fresh fruit imports are banana-exporting countries, and the Southern Hemisphere and NAFTA regions. The banana exporters — Colombia, Costa Rica, Ecuador, Guatemala, Honduras and Panama — are the largest providers of fresh fruit to the United States.

Together, these countries supply 36 percent of total U.S. fresh fruit imports, with bananas making up more than three-quarters of the fresh fruit value shipped by these equatorial countries to the United States. Southern Hemisphere countries — Argentina, Australia, Brazil, Chile, New Zealand, South Africa and Peru — supply 32 percent of U.S. fresh fruit imports.

The NAFTA region supplies 27 percent of U.S. fresh fruit imports.

Bananas, grapes and tropical fruit, including pineapples, mangos, papayas and guavas, accounted for nearly two-thirds of the value of U.S. fresh fruit imports in 2004-06, with bananas alone representing a 44 percent value share of the combined imports for these three major fruit products.

The structure of the U.S. fresh fruit import mix, however, has changed substantially, particularly since the 1990s, as grape and tropical fruit imports have grown faster than bananas.

Blueberries are a good example of an item that has grown quickly and hugely over the past decade. Other fruits and vegetables, such as asparagus from Peru, are also inching toward the list of items that are outpacing banana imports."

Americans must come to the realization that their Nation is being imploded from within by a deceptive villain who detests American ingenuity, the freedom associated with a free market system and above all else our Christian heritage. At this point in our Nation's history it is critically important that every American get involved in the turn-around of our Nation. If they do not, a 1930s Germany will be our final destination

180

and when it happens, Americans will go to bed in one nation and walk-up in another.

In a 1920 article Freemason Winston Churchill referred to so called Jews [Khazarian Talmudists] as "Terrorist Jews" he went on to further underline their role in Bolshevism, stating:

"There is no need to exaggerate the part played in the creation of Bolshivism... by these international and for the most part atheistical Jews. It is certainly a very great one."

Churchill's comments corroborate the views of successful Jewish business man, "Benjamin Freedman", who in 1961 delivered a speech which alarmed the Christian American majority to their core. Benjamin revealed what was at the time a relatively unknown history of Babylonian Talmudism, specifically Talmudists ancient hatred towards Jesus Christ and Christian America.

For those Christian American's who want to understand the ancient militant Antichristian nature of Babylonian Talmudism, Benjamin Freedman's speech may be read and watched in its entirety at **www.destroyers.us**. While reviewing Freedman's evidence it's paramount that you disregard your emotions, in their place focus on the facts. After you have reviewed the ample historical evidence I'm confident that you'll agree with the opinion that Babylonian Talmudists do not consider themselves American, European, etc. and they certainly have no allegiance to, or reverence for Jesus Christ, they're Talmudists first and foremost. And in a parasitical way they feed on their host nation with complete disregard for the nation's health and safety of its citizens. Historically Talmudists have been destroyers. In 1924 Maurice Samuel in his book 'You Gentiles', p.155 Harcourt, Brace, stated as such:

"We Jews, we, the destroyers, will remain destroyers forever. Nothing that you will do will meet our needs and demands. We will forever destroy because we need a world of our own."

On February, 1926, Marclis Eli Ravage in Century Magazine wrote:

"You have not begun to appreciate the depth of our guilt. We are intruders. We are subverters. We have taken your natural world, your ideals, your destiny, and played havoc with them. We have been at the bottom of not merely the latest great war, but of every other major revolution in your history. We have brought discord and confusion and frustration into your personal and public life. We are still doing it. No one can tell how long we shall go on doing it. Who knows what great and glorious destiny might have been yours if we had left you alone."

181

On February 9, 1883, The Jewish World Magazine published a statement which read:

"The great ideal of Judaism is that the whole world shall be imbued with Jewish teachings, and that in a Universal Brotherhood of nations – a greater Judaism in fact – all the separate races and religions shall disappear."

In Samuel Roth's prose, 'Jews Must Live' (1934), p.64, he states:

"So swiftly and surely is the instinct of anti-Semitism awakened in a man… there is not a single instance when the Jews have not fully deserved the bitter fury of their persecutors."

Why do you think Talmudists have been kicked out of more than 100 countries throughout history? In Russian Talmudists took over and killed more than 50 million innocent people. Then Talmudists instigated WWII and were able to kill millions of Germans and American Christians. In Armenia Talmudists took over and killed more than 2 million innocent people. In the Ukraine Talmudists inside of Russia orchestrated "Extermination by hunger" that resulted in the murders of more than 12 million innocent people. In 1933 Rabbi Stephen S. Wise provides us with an answer to the aforesaid question, stating:

"I am not an American citizen of Jewish faith. I am a Jew. I have been an American for sixty-three years, but I have been a Jew for 4000 years."

In 2015, Babylonian Talmudists are destroying America's ability to feed its citizens and if you personally do not prepare yourself and your family Talmudists will take great pride in watching you and your family die. Please prepare yourself today at **www.famfed.com**

Returning back to our examination of Walt Disney, I'd like to share with readers an interesting tidbit related to Walt's cartooning, specifically the term Walt coined, "Cels" to describe the media he used for backdrops. Since 248 AD the word "Cels" has been used to describe Celsus, an anti-Christian Greek philosopher who in c.177 AD mounted the earliest known comprehensive attack on Christianity through his work titled, "The True Word" (Alethes logos). Celsus was also an admirer of Ancient Egyptian religion and addressed the miracle of Jesus Christ, holding that "Jesus performed His miracles by sorcery". Much like the U.S. political and legal representatives of today Celsus believed that Christians should retain their beliefs but conform to the state religion.

182

Walt shared Greek philosopher Celsus' affinity for the Egyptian religion, choosing to debut his fairy tale animations at the, "Isis Theatre", located at Troost Avenue and 31st Street. Walt rode to the event in a car which contained a sign which read, "These pictures will be shown at the Isis Theatre Tomorrow Night."

Walt's first business was located near "Millionaires Row" this is what they called 31st and Troost. L.V. Harkness, and one of the largest stockholders in John D. Rockefeller's "Standard Oil" and Master Freemason lived on the 3100 block of Troost. Walt's lifelong love for railroads stems from his admiration for the railroad titan John D. Rockefeller. To Walt the Railroad was a symbol of wealth.

The 2nd Church of Christ Science was also located on 3101 Troost. Its founder Mary Baker Eddy based her "Christian" belief system on Hinduism which in fact believes man can become God and that the material world is an illusion. "...and ye shall be as Gods." [Satan] – Genesis 3:5. The idea that the material world is an illusion is fundamental to Walt Disney's universe, the idea that humans can do anything if they just believe in themselves and ignore God, "hath god said" [Satan] – Genesis 3:1, instead of believing in the promise that, "With men this is impossible; but with God all things are possible".

Walt Disney's "When You Wish Upon a Star" encapsulates what I refer to as the religion of Disneyism, parroted by fraudster pastors such as Oral Roberts, John and Joel Osteen, Rick Warren, Benny Hinn and thousands of others. These men are all too willing to deliver whatever a listeners "itching ears" [2 Timothy 4:3] want to hear as long as you, "give until it hurts!" After all, pain is what salvation is all about right? No, actually the Holy Bible tells readers that salvation in Jesus Christ is "rest", "Quietness" and "Strength.

Mary Baker Eddy's affinity for the occult is unsurprising considering Freemason Henry Steele Olcott, co-founder of Helena Blavatsky's "Theosophical Society" was an associate of Mary Baker Eddy. Blavatsky and Olcott met at one of the Eddy Brother's séances to communicate with the dead. As an aside one of Adolf Hitler's favorite books to read was 'The Secret Doctrine: The Synthesis of Science, Religion, and Philosophy' (1888) by Helena Blavatsky. Coincidently Blavatsky's grandmother was a daughter of Henrietta Adolfovna. What's fascinating about the Eddy, Olcott, Blavatsky, Freemason and as I'll expose shortly Walt Disney connection is that the Reichstag fire, which was pivotal in the establishment of Nazi Germany, was caused by a Freemason 2/27/1933. "I regard Christianity as the most fatal, seductive lie that ever existed." - Adolf Hitler

Mary Baker Eddy herself was married to a Freemason, the only secret society Eddy allowed her Christian Science members to join. The darling of Freemasonry, Eddy's Christian Science material was published in the Freemason's Monthly Magazine. Several Christian Science directors, board members and editors were Freemasons, including the President of the "Mother Church" in 1922-23 and 1923-24.

The connection between Christian Science, Freemasonry and the Knights Templars may be seen in the Christian Science insignia of a cross and crown [left]. Since antiquity the cross and crown logo has been associated with the historical degrees in freemasonry, knighthood of York, Scottish rites, etc.

One other 'Christian" group uses the cross and crown insignia, the Jehovah Witnesses. The founder of the Jehovah Witness church was Charles Taze Russell; he used the Red Cross and other features of the Knights Templar symbol which was borrowed from the stela of Nimrod [pg.18,"B"] by Freemason's c.926 AD. Charles Taze Russell's grave marker is even a Masonic pyramid with a Knights Templar cross affixed to the front.

Practitioner and teacher of Christian Science and 33rd degree Freemason, Samuel Greenwood, wrote a poem titled "What is our God" in it, Greenwood states, "OUR God is whatever we love the best. Be it good or evil, love or hate. Be it pleasure or power or rich estate." Greenwood's perception of God is identical to that of Satanist Aleister Crowley, who referred to himself as "The Great Beast 666". Crowley's Cult credo was, "Do What Thou Wilt shall be the whole of the law. Love is the law, love under will."

Mary Baker Eddy wrote that her cult had "mental powers" and those powers could be used as a "weapon". In one instance Eddy ordered her cult followers to stand outside her bedroom door to protect her from mental attacks. In 1882 Eddy claimed that her last husband had died of "mental assassination". And that anyone practicing "mental assassination" or "malicious animal magnetism" should be put to death. Several Christian Science members committed suicide while practicing Eddy's belief in 'malicious animal magnetism". One student threw herself out of a window. Another student of Eddy gassed herself to death. Later in life Eddy would become diagnosed with Psychotic Personality Disorder. Perhaps this was caused by her lifelong drug addiction to morphine or the fact that she worshipped Satan. Nonetheless, at the end of her wicked existence in 1910, Eddy believed that 50,000 people were trying to kill her by "projecting evil thoughts".

184

American author Mark Twain [Samuel Langhorne Clemens] who wrote "Adventures of Huckleberry Finn" and its prequel "The Adventures of Tom Sawyer" was the inspiration behind Walt Disney's iconic "Tom Sawyer Island" and "Fort Sam Clemens" located inside of Disneyland's "Frontierland", the only attraction designed solely by Walt himself. Mark Twain inspired more than just Disney; he was also a fan of Christian Science founder, Mary Baker Eddy, stating:

"… the most interesting woman that ever lived, and the most extraordinary." On 7/10/1861, Mark Twain became a master freemason of Polar Star Lodge No. 79, St, Louis Mo.

Today there are 1,700 Christian Science Churches in 76 countries. The Christian Science Monitor newspaper has won 7 Pulitzer Prizes to date. On 7/16/1921, the 100th anniversary of Eddy's birth, a 100-ton granite pyramid with 121 square foot footprint was dedicated to her at the site of Mary Baker Eddy's birth in Bow, New Hampshire. The pyramid was a gift from 33 degree Freemason, James F. Lord. "Christian Science" board of directors voted to demolish the pyramid because people were becoming aware of its occult meaning and that people were writing about it.

Mary Baker Eddy's birth monument contains a number of occult numerics, for instance the number of prime numbers up to 666 is 121, which is the square of 11. Belphegor's prime is the palindromic prime number that contains 666 and 13 zeros on either sides [1000000000000000666000000000000 0001]. Belphegor's prime is a number which is the same image forward and backward, just like the word "Illuminati" and is only divisible by itself and one. The name Belphegor refers to one of the 7 Princes of Hell, who was charged with helping people make ingenious inventions and discoveries. Like Eddy's Christian Science, the Illuminati, founded by Adam Weishaupt, was charged with creating a One World Religion and New World Order.

The images on pg.185 feature, Adolph Freiherr Knigge [top], the most effective recruiter for the Illuminati; Alexandre Gustave Eiffel, Freemason who constructed the Eiffel Tower in France and U.S. Statue of Liberty;.Babylonian Talmudist Karl Marx is featured in an Illuminati pose. Marx was both a Satanist as well as the founding father of Communism. Many people are uneducated about the core difference between Atheism and Satanism and therefore misrepresent Marx as an Atheist which is false and here's why. An atheist does not believe in the existence of God, whereas a Satanist believes in the existence of God in Heaven and Satan in Hell. A Satanist with his/her free will has made a conscious decision to follow Satan. Shortly after Karl Marx left high school he wrote a poem which stated in part, "I wish to avenge myself against the one [God] who rules above." This statement is consistent with a

185

Satanic declaration to stand with Satan against God. Finally we have Mary Baker Eddy's son, George Washington Glover II [bottom]. What these photographs illustrate is Eddy's knowledge of and involvement with the Illuminati. The hand inside of the jacket represents the "hidden hand" of the "Illuminati" [Church of Babylon].

On 12/24/1918, "The Concord Evening Monitor" published an article which featured elements of Eddy's birth pyramid monument including the writing found on each of the four sides stating, "On the west, the tablet bears the following... Novos Ordo Seclorum" this translates into "the New Order of the Ages" or New World Order. The top of Mary Baker Eddy's current burial monument inside of Mount Auburn Cemetery between Cambridge and Middlesex County, Massachusetts reads "DISCOVERER" associating her with the Prince of Hell, Belphegor.

The significance of all that you've read regarding Mary Baker Eddy's Cult of Christian Science is that Walt Disney and his family frequently attended and financially supported the Christian Science Cult.

In addition to Walt Disney's intimate association with Mary Baker's 2nd Church of Christ cult, there are several keys in the aforementioned information which seems to indicate that Walt Disney had a lifelong association with the Church of Babylon, these include the fact that Isis Theatre, and Walt's "Laugh-O-Gram Films" Corporate offices both shared the same 31st and Troost address. It will be remembered that Osiris was chopped into 13 pieces by Seth. Isis, the wife of Osiris, obsessed with her husband's penis, searched far and wide for it; we're told that Osiris' penis was eaten by a fish. Osiris' lost penis is symbolized in Egyptian obelisks which are commonly located inside of a circle, which represents female genitalia. Walt Disney knew that the Isis Theater was an occult alter built to honor the 'god' Osiris and his wife Isis and yet Walt Disney made the conscious decision to debut his first 6 cartoons here.

The picture above features the Isis Theater and Mary Baker Eddy's 2nd Church of Christ Science streaming the Star of Remphan between their buildings and all the way down Troost. It will be remembered that the six pointed Star of Remphan [Satan] contains dimensions which contain the "Mark of the Beast" 666.

Compounding the occult significance of the Isis building is its address, "31st". Since antiquity the number 31 has been associated with a three day festival named "Samhain" a festival dedicated to the Celtic lord of the dead. During the celebration men, women and children would be sacrificed to the sun god. One of the most popular Samhain celebrations occurs on October 31st [Halloween], where people blissfully carve pumpkins ["Jack-O-Lanters"]. During the Samhain celebration the Druids would create "Corpse Candles" ["Jack-O-Lanters"] and fill them with the fat of humans previously sacrificed to the lord of the dead. Druids would also go door-to-door yelling "Trick or Treat" and if the owner of the residence didn't offer up a "Treat" [a human sacrifice] they would receive a Star of Remphan [Satan] on their door a star with 6 points, inside of a circle (hexagram) painted with blood. Druids believed the 6 pointed star would cause those inside to be tormented by demons. It's interesting that "6" is the number of cartoons Walt Disney premiered at the Isis Theatre.

The popular children's game of "Bobbing for Apples" originated with the Druids as well. Druids would line their human sacrifices up around a boiling hot cauldrons filled with apples and give their captors a chance at freedom. If they successfully pulled the apple out

187

with one try they were free to live the rest of their lives with a deformed face. If they failed their first try they were beheaded, thrown into the cauldron and boiled down for "Corpse Candles".

Walt's "Scenario Editor" was Walt's childhood friend Walter Pfeiffer, who prior to joining Walt's team was working for IO Studios. It will be remembered that the Roman Numeral 'X', represents the number ten as well as the word 'IO' (pronounced EO) and in Greek the word 'IO' means Helios or Apollyon otherwise known as The Beast from the pit. Flash forward to the 1980s and we see Walt Disney Company further venerating Apollyon with the creation of the Disney attraction, "Captain EO" the 3D science fiction film produced by George Lucas, starring Michael Jackson. Ignoring the potential side effects e.g., convulsions, blackouts, etc. of 3D technology this film was shown at Disney theme parks from 1986 through 1996 and returned in 2010 to the "Magic Eye Theater", as a tribute to Michael Jackson's sacrifice, a fitting memorial to a man who venerated Lucifer in all that he did.

"I wanted to get hold of Satan personally and become his chief of staff. Satan Cry Aloud! Thou Exalted Most High! Oh My Father Satan! The Eye!" – Aleister Crowley

Michael Jackson was an admirer of Satanist Aleister Crowley, following the teachings inside of Crowley's book, "777 and other Qabalistic Writings of Aleister Crowley. In the book, Crowley suggests that when you look into a mirror you can look into yourself and channel the spirits before you. Following Crowley's advice Michael constructed a secret room full of mirrors to channel spirits. Michael Jackson states, "I have my own secret room with a moving wall and mirrors. This is where I talk to Liberace. I hear his voice in there, I feel his presence so very close to me. He's like my guardian angel. He even gave me permission to record his title, "I'll be seeing you" - Psychic News, 1987

For those readers who are unaware, Liberace was a flamboyant homosexual pianist. Liberace was also one of the first members of the Church of Satan and a close friend of its founder Anton Lavey.

Michael Jackson also stated that his hit songs were delivered to him by dream spirits. Morpheus is the God of Dreams and brother to Hypnos [Greek god of sleep] and Thanatos [god of death]. All of these figures are associated with the "Oneiroi." The Oneiroi were dark-winged Daimones of dreams. Ancient texts tell us that the Oneiroi would emerge every night, like a flock of bats from their caves in Erebos, the land of eternal darkness. When people hold up the "devil-horns" or "I love you" hand-sign, created by Satanist Helen Keller, they are in fact symbolizing the two gates the Oneiroi passed through to reach our world. The first gate made of two 'horns' represented prophetic god-sent dreams, while the second, made of ivory, represented nightmares or 'black dreams'. The leader of the Oneiroi was 'Morpheus', a god who appeared in the dreams of kings in the guise of a man, delivering messages from the gods. This ancient Greek 'God' is similar to the Church of Babylon manufactured Antichrist, "Maitreya", who has apparently unveiled himself to a number of world leaders, including former CIA Director and President George H.W. Bush.

The aforesaid is man's first ancient interpretation of this horn like hand sign. The second comes from the ancient Sanskrit language which first emerged circa 1,000 B.C. There are two hand-signs in Sanskrit, both of which have components found within the "I love you" and "Devil Horns" hand sign. The first Ancient Sanskrit sign represents the American Sign Language ('ASL') equivalent of the letter 'L'. In Sanskrit the fingers are pointed down towards the ground and are defined as follows, "Subjugates demonic passions;"

The "devil-horns" and "I love you" hand signs are an occult tool which deceives people into placing spells on one another. Occultists believe that by inverting the ancient Sanskrit hand sign, practitioners of these hand-signs are no longer suppressing demonic passions but expressing demonic passions.

Helen Keller, who wrote, "My Religion" proudly described her occult religious perspective on life and her enthusiasm for the teachings of Satanist Emmanuel Swedenborg. I know some people might be upset at the idea of Helen Keller being labeled a Satanist, unfortunately it's true. The book titled 'Light in My Darkness', originally published in 1927 as 'My Religion,' was a tribute to Satanist Emanuel Swedenborg whom Helen regarded as, "one of the noblest champions true Christianity has ever known." This book is regarded as Helen Keller's spiritual autobiography in which she openly declares, "the teachings of Emanuel Swedenborg have been my light, and a staff in my hand and by his vision splendid I am attended on my way."

Michael Jackson's first album on his own label, "MJJ Productions, was titled, "HIStory: Past, Present and Future, Book I" which featured a giant statue of Michael. On the armband [pg.190, top] of the statue is the number, "777" this is the title of Satanist, Aleister Crowley's, book, "777 and other Qabalistic Writings of Aleister Crowley." Crowley's 777 book is one of the most prominent books of the Qabalah [Kabbalah] in the western esoteric tradition. Kabbalah is a branch of Jewish [Khazarian Talmudism] mysticism [occultism]. Kabbalah is not a religion, and it never was. It originated around the 11th century as an outgrowth of earlier so called Jewish esoteric-occult traditions. Followers of this cult believe that with Kabalistic secrets in hand, they can construct magic words

189

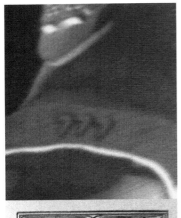

that will allow them to control demons. The 1998 movie, "Pi" featured malevolent Hasidic so called Jews [Khazarian Talmudists] searching for a way to decipher the true name of God. The movie, "Pi" coincided with a revival of mainstream interest in Kabbalah.

"Kabbalism is a system of Jewish mysticism and magic and is the foundational element in modern witchcraft. Virtually all of the great witches and sorcerers of this century were Kabbalists." -William J. Schnoebelen, The Dark Side of Freemasonry

In May of 1922 Walt Disney raised $15,000 ($186,358.73 in 2015) and leases the upper floor of the Scottish family owned McConahy Building at 1127, E. 31st st. in Kansas, City, Missouri. Interestingly in ancient times The McConahy Family were originally known as Clan Donnachaidh. A distinguished family, they were related to King Duncan I of Scotland who was killed by MacBeth of Shakespearean fame. The "Exclusive Agents" Walt Disney rented his office space from, worked for a German immigrant named Lawrence Baer. Baer operated L. J. Baer & Company, "Real Estate Managers of Income Property and Agents", with an office in the Grand Avenue Temple Building.

Temple Building Trivia: Baer's Temple Building is the same location Aviator Amelia Earhart gave a 10/17/1933 lecture in titled: "Flying for Fun" shortly before her disappearance.

In addition to being one of Walt Disney's earliest investors, Lawrence Baer was a Knights Templar whose ancestors were the founders of Switzerland's biggest and top Swiss bank. The Baer family banking roots date back to the 15th century approximately 185 years after the remaining Knights Templars disbanded from France and England in 1314, changing their name to Knights of Malta. The birthplace of the distinguished family name Baer is Austria, which was originally home to Celts who were conquered by the Roman Empire c.15 BC.

As of 2015, the Baer family manages more than one trillion 190 Swiss Francs in assets with offices in Frankfurt, Milan, Geneva, Dubai, Grand Cayman, New York, Singapore and Hong Kong. On

12/4/2008 Baer's CEO, Alex Widmer, was murdered. In 2011 the CEO of the Baer Swiss Empire, Julius Baer, was murdered at age 52, shortly after a wikileaks threat to disclose tax-evaders linked to the bank. The Baer Banking Dynasty has for centuries been a direct competitor to the Rothschild banking cartel, whose family members have espoused Luciferian doctrines including a "New World Order" system ruled by the Antichrist. Prior to the family patriarch changing their last name to Rothschild, their surname was Bauer. Variations of the surname Bauer include Baer.

MASONIC TEMPLAR HISTORY

Earlier I mentioned how Walt Disney has provided the public with very little information regarding his activities throughout France' Soissons region in 1919, and how there is a great deal of documentation regarding the significance of this region for the Knight's Templars, which is what we're going to examine next. In 1295 Gerard de Villiers joined the Knights Templars and by 1300 Villiers became the Knights Templar Master of France, head of economic affairs and head of the largest Templar order in Soissons France a region which enters written history under its Celtic name Noviodunum, meaning "new hillfort" and mentioned by Julius Caesar in 57 B.C. According to Templar trial records Gerard de Villiers was an evil man totally corrupting the Order of Templar Knights and incorporating Antichristian, blasphemous rituals. These included the requirement that all new Templars must deny the God of the Bible, spit on the Christian Cross, worship a severed head, practice magic and perform homosexual acts. All who denied Gerard de Villiers requests were held in a secret Templar prison and eventually put to death. According to ancient documents all but twelve Templar Knights were burnt to death. The twelve that escaped were led by Gerard de Villiers carrying with them Templar Treasure and artifacts of their cult to what is now Switzerland. This is why the Swiss Flag is that of a Freemason imposed, Knights Templar Cross.

In regards to the Knight's Templar's being charged with worshipping a severed head I would like to point out to readers that Walt Disney celebrates this ancient Templar tradition throughout his Haunted House. One of the most prominent elements to Walt Disney's Haunted Mansion is a character named "Madame Leota", a severed head, inside of a crystal ball, that floats above a table whose legs are serpents [pg.192, top]. During Madame Leota's performance she exposes guests to the following spell which is overtly serpent cult related:

191

"Horntoads and lizards, fiddle and strum. Please answer the role by beating a drum! Ghost fiends and furies, old friends and new! Blow in a horn, so we'll know whether it's you! Serpents and spiders, tail of a rat; call in the spirits, wherever they're at. Rap on a table; it's time to respond. Send us a message from somewhere beyond. Goblins and ghoulies from last Halloween. Awaken the spirits with your tambourine. Creepies and crawlies, toads in a pond; let there be music, from regions beyond! Wizards and witches, wherever you dwell, give us a hint, by ringing a bell!"

Madame Leota Trivia: Leota's table was given to Walt Disney by real practicing witches.

When we examine Walt Disney personal life we see that he enjoyed the company of fellow Satanist. For instance he was good friends with Sammy Davis Jr. [left]. In this picture Sammy is wearing a Knights of Malta [Knights Templar] cape holding up the "V" hand-sign. The "V" sign represents Adam Weishaupt's Illuminati and the "Law of Fives." What's more the Hebrew letter for V (Van) is "Nail" which is one of the secret titles of Satan within the brotherhood of Satanism. The "V" also symbolizes the pentagram and the five-fold salute used in Masonry and Withcraft. Sammy was also a member of Anton Lavey's Church of Satan and often wore a satanic pentagram necklace. Davis Jr. confesses to his Church of Satan membership in his autobiography, "Yes I Can". Davis Jr. also enjoyed promoting Satan on the big-screen and in his music. For instance Sammy Davis Jr. [pg.193, top] is featured playing The Devil in a movie titled: "Poor Devil".

Starring as the
POOR DEVIL

The popular entertainer also integrated the Masonic "As Above, So Below" into his dance performance. Reportedly Davis Jr's most popular song "The Candy Man" was secretly in praise of Satan. The Candy Man Can bring his disciples gifts such as illegal drugs e.g., heroin, cocaine, etc. and sexual favors.

Walt Disney's friend, Sammy Davis Jr., [left] is pictured here with both Church of Satan founder Anton Lavey on Sammy's left and Michael Aquino on Sammy's right. Aquino is the founder of The Temple of Set and former U.S. National Security General for the Army specializing in intelligence and psychological warfare.

Aquino's thesis "From Psyop to Mind War the Psychology of Victory" stated that enemy populations could be subdued by inflicting a state of psychological terror and feelings of eminent destruction. He discusses the use of psychotronic and electromagnetic weapons to influence the mind. Surrender could be induced without firing a shot. By extremely low frequency signals piggybacked on broadcasts of radio, TV or microwave communications in order to influence and manipulate the thoughts and feelings of the target population.

In the late 1980s Aquino was accused by the San Francisco Police Department of being involved in a Satanic child molestation ring centered at the daycare located on the San Francisco, CA Presidio military base where Aquino was stationed at the time. The 68 molested children contracted venereal diseases and twenty families filed $66 million dollars in claims against the Army however the U.S. Army protected the Satanist.

A central figure within the global child sex slave industry was the British, "Top of the Pops" host, Sir James Wilson Vincent [Jimmy Savile]. Decades of ramped pedophilia, necrophilia and Satanism led to the unmasking of a three decades long call boy ring fueled by British government officials, entertainers, government spies and royal palace workers.

The center of this investigation was on what is known as the, "Elm Guest House". It will be remembered from our examination of John F. Kennedy's sacrifice that he was murdered in Dealey plaza and that one of the three streets that make-up Dealey Plaza is named, "Elm" which is associated with Saturn or Satan.

The Elm [Satan] guest house in Great Britain fronted as a gay bathhouse however in reality it was where young children were transported from Ireland to Great Britain, where they would be violently molested and murdered by Masonic Babylonian elites during satanic blood sacrifice rituals. The Elm guest house revelation was so vast and damaging the British government declared the investigation a national security issue.

It is well documented that Sammy Davis Jr. and Walt Disney were such good friends that Walt invited Sammy and his Satanist friends to Walt's Palm Springs party house in the private gated community of Royal Carizzo Estates, were Romanesque orgy parties occurred. Other guests to Disney's Carizzo Estates included actor Ronald Reagan. Reagan and Disney were connected 'spiritually' and professionally, so much so that Reagan was present at the opening of Disneyland in 1955.

Another strategic partner of Walt Disney Company is Henry Kravis, "Kindercare." Henry Kravis, co-founder of (KKR) private equity firm, is a major contributor to the Church of Babylon's growing technocracy. Kravis' acquisition of GoDaddy.com in 2011 gave the Church of Babylon oversight on more than 45 million domain names worldwide or 40 percent of the global market. If you're a Christian business owner just getting started online, I ask that you consider purchasing your new domain name from an alternative domain registrar. If you currently own a domain through GoDaddy.com please consider transferring and/or renewing it under an alternative registrar. Alternative registrars can be found at **silvanusselect.com**. Additional KKR assets include: RJR Nabisco which distributes toxic GMOs; Former CIA Director and four-star Army general David Petraeus; Sun Microsystems which capitalizes on the elite created Spy-Cloud Computing control initiative; Hospital Corporation of America which capitalizes on the Rockefeller created GMO plague currently being managed by the elite devised predictive 'shock management' algorithm and bio-surveillance weapon named 'Obamacare'. KKR and Mitt Romney's Bain Capital purchased Toys "R" Us which distributes toxic estrogen mimicking plastic toys and baby formula, fire retardant clothing, occult themed movies and toys to our children.

194

SatanCare™

PROGRAMMING CENTERS

In December 2011 'KKR Capstone' executives (capstone referring to the top of an occult all-seeing-eye of Satan pyramid) took the Reins of GoDaddy.com. KKR owned Kindercare Learning Center [KLC] logo is a stylized pyramid and a capstone containing six notches. To Satanists the six notches inside of the capstone represent man above God. I have deconstructed the KLC logo [left] to illustrate the hidden design and meaning of KLC's occult pyramid logo. You'll notice that the [KLC] logo is identical to the occult pyramids flaunted by Sacramento Kings Basketball owner, Mark Friedman; The IRS Headquarters and former CIA Director/President, George H.W. Bush [pg.11]. **KinderCare is a leading child-care provider which operates 1,149 centers in 39 states and has child-care contracts with both The Walt Disney Company and The Lego Group.** KLC has been accused in the past of being part of an institutional pedophile ring. In 1999 a director for Kindercare [Martin Gibbons] was charged with two counts of 1st degree child molestation. KinderCare's Babylonian Talmudist owner, Henry Kravis, is very close friends with George H.W. Bush, Henry Kissinger, and the Rockefeller Family.

Other strategic interests of Walt Disney Company include the Freemason Naismith inspired, "National Basketball Association" who on 10/6/2014 announced long-term media deals with ESPN majority owner Walt Disney Co. On 1/26/2015 President Barack Hussein Obama invited Walt Disney's CEO, Robert Iger, and Sacramento Kings Basketball Team owner, "Vivek Ranadive" to meet with India's Prime Minister to discuss among other topics building nuclear power plants throughout India. Ironically this is during a time when nuclear power in America is ridiculed.

Walt Disney on a number occasions expressed strong favoritism for U.S. President Abraham Lincoln who was an advocate for what was during his lifetime a Christian America. President Lincoln expressed his position on several occasions stating:

"Take all that you can of this book upon reason, and the balance on faith, and you will live and die a happier man. (When a skeptic expressed surprise to see him reading a Bible)"— Abraham Lincoln

"But for this book we could not know right from wrong." — Abraham Lincoln

"I believe the Bible is the best gift God has ever given to man. All the good from The Savior of the world is communicated to us through this Book."
— Abraham Lincoln

On several occasions Walt Disney expressed great admiration for President Lincoln, however it was Walt Disney's idea to construct the Masonic, "Club 33" inside of Disneyland, Anaheim. Club 33 is named after Disney's mentor, Sovereign Grand Commander of the Supreme Council 33rd degree of Freemasonry, British spy, KKK founder and Grand Dragon and "Knights of the Golden Circle" founder, Albert Pike [left]. It was a member of Pike's Knights of the Golden Circle, "John Wilkes Booth" who assassinated President Lincoln 4/15/1865. Other notable members of the "Knights of the Golden Circle" include, Jessie James. In 1871 Pike outlined plans for three world wars that would bring about a 'New World Order'.

"In the third World War we shall unleash the nihilist and the atheists and we shall provoke a formidable social catechism which in all its horror will show clearly to the nations the effect of absolute atheism, origin of savagery and of the most bloody turmoil then everywhere the citizens obliged to defend themselves against the world minority of revolutionaries will exterminate those destroyers of civilization and the multitudes disillusioned with Christianity whose deistic spirits will from that moment be without compass or direction anxious for an ideal but without knowing where to render its adoration will receive the true light through the universal manifestation of the pure doctrine of Lucifer brought finally out into the public view. This manifestation will result from the general reactionary movement which will follow the destruction of Christianity and atheism both conquered and exterminated at the same time." -Albert Pike in a letter to Giuseppe Mazzini a 33 degree Grand Master freemason, founder of Italian Freemasonry, Revolutionary Terrorist Leader, Sicilian Gangster and founder of the "Mafia"

Yet another link in the long chain of Knight Templars who were associated with Walt Disney's success is Knight of Malta Jack Valenti, who for 38 years [1966-2004] was the Head of the Motion Picture Association of America. In response to the growing number of American's who were waking up to the fact that 1960s Hollywood was controlled by Babylonian Talmudists, Church of Babylonian elites placed corrupt former U.S. Senator Christ Dodd and high-ranking Knights of Malta Cult member as the head of the Motion Picture Association of America (MPAA). For those who are unaware of the MPAA history, connection with Walt Disney and impact on America culturally here is a short history.

The first member of the Motion Picture Association of America (MPAA) was Walt Disney Motion Pictures Group which of course was controlled by Knights Templar Walt Disney. According to Presidential Model, "Arizona Wilder" Walt Disney was a "sexual pervert" and "pedophile". Walt Disney's seventeen-member advisory board included a number of Knight's Templar's including President of Georgetown University, Leo J. O' Donovan. Walt Disney was also the man who created two 7 minute long propaganda cartoons in the 1940s which programmed American's into believing that they needed to "go file their tax returns".

(**NOTE:** For those American's who believe they're required to pay income tax please watch Aaron Russo's film: "America: Freedom to Fascism.")

In 1929 Greek shipping tycoon and Knight of Malta "Spyros Skouros" headed the Warner Brothers Theater Circuit. Skouros profited handsomely off the Great Depression which was of course caused by foremost short-seller of stock and Knights Templar Joe Kennedy. In 1933 Knights Templar William Randolph Hearst "the Chief" used his vast fortune to further the Antichristian motion picture monopoly. It's worth noting here that William Randolf Hearst was a proponent of Adolf Hitler and Mussolini both of which were controlled by The Church of Babylon. Walt Disney Company and Hearst Corporation also jointly own the following media assets: A&E, History Channel, H2, Military History, Crime & Investigation Network, FYI, and Lifetime Entertainment. If you subscribe to any of these channels you are financially contributing to the Church of Babylon.

In 1988 Warner Brothers entered into a five-year partnership with Walt Disney. Then in 1989 Warner merged with Time, Inc., creating Time-Warner. Coincidently Knights of Malta, Henry R. Luce, was a co-conspirator in the Kennedy assassination and cover-up. What's more Luce purchased Zapruder Film and was the founder of Time, Inc.,

The expendable inventory of Church of Babylon [Freemason's, Knights Templar's, etc.] is too long to list. A short list includes: Sicily born Frank Capra, the industry's leading producer during the 1930s; Anthony Quinn; Sidney Poitier, Jack Nicholson; Sylvester Stallone; Tom Cruise; Stanley Kubrick who depicted the Church of Babylon too accurately in his porn film, "Eye's Wide Shut"; Robert De Niro, who played the devil in "Angel Heart"; Al Pacino, who also played the devil in "The Devil's Advocate"; George Clooney, a Rockefeller puppet; John Malkovich; Nicolas "Coppola" Cage and Arnold Schwarzenegger, whose father was a Nazi.

197

WALT DISNEY'S TEMPLAR MANSION

From the enormous pool of names Walt had to choose from, during the creation of Mickey, Walt dubbed the character "Mortimer Mouse" which coincidently contains 13 letters. Allegedly at the behest of Walt's wife, Mortimer's name was changed to Mickey Mouse which interesting enough contains 11 letters. It will be remembered from previous text [pg.41] that the Church of Babylon associates the number 11 with Cain and their revenge of Lamech. Walt's association with the Knights Templars is further highlighted by the fact that he named his Mortimer Mouse character after his ancestor, a Norman Knights Templar, who according to an account which dates back to the Elizabethan Era [1558-1603], fought in the crusades and was distinguished in battle by the shores of the Dead Sea. The Mortimers were a powerful, Masonic dynasty during the Middle Ages and shared the same d'Isigny [Disney] bloodline. The Mortimer claims were transmitted to the House of York [1425] in the Wars of the Roses.

Additional evidence emphasizing Walt Disney's occult leanings are found in the Date Walt chose to open his Disneyland amusement park in Anaheim, CA. July 17, 1955 which is exactly twelve months and one day from the date he began construction (12+1=13). And out of the unlimited dimensions of his park Walt Disney chose to purchase 160 acres or **6969**600 square feet [666]. Coincidently when the remaining "6" in 160 acres is combined with the two remaining "9s", which are "6s" to the Church of Babylon, an additional "666" is created. Disneyland's **6969**600 sqft also contains the number "69" twice. The number 69 is important to Satanists because it represents Satanist Aleister Crowley's, "The Book of Lies, chapter 69 titled, "The Way to Succeed-and the Way to Suck Eggs!" which is a pun for the 69 sex position. The coordinates of Disneyland in Anaheim are 33.809 °N 117.919 °W. Both the Masonic "33" and Mark of the Beast "666" are contained within Disneyland's longitude and latitude geographic coordinates. What's more Walt Disney Company has labeled the Anaheim location, "Disneyland Resort, 1313."

The occult number 13 is featured throughout Walt Disney properties perhaps even more than Disney's "hidden Mickey's." For instance inside of the haunted mansion guests are presented with a clock whose 12th hour has been replaced with a 13 and paired with a stereotypical devil's tail [pg.198].

To members of the Church of Babylon the number 13 deifies the Egyptian god Osiris, who was cut up into 13 pieces. Isis, the wife of Osiris, searched for her husband's 13 pieces so that she may reassemble him. To her disappointment she is unable to find his penis. Osiris' penis is memorialized throughout America in the form of phallic shaped obelisks. For instance President Washington's phallic monument pays homage to Osiris. Unbeknownst to many Christian American's today, their church towers promote this occult practice. It's important for the Christian American majority to understand the mythology and ancient kinship Church of Babylon members have with Osiris and Isis. The number 13 also symbolizes man being above God and Satan himself.

Walt Disney began creating his Haunted House concept more than twenty years before it was constructed. Walt's stated goal was to create "a family park where parents and children could have fun- together" a ruse meant to convey good intentions. You know what they say, "hell is paved with good intentions". Twice in the Book of Proverbs [Proverbs 14:12 and Proverbs 16:25] it reads the same thing. "There is a way which seemeth right unto a man, but the end thereof are the ways of death." Contrary to his stated goal, Walt constructed a deceivingly innocent playground whereby "...the children of your father the devil." (John 8:31-44) and the seed of God come together. In the Walt Disney Universe, men are made feminine and women masculine. Disney has perverted marriage openly supporting the joining of men with men and women to women holding "Gay Days" at its theme parks. Disney promotes the murder of innocent children through their financing of Planned Parenthood Federation of America, Americas leading provider of abortions. Through Disney children are being subconsciously programmed to embrace the toxic passions of lustful pedophiles. Disney disconnects parents and children from spiritual values and redirects them on material desires and false gods. Through its subsidiaries of entertainment Disney mocks Christianity through films such as "Priest" and the ABC-TV show "Nothing Sacred". And in lock-step with the 1969 Planned Parenthood Memo which calls for an increase in homosexuality, Disney promotes the 'coming out' of the lead character and the increasingly homosexual story line of the ABC show Ellen and the publication by subsidiaries of books promoting homosexuality, such as "Growing Up Gay".

199

Before settling on the Haunted Mansion motif the title "Museum of the Weird" was proposed. This concept featured blatant occult elements celebrated by the Church of Babylon [Freemasonry] including a Babylonian demon Lilith character with a serpent wrapped around her leg and torso. This ancient Egyptian deity is also referred to the serpent god 'Sobek' [c.2181 B.C], a half-man, half-reptile figure commonly associated with Osiris and Ra. Both Hinduism and Buddhism promote the serpent cult through a serpent figure named 'Nagas' and the union of a human being and a female Naga. The particular serpent depicted inside of the Museum of Weird character set represents the Masonic doctrine of duality. It is written in ancient Hindu texts that this demigod was banished by the creator to the underworld with unimaginable riches and is allied with demons, a tradition which mirrors the legends associated with the Babylonian god Nimrod.

Many of the additional elements found throughout the "Museum of the Weird" involved serpent imagery symbolizing the Serpent Cult of Dann, including an androgyne creature which appears to be both male and female. The androgyne symbolizes the hermaphrodite principle of the two-faced entity or two-headed eagle. In the Cabala, this satanic amalgamation represents the feminine and masculine principle known as "Adam Kadmon," [Adam and Eve] otherwise known as Golem. This combination of opposites is part of alchemy, or hermeticism, which is beloved by the occult. In witchcraft, they refer to this principle as the joining of sun and moon, for which sacred sex rituals are shared. Other elements included a Lucifer clock, the Eye of Horus, Baphomet, the god Pan, The Double-Headed Eagle which the religion of Freemasonry considers "The Supreme Symbol", the Celtic horned god Cernunnos.

Out of the numerous structures around the world that Walt Disney could have based his iconic Cinderella's Castle on, he chose as one of his model structures the "Moszna" a 99 tower castle inside of Opole, Poland, a 365-room castle that once belonged to the Knights Templar in the Middle Ages and out of the limitless supply of American artists that could have been chosen to create the five intricately designed mosaic murals that adorn the inside of the Walt Disney World's Cinderella's Castle, Walt Disney Company chose a former Nazi of the Third Reich, "Hanns Scharff. In addition to Cinderella's Castle Hanns also created a mosaic for, "Land Pavilion" at EPCOT nearby two glass occult pyramids in "Journey into Imagination." Prior to working for Walt Disney Company, Hanns was famous within the Nazi Luftwaffe as the most prolific military interrogator not only within the Nazi world but the entire world. During WWII, Scharff was fluent in English which made him a logical choice for interrogating American soldiers who were captured. This isn't the only Nazi art on Walt Disney World property. A mural inside of Walt Disney Worlds, "Grand Floridian

Resort" features a Great Gatsby theme. Inside the mural there is a hotel which contains a Nazi SS storm trooper standing on the balcony.

Cinderella's Castle isn't the only property on Walt Disney property with a past. Out of the myriad of structures throughout America to base his haunted house design on Walt Disney chose the "Shipley-Lydecker" house in Baltimore, Maryland [left]. Walt's art director Harper Goff, or as Walt called them "Imagineers", created a concept for Walt that included a Christian Church, graveyard and Haunted House; however Goff's design was discarded. I'd like to point out here that Walt Disney chose to embolden the idea of Imagination while at the same time striking down Goff's idea of constructing a Christian Church on Walt Disney property. Walt's decision to place man's imagination above God, while at the same time denying a Christian Church, would have surely garnered praise from his Knights Templar handlers. The following are a few of the many Biblical versus that warn us of the eminent risk associated with being obedient to the exaltation of Imagination.

"Because that, when they knew God, they glorified him not as God, neither were thankful; but became vain in their imaginations, and their foolish heart was darkened." – Romans 1:21

"Casting down imaginations, and every high thing that exalteth itself against the knowledge of God, and bringing into captivity every thought to the obedience of Christ;" – 2 Corinthians 10:5

"They say still unto them that despise me, The LORD hath said, Ye shall have peace; and they say unto every one that walketh after the imagination of his own heart, No evil shall come upon you." – Jeremiah 23:17

What's interesting is that the original Shipley-Lydecker dwelling, Mill and vast estate was constructed, owned and named "Patapsco", after the Patapsco Indians which lived in the region (c.300-800 B.C.) by Dr. Charles Carroll, of Ireland who after settling in Annapolis purchased the plantation known as Georgia. The Irish Carroll Family's significance 201 stems not from their Mount Clare Iron Ore Mill wealth, but in the fact that the family was descended from the last Gaelic Lords of Eile in Ireland, Freemasons and Knights Templars. This is why Dr. Carroll's elder son Charles Carroll Barrister attended "The Honourable Society of the Middle Temple" (Middle Temple) in 1751. The Middle Temple is located in the wider Temple area of London and the headquarters of the Knights Templars until they were dissolved in 1312. Charles Carroll Barrister returned to Maryland in 1755 where he drafted the "Declaration and Charter of Rights and form of government for the state of Maryland" which served as Maryland's first new constitution on 11/3/1776.

There are too many markers throughout The Haunted Mansion to list which symbolize Walt Disney's knowledge of the Freemason/Templar Carroll Family and their Satanic Church of Babylon ancestry. The following are just of few of the most blatant associations.

Upon entering the Haunted Mansion guests are ushered into a large elevator called the 'Portrait Gallery' which features pictures that appear to stretch. On the ceiling of the elevator guests will find an abstract modification of the eight pointed star of Lilith [left] whose dark origins lie in Babylonian demonology. Lilith is said to have created prostitution and the degrading of sex. The demon was also notorious for seducing and killing young men and children.

Disney's abstract modification of the Babylonian star of Lilith is also referred to as the "8-Step Path of Enlightenment" by Satanists. The religion of Satanism teaches that a person must go through 8 separate steps in order to achieve full spiritual enlightenment, the eighth and final step being a Sex Act. Notice that the very center of this symbol is a very small octagon. This symbol represents the female. When the lightning and thunder effects begin in the elevator, the Babylonian star of Lilith disappears. Guests are then exposed to a corpse hanging by a rope, directly over the female symbol; the corpse in this instance represents a phallic symbol or male organ. The Babylonian demon Lilith theme is further amplified by the fact that the hanging corpse is of a man a recurring victim in ancient Lilith mythology. What's more placing a rope around a Freemason's neck during his initiation is customary in Lodges throughout the World.

In the "portrait hall" of Walt Disney's Haunted Mansion, while guests wait to board their 'doombuggies' the narrator informs guests:

"There are several prominent ghosts who have retired here from creepy old crypts from all over the world. Actually, we have "999" happy haunts here, but there's room for a thousand. Any volunteers?" It will be remembered that "999" symbolizes "666" to the Church of Babylon.

While guests are carried inside of "doombuggies" throughout the attraction they are presented with a suit of armor [left] featuring a red cross. This logo was first discovered by the Church of Babylon and then placed on the oldest Freemason logo in the world 926 AD. This icon may be seen on the Stela of Nimrod [pg.18, "B"]. This symbol would later be emblazoned across the chests of Knights Templars during the Church of Babylon orchestrated "Holy Wars." This same suit of armor features the face of an eagle and to the Church of Babylon the eagle represents the messenger of Zeus [Mercury], also known as Apollyon, the destroyer from the book of revelation. Lastly there are several encased "X's" on the knights shield. It's important to understand that the Roman numeral 'X' is a number 10; it also represents the word 'IO' [EO] which is Greek for Apollyon the sun god or Apollyon the destroyer from the Book of Revelation. Lastly the encased 'X' on this knights shield represents the Roman numeral for 1000, and 1000 in Greek is Helius, another name for Apollyon the destroyer [The Beast] from The Book of Revelation.

"And when the thousand years are expired, Satan shall be loosed out of his prison, And shall go out to deceive the nations which are in the four quarters of the earth, Gog and Magog, to gather them together to battle"
- Revelation 20:7-10.

Guests inside of Walt Disney's Haunted Mansion are also presented with an iconic Freemason image, a truncated pyramid staircase, which to the Church of Babylon represents "The Steps of Freemasonry" or Structure of Freemasonry [pg.204].

203

The Pirates of the Caribbean [pg.203, bottom] is rife with iconography associated with the Church of Babylon. The most obvious of these is a Masonic cross located on the ride entrance signage, which is identical to the one found on the Stela of Nimrod [pg.18, "B"]

One of the largest Knights Templar markers inside of Disneyland is hidden in plain sight across from Cinderella's Castle in the hub of Main Street [left].

All of these Masonic Babylonian symbols are reinforced by Walt Disney's 'Club 33' which I mentioned earlier, opened its doors 6 months after Walt's death 12/15/1966 at the age of 65 [666]. Freemason Presidents, dignitaries and celebrities have all visited Disney's Club 33 over the years.

Even Walt Disney's "Partners" statue features Walt and Mickey Mouse embraced in a Freemason handshake, even though publicly both Walt Disney and his family were vehemently opposed to placing a statue of Walt inside Disneyland. Walt's widow Lillian Disney once told sculptor Blaine Gibson that "She didn't ever want a bust or a portrait or a statue of Walt to be done." Babylonian Talmudist Michael Eisner ignored her wishes and placed a statue of Walt anyway.

When one honestly inventories the colossal volume of occult elements throughout the Disney Universe, it's really not that shocking to learn that deaths, associated with many of these facilities, would coincide with occult numerics. For instance:

"On September 5, 2003, Marcelo of Gardena, California was riding in the front car of Big Thunder Mountain Railroad when the locomotive became separated from the rest of the cars and derailed. Marcelo died on the scene from blunt force trauma to the chest. The train crashed on the 13th ride."
- "Disney Declassified: Tales of Real Life Disney Scandals, Sex, Accidents and Deaths," - Aaron H. Goldberg

Goldberg's book also describes several brain injury deaths associated with Disney's, "Indiana Jones" attraction, a collaborative venture involving Walt Disney Company and George Lucas. One of the most noticeable occult elements within this attraction is an all-seeing-eye of Satan which guests are exposed to prior to the ride vehicle entering the main attraction, which in addition to other occult relics contains a giant serpent. Another Disney/ Lucas attraction killed someone in 1987. While a maintenance worker was inside of the "Star Tours" attraction he mysteriously fell 8ft to his death.

Additional attractions which have claimed the lives of visitors include: The Matterhorn, Roger Rabbit's Car Toon Spin, The Monorail, The People Mover, Tom Sawyer's Island, Carousel of Progress and America Sings, Space Mountain, Rivers of America, It's a Small World, Toy Story Midway Mania, Mark Twain Landing.

WALT DISNEY'S "MARK OF THE BEAST" 666

"To be honest about the matter, when our gang goes into a huddle and come out with a new Mickey Mouse story, we will not have worried one bit as to whether the picture will make the children better men and women." – Overland Monthly, published 1933, titled: "The Cartoon's Contribution to Children, by Walt Disney.

Beginning in the 1880s, Overland Monthly featured contributors like Disney and fellow occultist and Mary Baker Eddy confidant Mark Twain. In this same October, 1933 Overland article Walt Disney gloats about his Socialist, Communist admirers Mussolini and Hitler stating, "Mr. Mussolini takes his family to see every Mickey picture" and that "Mickey is going to save Mr. A Hitler." A mutual admiration between Disney and Hitler was verified by Adolf Hitler's propaganda minister Joseph Goebbels' diary entry for December 22, 1937, which states, "I am giving the Fuhrer...18 Mickey Mouse films (as a Christmas gift). He is very excited about it. He is very happy about this treasure."

For generations Walt Disney's cartoons and movies have been subliminally influencing the morality of American Children. In 2004 researchers, Erin L. Ryan and Keisha L. Hoerrner compiled a list of instances where Walt Disney products were complicit in facilitating a lockstep mindset that has proven to be detrimental to the physical and spiritual wellbeing of young minds. Their thesis was titled, "Let Your Conscience Be Your Guide: Smoking and Drinking in Disney's Animated Classics". According to their paper, Ryan and Hoerrner "analyzed 24 Disney G-rated, animated, feature-length motion pictures from 1937 to 2000, looking for instances of tobacco and alcohol use. They found 381 instances of substance use with no antiuse messages in the films." What this study shows is that Walt Disney products have in fact assisted with the behavioral modification of American children.

One needn't possess the power of precognition to effectively predict what is best described as predictable consequences associated with exposing young children to Walt Disney products, specifically the negative affects these products have on their physical health. Next we're going to examine what this author believes to be a far greater threat to our Nation, which is the influence Walt Disney products are having on our Children's spiritual health.

I realize there will be a number of readers who may not subscribe to the religiously ambiguous spectrum of 'spiritualists' inhabiting our Nation, much less a leader for Christ, like this author. However, with the aforesaid contrast in mind, I ask readers to objectively contemplate the following question once you've had an opportunity to review the subsequent data.

If God and Satan do not exist, if the Holy Bible is nothing more than a compilation of scribbles by cave dwellers, why are those, who possess the vast majority of knowledge, wealth and control throughout the world, extravagantly endorse what Biblical prophesy states as being "The Beast" [Satan]?

The following are examples of how Walt Disney Company promotes iconography associated with the Church of Babylon. We begin with the seemingly innocent Disney television cartoon, "Gravity Falls", which presents a reptilian, all-seeing-eye of Satan to children in its intro, the skeleton of Satan, the conjuring of demons from flames, and a number of additional occult related icons. The picture below flashes for just a second during the introduction, however, you can clearly see the Satanic, alchemical, and magical suggestions being promoted to our children by Walt Disney Company.

Even the wildly popular children's cartoon, "Phineas and Ferb" features occult imagery as well a direct connection with the crucifixion of Jesus Christ. The vast majority of Americans watching this cartoon will be unaware of the connection between the ancient Prophet, "Phinehas" [Phineas] who is said to have forged the, "Spear of Destiny" with the powers inherent in the blood of God's Chosen People.

The Spear of Destiny pg.208] had been raised in the hand of Joshua when he signaled the great shout that would cause the crumbling of the walls of Jericho. Herod The Great held this insignia of power over life and death when he ordered the massacre of 2,000 innocent babies throughout Judea during his mission to locate and murder the Christ Child who was prophesied to grow up and become "King of the Jews". Following Christ's crucifixion, the son of Herod The Great now carried the spear of Destiny as a symbol of authority, to crush the bones of the recently crucified Jesus Christ.

207

Ancient text tells us that when the Temple Guard arrived at the sight of the crucifixion, the Roman Soldiers turned their backs in disgust. The Roman Centurion Gaius Cassius watched as the Jewish High Priests clubbed and crushed the skulls and limbs of Gestas and Dismas, the two men nailed to crosses on either side of Jesus Christ. The Roman Centurion was so repelled by the mutilations caused by the Jewish High Priests, he is said to have rushed up to the central cross holding Jesus Christ and thrust The Spear of Destiny into the side of Jesus Christ, fulfilling the prophecy of Zechariah:

"And I will pour upon the house of David, and upon the inhabitants of Jerusalem, the spirit of grace and of supplications: and they shall look upon me whom they have pierced, and they shall mourn for him, as one mourneth for his only son, and shall be in bitterness for him, as one that is in bitterness for his firstborn."
- Zechariah 12:10

Thrusting a spear into the side of one's enemy was a Roman soldier's method of verifying the death of a foe, because blood ceases to flow from a lifeless body. To the surprise of the Roman Centurion Longinus:

"But one of the soldiers with a spear pierced his side, and forthwith came there out blood and water." - John 19:34

Charles the Great (Charlemagne) the first Holy Roman Emperor and heir to Constantine wrote about the spear c.774:

"It is a treasure by which God binds the earthly and the celestial to ensure victory over visible and invisible foes:"

For one brief moment in history, Adolf Hitler stood at the pinnacle of power. He firmly believed that the secret powers of the Spear of Destiny, which he possessed, was responsible for his incredible success. Ten days after the fall of Nuremberg in April, 1945, the American military intelligence agents had failed to discover the hiding place in the Oberen Schmied Gasse. It was not until April 30, the day that many people believe Adolf Hitler committed suicide in Berlin, that the secret passage in Blacksmith's Alley was unearthed.

None of the American senators who came to postwar Europe in droves, or the senior United States generals who travelled to Nuremberg to see the vast display of Nazi loot in the underground bunker in the Oberen Schmied Gasse, showed the least interest in the age-old legend of the Spear of Destiny. The only exception was General George "Blood and Guts" Patton, one of the most colorful characters and possibly one of the best Allied Commanders of World War II. General Patton, who had a historically orientated cast of mind and had made a study of the search for the Holy Grail, appears to have been totally fascinated at the sight of the Spear of Destiny. It is said that General Patton took the Spear from its leather case and removed the golden sleeve which held the two separate parts of the Spear of Destiny. General Patton was the only American general who realized the true significance of the fact that the United States was now the official possessor of the Spear of Destiny.

In the first week of 'Phineas and Ferb' airing on television, I was immediately concerned to see one of Phineas and Ferbs' main characters 'Dr Doofenshmirtz' making fun of a handicap person, calling him "weak". This is an obvious endorsement for eugenics. During the second week of the program one of the characters said something is "as insane as organized religion". Walt Disney's Phineas & Ferb also dedicated an entire episode to the religion of evolutionism, a myth which I addressed previously.

There is a long list of examples that I could point to in which The Walt Disney Company has intentionally injected subliminal messaging based on Jungian psychology and inappropriate content into its television programs, films, advertising and corporate culture.

The following are just a sampling of the hundreds of blatant attempts by the Church of Babylon to compromise the innocence of our Christian children through subliminal messages and perception in film, toys, etc.

"The new medium of film was capable of evil, having power for it, the greater because of the attractiveness and manner of exhibition" - Irish American Justice Joseph McKenna (U.S. Supreme Court 1915) U.S. Mutual Film Corporation vs. Ohio Industrial Commission

An example of how Michael Swift's gay manifesto 'Gay Revolution' **www.gayrevolution.us** is helping to shape the overt Homosexual programming in boys toys is illustrated in the picture of a Marvel Comics inflatable Wolverine 'bop hammer' [pg.210, top]. As you can clearly see the toy features a phallic looking blow up valve between the characters legs.

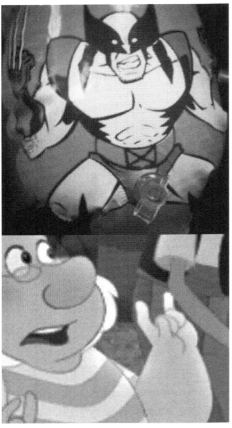

Readers should be aware of the fact that in 1999 [666] four of Hollywood's gay A-listers were accused of sexually abusing teenage boys. They include: X-Men Movie Director Bryan Singer; Former President of BBC Worldwide America and head of programming for FOX, NBC and Warner Brothers Garth Ancier; Gary Goddard the head of a Los Angeles based entertainment design group 'The Goddard Group'; and former President of Disney T.V. David Newman. Newman previously worked with the ringleader of the aforesaid perversion, Mark Collins-Rector, who is best known for founding the notable dot-com failure 'Digital Entertainment Network' a precursor to YouTube. Rector's former business partners were boyfriend Chad Shackley and former child star Brock Pierce who is now a board member of the Bitcoin Foundation. Rector hosted lavish homosexual parties whose guests included the gay entertainment mogul and Babylonian Talmudist David Geffen who along with Babylonian Talmudists Jeffrey Katzenberg and Steven Spielberg founded DreamWorks SKG. It was at those parties that Collins-Rector and others allegedly sexually assaulted half a dozen teenage boys, according to two sets of civil lawsuits, the first filed in 1999–2002 and the second in 2014.

Disney's Jake and the Neverland Pirates, episode 'Follow the Bouncing Bumble' features the character 'Smee' flashing Devil Horns on multiple occasions [center].

Disney owned Marvel Comics manufactures a Spiderman action

figure [pg.210, bottom] which promotes devil horns and masturbation. The Church of Babylon worship all types of Babylonian gods, however, their god of choice is the sexual pervert Pan. The god Hermes is said to have invented masturbation for his son, the god Pan. Pan in turn taught the habit to young shepherds.

"America is like a healthy body and its resistance is threefold: Its patriotism, its morality, and its spiritual life [Christianity]. If we can undermine these three areas, America will collapse from within." – Joseph Stalin, Babylonian Talmudist, changed his name from Joseph David Djugashvili. In the Georgian language, "Shvili" means, "son" or "son of" and "Djuga" means "Jew" so Joseph Stalin's real last name means, "Son of Jew" or "Jewison."

Walt Disney's Beauty and the Beast (1991) features two scantily clad women flashing, "Devil Horns" and another woman flashing, "Devil Horns" [below]. In the Babylonian Talmud, Abodah Zarah 36b, non-Jewish women are described as being, "in a state of niddah (filth) from birth. Non-Jewish women are regarded as slaves, heathen and whores." Is this how you view your mother, sister or daughter? Babylonian Talmudists do.

Walt Disney's Beauty and the Beast is based on the writings of a collage of writers, however Babylonian Talmudist, Gabrielle-Suzanne Barbot de Villeneuve, wrote the original titled, "La Belle et la Bête" in 1742. Villeneuve's original story involved a genuinely savage e.g., "stupid beast," not merely a change of appearance. The Babylonian Talmud, Baba Mezia 114b reads,

"The Jews are called human beings, but the <u>non-Jews</u> are not humans. They <u>are beasts</u>." Babylonian Talmud, Yebamoth 98a reads, "<u>All gentile [Christian] children are animals</u>."

"If I wanted to put satanic messages in a movie, you would see it."
– Tom Sito, Disney animator for The Little Mermaid

Walt Disney's 'The Little Mermaid' (1989) movie design elements include a number of penis shaped spires in the film's castle [below]. This is yet another example of Michael Swift's gay manifesto 'Gay Revolution' read their plans for your children at: **www.gayrevolution.us**

The Walt Disney themed Product Ad on your left features Minnie Mouse wearing a penis shaped dress. Mickey Mouse' hand is wrapped around the penis shaped dress.

The Rescuers Down Under (1990) Features a Topless Woman in Window

Walt Disney's Ducktales features an eye chart that reads "Ask Illuminati," referencing the occult organization whose founder, Adam Weishaupt, stated as his primary goal the elimination of Christianity.

Walt Disney's Mickey Mouse Club House featured an All Seeing Eye of Satan on Goofy's skateboard, symbolizing the Egyptian god Ra. The Crown represents Antichrist.

Walt Disney's "Kick Buttowski: Suburban Daredevil" flashing devil horns.

The following image features a merchandise sticker from 'The Art of Disney' in Walt Disney World USA. Do you see the 666 Mark of the Beast which deceptively forms the iconic Mickey Ears?

In the 1992 Disney animated film Aladdin "Good Teenagers Take Of Their Cloths" can be heard right as the movie's young character Jasmine appears with a startled look on her face..

16 min 12 sec into Walt Disney's Sophia The First, Season 2, Episode 18 titled, Bailey Whoop exposes children to a double-headed snake coiled into a double helix the most ancient symbol for the Serpent Cult of Dann. Adjacent to the Serpent Cult image is writing which contains "666" throughout the page. This episode of Sophia is #18 [6+6+6=18] "666."

Walt Disney Company owned, Marvel Comics released a comic book in 2015 titled, "CAPTAIN AMERICA SAM WILSON #1." in their book Americans, who identify with American sovereignty , the U.S. Constitution and Bill of Rights, are portrayed as a right-wing terrorist group called, "The Sons of the Serpent," another reference to the Serpent Death Cult of Dann. By the way, if you happen to be an American who admires the liberties associated with the U.S. Constitution and Bill of Rights, please consider boycotting all of Walt Disny's assetts including thier ABC and ESPN networks.

214

Walt Disney's children show 'Sophia the First' produced an episode titled 'When You Wish Upon A Well'. At 11min 23sec one of its main characters 'Cedric the Sorcerer' was programmed by designers with praying hands, while standing in front of a wall containing the Mark of The Beast (666). On a subconscious level this scene is programming children to pray to "The Beast" [Satan].

Walt Disney Company would never explain the meaning behind the satanic symbols they're exposing children to; executives for Disney on the other are unapologetic about their current Antichristian, human exploitation programming targeting young impressionable girls. Senior Vice President of original programming and general manager of Disney Junior World Wide had this to say about the scheme behind Disney's "Sophia the First" character, "We knew we didn't want it to be a young woman looking for a man." This is a blatant example of how Walt Disney Company leverages its identity to perpetuate Planned Parenthoods 1969 memo, which called for, degradation of America's nuclear family which once flourished under the umbrella of Christianity.

The Holy Bible contains 177 verses which instruct how and why husbands and wives should cherish the sanctity of marriage, such as:

"For by means of a whorish woman a man is brought to a piece of bread: and the adulteress will hunt for the precious life." - Proverbs 6:26

God wants His creation [Man & Woman] to have a "precious life" and He defines a precious life as being a lifelong, monogamous marriage, between one man and one woman. However, the Babylonian Talmudist element controlling Walt Disney Company seeks to undermine and destroy Gods' Basic Instructions Before Leaving Earth [B.I.B.L.E.]

One of Hollywood's most successful "precious life" retardants was the widely popular TV show and movie 'Sex and the City'. This was a show about four desperate aging women seeking husbands. The recurring theme throughout this show was that the characters are 215 emotionally and spiritually incompatible with all of the men they come across. Anyone who is keen to Hollywood's human exploitation psychology programming will recognize the blatant feminist/lesbian undertones that men and women are identical.

The 'Sex and the City' characters found themselves in a very confusing lifestyle, mainly because they wanted to control the men they were pursuing, while at the same time wanting to be possessed. Like many American women today, these characters have been programmed by the Church of Babylon to resist their God given femininity. The resulting effect is a group of depressed, angry, emotionally and physically unfulfilled women, who engage in fruitless sex acts with countless men, all the while growing older and bitterer. The overarching dysfunctional theme of the show is that it's OK that you're a shallow, materialistic whore so long as you have your girlfriends to sit with in a coffee shop, complaining about what's wrong with everyone else.

It should come as no surprise that the creator of "Sex and the City" was Darren Starr, a homosexual. Starr's "Sex and the City" program was in lockstep with the psychological warfare research and Freudian Psychotherapy based Tavistock Institute, who through funding and support by the Rockefeller Foundation, Stanford Research Institute, The U.S. Office of Naval Research, the Science Policy Research Unit in England, MIT, Heritage Foundation, U.S. Air Force Intelligence, Wharton School, Institute for Policy Studies, Hudson Institute, Brookings Institute and Rand Corporation, a group who was once accused of being commissioned by the USSR (Russia) to work out terms of surrender of the United States Government have all supported initiatives necessary to maintain dominion over the minds and emotions of Americans.

Social manipulation, moral decline, and de-industrialization has all been achieved through TV programming and has resulted in the growing rate of illegitimacy, petty lawlessness, drug addiction, welfare, STDs, and mental illness. One of Tavistock' key methods of destabilizing a victim's character and inducing a target with mental illness was repeatedly shown throughout the "Sex and the City" program and Walt Disney's Sophia the First. For instance, "Sex and the City" victims were repeatedly advised throughout the show to 'establish new rituals of personal interaction', that is, to indulge in brief sexual encounters which actually set the subjects adrift with no stable personal relationships in their lives, destroying their ability to establish or maintain a family. What's more, the show repeatedly characterized married women as nagging, cheating, materialistic whores who cannot be trusted. This message is parroted throughout Hollywood which promotes the idea that men should physically and mentally abuse women which is the opposite of what the Holy Bible teaches:

216

"Husbands, love your wives, and do not be harsh with them."
- Colossians 3:19

"Husbands, love your wives, as Christ loved the church and gave himself up for her," - Ephesians 5:25

"Let marriage be held in honor among all, and let the marriage bed be undefiled, for God will judge the sexually immoral and adulterous."
- Hebrews 13:4

Hollywood also indoctrinates men and women into the idea that sharing their marriage bed with multiple partners is healthy. What's more men are characterized as being weak, impotent, stupid animals which Hollywood programmers know sow the seeds of low self esteem and self hatred. God tells man to be watchful and aware of Satan's trickery, stand firm in your Christian faith, act like men and be strong!

"Watch ye, stand fast in the faith, quit you like men, be strong."
- 1 Corinthians 16:13

A resulting effect of the aforementioned human exploitation is that the percentage of American women using antidepressant drugs is higher than in any other nation in the world. These are drugs which contain warnings such as "suicidal thoughts" should be expected. Predictably, prescription drugs kill more people in the United States than guns, terrorists and car accidents combined every year.

"Here is wisdom. Let him that hath understanding count the number of the beast: for it is the number of a man; and his number [is] Six hundred threescore [and] six." - Revelation 13:18

Walt Disney used the above 1942 signature until his death 12/15/1966. Clearly there's a difference between the strategically altered 1971 Walt Disney World "666" version [pg.218, top]. Today the "Mark of the Beast" is featured throughout a number of Walt Disney Company properties including Downtown Disney's, "Disney Quest" [pg.218]. The Disney Quest logo also contains the number "69." The number 69 is important to Satanists because it represents Satanist Aleister Crowley's, "The Book of Lies, chapter 69 titled, "The Way to Succeed-and the Way to Suck Eggs!" which is a pun for the 69 sex position. 217

If you look closely, at the "6" and "9" in the Disney Quest logo [above], you'll notice that these individual numbers are even placed in a way which represents the 69 sex position. Please keep in mind that it was Walt Disney Company designers and executives who signed off on the idea of exposing millions of children to this toxic, subconscious exploitation psychology. The Disney cartoon, Henry Huggle Monster, is chuck-full of "666". The walking path stones leading up to Henrys' house are the most obvious. The video game, "Henry's Roarsome Rescue" rewards children for collecting elements which contain "666."

SATAN WARS

In 1971 George Lucas directed his first film titled 'THX 1138' alongside Francis Ford Coppola. The film depicts a dystopian future where social order is enforced by android police. Sexual intercourse is illegal and the populous is forced to consume mind-altering narcotics which enable people to perform life threatening assignments. Lucas' THX 1138 has eliminated God and the populous worship a god named 'OMM 0910' [Satan] in 'Unichapels'. Employment in THX 1138 consists of men and women keeping surveillance on their fellow slaves and answering questions related to proper drug use.

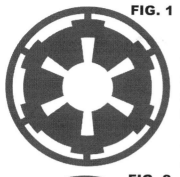

FIG. 1

FIG. 2

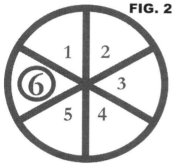

FIG. 3

FIG. 4

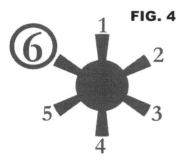

People reading this may be saying to themselves, "this reads like a nightmare future", unfortunately the aforesaid is already upon us. Consider the fact that Chinese sourced mind altering toxins like fluoride are placed into the American water supply and estrogen mimicking GMO Soy is a pervasive ingredient found throughout our U.S. food supply. It's GMO soy which is feminizing our young boys and causing impotence, erectile dysfunction (E.D.), gynomastia and 'male menopause'.

Lucas films are riddled with Luciferian cryptograms and what esoteric Satanists like Aleister Crowley considered being the mystical significance of number 23. For instance, the cell in which Princess Leia was held in the original Star Wars movie was AA23 and George Lucas' first film, THX 1138, included a police robot numbered 23. Most troubling of all is the fact that both George Lucas' Star Wars and Satanism glorify 'The Force'. The King James Holy Bible notifies readers that the Antichrist will be 'the God of forces" - Daniel 11:38. And what should be blatantly obvious to anyone who has read their bible is that the title 'Star Wars' is mentioned in, "Revelation 12:4," which describes Satan's star war with God:

"And his [Satan's] tail drew the third part of the stars of heaven, and did cast them to the earth".

A central figure inside of Star Wars is the character 'Yoda' and to Church of Babylon members 'Yota' is a hidden master with a direct lineage to ancient Babylon. Satanism is promoted throughout Star Wars including the Imperial Logo cryptogram [FIG.1] which is the 'Mark of The Beast' 666 [FIG.2-4]. FIG.4 is also an abstract modification symbolizing the Babylonian sun god Shamash [pg.19]. What's more, Lucas Arts logo [FIG.5, pg.220] contains both a pyramid and an all-seeing-eye of Satan.

219

FIG. 5

Star Wars uses 19th century German philosopher Georg Wilhelm's Hegelian Dialectic to deceive viewers into accepting the "light side" or "dark side." The reality is both white and black magic are tools of Satan, and they were designed to draw our attention away from the light of Jesus Christ. As stated in John 1:3, God is the force behind all things.

As I mentioned earlier, George Lucas was executive producer for the Walt Disney story idea 'Captain EO' the 3D science fiction film starring Michael Jackson. Ignoring the potential side effects e.g., convulsions, blackouts, etc. this film was shown at Disney theme parks from 1986 through 1996 and returned in 2010 to the 'Magic Eye Theater', as a tribute after Michael Jackson's death.

It will be remembered that the Roman Numeral X represents the word 'IO' (pronounced EO) and in Greek the word 'EO' means Helios or Apollyon otherwise known as The Beast from the pit.

"And they had a king over them, which is the angel of the bottomless pit, whose name in the Hebrew tongue is Abaddon, but in the Greek tongue hath his name Apollyon."   - Revelation 9:11.

Captain EO featured a song titled, "We Are Here to Change the World," the same promise made by Satan six thousand years ago, "I [Satan] will ascend above the heights of the clouds; I [Satan] will be like the most High." - Isaiah 14:14.

Walt Disney Company purchased Lucasfilm 10/30/2012 for $4.05 billion dollars. 10/30 is the **303**rd day of the year [**33**]. Babylonian Talmudist CEO Bob Iger announced that Star Wars Episode VII" is set for release in December 2015. Prior to its acquisition, LucasArts was developing a video game titled, "Star Wars 1313." Please keep the aforesaid in mind when faced with the decision of paying $8.00 for a Star Wars movie ticket or $29.00 for a Star Wars figure set. Know that if you do purchase that merchandise you're supporting the Church of Babylon.

Walt Disney's, "The Lion King" [1994], starring James Earl Jones, is riddled with sexual innuendos and occult overtones intended to promote sexual promiscuity and the Church of Babylon. An example of this is 6min 24sec into the film, where one of the film's main characters named 'Scar' is featured forming devil horns with his paw [pg.221, top].

James Earl Jones was the voice of the iconic figure Darth Vader in George Lucas Star Wars franchise now owned by Walt Disney. James Earl Jones also provided the voice of "Mufasa" in Walt Disney's 'The Lion King' and its 1998 sequel, 'The Lion King II: Simba's Pride'. He was also an international host for Fantasia 2000. He also voiced Satan Claus in 'Recess Christmas: Miracle on Third Street'. He also voices Darth Vader in the Star Tours attraction at Disneyland and DisneyWorld's Hollywood Studios. He was also the narrator in 'Judge Dredd'.

In 1982 African-Irish American actor James Earl Jones appeared in 'Conan the Barbarian' aside Arnold Schwarzenegger. Conan the Barbarian represented more than just a muscled Barbarian; it depicted the Serpent Cult of Dann. In fact James Earl Jones evil wizard character, "Thulsa Doom," [left] represented Dann. Jones' character, was the leader of the snake cult and is featured in the film transforming himself into a giant serpent [Satan]. 1hr 56min into the film Jones is shown standing in front of the 'All-Seeing-Eye' of Satan, which is also associated with Osiris, Horus and the Serpent Cult while stating:

"...those who have corrupted the earth shall all be cleansed [murdered]"... In your hand you hold my light, the gleam in the eye of Seth"... "Burn you the way to paradise"... "Who gave you the will to live? I am the wellspring, from which you flow. When I am gone you will have never been."

There are a number of overtly satanic, pro New World Order elements to this scene. First, Jones character's statement that "those who have corrupted the earth shall all be cleansed [murdered]" is a recurring theme found throughout 'Agenda 21' propaganda. Agenda 21 policies, date back to the 1970s, however it really kicked into high-gear in 1992 at the Earth Summit in Rio de Janeiro. That's when Former CIA Director/President, George H.W. Bush and Prince Charles signed onto it. President and Mrs. Clinton saw to it that Agenda 21 infected the entire U.S. Government.

NOTE: Please visit **americanpolicy.org** to learn more about Agenda 21.

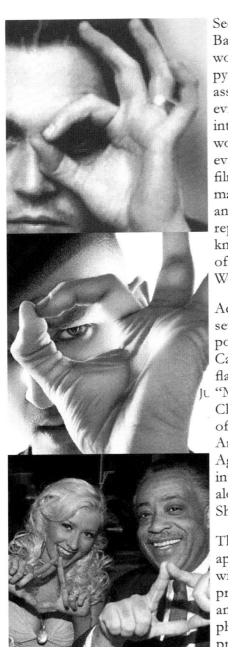

Second, ancient texts tell us that the Babylonian god Nimrod promoted the worship of fire and sacrifice and ancient pyramid writings tell us that Seth was associated with active chaos and universal evil. After murdering Osiris, Seth [Satan] introduced 'divine moral evil' into our world. This is why we see nothing but evil and chaos throughout Hollywood films and the music industry. The vast majority of celebrated writers, producers and directors throughout these industries represent the Church of Babylon and are knowingly participating in the reemergence of Satan's One World Religion and New World Order.

Actor Johnny Depp has appeared in several Walt Disney assets including the popular movie franchise 'Pirates of the Caribbean. Johnny Depp [top] is shown flashing the satanic 666 hand-sign. Former "Mouseketeer" in The Mickey Mouse Club, Justin Timberlake [center] is fond of the all-seeing-eye of Satan as well. Another former Mouseketeer, Christina Aguilera [bottom] is shown flashing the international gang sign for the Illuminati, alongside Prince Hall Freemason, Al Sharpton.

The occult structure to which Walt Disney apparently belonged to was based on witchcraft, alchemy and magic. Like his predecessors Walt Disney both secretly and overtly endorsed freemasonry's philosophy of "Universal Motion", the practice of deliberately causing chaos so that order may come out of two dynamic competing forces ["Ordo Ah Chao"]. When we study Walt Disney's lifestyle and relationships there is no doubt this was Disney's 'Great Work'.

Throughout his attractions and films we see the deliberate altering of God's creation [Man], into a "reptilian brain" serpent-being, devoid of morality and righteousness.

222

What Walt Disney's movies, cartoons and amusement parks promote subconsciously is a materialistic habitat occupied by utilitarian zombies determined to change heaven and earth into hell through chaos and destruction. "The Will of Satan shall be done on Earth as it is in hell," is the Church of Babylon's mantra or "Royal Secret".

"The High Priest told us that demons love to see humans die, and especially in times of war. And when they have great battles and a lot of people die, they have a celebration over it." – Roger Morneau, former Luciferian Priest

The Disney Universe, in which Walt was instrumental in creating, suggests that Walt embraced the theory of Universal chaos and welcomed the emergence of the Church of Babylon's, "Holy Empire of true Masonic Brotherhood", ruled by the Antichrist.

Grand Commander of Freemasonry Albert Pike was quite clear about his cult's objective on pg.861 of his book "Morals and Dogma" which reads:

"From the mutual action and re-action of each of these pairs of opposites and contraries results that which with them forms the Triangle, to all the Ancient Sages the expressive symbol of the Deity; as from Osiris and Isis, Har-oeri, the Master of Light [Lucifer] and Life, and the Creative Word... Such, my Brother, is the True World of a Master Mason; such the true ROYAL SECRET, which makes possible, and shall at length make real, the HOLY EMPIRE of true Masonic Brotherhood. GLORIA, DEI EST CELARE VERBUM. AMEN."

DISNEY'S CORRUPTIVE UNIVERSE

Many of the people who profess and/or reject the existence of God and his creation, "Satan" are unmindful of the fact that Satan's original appearance was anything but unsightly. On the contrary, the Holy Bible tells us that Satan was one of God's most beautiful creations, covered in precious stones and mentally equipped with an immense database of knowledge. Ezekiel 28:13,17 reads:

"Thou hast been in Eden the garden of God; every precious stone was thy covering, the sardius, topaz, and the diamond, the beryl, the onyx, and the jasper, the sapphire, the emerald, and the carbuncle, and gold: the workmanship of thy tabrets and of thy pipes was prepared in thee in the day that thou wast created... Thine heart was lifted up because of thy beauty, thou hast corrupted thy wisdom by reason of thy brightness: I will cast thee to the ground, I will lay thee before kings, that they may behold thee."

"… and it is at the option of every Brother to procure or not to procure, as he pleases, the dress, decorations, and jewels of any Degree other than the 14th, 18th, 30th, and 32d." – Albert Pike, Morals and Dogma, pg. 329

For over six millennia Satan's primary objective has been to transform God's creation e.g., earth, man, etc. into what God transformed Satan into, an immensely corrupt creature morally, spiritually and physically. Through the conduit of Walt Disney Company, the "father of lies," corrupts young lives and subconsciously indoctrinate them into magic, wizardry, witchcraft, homosexuality, etc. Since his encounter with Knights Templars in Soissons, France in 1919, Satan's aim became Walt Disney's master opus throughout his entire life.

The Holy Bible teaches us to judge an individual by their fruits [Matthew 7:20] and when we examine the fruits of Walt Disney's labor we discover that his creation has given rise to the feminization of men and has been instrumental in portraying women in a masculine or whorish light. Consider the fact that Both Disneyland and Disneyworld endorse 'Gay Rights' parties on their properties, which blatantly promote the abolition of biblical marriage and the destruction of the 'Nuclear Family'. What's more, Walt's universe has created an environment in which Disney employees and strategic partners engage in pedophilia, child sex trafficking, etc.

"And he caused his children to pass through the fire in the valley of the son of Hinnom: also he observed times, and used enchantments, and used witchcraft, and dealt with a familiar spirit, and with wizards:

he wrought much evil in the sight of the LORD, to provoke him to anger."
- 2 Chronicles 33:6

Walt Disney's Universe fully embraces the meaning of the Masonic double-headed eagle, the androgynous joining of man and woman into one species, the combination of the 'yin and yang', this is what the checkerboard, black and white floors inside of a Masonic Lodges represent. The mirror images of the Rosicrucians, the sulphurous tale of Beauty and the Beast; the witches parable of the lovely lady vs. the crone on her broom; the Druid/Satanic/Catholic alternating of black and white priest vestments; the front and obverse (hidden) sides of the Great Seal of the United States; the reversing of the cross and the reading of the Lord's Prayer backwards in satanic worship, etc. What this reveals is that Walt Disney's Universe was created to assist in the destruction of God's creation [man]. This is why we see the transmission of negative taboos into things which are positive and acceptable throughout Disney films and cartoons. The end-goal of the Church of Babylon is that, "Bad shall be good. Black shall be white. The ugly shall be deemed beautiful and the beautiful is to be

224

spoiled, scarred, and made repugnant and revolting. God shall be debased and Satan exalted.

> "I [Satan] will ascend above the heights of the clouds; I will be like the most High [God]. – Isaiah 14:14

Earlier I discussed how Walt Disney Company purchased George Lucas' Lucasfilm 10/30/2012 for $4.05 billion dollars. I also shared the occult numerics associated with Star Wars 666 logo, the Lucasfilm acquisition, 10/30 the **303**rd day of the year [**33**] and that Prior to its acquisition, LucasArts was developing a video game titled, "Star Wars 1313." I reiterate this to bring to light the true origins of George Lucas' "creative genius," a man who once said:

> "I've always tried to be aware of what I say in my films, because all of us who make motion pictures are teachers with very loud voices."

In large part Lucas' cinematic beauty, corrupt wisdom and riches were acquired through resources provided to him by the Church of Babylon, namely Joseph Campbell, a famous Freemason writer on the mythology surrounding Newgrange in Ireland. One can only speculate that it was Campbell who influenced Lucas to create reptilian humanoids named 'Trandoshans', 'Barabels' and 'Ssi-ruuk' for his Star Wars franchise, whose features are similar to that of the Babylonian priest's Oannes [Satan] and the Rothschild's Nimrod. What's unmistakably clear is that, like Walt Disney and many other "celebrities," George Lucas is a card carrying Church of Babylon member, complicit in the pilfering and corruption of ancient Celtic and Pictish knowledge.

To understand why the progeny of ancient Celts and Picts, which make up more than 50% of the founders of the United States, have been sacrificially targeted by the Church of Babylon, all one must do is study, "The Declaration of Arbroath," the predecessor to the 9/17/1787 United States Constitution, written April 6, 1320. In part this, the world's first written declarations of independence, states:

> "We know, Most Holy Father and Lord, and we find it written in the records and histories of the ancients, that amongst other peoples of renown our Scottish nation has been distinguished by many tributes to their fame. Within this our realm there have reigned one hundred and thirteen Kings of our native royal dynasty, and not one of alien birth. If proof be needed of the quality and worth of our people, it shines forth for all to see in this that the King of Kings, our Lord Jesus Christ, after His Passion and Resurrection, chose us as almost the first to be called to His most holy faith, though we dwelt in the uttermost

225

parts of the earth, and He would not that we should be confirmed therein by anyone except the first of His Apostles by calling, though the second or third in rank, Andrew the Meek, the brother of blessed Peter, whom He appointed to be our leader and patron Saint for ever."

This historic document reveals to the descendants of ancient Celts and Picts that St. Andrew was specifically charged with a mission to carry the message of Christ to Scotland by Jesus Christ Himself. Why? Because God in the flesh [Jesus Christ] was aware of ancient Caledonia [Scotland] and its participation in the destruction of the Church of Babylon and considered its people of sufficient importance to send a leading Apostle to its lands.

I believe the above quote along with the supporting evidence, contained in the previous pages, supports my thesis that the ancient Celtic ancestors of nearly 50 million Scots/Irish throughout the U.S., Scotland, and Ireland created coded family crests, shields, and oral traditions containing cautionary tales of an ancient Old World Order system, to ensure their descendants, who are not "Willingly ignorant" [2 Peter 3:5], would be able to decipher the hazards and triumphs of their ancient ancestors over the once powerful global control system of the Church of Babylon. Those Celts, whose family trinkets, customs, crests, or shields have incorporated into them one of the principle marks of Nimrod are descendants of mariners, messengers, and warriors who brought forth ancient technologies and knowledge to the, "four quarters of the earth" [Revelation 20:8] in ancient times, resources that were instrumental in destroying the Church of Babylon's old world order system. If you are of Scottish, Irish, etc. descent research your Family Crest at: **rummle.com**

Given that more than half of America's founding fathers were Scottish I would like to point out the similarities between the ancient world order of the Church of Babylon and the Americas, which are too many to list and too striking to be coincidence. Consider the parallels between the first step pyramid of Egypt and the ancient Mexican 'Pyramid of the Sun', an obvious reference to one of Nimrod's principal demon gods, 'Shamash', the 15ft tall giant sun god [pg.19]. Further evidence connecting Mesoamerica to the ancient Church of Babylon and their god Nimrod can be found in the flag of the Nation controlled by said ancient order, Great Britain.

The following images are components of the British Flag "Union Jack," [pg.227, top] which is a combination of two ancient Babylonian symbols. Given that it's interconnected with our examination of the Union Jack, I'm obligated to disclose my family's connection with the following data, which has been part of my Scottish ancestry for centuries and passed down through the generations to this author from my Scottish ancestor, "Tom Bog." According to family records

226

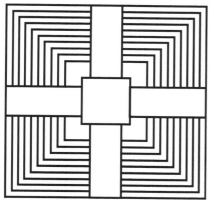

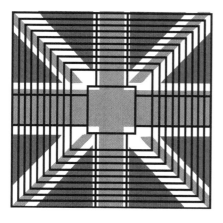

Tom was a 92nd, out of a possible 360th, degree Freemason, who shortly before his death c.1460 renounced his relationship with the order. Records also show that the 5th generation of Tom Bog married, "Elizabeth Cockburne" c.1612 the ancestor of Sir Alexander de Cockburn, who was known as, "The Keeper of the Great Seal of Scotland". More famously, Admiral Cockburn conveyed Napoleon Bonaparte to his exile on St. Helena 1815 following Napoleon's defeat at the Battle of Waterloo, which gave rise to the Babylonian Talmudist Rothschild Family. It's noteworthy to mention that the British hammer, Irish born, Protestant, Arthur Wellesley [Duke Wellington] used to smash Napoleon's forces was a composite of warriors 1/3 [33%] of which were Irish men. In recognition of Wellington's long ties to the Church of Babylon, his regiment was named, "33rd Regiment of Foot." Ironically the Cockburne's were also ardent supporters of Mary, Queen of Scots a Catholic whose son King James I, would go on to embolden those protesting [Protestants] against the Catholic Church.

The first symbol within the British Flag is said to be St. George's Cross, which in reality did not originate with St. George, Knights Templars or the 'Holy Wars,' rather it's based on the cross found within the world's oldest Freemason Lodge logo c.926 A.D. [pg.17] whose origins date back to ancient Babylon, specifically the Stela of Nimrod [pg.18, "B"]. The second symbol is the 'X' flag of Scotland which again has nothing to do with the people of Scotland; rather it's the mark of the Serpent Cult of Dann. What's more the letter "X" contains two 7s. It will be remembered from [pg.41] that the Church of Babylon teaches its members that the founder of Freemasonry was, "Hiram Abiff" and that Abiff's ancestors were Cain, father of TubalCain, Lamech and the "Tribe of

227

Naphtali", an ancient tribe of Pharisee worshipping Talmudists [Khazars] who along with the demon god Pazuzu and Lucifer built King Solomon's Temple.

"If Cain shall be avenged sevenfold, truly Lamech seventy and sevenfold. [777]" - Genesis 4:24

The number 7 is considered 'magical' by the Serpent Death Cult and is associated with The Church of Babylon's revenge of Lamech. This resonates 7, 11, and 77 because Lamech's revenge of 77 is 11 times Cain's 7. This is why both the 'Cross' and 'X' of the Union Jack contain double 7s. Double 7s appear in 7 of our 26 letter alphabet which was originally introduced by Irish missionaries [c.9th century] after Runes were banned under King Cnut. Single 7s appear in three additional letters, these include: A, E, H, K, L, M, N, T, X, Z. This knowledge along with basic principles in perspective and geometry have been hidden from the world for over 1,000 years. The Church of Babylon conceals this intelligence inside of symbols to maintain power and position over global populations. These symbols allow them to spread and control fear, war, famine, death, disbelief, disinformation and misdirection. Above all else it provides them with the tools necessary to deceive the human race away from God and towards Satan, who since the beginning of Creation has wanted to become God:

"I [Satan] will ascend above the heights of the clouds; I [Satan] will be like the most High [God]." – Isaiah 14:14.

A E H K L
M N T X Z

The above anagram creates a handful of names associated with historically significant figures, events and locations. Just a few of these include: Lamek, as in the revenge of Lamech and Azel a descendant of King Saul the first King of Israel [1 Chronicles 8:37; 1Chronicles 9:43-44. Reluctantly anointed by Prophet Samuel, Saul lost favor with Samuel, committed suicide by falling on his sword and was succeeded by his son-in-law, King David [Books of Samuel] who was succeeded by King Solomon [1 kings 1-11, Chronicles 28-29, 2 Chronicles 1-9]. Solomon's wisdom, wealth and power and sins which included idolatry and turning away from God led to the kingdoms being torn in two during the reign of his son Rehoboam. The Knights Templar's were originally named "The Poor Fellow Soldiers of Christ and of the Temple of Solomon.

228

The word "Mt. Hekla" is also mentioned in this anagram. Hekla is one of the most active volcanoes in the South of Iceland. It is known as the "Gateway to Hell." Built in 1872, the Norwegian whaler Hekla takes her name from Mt. Hekla. The ship was purchased in 1902 by Britain's most famous polar scientist and Freemason, Scotsman William Spiers Bruce [8/1/1867-10/28/1921] for use by the Scottish National Antarctic Expedition. Bruce spent most of the 1890s engaged on expeditions to the Antarctic and Arctic regions confirming ancient knowledge regarding earth's physical characteristics, namely the ancient belief that earth is a flat surface, contained by a circle of ice and covered by a crystal dome or firmament, "The heavens declare the glory of God; and the firmament sheweth his handywork." [Ezekiel 1:22]. A comprehensive series of essays which use scripture, reason and fact to argue in favor of a 'flat earth' was published in 1901 by a contemporary of Bruce, Scotsman David Wardlow Scott, in his book, "Terra Firma: the Earth Not a Planet, Proven from Scripture, Reason, and Fact.

The word "menthal" is also represented in this anagram. Menthal is an organic compound which has been used by Babylonian Talmudists as a poison for thousands of years. This is why Babylonian Talmudist founded and controlled Philip Morris [Altria since 2003] sell menthal cigarettes to goyim [non-Jews]. The toxin Menthol is also used as a flavoring agent inside of candy, cough drops, cold sore medications, gum, inhalants, mouthwashes, Ben-Gay, Mineral Ice, etc. Currently menthol cigarettes comprise about 30% of the total cigarette market, however over 80% of African-Americans consumes menthols. Philip Morris was born in Whitechapel, United Kingdom [1835], a fitting location considering this was the location of the infamous Whitechapel Murders by Jack the Ripper [1880s]. Jewish Politician Rep. Eric Cantor's "legislative career is marked by his tireless advocacy of the tobacco industry…he has gone out of his way to help shield the tobacco industry – and Philip Morris, in particular – from legal responsibility for its actions" – Jewish Daily Forward. Cigarettes have killed millions of Americans and still cause the deaths of more than 400,000 Americans per year. Philip Morris holdings include: Marlboro, Virginia Slims, Benson & Hedges, Merit, Miller Brewing Company, South African Breweries, General Foods, Kraft Foods, Smokeless Tobacco Company, Skoal, Copenhagen, Chateau Ste. Michelle Wine Estates.

Speaking of South Africa, the "White separatist" group, "Afrikaner Weerstandsbeweging" founded in 1973 by alleged anti-communist Eugène Terre'Blanche, glorified the Church of Babylon's "revenge of Lamech" [777] on their flag [pg.230, left]. This flag was obviously inspired by Adolf Hilter's Nazi Flag [pg.230, right], which also contained the Serpent Cult's "X" in the center along with four 7s.

The name "Max Lenz" is also represented in this anagram. Max Lenz - [6/13/1850-4/6/1932] was one of the most important historians in Berlin, German. He was an admirer of the Protestant Reformation. He published a biography of Martin Luther in 1883. Lenz advocated complete objectivity and neutrality in the study of history. He was a bitter opponent of Karl Gottfried Lamprecht [2/25/1856-5/10/1915] who wrote his Doctor's thesis about Alexander the Great. Lamprecht worked for Karl Von Hegel [6/7/1813-12/5/1901] the son of Georg Wilhelm Friedrich Hegel [8/27/1770-11/14/1831] the German philosopher who influenced Karl Marx, Nietzsche, subjective consciousness, existentialism and psychoanalysis. George Wilhelm was strongly influenced by German Satanist Jokob Bohme [1575-11/17/1624] who subscribed to Satan's plan of destroying man, Bohme wrote, "the fall of man was a necessary stage in the evolution of the universe."

The name "Ken Ham" is also represented in this anagram. Ken Ham is a young earth creationist, Christian fundamentalist and President of Answers in Genesis (AiG), a Creationist apologetics ministry that operates a Creation Museum. According to Ham: "[My father] was always very adamant about one thing - if you can't trust the Book of Genesis as literal history, then you can't trust the rest of the Bible. After all, every single doctrine of biblical theology is founded in the history of Genesis 1-11. My father had not developed his thinking in this area as much as we have today at Answers in Genesis, but he clearly understood that if Adam wasn't created from dust, and that if he didn't fall into sin as Genesis states, then the gospel message of the New Testament can't be true either." – Raising Godly Children in an Ungodly World: Leaving a Lasting Legacy, New Leaf Publishing Group, by Ken Ham (2008).

Returning back to our examination of the British Flag "Union Jack," the second image [pg.227, center] is an aerial view illustration of the pyramid at Chichen Itza. And finally the third image [pg.227, bottom] is of the two images combined which match perfectly. Legend tells us that Scotland's 'X' flag represents St. Andrew who is said to have been martyred by crucifixion at the city of Patras (Patræ) in Achaea, on the northern coast of the Peloponnese. However the Acts of Andrew known to

Gregory of Tours c.538, refute these claims describing St. Andrew as being bound, not nailed, to a Latin cross of the kind on which Jesus was crucified; however, when Knights Templar's, representing the Serpent Cult of Dann and possessed with Babylonian demon gods, escaped execution in France and arrived in Scotland c.1314 they developed the blasphemous tradition throughout Scotland that St. Andrew had been crucified on an X-shaped cross signifying the Serpent Cult of Dann a mark which is represented on the Stela of Nimrod [pg.18, "C"], which is now commonly known as "Saint Andrew's Cross."

There are a number of groups and Nations throughout the world today who brandish the mark of Dann or X of Nimrod, these include: The Nazi Flag; The Confederate Flag; Flag of Northern Ireland; Flag of Iceland; Flag of Georgia [Five Cross Flag]; etc. The Holy Bible informs us that the tribe of Dan left its "mark" wherever they travelled. Judges 18:29 reads, "And they called the name of the city Dan, after the name of Dan their father, who was born unto Israel: howbeit the name of the city was Laish at the first." There is physical evidence that suggests prominent nations around the world have maintained their allegiance to the Serpent Cult of Dan. This loyalty is flaunted in the names of such countries as ScanDanavia; Danmark; Danube River; LonDan; etc.

For those readers who are reluctant to believe my theory regarding an ancient demonic force, who for centuries through occult rituals have existed off the life-force of ancient Irish and Scottish bloodlines, please read the following 2009 Canadian TV interview of Academy Award winning Irish American actor, "Randy Quaid". Randy provides those who are asleep and unaware a sobering depiction of The Church of Babylon and their control methods over America. Randy, who is best known for his roles in National Lampoon's Vacation and Independence Day, is brother to Dennis Quaid and Uncle to Jack Quaid, an American actor who rose to prominence after portraying the character, "Marvel" in the film, "The Hunger Games."

"For the past twenty years my wife Ebbie and I have been the victims of criminal activities perpetrated by a small network of individuals who are out to destroy us personally professionally and financially. This network of individuals is manipulating the banking system and the criminal justice system for the purpose of sabotaging our credit and our credibility.

Three of these individuals are Hollywood lawyers and a business manager all of whom I hired twenty years ago to handle my legal and business affairs. They're Allen Watmaker, my financial estate planner, Warren Grant, my former business manager, and Lloyd Brawn, my ex-attorney. These three along with a few others whose professional services I've engaged over the years have conspired together to

231

steal my property, my money and with the aid of specific individuals at two major studios - Bruce Berman certainly being one - have gained access to my royalties revenue stream. These people have been able to do these things through the creation of a phony probate file, phony living trusts, secret bank accounts, fake loans, bogus corporations, smear campaigns and false arrests of my wife and me.

They've been aided and abetted in their schemes by the entertainment division of City National Bank's Roxbury Branch in Beverly Hills. This particular branch is a major financial hub for the entire Hollywood industry. With the cooperation of certain individuals within City Nation's entertainment division, business managers, lawyers and agents have been able to misappropriate my assets, life insurance policy and royalties, through various client trust accounts and bogus loans taken out in my name without my knowledge. The President of the Bank's estate planning division told my wife that the Bank: 'Prefers dead actors because they don't get in the way'

These former employees of mine have further reached out to their relatives and contacts in Santa Barbara County to take civil disputes and turn them into criminal complaints against us. To be clear, we did not defraud an innkeeper and we did not trespass on our own property. Up until a year ago, Ebbie and I had never had any run-ins with the law whatsoever. We are not criminals nor are we fugitives from justice. Nor are we crazy. We are simply artists and film makers who are being racketeered on by what we believe to be a malignant tumor of 'star whackers' in Hollywood.

How many people do you know personally who have died suddenly and mysteriously in the past five years? I have personally known eight actors, all of whom I have worked with and was close to. Heath Ledger, Chris Penn, David Carradine and others. I believe these actors were 'wacked' and I believe that many others, such as [Scottish American Musician] Brittany Spears, [Irish American Actress] Lindsey Lohan and [Scottish American Actor/Director] Mel Gibson are being played to get at their money. In the meantime many celebrities' image and marketability is being co-opted and destroyed. Google helps out by keeping the negative stories at the top of their celebrities' webpage, because it's the negativity that brings in the advertising revenue.

In my own case, my ex attorney Lloyd Braun has joined this tribe of bottom feeders by creating his own celebrity gossip website. What is wrong with that picture? When your own attorney starts defaming you, who do you turn to, to defend you? Lloyd Braun also claims to have 232 come up with the idea of the Sopranos. So he's obviously familiar with the ways and means of organized crime. Unfortunately my brother Dennis has made matters worse by buying a house from Mr. Braun on property Braun originally bought with money that he embezzled from me. I recently discovered much to my surprise that Dennis was also on the deed to my Santa Barbara property. This is also the work of Mr. Braun further confounding the validity of the transfer of my fully furnished property in 1992 to Mr. Bruce Berman. I have earned approximately $40 million dollars throughout my career. I have profit participation in some of my films. I am being embezzled from this monstrous ring of accountants, estate planners, and lawyers who are mercilessly slandering me and trying to kill my career and I believe murder me in order to gain control of my royalties."

Randy Quaid is one of only a few Hollywood Celebrities to not only acknowledge the existence of a secret society subculture throughout Hollywood. Quaid describes in detail their subjugation methods. What Quaid describes in the aforesaid quote is the hallmark of Khazarian Babylonian Talmudist Supremacists, who believe all non-Talmudists ["goyim"] are here to serve the Talmudists and killing a non-Talmudist to gain access to his/her body and money is sanctioned by their "Holy Book," the Babylonian Talmud. For instance, Ikkarim IIIc, 25 reads:

"It is permitted to take the body and the life of a non-Jew."

This parasitic nature is endorsed by leaders within the Talmudist community as well. Rabbi Ovadia Yosef, senior Sephardic posek and head of the Shas Council of Torah Sages during a sermon on the laws regarding non-Jews stated, "Goyim [Christians] were born only to serve us. Without that, they have no place in the world - only to serve the People of Israel... With gentiles [Christians], it will be like any person - they need to die, but [God] will give them longevity. Why? Imagine that one's donkey would die, they'd lose their money. This is his servant... That's why he gets a long life, to work well for this Jew [Talmudist]. Why are gentiles [Christians] needed? They will work, and they will plow, they will reap. We will sit like an effendi and eat. That is why gentiles were created." - Jerusalem Post, October 18, 2010

Unfortunately, with every person who escapes the grasp of The Church of Babylon there are many who are not so lucky. Michael Jackson was one of these deceived souls who unwittingly became a lifelong target of The Church of Babylon until his death at the hands of Dr. Conrad Murray [pg.234, top], a cardiologist who until securing an exclusive $150,000 per month relationship with Jackson managed a small practice in which he made house calls to high-profile clients in Las Vegas and Washington D.C. Piecing together all of the reports that we've heard regarding Michael Jackson's heightened sense of awareness about those who

233

in his words were "trying to kill me" it begs the question. How does a virtual nobody doctor gain access to one of the wealthiest entertainers in the world [$1.3 billion in 2007] and the recipient of dozens of U.S. chart records and achievements? The answer can be found in the following June 6, 2009 Fox News report regarding Conrad Murray's affiliation with Freemasonry:

> "Three years ago, Murray joined the Freemasonry, the international fraternal society that dates back to the early 17th century [9th century actually]. His friends say this new network galvanized his growing side business."

The fact is Murray was recruited and groomed by The Church of Babylon to befriend Jackson and then sacrifice him. Why? Because of Michael's long-standing insolence towards the secret order Randy Quaid identifies as preferring "dead actors because they don't get in the way."

When Jackson discovered who he was enriching and what their true intensions were on this planet, he began creating art which flew in the face of Babylonian Talmudists and by all accounts returned his life to the one true God. It was shortly after this transition Michael Jackson became the target of child molestation charges. In the summer of 1993 Evan Chandler accused Michael Jackson of sexually abusing his 13-year-old son. In January 1994 the criminal investigation was closed due to lack of evidence. Five months after Jackson's death, Evan Chandler 'committed suicide.

Reflecting back on all that you've learned so far, I invite you to consider the preceding knowledge as an example of synchronicity. Namely, the recurring relationship between ethnic cleansing and the Church of Babylon's ancient system of subjugation in what has become a favorite pastime for Talmudists. Regular contestants in this arena are Steven Spielberg, George Lucas, and Stan Lee, the owner of 'Marvel' Comics. Like Spielberg and Lucas, Lee sourced much of his popular character base from ancient Celtic traditions, namely the struggle between Celtic tribes, Nimrod and the "Tuatha De **Dan**ann" [Dann].

Evidence of Stan Lee's reliance on these historic events can be found on Marvel.com where it states: "The Tuatha De **Dan**ann and 234 the Asgardians [Oden, Thor, etc.] joined forces to defeat Seth, the Egyptian god of evil." Marvel Comics actually features a character named, "Nimrod" in their Comic Book titled, "Uncanny X-Men #191" [March 1985]. What's curious about Marvel's depiction of the Tuatha De **Dan**ann is its relationship with the yet to be fulfilled prophecy from ancient Irish legends which states that the Tuatha De **Dan**ann will return to liberate the inhabitants of Ireland from a plague of absentmindedness. It is said that the coming of Tuatha De **Dan**ann will be at a time when:

> "Symbols will be more real than the things they represent, when people no longer have control over their thoughts and their state of illusion is stronger than their intuition. Their coming will be at a time when our planet has focused the majority of its existence on materialism and destroying itself in exchange for possessions, control, and monetary gain."

Stan Lee even uses this premise for a series of stories in Thor (1986) which actually featured the Tuatha De **Dan**ann as the main characters.

I believe the above ancient Celtic prophecy of the Tuatha De **Dan**ann reveals an underlying pattern of a much larger framework. It's yet one more example of how descendants of ancient Celts are being provoked out of their state of absentmindedness and provided very clear examples of how Satan will use his proxies to deceive people into accepting The Antichrist. An example of this is Stan Lee's depiction of Nimrod' Tuatha De **Dan**nan as liberators who should be welcomed as allies to defeat Seth. This is telling when you consider both sects are of Satan. Seth' siblings included Osiris and Isis and Seth' homosexual episodes with Horus resulted in the creation of the moon god Thoth, an ancient reproduction of the Babylonian moon god 'Sin', son of Enlil, and one of Nimrod' principle demon gods. The Serpent Cult also believe that Enlil is the Chief god of the Earth "Lord of 7". It will be remembered from our examination of the World Trade Center buildings in New York City [pg.41] that the serpent cult also associate Cain with the number seven, "If Cain shall be avenged sevenfold, truly Lamech seventy and sevenfold [777]. - Genesis 4:24

It too will be remembered that Satanist Aleister Crowley wrote a book titled, "777 AND OTHER QABALISTIC WRITINGS OF ALEISTER CROWLEY."

Crowley's all-seeing-eye of Satan permeates popular culture and the moon god is depicted throughout many corporate logos including DreamWorks Animation, owned by Babylonian Talmudists Jeffrey Katzenberg and Steven Spielberg.

235

Spielberg and Katzenberg represent a short list of elite Talmudist Billionaires whose actions arrogantly proclaim a steadfast allegiance to the Church of Babylon's goal of eradicating any evidence of Jesus Christ and according to President Barack Hussein Obama, Spielberg and Katzenberg are central to achieving this goal:

"Believe it or not, entertainment is part of our American diplomacy. You helped shape the world culture. Tolerance, diversity and creativity" – President Barack Hussein Obama 2013 DreamWorks Animation Campus

Whether you believe in the existence of God does not matter to the Church of Babylon who accepts as true and worships the "father of lies" [Satan]. In actuality if you deny the existence of either one it makes their job of deceiving and killing you that much easier. I hope that in some measure I have provided enough evidence throughout the preceding pages to illustrate this fact.

With all of the aforesaid evidence in mind, please allow me to introduce you to a multi-billionaire Scotsman, who under the guise of preservation is working hard to destroy the only resource available to mankind that's capable of extinguishing Satan's triad of malevolence.

Rupert Murdoch's
Empire of
Remphan

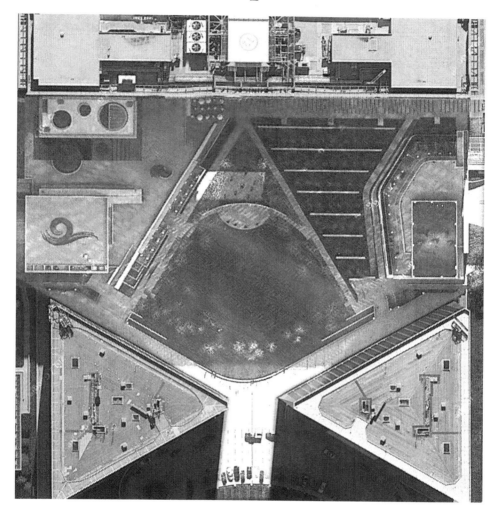

"The real Satanist is not quite so easily recognized as such" - Anton
Szandor LaVey, The Satanic Bible

The previous photograph [pg.237] is an aerial view of Century City business center located between Avenue of the Stars, Constellation Blvd, Olympic Blvd and Century Park E. in Southern California. I would like to point out the obvious in this picture, and then we'll discuss the not so obvious. The first image your eyes should be drawn to is the giant pyramid encasing an all-seeing-eye of Satan. The eye here also represents a profile view of what planet earth looks like from outer space. In geometry this is a semicircle. What the Church of Babylon is hiding here in plain sight is the knowledge that earth's profile is not a ball but a semicircle.

"I wanted to get hold of Satan personally and become his chief of staff. Satan Cry Aloud! Thou Exalted Most High! Oh My Father Satan! The Eye!" – Aleister Crowley

The second images you should see are two large pyramid buildings flanking either side of the giant all-seeing-eye of Satan. The most concerning aspects of this satanic alter is not what you can see, rather it's what you don't see and that's what we're going to discuss next.

Geometrically the two large pyramid shaped buildings flanking either side of the giant all-seeing-eye of Satan are identical to the two pyramids which make up the six pointed Star of Remphan/Molech [Satan] shown below:

"But ye have borne the tabernacle of your Moloch and Chiun your images, the star of your god, which ye made to yourselves." - Amos 5:26

Yea, ye took up the tabernacle of Moloch, and the star of your god Remphan, figures which ye made to worship them: and I will carry you away beyond Babylon. - Acts 7:43

To the Church of Babylon the top pyramid represents Man whereas the bottom pyramid represents god. In other words those who worship this symbol believe Man is above God. The first mention of this star was in c.922 BC, this is when King Solomon rebelled against God and began practicing magic, witchcraft, etc. Prior to King Solomon, the Egyptians used the star in pagan rituals, followed by the Arabs who used it for pagan ceremonies.

The logo became exceedingly popular during the Middle Ages c.1066 AD by Druids, for something they called the 'highest Sabbath of the witches', what is now commonly referred to as Halloween. In the late

1500s the anti-Christian, anti-Torah Talmudist patriarch of the Rothschild family, Izaak Elchanan Rothschild [born in 1577] would adopt the satanic emblem as the official family logo. The vast majority of spiritually re-mastered Christians living throughout America have been brainwashed into believing that this logo represents the 'Star of David' or the Judaic people. The problem with this 'Big-Lie' is that The Holy Bible only references the "Shield of David", not a satanic hexagram of Rothschild which this clearly is. This satanic emblem was imposed onto Judaic people by the demonic Rothschild family. The menorah is in fact the oldest sacred symbol of the Jewish people:

"And thou shalt make a candlestick of pure gold: of beaten work shall the candlestick be made: his shaft, and his branches, his bowls, his knops, and his flowers, shall be of the same. And six branches shall come out of the sides of it; three branches of the candlestick out of the one side, and three branches of the candlestick out of the other side:" - Exodus 25

The Rothschild Family has known for centuries that the hexagram symbol is associated with Satan. What should concern every Christian and Judaic person in the world is that the Rothschild hexagram is comprised of two large pyramids with a total of 6 sides, 6 smaller pyramids and 6 points [666] 'mark of the beast'.

"Here is wisdom. Let him that hath understanding count the number of the beast: for it is the number of a man; and his number is Six hundred threescore and six [666]." - Revelation 13:18

The second aerial view of Century City business center that I would like to share with readers features a portion of the business center that's located on Avenue of the Stars [below]. What has been constructed here is an all-seeing-eye of Satan, with a water fountain feature in the middle, which creates the number 69. The number 69 is important to Satanists because it represents Satanist Aleister Crowley's, "The Book of Lies, chapter 69 titled, "The Way to Succeed-and the Way to Suck Eggs!" which is a pun for the 69 sex position. It will be remembered from pg.217 that the Disney Quest logo

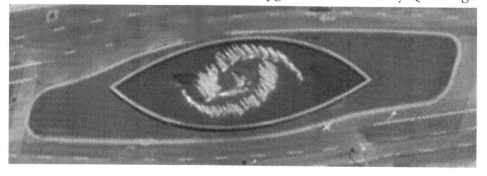

HSBC
The world's local bank

in Downtown Walt Disney World contains a similar design.

In 1961, 180 acres of the Century City business center was sold to Alcoa Inc. (Aluminum Company of America) whose aluminum is used in cookware, soft drink cans, our atmosphere, etc. Coincidently, ALCOA' logo [left] contains one large pyramid and two smaller pyramids that when combined make up the Star of Remphan, as does the Rothschild controlled HSBC Bank [left], who in 2014 demanded to know how their customers were spending their money. HSBC, along with Goldman Sachs, Coca-Cola, healthcare giant Tenet, Ukrainian steel magnate Victor Pinchuk, the governments of Oman, Kuwait and the United Arab Emirates, are major donors to the Bill, Hillary and Chelsea Clinton Foundation.

It's worth mentioning that multiple studies going as far back as 1885 have shown that aluminum is toxic to the nervous system of animals.

For years the Century business center has played host to a large number of executives associated with the anti-Christian film, television, and music industries, and is a former back-lot of 20th Century Fox Studios, whose most famous actresses included Church of Satan members Marilyn Monroe and Jayne Mansfield.

Century City still contains Rupert Murdoch's News Corp. Fox back-lot and FOX headquarters. This is the same Rupert Murdoch, by the way, who is a major shareholder in Genie Israel Holdings, Ltd., along with anti-Christian Lord Jacob Rothschild. It's noteworthy to mention that Genie Energy's Chairman is a General in the Israeli Army who in a 2004 interview with The New Yorker said about all Palestinians 'We will have to kill them all'. In short what Christian Americans must realize is that Rupert Murdoch and the Satanic Rothschild Family have a vested interest in perpetual war between the Christian majority of America and the entire Middle East. This is why the Talmudist owned and controlled movie, television and music industry continue to associate satanic, godless logos, namely the eye of Satan and Nimrod with America. The Century City business center has hosted a number of celebrities such as the Apollo 11 moon landing astronauts including Freemason Buzz Aldrin who brought a Masonic flag to the moon in 1969. Coincidently, Apollo [Apollyon] is the name of

240

the Beast in The Book of Revelation. Apollo's rockets were named Saturn rocket boosters. Saturn in old Latin is the same word as Satan. Furthermore, the Apollo 11 rocket booster had on one side a 6, the top of it a 6, and on the other side a 6 [666]. And let's not forget that the Saturn rocket booster was invented by Wernher von Braun, Adolf Hitler's top Nazi Scientist and NASA's Deputy Associate Administrator for Planning. Additional visitors to Century City business center include New Age practitioners President and Mrs. Reagan, and President Johnson, the same President who reversed President JFK's Executive Order 11110 which stripped all power away from the Rothschild/ Rockefeller/JP Morgan founded and controlled Federal Reserve Corporation. Moreover, President Johnson is the same President featured on a previous page forming a pyramid with his eye-glasses. The massive Century City monument dedicated to Satan is centered between Avenue of the Stars, Constellation Blvd., Olympic Blvd. and Century Park E.

What Christian Americans must know is that Rupert Murdoch's motivation to become a U.S. Citizen at 54 was simply so that he could meet the legal requirement necessary for owning a U.S. television station. What should be deeply disturbing for each and every Christian American is that Murdoch owns HarperCollins, the publisher of "The Satanic Bible" and "The Satanic Rituals - Companion to The Satanic Bible" by Church of Satan founder Anton Lavey. Rupert Murdoch's HarperCollins is also the publisher of 'The Joy of Gay Sex' and anti-Christian Richard Dawkins. Furthermore, in 2010 Murdoch's HarperCollins bought educational publisher Letts and Lonsdale, the leading publisher of revision guides to Home Schools and online education throughout Great Britain with an emphasis on Scotland. Most troubling of all is that Rupert Murdoch's publishing house which offers The Satanic Bible and Satanic Rituals, purchased the Christian book publishers Zondervan in 1988 and Thomas Nelson in 2011, which resulted in the elimination of approximately 700 jobs. Thomas Nelson is a Scottish Christian Book Publisher founded in 1798 and is the world's largest Christian publisher and leading producer of Christian live events. Further, HarperCollins purchased 'Chronicles of Narnia' written by Irish Christian apologist and novelist C.S. Lewis. With these acquisitions, Murdoch's HarperCollins now controls more than 50 percent of the Christian publishing market e.g., The Holy Bible, Christian Authors, Christian live events, etc.

Murdoch has wasted no time leveraging his strength in Christian media to recruit hundreds of Christian mystics in an effort to promote anti-Christian One World Religion directives. For instance, HarperCollins/ Zondervan author and American evangelical Christian pastor Rick Warren's blatant dismissal of ancient Christian doctrine smacks of Theosophy. As I mentioned in an early chapter Warren said that he: "Apologizes 241 to his homosexual friends for making comments in support of

California's Proposition-8 same-sex marriage ban."

The Holy Bible is quite clear about homosexuality. With that said, which 'god' is Rick Warren representing when he apologizes for his stance on same sex marriage? If we study who Rick Warren's publisher and fellow authors are e.g., Church of Satan Founder Anton LaVey, 'The Joy of Gay Sex' and the agenda they're associated with, it doesn't take a rocket scientist to figure out who men like Rick Warren are representing.

"And account [that] the longsuffering of our Lord [is] salvation; even as our beloved brother Paul also according to the wisdom given unto him hath written unto you; As also in all [his] epistles, speaking in them of these things; in which are some things hard to be understood, which they that are unlearned and unstable wrest, as [they do] also the other scriptures, unto their own destruction. Ye therefore, beloved, seeing ye know [these things] before, beware lest ye also, being led away with the error of the wicked, fall from your own stedfastness." - 2nd Peter 3:15-17

Rupert Murdoch's One World Religion Bible:

"Think not that I am come to destroy the law, or the prophets: I am not come to destroy, but to fulfil. For verily I say unto you, Till heaven and earth pass, one jot or one tittle shall in no wise pass from the law, till all be fulfilled. Whosoever therefore shall break one of these least commandments, and shall teach men so, he shall be called the least in the kingdom of heaven: but whosoever shall do and teach [them], the same shall be called great in the kingdom of heaven." - Matthew 5:17-19

Although McArthur's writings are fittingly critical of New Age Christian Rick Warren, Scottish American John MacArthur is himself responsible for inventing Thomas Nelson's best-selling modernist 'MacArthur Study Bible' which was recently paired with Zondervan's 2011 updated heretical New International Version (NIV) Bible, which refers to Jesus Christ as Satan and promotes a New World Order "...Until the time of The New Order." – Hebrews 9:10 (NIV):

In the King James Holy Bible we find just one reference to Satan and he is given the name 'Lucifer' and the title 'son of the morning'. It reads:

"How art thou fallen from heaven, O Lucifer, son of the morning! how art thou cut down to the ground, which didst weaken the nations!" – Isaiah 14:12

242 The King James Holy Bible also provides readers with the title of Lord Jesus Christ. It reads:

"I Jesus have sent mine angel to testify unto you these things in the churches. I am the root and the offspring of David, and the bright and morning star." – Revelation 22:16

With the aforesaid in mind now read how the New International Version (NIV) Bible casts Jesus Christ out of heaven and not Lucifer:

"How you have fallen from heaven morning star, son of the dawn! You have been cast down to the earth, you who once laid low the nations!" - Isaiah 14:12 (NIV)

Zondervan's senior vice-president and publisher of bibles Chip Brown says about MacArthur's modernist Study Bible:

"He is just unpacking what the text says and how that fits into our lives,"... "in an information age [WWW=666] more readers will be looking for this kind of expertise to accompany their bibles." – Chip Brown

For those people who may not be aware of the fact that each Hebrew letter has a numerical value. The letter 'W' happens to be '6', so even though WWW equals 18 it reads '666'.

I would like to point out that the above verse from the Holy Bible calls those who alter The Holy Bible in any way 'wicked'. Moreover, the context of the word "steadfastness" in this verse clearly commands Christians to be doctrinally sound in the promises of Lord Jesus Christ, not the study bible notes of John McArthur or Rupert Murdoch's NIV.

One of the most glaring anti-Biblical aspects of the NIV and New King James Version (NKJV) Bible which was created in 1983 is they deceive Christians into rebelling against God's command to be divided by truth, rather than be united by error [2 Corinthians 6:14-17]. Here is just one of many examples:

Is Jesus God's "Son" or God's "servant"? In Acts 3:26, the Antichristian Thomas Nelson NKJV calls Jesus God's "Servant." The preserved words of God in the King James Version (KJV) correctly call Him God's "Son." The definitional divide between 'Servant' and 'Son' can be measured in yottameters. Which one is Jesus Christ? Satan knows that if he can deceive man into believing Jesus Christ is God's 'servant' Jesus Christ is marginalized and over time can be relegated to the status of 'Prophet'. However, Christ isn't God's 'servant' Jesus Christ is God's Son, therefore he is exalted above all including the one who wishes to be God [Satan].

243

"All things are delivered unto me of my Father: and no man knoweth the Son, but the Father; neither knoweth any man the Father, save the Son, and he to whomsoever the Son will reveal him." - Matthew 11:27

In order for God's people to be an impenetrable spiritual force capable of defending itself against all of its ancient foes deceptions, it's imperative for Christians to understand the history behind the organizations they support and realize that one should never underestimate the deceptions of Satan and know that he always attacks truth and especially what affects our salvation.

This brings us to origins of the anti-Christ NKJV Bible. The NKJV is in fact the brainchild of a man named Sam Moore [real name Sam Ziady] a 54 year old native of Beirut Lebanon and his 10 year old child, who told his father 'he could not understand the King James Bible'. Describing his upbringing and lifestyle while in Lebanon and prior to becoming a born again Christian at 54 years old, Sam Ziady is quoted as saying:

"I was living for the devil." - Associated Press June 24, 1985

Upon arriving in the United States Sam Ziady began working for CHASE Bank which is owned by the anti-Christian Babylonian Talmudic Freemason David Rockefeller. Keep in mind while you're reading this that David Rockefeller founded International Advisory Committee (IAC) in 1960:

"...the peak body responsible for advising UNESCO on the planning and implementation of the Programme as a whole" - UNESCO Website.

As an aside, members of David Rockefeller's IAC included prominent and respected businessmen from Sam Ziady's native Lebanon. Following his employment at Rockefeller's CHASE Bank, Sam's occupation became that of a door-to-door Bible Salesman where he worked 75 hours a week saving an estimated $2,500. In 1969 [666] Sam had developed a booming business in the heart of the 'Bible Belt' selling King James Holy Bibles, capturing the attention of the world's largest Christian Publisher and distributor of King James Bibles, Thomas Nelson & Sons. During a meeting the 170 year old Scottish Christian publishing company offered Sam a job to head up Thomas Nelson & Sons American Division.

We're told that Sam, who is quoted in a June 24, 1985 AP article that he: "feels more at home with a balance sheet than a religious book", surprised Thomas Nelson & Sons when he counter offered with a buyout offer for Thomas Nelson & Sons American Unit for $2.5 million. Coincidently, Sam Ziady's capital resources included Morrow

244

Graham, mother of Billy Graham who is in fact a client of Sam Ziady's Thomas Nelson Publishing. Taken at face value the investment by Morrow Graham into a Bible manufacturer doesn't seem extraordinary, however, in context with all of the aforesaid and subsequent knowledge, the association is questionable. Suffice it to say this was a surprising revelation as I reflected back on a book that I had read by a man named Jim Shaw, one of the highest ranking Freemasons to have ever defected from the Church of Babylon [Freemasonry] to Christianity. In his book titled: 'The 'Deadly Deception', pg.104, Jim Shaw states Billy Graham took part in Reverend Jim Shaw's 33rd Degree Masonic initiation.

In 1983 Sam Moore, the man whose real last name was Ziady, the man who was once 'living for the devil' in Lebanon, the man who once worked for the anti-Christian Rockefeller Family, and the man who says he is 'more at home with a balance sheet than a religious book' announced that he was investing $4.5 million dollars and seven years to completely change the preserved words of God found inside of the apostolic, Antiochian line that progresses from the Christians at Antioch of Syria to the King James Holy Bible.

"And when he had found him, he brought him unto Antioch. And it came to pass, that a whole year they assembled themselves with the church, and taught much people. And the disciples were called Christians first in Antioch." - Acts 11:26

Why did Sam Ziady relegate Lord Jesus Christ from being the Son of God to a 'servant'? Because God's words confused his 10 years old son. In truth, Sam's investment was the continuation of the Serpent Cult's ancient agenda against Christianity. We begin to see the attacks on Thomas Nelson by Freemasons c.1878, this is when The Church of Babylon burned down the Christian Publishers, "Hope Park Works" in Edinburgh, Scotland with

the intention of destroying all works by writers who espoused an Anti-Serpent Cult message, specifically all evidence of a book titled: 'Legions of Satan' by Scottish born Jonathan William.

Jonathan Williams [left] is one of Christian America's biggest unsung historical figures, primarily because the Church of Babylon has gone to great lengths to delete what he wrote 232 245 years ago. What historians have concealed for centuries is that Williams was a close trusted friend and officer in one of General George Washington's artillery regiments. It's well documented that Washington along with many of his contemporaries were ardent critics of Adam Weishaupt's Illuminati and yet he is promoted in both paintings and literature as being a Satanic Freemason, which begs the question... Was President George Washington truly a Freemason or was he merely painted into historical archives as one by The Church of Babylon to suit their agenda? Also consider the fact that President Washington was bled to death by a Freemason doctor to balance the 'four humors' in Washington's blood. Even more mystifying is the fact that General Washington's wife Martha is on record having owned hundreds of Class A stock in the Bank of England, a financial institution whose capitalization was based on the appropriated wealth of Church of Babylon created "Templar Knights".

Read what President George Washington wrote, thirteen years after the Illuminati had allegedly been outlawed in Bavaria:

"I have heard much of the nefarious, and dangerous plans, and doctrines of the illuminati. It was not my intention to doubt that, the doctrines of the illuminati, and principles of Jacobinism had not spread in the United States. On the contrary, no one is more truly satisfied of this fact than I am. The idea that I meant to convey, was that I do not believe that the lodges of Freemasons in this country had, as societies, endeavored to propagate the diabolical tenets of the first, or pernicious principles of the latter if they are susceptible of separation that individuals of them may have done it, or that the founder or instrument employed to sound, the Democratic societies in the United States, may have had these objects, and actually had a separation of the people from their government in view is too evident to be questioned" – President George Washington, 1797

Flash forward sixteen years after the death of President George Washington to June 19, 1815 the day after Napoleon's defeat at Waterloo. Baron Nathan Rothschild, a self proclaimed direct descendant of the Serpent Tribe of Dann, has incited rumors throughout England's investment community that Napoleon had in fact won the battle at Waterloo. This lie perpetrated by Baron Rothschild allows the Baron to take full control of the Bank of England, the epicenter for International Commerce, ensuring the Rothschild Family's ownership of all future central banks worldwide including the illegally established, unconstitutional Federal Reserve Inc. in America.

246   In his book officer Jonathan Williams writes that he was the man who received General Cornwallis' letter of surrender following Cornwallis defeat to General Washington in Yorktown, Virginia 1781. It was

during this time period that Jonathan Williams wrote his book titled 'Legions of Satan', in it he notes a provocative warning made by General Cornwallis to General Washington. He states:

"A Holy War will now begin on America, and when it is ended America will be supposedly the citadel of freedom, but her millions will unknowingly be loyal subjects to the Crown... Your churches will be used to teach the Jews' [Khazarian Talmudism] religion, and in less than two hundred years the whole nation will be working for divine world government. That government that they believe to be divine will be the British Empire. All religions will be permeated with Judaism [Talmudism] without even being noticed by the masses, and they will all be under the invisible all-seeing eye of the Grand Architect of Freemasonry." - Jonathan Williams, c.1781

To celebrate the destruction of Thomas Nelson's Edinburgh location, Babylonian Talmudist Freemasons erected Freemason stone pillars at the east end of Melville Drive. By the early twentieth century, Thomas Nelson had become thoroughly infected with the Church of Babylon, including a number of esoteric Christian mystics such as Arthur Conan Doyle. American historian of science Richard Milner postulates that Doyle perpetrated the Piltdown Man hoax of 1912, creating the counterfeit hominid fossil that fooled the scientific world for over 40 years and promoted the false religion of evolutionism. What was Doyle's motive? Revenge on the scientific establishment for debunking one of his favorite psychics.

What should concern Christians about the most recent acquisition of Thomas Nelson by Rupert Murdoch's HarperCollins, which distributes Anton LaVey's Satanic Bible, is that it has deceived over 400 million people into buying the aforesaid modernist 'bibles', which drastically change, even delete the messaging found throughout The King James Holy Bible. Moreover, the NIV and New King James Version (NKJV) Bible has deleted nearly 65,000 words found in the King James Bible destroying The Principle of First Mention.

For instance, the King James Bible declares the 'Godhead' three times whereas the NIV Bible has completely deleted 'Godhead'. You'll no longer find the word 'propitiation' in the NIV Bible. As a matter of fact, here is a short list of all the words that no longer exist in the New World Order International One World Religion 'bible': Jesus in 38 locations, Holy Ghost, damnation, brimstone, Jehovah, omnipotent, bottomless pit, Calvary, mercy seat, remission, infallible, immutable, regeneration, quickened, Comforter, trucebreakers, winebibbers, carnal, slothful, unthankful, , backbiting, vanity, and lasciviousness. What's telling is the deletion of the last few words from the NIV Bible.

Reflecting upon what you've learned so far about Planned Parenthood's 1969 memo e.g., increasing homosexuality throughout America, etc. [http://tinyurl.com/homoamerica] and Michael Swift's 1997 Gay Manifesto titled, "Gay Revolution" [**www.gayrevolution.us**], it's unsurprising to learn that Rupert Murdoch's HarperCollins omitted the words: effeminate and sodomite, after all Rupert Murdoch's HarperCollins is the publisher of 'The Joy of Gay Sex'.

Knowing what you now know about The Century City business center containing FOX Headquarters, it should come as no surprise that Rupert Murdoch's HarperCollins has also removed the words: Lucifer, devils, hell in 40 places, whoredom and fornication from their New World Order International One World Religion 'bible'. Why? Because Luciferians do not want their god Lucifer and his legion of demons referenced negatively. In fact Rupert Murdoch is such a good steward, for the father of lies, that he will be airing a series over the FOX network in 2016 devotedly named "Lucifer." The Luciferian NIV bible's most blasphemous omission is in John 3:16 where Jesus is no longer proclaimed as the "only BEGOTTEN Son of God."

When you consider all that you've learned up to this point and couple that with a deal Rupert Murdoch's 20th Century Fox signed with Babylonian Talmudist, Jeffrey Katzenberg's DreamWorks Animation in August 2012, it's not surprising to see such a large volume of pro-Lucifer imagery throughout Hollywood. After all this is the same Jeffrey Katzenberg who was business partners with media mogul David Geffen, who in 1971 was allegedly involved with the CIA's MK-Ultra mind control slave operation in Laurel Canyon. Geffen was also alleged to have played a role in the sacrifice of Scotsman Musician John Lennon and in 1999 was associated with homosexual parties, where teenage boys were sexually abused. Given the company he keeps and his blatant pro-Lucifer views it's not surprising that we find many Antichristian references throughout both Disney and DreamWorks children's films. Allow me to deviate from our current trajectory for a moment to share with you the Antichristian works of Dreamworks Animation.

SATANWORKS

ANIMATION 666

"If the movie works, I don't think it will hurt him. People here will work with the Antichrist if he'll put butts in seats," - John Lesher, agent with Endeavor.

Film producer Jeffrey Katzenberg is the Chief Executive Officer of DreamWorks Animation. It's under the roof of DreamWorks where Katzenberg, David Geffen and Steven Spielberg produce bigoted, blasphemous, anti-Christian heresy. Katzenberg is best known for his period as chairman of Walt Disney Studios [1984-1994].

As an aside Christopher Carradine was vice-president for Walt Disney Imagineering during this same period. There is indisputable evidence that Christopher' father, John Carradine, was associated with Church of Satan's founder Anton Lavey. During Katzenberg's and Carradine's time at Disney, the company produced 'The Little Mermaid', featuring a penis castle and other perverted imagery, 'Beauty and the Beast' which featured a woman flashing satanic devil horns and a number of depraved images, Aladdin and The Lion King, both featuring a number of inappropriate metaphors.

As both founder and CEO of DreamWorks Animation, Jeffrey has overseen the production of Shrek, Madagascar, Kung Fu Panda, Monsters vs. Aliens and How to Train Your Dragon. Given Katzenberg's pervasive anti-Christian track record while at Disney, the following perversions should come as no surprise. DreamWorks most recent version of 'Madagascar 3: Europe's Most Wanted' actor Ben Stiller plays the voice of Alex the lion. While Ben Stiller' character is standing in the Roman Coliseum, he makes the following anti-Christian comment 31min 28sec into the film:

"You know... My ancestors use to perform here... Yeah... Every show had a captive audience... Apparently they killed."

To which the character, Marty the zebra, played by actor/comedian Chris Rock responds... "Sounds like a great gig".

What makes these comments during the film reprehensible is the fact that literally thousands of Christians each day were brutally murdered in the Roman Coliseum, not only by lions, but all types of beasts, during the reign of Emperor Nero. The fact that DreamWorks Films chooses to celebrate and make light of this Christian holocaust is deplorable. Christian's around the world should boycott anything Jeffrey Katzenberg, David Geffen, Steven Spielberg, Ben Stiller and Chris Rock are associated with.

For those people who are unaware, Nero performed the worst atrocities upon Christians, a predictable occupation considering ancient historical records that indicate Nero was a descendant of the Serpent Cult of Dann bloodline dating back to the first century B.C.

249

Atia Balba Secunda [85 BC – 43 BC] was the daughter of Gaius Julius Caesar's sister [Julia Caesaris], the mother of the Emperor Augustus, step-grandmother of the Emperor Tiberius, great-grandmother of the Emperor Claudius, great-great grandmother of the Emperor Caligula and Empress Agrippina the Younger, and great-great-great-grandmother of the Emperor Nero.

Suetonius' account of Augustus describes the impregnation of Augustas' mother by a serpent as well as the occult omens before and after Augustus' birth:

"When Atia had come in the middle of the night to the solemn service of Apollo, she had her litter set down in the temple and fell asleep, while the rest of the matrons also slept. **On a sudden a serpent glided up to her and shortly went away. When she awoke, she purified herself, as if after the embraces of her husband, and at once there appeared on her body a mark in colours like a serpent, and she could never get rid of it; so that presently she ceased ever to go to the public baths. In the tenth month after that Augustus was born and was therefore regarded as the son of Apollo.** Atia too, before she gave him birth, dreamed that her vitals were borne up to the stars and spread over the whole extent of land and sea, while Octavius dreamed that the sun rose from Atia's womb. The day he was born the conspiracy of Catiline was before the House, and Octavius came late because of his wife's confinement; then Publius Nigidius, as everyone knows, learning the reason for his tardiness and being **informed also of the hour of the birth, declared that the ruler of the world had been born**."

It is believed the Apostle Peter was martyred under Nero as well as the Apostle Paul. In 64 A.D. the Roman Emperor Caesar Nero attempted to systematically exterminate all people who professed faith in Jesus Christ. Under Serpent Death Cult rule, Romans witnessed the worst atrocities upon Nero's victims; he did not just kill Christians, he made them suffer extremely. Nero enjoyed dipping Christians in tar or wax, and impaling them on poles around his palace; he would then light them on fire, and yell: "Now you truly are the light of the world."

Nero also performed many other kinds of torture, often killing Christians in the Circus Maximus in front of large crowds of spectators where he did some of his most gruesome murders. Here he would wrap Christians up in animal skins and throw them to lions, or dogs who would then tear these men and women apart in front of thousands of entertained spectators. At other times he would crucify them, and after the crowd would get bored, he would set the Christians on fire.

250

We have no idea how many Christians lost their lives under the Neronian persecution, but Historian Harold Mattingly tells us: "Nero's persecution lasted several years, was not confined to Rome but was practiced throughout the Empire, and cost the lives of a very large number of Christians."

We also know that Nero's policy of persecution was practiced by many subsequent Emperors such as: Domitian, Valerian, and Dioclesian, who instituted the great persecution which would see millions, go through the worst kinds of tortures. One very interesting thing is that those Christians who were Roman Citizens did not face the same terrible death as Christians who were not. The Roman Government, by law, could not torture Roman citizens. Among other diabolical whims, Nero ordered that the city of Rome should be set on fire, which was in fact executed by his officers, guards, and servants. The Roman historian Tacitus, a few years after the event, wrote:

"Consequently, to get rid of the report [that Nero set the fire], Nero fastened the guilt and inflicted the most exquisite tortures on a class hated for their abominations, called Christians by the populace. Christus, from whom the name had its origin, suffered the extreme penalty during the reign of Tiberius at the hands of one of our procurators, Pontius Pilatus... An immense multitude was convicted, not so much of the crime of firing the city, as of hatred against mankind. Mockery of every sort was added to their deaths. Covered with the skins of beasts, they were torn by dogs and perished, or were nailed to crosses, or were doomed to the flames and burnt, to serve as a nightly illumination, when daylight had expired."

Nero was declared a public enemy by the Senate and with mobs coming to kill him; he committed suicide on June 8, 68. His last words were: "What an artist dies in me!"

Nero became one of the many historical figures who, through the use of "secret knowledge," black magic and human sacrifice, was deceived into believing his behavior would create riches and fame. Nero rejected centuries of evidence demonstrating how the father of lies and his fallen angels [demons] exploited God's creation [man/woman] as disposable assets. Once they [demons] no longer had a use for Nero they discarded him and the social experiment which he birthed, in the same way they scrapped the Babylonians, Egyptians, Greeks, Romans and Germans and if it continues on its profane path, America will follow. The good news is, God provides His creation with an easy to follow instruction manual on how to repair a broken Nation and it reads, "If my people, which are called by my name, shall humble themselves, and pray, and seek my face, and turn from their wicked ways; then will I hear from heaven, and will forgive their sin, and will heal their land." - 2 Chronicles 7:14

251

DreamWorks is the creator of the children's film Shrek whose title character is voiced by Scottish/Irish Canadian actor Michael Myers. At 25 minutes 16 seconds into the film Shrek's left hand is contorted into the Satanic 666 hand-sign by DreamWorks programmers. The 666 hand-sign is made by extending three fingers and forming a circle with your remaining fingers, thus creating three sixes, [666]. It symbolizes the unholy trinity e.g., horned God, Goddess, and offspring (anti-Christ).

At 32 minutes 4 seconds into 'Shrek The Third' the young King Arthur's character is featured flashing devil horns to an auditorium full of high school students. At 26 minutes 9 seconds into the film, there are two young boys jumping out of a smoke-filled van, speaking as though they are under the influence of drugs an obvious endorsement of illegal drug use.

"I am the Snake [Satan] that giveth knowledge and delight and bright glory, and stir the hearts of men with drunkenness. To worship me take wine and strange drugs..." – Satanist Aleister Crowley, Book of the Law

DreamWorks 'Shrek The Third' whose main character 'Shrek' is based on the Russian born theosophist Maurice Tillet, is shown 42 minutes 55 seconds into the film, pointing devil horns at the back of the character named "King Arthur." Ancient Celtic chronicles portray Arthur as a descendant of Christian Galatians [Gaul], who received one of Apostle Paul's letters [c.40 AD], and a Gaul military commander who slaughtered demon possessed witches and marauding giants. DreamWorks 'Shrek The Third' at the 57 minutes 20 seconds mark provides its young viewers with the following collection of Antichristian imagery [pg.253]: number 1 is the All-Seeing-Eye of Satan; number 2 "Mead" is an ancient beverage created by those who practiced the Vedic religion; like the

252

Babylonia god Nimrod, their mode of worship was that of fire; number 3 features a witch walking under both logos. All forms of horoscopes, Tarot cards, psychics, palm readings, fortune telling, crystal balls, Ouija boards, astrology, worshipping or contacting the dead (necromancy), witchcraft, magic and sorcery are of Satan. Astrology, fire worship and magic were all promoted by the Babylonian god Nimrod.

"And he caused his children to pass through the fire in the valley of the son of Hinnom: also he observed times, and used enchantments, and used witchcraft, and dealt with a familiar spirit, and with wizards: he wrought much evil in the sight of the LORD, to provoke him to anger."
- 2 Chronicles 33:6

Ever since President Bill Clinton strategically introduced his transgender Presidential advisor to the Nation, the American public has been both covertly and overly indoctrinated into believing a transgender lifestyle is 'normal'. Homosexual and transgender behavior has been considered psychopathological for centuries. The Diagnostic and Statistical Manual of Mental Disorders (DSMMD) once listed homosexual and transgender behavior as 'Psychopathological'. In 1980 a Church of Babylon backed homosexual attorney argued for its removal and won. As of December 1, 2012, a transgender is no longer classified as having a mental disorder.

One of the biggest contradictions in terms is someone who practices 'Christian mysticism' it's second only to the field of 'Christian Psychology' which is the antithesis of Christianity. Why? Because the father of psychology, Wilhelm Maximilian Wundt, was an avowed atheist. Furthermore, his pseudoscience has been the catalyst through which satanic global elites have amassed vast resources with the expressed goal of abolishing Christianity.

Why? So that they can be worshipped like gods. This didn't stop the director of the Society for Christian Psychology from telling the Christian American majority on December 12, 2007:

"if any model of humanity would lead to a compassionate stance towards those with same-sex attraction [Psychopaths], as well as pedophilia [Psychopaths], one would think Christianity would. Gay people deserve our respect and love" - Eric L. Johnson   253

It's New Age Christian Mystics like Eric Johnson who are responsible for the increase in Psychopathological imagery throughout Hollywood and Television. Christians like Mr. Johnson are also the reason why DreamWorks felt it was appropriate to feature this overtly flamboyant gay/transgender character named 'Doris' inside of the children's movie 'Shrek The Third' 34 minutes 7 seconds into the film [left]. It should come as no surprise that the voice of Doris is the anti-Christian Talmudist Larry King. The Christian American majority must realize that they are on the receiving end of the largest 'Psyop' in world history whose ultimate goal is to persuade, influence and change the United States. Wake-up America, silence is acceptance!

"From a medical and scientific perspective there is no such thing as a "transgendered" person. People who identify themselves as "transgendered" are mentally ill or simply unhappy. Hormone therapy and surgery are not appropriate treatments for psychosis or unhappiness. The medical treatment of delusions, psychosis or emotional happiness is not surgery." - Prominent Toronto psychiatrist Dr. Joseph Berger 1/11/2013

The following finds were disappointing considering the association Big Idea, LLC, a.k.a. VeggieTales has with Christianity. The movie titled 'ROBINGOOD and His Not-So-Merry Men" 8min 41sec into the DVD contains a winged solar disk on the refrigerator [pg.255, top]. In addition to its association with Babylonian gods, the winged solar disc is a form the Egyptian god Horus took into battle with Seth. Furthermore, the tiles on the kitchen wall contain the "Mark of The Beast" [666] in a number of places [pg.255, center].

The Mark of the Beast [666] also appears 19min 28sec into "Merry Larry and the True Light of Christmas" [pg.255, bottom] a VeggieTales DVD featuring the voice of Scottish American "Si" Robertson of Duck Dynasty fame. Some will argue this is the ancient Celtic "Triple Spiral" which I demonstrated [pg.141-142] is also associated with the Serpent Cult of Dann.

254 What is most unique about this particular Veggie Tales character, are its design elements, specifically the lime green and dark emerald green colors used to accentuate the "666."

Within the CIA's "MK-Ultra" Monarch mind control slave program the color code light green is associated with the gods and goddess alters which are triads which function in Illuminati ceremonies, whereas the dark emerald green color code is assigned with the Antichrist-Satan alter(s). Green is the occult color for Satan and happens to be the most sacred color. Few people outside of Satanists know that green is more sacred for them than any other color.

"Nazi SS officer, Joseph Mengele, and the programmers who worked with and under him, used a large dollhouse with 26 rooms. Each of the rooms were painted with one of the 13 different programming colors in order to build into the child's mind, the 13 front and 13 back personalities. During the programming a black box with needles and wires which attach to the body for electroshock is used. While electro shocking the victim, colored scarf's coming out of a box are shown to the child... The memory storage area for the computers [personalities] include the Emerald City Library... In line with what is being done by the Illuminati around the world with their network of computers—the computers have access codes similar to 666 666 666, and back out and close down similar to 999 999 999. These are the codes that the UNIX universal system uses and the Monarch slaves are being created with codes that interface with the

255

UNIX system for computers… The UNIX system is being used to allow the New World Order's big BEAST computers to communicate with any known computer, including the minds of their Monarch mind-controlled slaves." – "The Illuminati Formula to Create an Undetectable Total Mind Control Slave, Chapter 11, Internal Controls, by Fritz Springmeier & Cisco Wheeler

9min 10sec into the VeggiesTales movie, 'Veggies In Space The Fennel Frontier' features a flag containing the planet Saturn [bottom]. Saturn in old Latin is the same word as Satan. The flag is also an abstract modification of the Babylonian god of the moon 'Sin'.

Like Rat Poison, whose active ingredient is only .005%, a few blasphemous story lines or visuals inside a body of work whose content is largely positive, can be highly toxic to the minds of our children. Parents must be mindful of the subliminal messaging in VeggieTales, especially now that Big Idea's parent company, Classic Media, was acquired by Babylonian Talmudists Jeffrey Katzenberg, David Geffen and Steven Spielberg and their DreamWorks Animation on July 2012.

Returning back to our examination of Rupert Murdoch's Antichristian "bible", I would like to share with readers what the Holy Bible states, regarding anyone who alters its text.

"For I testify unto every man that heareth the words of the prophecy of this book, If any man shall add unto these things, God shall add unto him the plagues that are written in this book:" - Revelation 22:18

If people are to live for God, then they need every word provided to them by God, not the study bible notes of John McArthur or Rupert Murdoch's NIV. What's telling about John MacArthur is how he describes himself as being a Cessationist e.g., someone who believes God no longer provides his followers with divine guidance, miracles, etc. because that guidance or miracle may accredit new doctrine or add to the New Testament canon. What do you call it when a man pride fully suggests that he knows what God is really trying to say through his MacArthur Study Bible notes? Isn't creating a 'study bible' with notes accrediting new doctrine? Furthermore, MacArthur subscribes to the pre-tribulation rapture which is a late 19th century invention by New Age Theosophist Cyrus Scofield.

Many Christians may be unaware of the fact that Cyrus Scofield was the inventor of his own modernist bible named the Scofield Reference Bible. Moreover, Scofield was a questionable lawyer funded by New York Babylonian Talmudists.

NOTE: Watch the video titled: "After The Tribulation" and "Marching to Zion" by Pastor Steven Anderson at: **www.marchingtozion.com**

What is most concerning about Rupert Murdoch's golden boy MacArthur is his proclivity towards fulfilling all the covenant promises made to the "Jews". The question the Christian Majority should be asking itself is… Which 'Jews' is McArthur referring to? Is he referring to the Jews of The Holy Bible who doggedly adhere to God's Holy Torah or is he naively championing the Babylonian Talmudists wrapped in a Torah? If McArthur chooses to enrich those who worship satanic alters to the Babylonian god Nimrod and the satanic red shield of Rothschild. If McArthur chooses to champion the efforts of men and women who worship the tabernacle of Moloch and whose stated goal it is to eliminate Christianity… If McArthur remains complicit in the scheme to march the Christian American majority one step closer to creating a Christian version of the Anti-Torah Talmud, just as the Pharisees and proponents of the Church of Babylon have done to Judaic people, then I can only surmise that his intentions are to expand Rupert Murdoch's anti-Christian Empire and its obvious goal of distancing Christians from the true word of Lord Jesus Christ.

"Yea, ye took up the tabernacle of Moloch, and the star of your god Remphan, figures which ye made to worship them: and I will carry you away beyond Babylon." - Acts 7:43

It's worth mentioning that Anti-Christian, Arab Prince, Alwaleed bin Talal, who is a "Donmeh" Crypto-Jew Muslim, is the second-largest voting shareholder in News Corp., [19.9%] after the Murdoch family and one of the largest shareholders in Citigroup a bank that in 2009 sold 36% of its equity to the U.S. Government and where Zambian-American-Israeli economist Stanley Fischer left to head up Israel's central bank of Rothschild. Prince Alwaleed is also one of the largest shareholders in the Walt Disney Corp. Why is Prince Alwaleed relevant? Because the Saudi minister of education Prince Faisal Bin Abdullah Bin Muhammad al-Saud and Prince Alwaleed are King Abdullah's nephews. The education minister has publicly acknowledged that reform of grade 1-12 textbooks is needed however it was not a government priority. The type of information found inside Saudi Government funded textbooks deemed insignificant to the Saudi Government include:

257

"The Jews and the Christians are enemies of the believers [Muslims], and they cannot approve of Muslims."

"The struggle of this [Muslim] nation with the Jews and Christians has endured, and it will continue as long as God wills."

"As was cited in Ibn Abbas, and was said: The Apes are the people of the Sabbath, the Jews; and the Swine are the infidels of the communion of Jesus, the Christians."

Prior to Rupert Murdoch's acquisition of Scottish Christian Book Publisher Thomas Nelson for $200 million in 2011, the private equity firm InterMedia paid $473 million for Thomas Nelson in 2006. Aside from what appears to be the intentional $273 million dollar devaluation of one of the largest Christian Book Publishers in the world... The resume of Intermedia's CEO Leo Hindery provides the Christian American majority with a profile which is the antithesis of someone friendly to Christianity. For instance, Hindery is Director of the Library of Congress aside Dr. James Hadley Billington. In short Billington is an anti-Christian, anti-American, pro-communist sympathizer who has been honored with multiple awards by the Communist Russian Government. As a matter of fact, Billington was awarded the Order of Friendship by the President of the Russian Federation Dmitry Medvedev in 2008, the highest state order that a foreign citizen may receive. Like Ronald Reagan, the Bush family, the Clintons and Obama, Medvedev supported the creation of an anti-Christian New World Order. Medvedev was not only a proponent of the New World Order he envisioned Russia being a 'cofounder':

"...We are living in a unique time. And we should use it to build a modern, flourishing and strong Russia ... which will be a cofounder of the new world economic order." – Dmitry Medvedev, June 18, 2010

I address Dr. James Hadley Billington in subsequent chapters and detail his cadre of atheists and anti-Christian associations. The proceeding data on the good Dr. should make the Christian American majority very nervous. For example, I show how Dr. Hadley is associated with 'UNESCO', a group which is controlled by David Rockefeller, a former employer of Sam Ziady, one of Thomas Nelson's previous owners. The massive red flag in Leo Hindery's resume, however, is the fact that the man who purchased one of the world's largest Christian book publishers is a member of the Council on Foreign Relations (CFR). I've cited many of CFR's more infamous New World Order quotes and members in subsequent chapters; however, for those Christians who are unfamiliar with CFR, here is a condensed overview. CFR was founded on July 29, 1921, in New York City by Church of Babylon member Col. Edward Mandell House, chief adviser to President Woodrow, Wilson, the same President who allowed the Rothschilds, Rockefellers and Morgans to create the unconstitutional Federal Reserve Bank Inc. Self avowed communist, Col. Edward Mandell Haus played a major role in a conspiracy to gain control of both the Republican and Democratic parties with the stated goal of using them as instruments to create a One World Government. Since its creation, nearly 80 percent of their memberships have been anti-Christian Babylonian Talmudist Freemasons.

In summation, the Corporate Headquarters of one of the world's richest men [Rupert Murdoch] and the property owner of one of America's oldest and largest Corporations [Alcoa] resides inside of a business park which contains a massive all-seeing-eye, which pays homage to Satan. Moreover, this giant alter to Satan is flanked by two pyramid shaped buildings that when combined create a massive satanic Rothschild hexagram which contain 'mark of the beast' dimensions e.g., 6 points, 6 small inner pyramids and 6 total sides [666], these same dimensions exist in Alcoa's Corporate logo. Furthermore, Murdoch is the publisher of "The Satanic Bible" and "The Satanic Rituals - Companion to The Satanic Bible" by Church of Satan founder Anton Lavey. In addition, Murdoch's company also publishes the anti-Christian book titled 'The Joy of Gay Sex', all the while controlling 50% of the Christian publishing market, e.g., The Holy Bible, Christian Authors, Christian live events, etc. Moreover, the second largest shareholder in Murdoch's company is an Arab Prince whose government prints anti-Christian, anti-Jewish educational materials, and yet Rupert Murdoch is a major shareholder in Genie Israel Holdings, Ltd., along with anti-Christian Satanist Lord Jacob Rothschild, whose Israeli General Chairman wants to kill all of the Palestinian people using the likes of veteran special operators such as Babylonian Talmudist Aaron Cohen, founder of Israeli Military Specialists (IMS) Security. When he's not capturing and killing Palestinian militants in the West Bank, Cohen oversees the only private security firm in America specializing in Israeli-style protection to Corporate America and Hollywood. Employing a staff of 22, Cohen rotates in new Rothschild owned and controlled Talmudic special forces every 1 1/2-2 years to guard the likes of Brad Pitt, Eva Longoria and Jackie Chan. In addition to making a lucrative career in the United States, Cohen also works abroad neutralizing targets which pose a threat to Satanic Rothschild Family assets and associated proxies. Cohen recently began soliciting money on the crowd-funding website indiegogo to fund 'The Counter Terror Project - Kenya' a response to the September 21, 2013 attacks against the Rothschild owned mall in Nairobi, Kenya. President Obama's make believe homeland.

If that's not convoluted enough, Murdoch's second largest shareholder, Prince Alwaleed bin Talal's family's wealth is based on 259 the dissolution of John D. Rockefeller's Standard Oil Trust by the

U.S. government in 1911. Following the dissolution, Rockefeller shared his proprietary oil drilling techniques with the Saudi government creating Aramco in 1921 and by 1980 the Rockefellers had liquidated 100% of their equity in Aramco to the Saudi Arabian government, while maintaining complete control of the company. Remember John D. Rockefeller's principle Golden Rule: "Own nothing, but control everything." The most thorough explanation of the Rockefeller's Standard Oil Company was written by Ms. Ida M. Tarbell in her book titled: "The History of The Standard Oil Company" (2 Volumes in 1).

Irish American Bill O'Reilly is a host for Rupert Murdoch's Fox News and one of Murdoch's highest-rated assets, with an estimated 3.206 million total viewers, earning O'Reilly a personal income of over $20 million a year. On September 24, 2013 O'Reilly released his book 'Killing Jesus: A History' which O'Reilly suggests one evening he was directed by the 'Holy Spirit' to write. My question is... Who was O'Reilly's 'Holy Spirit'? "And no marvel; for Satan himself is transformed into an angel of light." [2 Corinthians 11:14]. Before Bill O'Reilly invokes the 'Holy Spirit', as his source of inspiration, he should first educate himself about the true origins of this term 'Holy Spirit'. In the 1940s the freemason controlled Vatican deleted the last name from the Holy Trinity, that of God the Father, the Holy Ghost. During World War II, Saint Lucia warned: "It is with a certain trepidation because if you despise and reject this ultimate means, we will not have any more forgiveness from Heaven, because we will have committed a sin which the Gospel calls the sin against the Holy Ghost. This sin consists of openly rejecting, with full knowledge and consent, the salvation which He offers." - Sister Lúcia Santos, 1957

"But he that shall blaspheme against the Holy Ghost hath never forgiveness, but is in danger of eternal damnation:" - Mark 3:29 (KJV).

Like Rupert Murdoch's NIV and NKJV Bible, O'Reilly's 'Killing Jesus' is fraught with anti-biblical sentiment, leaving me to believe that O'Reilly is woefully inept with regards to the scores of esoteric Christian mystics and Satanists, who over the years have made similar claims prior to wailing in torment throughout the night, consumed by demons to which they succumb. Such was the case with Emanuel Swedenborg, Poet William Blake, Oscar Wilde, Helena Blavatsky, Aleister Crowley, Anton Lavey, and Adolf Hitler. Consider the following statement made by the inventor of Satanic Theosophy [Helena Blavatsky] who said:

"I am here in this country [America] sent by my Lodge [Church of Babylon] on behalf of Truth [Satan] in modern spiritualism, and it is my most sacred duty to unveil what is, and expose what is not."

The Holy Bible, according to Bill O'Reilly ['Killing Jesus'], is an esoteric version of the truth, and like his Church of Babylon predecessors, I believe O'Reilly's texts seek to marginalize facts surrounding Jesus Christ's life and message. How? By omitting crucial text, questioning the accounts made by Jesus Christ's contemporaries and categorizing Jesus Christ as a mere 'Man', a mortal historical figure, not the Messiah or Son of God, a title He is respectfully owed but not given. Reflecting back on all that I've shared with you regarding Rupert Murdoch's HarperCollins, I invite you to analyze O'Reilly's subsequent statements in context with Murdoch's transgressions. In doing so, I believe you will see that 'Killing Jesus' is in no way inspired by the 'Holy Ghost' of The Holy Bible. Case in point, O'Reilly omits the most famous statement made by Jesus Christ while on the cross, namely "Then said Jesus, Father, forgive them; for they know not what they do." [St. Luke 23:34]. Why? O'Reilly states:

"Because you couldn't say something like that, audibly that people would hear. He, you die on a cross from being suffocated. That your lungs can't take in anymore air. You can hardly breathe. We believe Jesus said that, but we don't believe he said it on the cross, 'cause nobody could've heard it... Well you believe what you want. If you want to take the Bible literally, then that's your right to do that." - Bill O'Reilly, 60 Minutes interview with Norah O'Donnell 9/29/2013

O'Reilly posits his esoteric Bible, according to Bill, was in part inspired by historical accounts found throughout Muslim sources, Roman sources, and Jewish sources. Which 'Jewish sources' is he referring to? The Holy Torah [Old Testament] or the Pharisee created anti-Christian Talmudic text which states: Talmud, Gittin 57a - Jesus is in hell where he is boiling in hot urine.

Lastly, what 'Muslim sources' would O'Reilly be referring to when he pontificates about Jesus Christ's final Message while nailed to the cross? Islam didn't exist until c.632 AD, nearly 600 after Jesus Christ's crucifixion. What's more, Muslims believe Jesus Christ was a mere 'Prophet', they do not recognize [King James Version]: Matthew 16:16; Matthew 26:63; Mark 1:1; Luke 4:41; Luke 11:17; John 6:69; John 11:27; John 20:31; Acts 8:37; Acts 9:20; 1 Corinthians 1:9; 2 Corinthians 1:19; Galatians 2:20; Galatians 4:7; Ephesians 4:13; 1 John 5:20; 2 John 1:3; 2 John 1:9, which all state Jesus Christ is 'The Son of God'. When O'Reilly claims that he referenced 'Muslim sources' it makes him seem like nothing more than a religious and political carpetbagger. I find O'Reilly's claims puerile, shallow, and Incredulous. This however, is a recurring theme throughout O'Reilly's work.

Take for instance an interview between Bill O'Reilly and Russell Simmons, Cofounder of 'Def Jam' and proponent of Transcendental Meditation ['TM'] 3/10/2014.

Simmons: "I want to put meditation in schools".

Bill O'Reilly: "I agree with you on that and I support the David Lynch Foundation, which does just that".

Simmons: "I'm on the board".

O'Reilly: "And I give you a ton of money".

O'Reilly then asks Simmons his opinion on 'forcing' children to participate in 'TM' in schools to which Simmons responds:

Simmons: "There is no religious... Or any kind of agenda that should separate you from any religious ideas".

Christians should be aware of the fact that The David Lynch foundation teaches children the religion of Transcendental Meditation ['TM'] a.k.a. The 'Science of Creative Intelligence', as promoted by Yogi Maharishi Mahesh, in U.S. public schools where Christian prayer is not allowed. What Bill O'Reilly has failed to mention to his Christian viewers is that he is investing "a ton of money" in Antichristian 'New-Age' concepts which are firmly rooted in Hindu principles and practices which contradict The Holy Bible. Christians must understand that performing any mental or physical techniques, religious or health protocols which invoke the idea that you are 'God' is blasphemous... "...and ye shall be as gods" - Satan, Genesis 3:5. Yet this is a fundamental concept of Hinduism and the theory on which Yogi Mahesh' TM is based.

"Malnak v. Maharishi Mahesh Yogi. The 'Science of Creative Intelligence - Transcendental Meditation' was 'religious in nature'..." - Harvard Journal of Law and Public Policy.

"Under the most recent Supreme Court pronouncement in this area, Committee for Public Education v. Nyquist, 413 U.S. 756, 773, 93 S.Ct. 2955, 37L.Ed.2d 948 (1973), the Court reiterated the three criteria within which to scrutinize the involved governmental action. To pass muster, the action in question must: (1) reflect a clearly secular legislative purpose; (2) have a primary effect that neither advances nor inhibits religion; and (3) avoid excessive government entanglement with religion. The district court applied the Nyquist test and determined that the SCI/TM course has a primary effect of advancing religion and religious concepts, School District of Abington Township v. Schempp, 374 U.S. 203, 83 S.Ct.

262

1560, 10 L.Ed.2d 844 (1963); Engel v. Vitale, 370 U.S. 421, 82 S.Ct. 1261, 8 L.Ed.2d 601 (1962), and that the government aid given to teach the course and the use of public school facilities constituted excessive governmental entanglement with religion. Lemon v. Kurtzman, 403 U.S. 602, 91 S.Ct. 2105, 29 L.Ed.2d 745 (1971). – Malnak v. Yogi.

"Essential to the practice of Transcendental Meditation is the "mantra"; a mantra is a sound aid used while meditating… a meditator must attend a ceremony called a "puja." During the puja the student stood or sat in front of a table while the teacher sang a chant and made offerings to a deified "Guru Dev"… the chant invoke the deified teach, who also was a Hindu monk, of Maharishi Mahesh Yogi. – Malnak v. Yogi

"Once SCI/TM is found to be a religion, the establishment resulting from direct government support of that religion through the propagation of its religious ideas in the public school system is clear. Whatever its merits the program under consideration here, endorsed, as it is, by the State of New Jersey and the Department of Health, Education and Welfare, is forbidden by the first amendment. As such, it cannot stand." – Malnak v. Yogi

President of Fox News and Chairman of Fox Television [Roger Ailes] recently announced his desire to create a "history channel" along with Bill O'Reilly that would teach our children "the real stuff". After reading the previous twelve pages would you trust Rupert Murdoch, Arab Prince Talal, Roger Ailes and Bill O'Reilly to educate our Christian American children about history? Before you answer that question, consider the fact that the Satanic Babylonian Talmud based Kabbalistic numbering system known as gematria (10-220 A.D.) associates a number with every letter of the alphabet. For example 1=a,j,s; 2=b,k,t; 3=c,l,u; 4=d,m,v; 5=e,n,w; 6=f,o,x; 7g,p,y; 8=h,q,z; 9=i,r. Notice that Rupert Murdoch chose to name his empire 'FOX' and based on the ancient Babylonian numbering system FOX has a value of 666. Additional Church of Babylon holdings associated with the value 666 include: eXXOn, XbOX, etc. and according to ethnomathematician Claudia Zaslavsky's book 'Tic Tac Toe' the pencil game played by young children with the goal of placing 3 X's (666) horizontally or vertically 'could originate back to ancient Egypt'.

Given the Church of Babylon's stated goal of murdering all, "Goyim" it's predictable that we would find a smorgasbord of Khazarian Bablyonian Talmudists spewing militant Antichristian hate speech with no resistance from Talmudist owned media outlets. For instance in 2006 comedian, Sarah Silverman released a movie titled, "Jesus is Magic," where she stated:

"Good! I hope the Jews did kill Christ, I'd do it again. I'd Fucking   263
do it again in a second!"

Silverman, [left] is pictured holding a board containing the image of Jesus Christ, is featured regularly on the cable channel "Comedy Central". In addition to the image of Christ on the cross there are some articles of clothing. These include a Satan outfit, women's clothing, etc. The inference here is that Lord Jesus Christ is gay and/ or Satan. This picture echoes what is taught in the racist, Pharisee created, Antigoyimite Babylonian Talmud about Jesus Christ and his followers. Other militant Antigoyimite comics on Comedy Central include Jonathan Stuart Leibowitz (Jon Stewart - The Daily Show) who referred to the nativity as the "Vagina Manger". Leibowitz then refers to Jesus' mother as the "Vagina Mary". Comic Kathy Griffin, while receiving an Emmy Award, Pompously stated "Suck it, Jesus! This award is my god now."

As an aside, Comedy Central is owned by Babylonian Talmudist Sumner Redstone [Rothstein]. Redstone also controls CBS Corporation, Viacom, Paramount Pictures, Simon & Schuster, MTV, VH1, TV Land, Nickelodeon, Nick Jr., Nicktoons, TeenNick, Nick and Nick at Nite.

Redstone's Nickelodeon aired an episode on 3/5/2015 of the animated series "Oggy and the Cockroaches". During this episode an image of a topless woman sunbathing is shown to children [above].

Featuring lewd imagery to our children is no accident, after all the Babylonian Talmud teaches its adherents that, "All gentile [Christian] children are animals" [Talmud, Yebamoth 98a] and "Gentile girls are in a state of niddah (filth) from birth. Christian women are regarded as slaves, heathen and whores." [Talmud, Abodah Zarah 36b].

The main attraction for members of the Church of Babylon e.g., Serpent Death Cult, Masonic Babylonian Talmudists, Satanism, etc. is that as a member you are promised the secret of immortality. What is this secret? It's that immortality is conveyed through tantric sex-magic and the kind of sex-magic that's required to achieve immortality is the brutal violation of a small child mentally and physically, otherwise known as, "Transuguthian Magic" which is magic that goes into transplutonian space.

"A white male child of perfect innocence and intelligence makes the most suitable victim." – Satanist Aleister Crowley

They believe that every time they defile an innocent little child they steal that child's youth. They believe that this allows them to access alternate Universes whereby they become "… as gods." [Genesis 3:5]. Satanists like Sumner Redstone [Rothstein] endorse this ideology every time they broadcast sexually charged imagines and distribute spiritually toxic merchandise to small children. What the above-mentioned reveals is that Sumner Redstone [Rothstein] is a practitioner of vampirizing little children sexually participates in the worship of the brother of the Ancient Serpent and the Light bearer.

"… Satan is not a Person, but a Force, created for good, but which may represent evil. It is the instrument of Liberty or Free Will. They represent this Force… under the mythologic and horned form of the God Pan; thence came the he-goat of the Sabbat, brother of the Ancient Serpent, and the Light-bearer…" – Albert Pike, Morals and Dogma

The following is an example of how Sumner Redstone [Rothstein] is waging psychological warfare against our children through the creation of toys meant to psychologically, emotionally and intellectually manipulate them into a state of mind which is causing them to disconnect from God as well as lose their human qualities and freedom of mind without even being aware that's it happening. The most effective way of protecting yourself and your children from what I refer to as, "human exploitation psychology" is to understand that what the conscious mind believes the subconscious acts on. Just like with a computer program when a user inputs date into an application and hits 'enter' the computer executes the command. However if the data fed into the computer is corrupted or wrong the computer still acts upon the incorrect data. Likewise if a person believes something that's not true the subconscious mind does not correct the error but acts on it. Repetition is one of the simplest ways to convince children into doing something. When they hear or see something multiple times, they tend to believe what they see and hear more. Whatever this 265 object of statement is becomes familiar and safe even though what they're seeing and hearing is anything but. Repetition of an audible or visual message convinces children into carrying out what they're seeing and hearing regardless of whether or not what they're considering is logical. What's more programming our children is made easier if the visual or audible message is simpler in nature rather than complex, if the truth is more complex the human mind will gravitate towards an easier explanation.

When it comes to the confusion, disorganization and degradation of our children no other form of programming is more popular than the entertainment, fashion and music industry's. Here sexual promiscuity, lack of self control, violence, death and homosexuality is rampant. An example of how Sumner Redstone [Rothstein] uses seemingly innocuous children's toys to create a toxic cult of personality let's examine the follow children's toy which covertly leverages human exploitation psychology through effigy's and cleverly stylized iconography.

sumner rothstein's
GOYIM SUICIDE SEWER
TURTLES

fig.1

The packaging for Sumner Redstone', "nickelodeon TEENAGE MUTANT NINJA TURTLES," states that these products are meant for "AGES 4+" and that purchasers are cautioned "WARNING CHOKING HAZARD – Small parts not for Children under 3 years." The twisted insincerity of this warning is that inside of nickelodeon's 4+ children's product titled "TEENAGE MUTANT NINJA TURTLES SECRET SEWER LAIR PLAY SET,"exists an effigy of a figure hanging from a rope with five stab wounds in the chest cavity [fig1] and a trash can play area [fig2, pg.266]. Why a trash can? Because Khazarian Babylonian Talmudists believe your "Goyim" boys are "animals"and your little daughters "Shiksa" [whores] are "in a state of niddah (filth) from birth" so what better play set for Goyim children than

fig.2

fig.3

fig.4

fig.5

a Ninja Turtle 'SEWER', Trash can and hanging corpse.

The above-mentioned is a textbook example of how The Church of Babylon is leveraging human exploitation psychology to visually stimulate your 4 year old child's conscious mind so that later in life his/her subconscious mind will not hesitate on executing the act of suicide and because your child was just 4 years old and playing with this safe and familiar image at the time he/she was effectively programmed to believe that the act of suicide is familiar and safe. The wickedness of Sumner Redstone's effigy doesn't stop there. When one studies the face on this hanging corpse they will notice that it contains the universally excepted symbol of death e.g., two X's where the eyes should be, illustrating this individual is dead. It will be remembered that the origins of the 'XX' mark is satanic in nature and misunderstood by the vast majority of Americans including most if not all church leaders.

It is most important that the reader should have a clear idea of what this mark means, and as it is rather a difficult point to explain accurately, I must ask the reader to give me his/her best attention; and I cannot refrain from adding the hope that if the reader succeeds in mastering the explanation of this mark, the reader will abstain from glorifying it in the future. Most people know that the Roman Numeral 'X', represents the number 267 ten however many will be surprised to learn that the Roman Numeral X also represents the word 'IO' (pronounced EO) and in Greek the word 'IO' means Helios or Apollyon otherwise known as The Beast from the pit [Revelation 9:11].

In addition to being associated with Apollyon, the 'X' or 'IO' is linked to Serpent Death Cult of Dann as well as the god of Babylonian Talmudists, "Nimrod." Nimrod [Hebrew for "we will rebel"] was worshipped like a god and constructed the Tower of Babel with the intention of eliminating God. Like Satan, The Serpent Cult of Dann and Nimrod rebelled against the will of God and beguiled men into a satanic religious order that insidiously controlled their minds. Nimrod promoted diverse and erratic superstitions and led his followers to be governed by the signs in the stars. Nimrod was eventually smote by God circa 2200 B.C. and all those who worshipped him were divided into 70 different Nations, all speaking in different tongues. Nimrod is the fountainhead from which the Sumerians Marduk and Gilgamesh, the Greeks Apollo the Egyptians Osiris, The Babylonian Talmud, Kabbalism, Freemasonry and satanic theosophy all sprung.

"And Cush begat Nimrod: he began to be a mighty one in the earth. He was a mighty hunter before the LORD: wherefore it is said, Even as Nimrod the mighty hunter before the LORD. And the beginning of his kingdom was Babel, and Erech, and Accad, and Calneh, in the land of Shinar." - Genesis 10:8-10

The 'XX' placed on Sumner Redstone's nickelodeon effigy also means to double-cross or betray. Fundamentally speaking it indicates one's willingness to betray on behalf of Satan. When individuals, companies, corporations, etc. feature the 'XX' on their person, in their logo or on their products they are invoking satanic energy. For instance, the members of the Rockefeller Family are fully aware of the 'XX' meaning that is why the family of Standard Oil fame named their Corporation "Exxon". The Thule Society also featured the double-cross [XX] inside their logo. This was a German occultist group which was later reorganized by Adolf Hitler into the Nazi Party.

Within the "Teenage Mutant Ninja Turtles Secret Sewer Lair Play Set" there is a sticker set which contains a number of satanic icons for instance, "Antonios' Pizza-Rama" [fig.3, pg.265] features a man showing only one eye an overt symbol for the global death cult 'The Illuminati' in addition this character is holding up the satanic 'OK' hand-sign which is made by extending three fingers and forming a circle with your remaining fingers, this creates three six's, [666]. To Satanists this symbolizes the unholy trinity e.g., horned God, Goddess, and offspring (anti-Christ). In other words this product, being offered to 4 year old children, is subconsciously indoctrinating these young people into accepting the,

"Mark of The Beast", [666] so that when The Antichrist reveals himself they will be familiar with his mark and feel safe even though what he'll be offering is anything but safe. Additional images within the sticker pack include a little boy whose shadow is that of a Devil along with the number 13 [fig.4, pg.265] and a women's severed head [fig.5, pg.265].

When you pay $78.99 for Sumner Redstone's "Teenage Mutant Ninja Turtles Secret Sewer Lair Play Set" or $39.96 for a Teenage Mutant Ninja Turtles: Danger of the Ooze video game, etc. you are in fact enriching and strengthening Corporations and Company's whose business owners belong to the Church of Babylon.

With the stated goal of sexualizing preteen Goyim, Sumner Redstone's Nickelodeon hired porn film writer/director, Irish/African American Jonathan Butler [1/17/2015] to produce the popular teen sitcom, "Bella and the Bulldogs." Butler's production company, "Mythological Beast" logo features a Minotaur, the legendary child-eating beast, born of a woman and a bull. The bull here also represents the Babylonian demon god Ashur who also symbolizes the goat gods such as Pan. The porn film Butler produced, prior to creating Bella and the Bulldogs, was named "The Cuckold" which refers to an adult sex fetish where mentally unstable husbands watch their depraved wives having sex with other men. Butler's film features a black man, known in the "Cuckold" fetish subculture as a "Bull," having sex with white married women. Many of the same sadomasochistic sex rituals featured in Butler's adult porn film were sneakily injected into his teenage sitcom Bella and the Bulldogs. For instance the dominant black teen football player [Troy Dixon] wins the affection of the strong, white, blonde, female character [Bella] over Troy's weak, emasculated white male rival [Newt]. Bella is featured in one episode blindfolded, in a candle lit basement, while Troy stands behind her wearing a bull horned helmet on his head. Around Bella's neck are two key's a larger black key and a smaller white key. While in the dark basement Troy directs Bella over to a bull and orders her to slap it. Both keys and blindfolds are accessories in the "Cuckold" fetish. Butler then features an adult black man standing behind the teen Bella and behind the adult male is a poster of a white baby, crying, with a large red "X" over the infant. Butler and Redstone's child porn "Bella and the Bulldog" is clearly a manifestation of Rabbi Rabinovich's 1/12/1952 Council of European Rabbis racist hate speech in Budapest Hungry, where he declared:

"I can state with assurance that the last generation of white children is now being born. Forbid the Whites to mate with Whites. The White Women must cohabit with members of the dark races, the White Men with black women. Thus the White Race will disappear, for the mixing of the dark with the White means the end of the White Man, and our

269

most dangerous enemy will become only a memory. We shall embark upon an era of ten thousand years of peace and plenty, the Pax Judaica, and our race will rule undisputed over the world. Our superior intelligence will easily enable us to retain mastery over a world of dark peoples."

Sumner Rothstein isn't the only Babylonian Talmudist peddling human exploitation psychology to young children under the guise of innocent fun. Rothstein isn't the only Talmudist associating our children with a sewer system either. In 2015 the Cartoon Network endorsed a video game titled, "The Amazing World of Gumball: Sewer Sweater Search Game." It will be remembered that the Babylonian Talmud teaches "Jesus is in hell where he is boiling in hot excrement." [Talmud, Gittin 57a]. Given the fact that nearly 80% of the U.S. identify themselves as followers of Jesus Christ; Talmudists uses these thinly veiled sacrileges to degrade the sanctity of Jesus Christ in the minds of Christian children.

The Founder of "Cartoon Network," Betty Cohen [1992-1997] fashioned her Cartoon Network identity after the Masonic Babylonian black and white checkerboard which to Masonic Babylonians symbolizes duality and has been used for generations by the CIA's "MK-Ultra" mind control slave program. Satanist Aleister Crowley used the checkerboard symbolism for human and animal sacrifice rituals. Like other Masonic Babylonian symbolism the checkerboard represents one eye shut and one open [all-seeing-eye] in short this represents the all-seeing-eye of Satan. Under her leadership at Cartoon Network, Betty Cohen, "greenlit" [endorsed] cartoons such as, Grim & Evil" which featured two young children [Billy and Mandy] who according to cartoon network wiki, befriend the Grim Reaper and "venture into supernatural locations or environments, such as the underworld, inhabited by an assortment of grotesque monstrous beasts." Cohen's Cartoon Network helped launch the career of Scottish/Irish American Seth MacFarlane who is descended from the ancient Christian Chief Allan [Clan Allan], son of Farlane in Aberdeenshire [9th century AD]. Seth is also the creator of The Family Guy, American Dad! and The Cleveland Show. MacFarlane's militant Antichristian "Family Guy" cartoon is notorious for projecting hedonistic, satanic, imagery associated with Masonic Babylonian Talmudism and predictive programming. For example MacFarlane features God inside of the Garden of Eden with pornography behind the tree of knowledge. MacFarlane also features a stereotypical image of Jesus Christ as a magician while flashing the 666 hand-sign with his arms in a "V" formation [pg.271]. The "V" sign represents Adam Weishaupt's Illuminati and the "Law of Fives." What's more the Hebrew letter for V (Van) is "Nail" which is one of the secret titles of Satan within the brotherhood of Satanism. The "V" also symbolizes the pentagram and the five-fold salute used in Masonry and Witchcraft.

The "V" sign also signifies the Vulcan sun deity who was associated with fire, thunderbolts and light. The Vulcan deity was made popular during the original Star Trek series 1966-1969 [666 x2. The creator of Star Trek, Gene Roddenberry, was both a Babylonian Talmudist [mother, Caroline Goleman] and 33rd degree Scottish-Rite Freemason. Babylonian Talmudist, Leonard Nimoy, played the half-Vulcan character, "Mr. Spock," on the original Star Trek television series where he devised the "Vulcan Salute" hand-sign which is a "V" representing the Hebrew letter for V (Van) or "Nail" the title of Satan within Satanism. Roddenberry named his central Star Trek character, "Captain Kirk," because "Kirk" is a Scottish word meaning a Church and Roddenberry's Church was the Church of Vulcan or Church of Satan.

The festival in honor of the Vulcan sun deity was called the Vulcania in which human sacrifices were offered. Vulcan also bears a family relationship to the Christian devil. Vulcan married Venus, another name for Lucifer or the devil. Vulcan is adored in Masonry under the name of Tubal Cain. In the Masonic Quiz Book the question is asked: "Who was Tubal Cain?" The answer is: "He is the Vulcan of the pagans." In Masonry, Tubal Cain is the name of the password for the Master Mason (or third) degree. In regards to Vulcan's influence over Masonry, occultist and Freemason, Manly Palmer Hall, states, "When the Mason learns that the key to the warrior on the block is the proper application of the dynamo of living power, he has learned the mastery of his craft. The seething energies of Lucifer are in his hands and before he may step onward and upward, he must prove his ability to properly apply energy. He must follow in the footsteps of his forefather, Tubal-Cain, who with the mighty strength of the war god hammered his sword into a ploughshare."

There is also a sexual connotation associated with Vulcan and Tubal Cain. Former Mason, Bill Schnoebelen, explains, "For Masons who wish to conceal their membership from non-Masons, but still advertise it to their Lodge brothers, there is a special pin (or tie tack) they can wear. It looks like an upside down golf club with two balls near the top....Many people assume the person is a golfing enthusiast, but it is actually a visual Masonic pun. This is called the 'Two Ball Cane,' and is a pun on the secret password of a Master Mason, 'Tubalcain'...It is also an all-too-obvious pun on the 'god' of Masonry, the male reproductive organ. Nice, eh?...especially when many men wear these wretched things to church on Sunday!"--

Masonic and Occult Symbols Illustrated, pp. 233-238, 2008.

In 2007 The Parents Television Council named Family Guy the worst program for young audiences. PTC President, Tim Winter said, "… shows like American Dad and Family Guy are serving up some of the most inappropriate content on broadcast television that kids are consuming." It's no wonder a belief in God has plummeted among millennial generation. Protocol No.4 within the Protocols of the Learned Elders of Zion [HERE] states, "WE SHALL DESTROY GOD."

In an episode of "Family Guy" titled, "One if byClam, Two if by Sea," MacFarlane featured a caricature of Babylonian Talmudist henchman, "Benjamin Disraeli." Disraeli was the first and thus far only Jewish [Talmudist] Prime Minister of the United Kingdom. Disraeli harbored a deep hatred for the Irish and Scottish people and was complicit in the murder of five million Irish men, women and children. In 1836 Disraeli expressed his disgust stating:

"The Irish hate our order, our civilization, our enterprising industry, our pure religion [Talmudism]. This wild, reckless, indolent, uncertain and superstitious race have no sympathy with the English character. Their ideal of human felicity is an alternation of clannish broils and coarse idolatry. Their history describes an unbroken circle of bigotry and blood." - "How the Irish Saved Civilization: The Untold Story of Ireland's Heroic role from the Fall of Rome to the Rise of Medieval Europe," by Thomas Cahill

What a far cry from MacFarlane's Puritan Separatist ancestor, William Brewster, who was a passenger on the Mayflower [1620].

"Neither filthiness, nor foolish talking, nor jesting, which are not convenient: but rather giving of thanks." – Ephesians 5:4

Most recently Betty Cohen served as CEO for Walt Disney Company's, Lifetime Entertainment, "a leader in women's television." Lifetime's reality TV show, "Preach" features extreme female false prophets [Matthew 24] who instead of promoting the "Holy Ghost," [Matthew 28:19] promote the "kundalini spirit" and blaspheming. The Hindu/Yoga Kundalini is described as being the "coiled one" at the base of the spine, represented as a sleeping serpent waiting to be awakened. "… then your eyes shall be opened, and ye shall be as gods," [Satan] – Genesis 3:5. Like all of the preceding data that I've shared with you, Lifetime's "Preach" is nothing more than a bully pulpit for the Serpent Death Cult. Lastly let's read the warnings found inside of The Holy Bible regarding female preachers:

272

"In like manner also, that women adorn themselves in modest apparel, with shamefacedness and sobriety; not with broided hair, or gold, or pearls, or costly array; But I suffer not a woman to teach, nor to usurp authority over the man, but to be in silence. For Adam was first formed, then Eve. And Adam was not deceived, but the woman being deceived was in the transgression. Notwithstanding she shall be saved in childbearing, if they continue in faith and charity and holiness with sobriety."
— 1 Timothy 2:9-15

Sumner Rothstein and Betty Cohen aren't the only Talmudists in town. According to a 12/19/2008 L.A. Times article by Talmudist Joel Stein:

"When the studio chiefs took out a full-page ad in the Los Angeles Times a few weeks ago to demand that the Screen Actors Guild settle its contract, the open letter was signed by: all eight major film studios are run by men who happen to be Jewish." Stein goes on to detail the extent to which Talmudists have monopolized Hollywood, stating: "News Corp. President Peter Chernin (**Jewish**), Paramount Pictures Chairman Brad Grey (**Jewish**), Walt Disney Co. Chief Executive Robert Iger (**Jewish**), Sony Pictures Chairman Michael Lynton (surprise, Dutch **Jew**), Warner Bros. Chairman Barry Meyer (**Jewish**), CBS Corp. Chief Executive Leslie Moonves (so **Jewish** his great uncle was the first prime minister of Israel), MGM Chairman Harry Sloan (**Jewish**) and NBC Universal Chief Executive Jeff Zucker (**mega-Jewish**). If either of the Weinstein brothers had signed, this group would have not only the power to shut down all film production but to form a minyan with enough Fiji water on hand to fill a mikvah. The person they were yelling at in that ad was SAG President Alan Rosenberg (take a guess) [**Jew**]. The scathing rebuttal to the ad was written by entertainment super-agent Ari Emanuel (**Jew** with Israeli parents) on the Huffington Post."

Another militant Antichristian, Khazarian Babylonian Talmudist is Larry David the creator of both "Seinfeld" and "Curb Your Enthusiasm." In October 25, 2009, an episode of Curb Your Enthusiasm aired titled "The Bare Midriff." In this episode Larry David features himself urinating on a picture commonly associated with Lord Jesus Christ [above]. This is obviously an endorsement of the Talmud, Gitten 57a which states Lord Jesus Christ is in hell "boiling in hot urine".

Through his career, Larry David has not only attacked the Christian American majority, he has also shown a propensity towards the hatred of conservative so called Jews who eschew the satanic Talmud. On April 28, 1994 millions of viewers tuned into Seinfeld to watch a two-part episode written by Larry David. The title of this episode was "The Rain Coats". In it Jerry Seinfeld's character is featured groping and kissing his girlfriend inside of a movie theater, while the movie Schindler's List is playing. It begs the question. Why would self ascribed Jewish actors, writers and directors feature lustful, celebratory acts during the showing of a film which depicts the extermination of millions of Jewish people? The explanation is quite simple if you understand what the Talmud says about "am ha'aretz" or Jews who deny the Pharisee written Talmud.

Another example of a militant Antichristian Khazarian Talmudist is the exceedingly and stereotypical Jewish comedienne, Sandra Bernhard who while performing at the leading Jewish theater in Washington, D.C. viciously attacked Sarah Palin as a "Goy whore," and threatened the mother of five with gang rape by Black males.

Goy [goyim], as you should be aware by now is an unflattering word Jews use for Gentiles [Christians], in other words, all non-so called Jews. Bernhard also warned Palin not to reference the Old Testament and condemned the New Testament as "crappy bullshit". Bernhard further stated, "Turncoat bitch! Don't you fukin' reference the Old Testament, bitch! You stay with your New Goyish, crappy, shiksa, funky bullshit! Don't you touch my Old Testament, you bitch!"

Christians are not the only ones who have been deceived by Church of Babylon doctrines. The anti-Torah Talmud has deceived countless generations of so called Jewish people into following the teachings of mortal sages and Pharisees, over the Holy Torah. One of many examples of this is the Chief Rabbi of Prague who once stated, "It appears to me, since the heretics (Christians) also study Bible for their own purposes, if your son studies Bible without supervision, he may have a teacher who is one of them, and he will follow after their empty beliefs." – Rabbi Yechezkel Landau (circa 1760)

It is militant Antichristians such as Rabbi Yechezkel which caused the governor general of Kiev, a man named Drenteln, in 1881 to present a plan to the Emperor of Russia, Alexander II. His plan called for the immediate suppression of all Talmudist mercantile activity. The governor general felt that it was necessary for the Christian Emperor to, "Shield the Christian population against so arrogant a tribe as the Jews [Talmudists], who refuse on religious grounds to have close contact with the Christians"

274

Actions taken by the Emperor to protect Christians from what he referred to as a destructive 'Liberal' agenda included important changes to Russia's legislation concerning industry and commerce. Moreover, the Emperor signed the emancipation of the serfs [slaves of Russia]. Serfdom was the dominant form of relation between peasants and nobility in the 17th century and by the 19th century the peasant class population totaled more than 49 million. As an aside the same year [1881] the Emperor made changes to Russia's legislation concerning commerce he was assassinated by the Rothschild Family; just sixteen years prior to the assassination of U.S. President Abraham Lincoln by Albert Pikes, "Knights of Golden Circle" member, John Wilkes Booth. It will be remembered from previous chapters where I presented information which suggests Lincoln's assassination was due to his repeal of the Rothschild's business plan to build what we now refer to as the Federal Reserve Bank Inc. As of 2013 the only countries left without a Central Bank owned by the Rothschild Family are Cuba, North Korea and Iran.

Because of the ample spiritual discrepancies between the Talmud - created 1st century A.D. in the Babylonian Talmudic Academies of Iraq - and the God inspired Holy Torah, Karaite Jews are a growing sect of Judaic people who only follow the God inspired Holy Torah or what the Christian American majority refers to as the Old Testament. Karaite Jews rightly eschew the Satanic Talmud, which they have shown to be nothing more than a collection of man-made laws verbally handed down by anti-Torah Rabbis. It should also be noted that Talmudists in these regions used 'Seleucid Era' dating also known as the 'Anno Graecorum' [AG] or 'Era of Contracts'. This begs the question: With whom were Talmudists creating contracts with? Based on their bigoted, anti-Christ rhetoric it's quite clear their contracts were with Lucifer and the demon god Pazuzu.

"Jesus saith unto them, Did ye never read in the scriptures, The stone which the builders rejected, the same is become the head of the corner: this is the Lord's doing, and it is marvellous in our eyes? Therefore say I unto you, The kingdom of God shall be taken from you, and given to a nation bringing forth the fruits thereof. And whosoever shall fall on this stone shall be broken: but on whomsoever it shall fall, it will grind him to powder. And when the chief priests and Pharisees had heard his parables, they perceived that he spake of them." - Matthew 21:42-45

In the above Biblical quote, it is clear Jesus Christ is referring to the minority Judaic heretical movement of his day, whose goal it was to develop a sacrilegious, self serving rabbinic movement. It's of vital importance for both the Christian American majority as well as the Judaic American population to be aware of the verbiage throughout 275 the anti-Torah Talmud, which places the Babylonian Talmud above The Holy Bible. In the book titled From Torah to Kabbalah: A Basic Introduction to the Writings of Judaism (Page 40), R.C. Musaph Andriesse writes, "The authority of the Babylonian Talmud is also greater than that of the Jerusalem Talmud. In cases of doubt the former is decisive."

What's more, the Babylonian Talmud teaches that "The Almighty Himself" is inferior to the sages, Pharisees and Rabbis, "The realization of the difference between written and oral regulations finds expression in the appraisal that 'The Sages safeguarded their own enactments more than those of the Torah' and in the hyperbolical statements concerning the supreme authority of the expositions and decisions of the Rabbis. The Almighty Himself is bound by them." - Pesiqta de-R. Kahana, Para, ed. Mandelbaum, p. 73

Christians exist only to serve Jews [Khazarian Talmudists]:

"Goyim [Christians] were born only to serve us. Without that, they have no place in the world - only to serve the People of Israel... With gentiles [Christians], it will be like any person - they need to die, but [God] will give them longevity. Why? Imagine that one's donkey would die, they'd lose their money. This is his servant... That's why he gets a long life, to work well for this Jew [Talmudist]. Why are gentiles [Christians] needed? They will work, and they will plow, they will reap. We will sit like an effendi and eat. That is why gentiles were created."

Rabbi Ovadia Yosef, senior Sephardic posek and head of the Shas Council of Torah Sages. Sermon on the laws regarding non-Jews. Source: "Yosef: Gentiles exist only to serve Jews," Jerusalem Post, October 18, 2010.

"The best among the Gentiles deserve to be killed."
– Talmud, Rabbi Simeon BenYohai

A real world example which demonstrates Talmudist Rabbi Yosef, BenYohai and Rabinovich's aforesaid militant Antichristian, racist hate speech can be found in the actions of Talmudist Rabbi Isaac Rosenbaum. Rabbi Rosenbaum, along with five additional Talmudist Rabbi's, was arrested in 2009 for running the largest organ trafficking scheme in America. Victims were flown into the United States from predominately impoverished Christian majority nations such as Moldova, once in the U.S. their organs were cut out of their bodies and sold to the highest bidder. In connection with the crime Talmudist real-estate developer Solomon Dwek was arrested for $50 million in bank fraud. As an aside, Dwek's family founded the Deal Yeshiva, an educational institution that focuses on the study of the anti-Christian Babylonian Talmud.

The following are just a few of the blasphemous teachings a Christian will find in the Talmud and those who teach its militant anti-Christian heresy. For instance, in the book titled Jewish History, Jewish Religion, (Pages 97-98, 118) Dr. Israel Shahak writes, "The Hebrew form of the name Jesus--Yeshu--was interpreted as an acronym for the curse, 'may his name and memory be wiped out,' which is used as an extreme form of abuse. In fact, anti-zionist Orthodox Jews (such as Neturey Qarta) sometimes refer to Herzl as 'Herzl Jesus' and I have found in religious zionist writings expressions such as "Nasser Jesus" and more recently 'Arafat Jesus."

The Antichristian, Antitorah Talmud contains disturbing edicts which the Christian American Majority must be made aware of. Understand that all of the above sacrilegious Talmudic laws, targeting Lord Jesus Christ and Christians, are celebrated by Hollywood writers, directors, actors and actresses in both feature films and on television, as well as business moguls throughout Corporate America. Consider The Walt Disney Company's Lifetime Channel "Television for Women" which depicts daughters of Christian preachers exhibiting lewd behavior in the TV Show 'Preachers' Daughters'.

In the book titled "Judaism's Strange Gods" writer Michael Hoffman (**www.revisionisthistory.com**) shares with his readers what many of the leading Babylonian Talmudic leaders subscribe to, namely the murder of anti-Talmud conservative Jews. On pg. 37 of his book Mr. Hoffman cites the Talmudic views of Lubavitcher Rebbe on the subject of the Jewish Holocaust. Keep in mind, that Rebbe is the so-called 'King Messiah' of the largest Jewish organization in the world.

"Rebbe...compare(s) God to a surgeon who amputates a patient's limb in order to save his life. The limb 'is incurably diseased... The Holy One Blessed Be He, like professor-surgeon... seeks the goo of Israel, and indeed, all He does is done for the good... In the spiritual sense, no harm was done, because the everlasting spirit of the Jewish people was not destroyed."

According to Rebbe's man-made anti-Torah Talmud the murder of conservative Jews who eschew the Talmud is justified and Hitler was a 'servant of God'.

When militant anti-Christian Corporations, such as HBO, defend 'men' like Larry David they promote Rebbe's vitriol. What's more, they inspire the notion that it's perfectly fine to urinate on the divinity of Lord Jesus Christ. Urinating on Lord Jesus Christ is not "playful"? And if you're a Christian reading this, who currently subscribes to HBO, I hope that you will consider cancelling your membership and boycott any project the anti-Christian Larry David is associated with.

The American entertainment and fashion industries, especially music and films, have been normalizing misogynistic language and imagery, as well as child pornography for the past fifty-years. Dr. Jason D. Kovar's documentary titled: "Hollywood Unmasked" exposes the demonic influence over Hollywood and provides quotes from the vast majority of Hollywood actors and actresses proclaiming their allegiance to Lucifer. Dr. Kovar's video can be purchased at: **www.hollywoodunmasked.com**.

Beginning in the late 1970's, verbal and visual attacks against the sacredness of our Christian American young girls and women reached epidemic proportions. In 2011 however, we begin to see a level of satanic propaganda which surpasses all previous levels of depravity. It's in 2011 that ABC Television, Inc. - whose core viewership is sadly Christian – announces its plan to release a show titled "Good Christian Bitches". It's these types of show titles which support militant anti-Christian Talmudic teachings such as Abodah Zarah 36b which reads "Gentile girls are in a state of niddah (filth) from birth". Companies like 'American Apparel Clothing' further endorse Abodah Zarah 36b when they promote pornographic messaging on clothing made for little girls and women. Examples include: "Who needs brains when you have these", "Must be 21 to enjoy this ride", "Contains strong sexual content."

It's messaging like this which makes our young Christian girls and women look like mindless pieces of meat. Free speech is the foundation of our Republic. So too is the freedom of choice. To eliminate anti-Christian organizations such as American Apparel Company from the free market, all the Christian American majority must do is simply not buy goods and/ or services from them. These types of blatant satanic attacks against our Christian women should have our Christian American Majority up in arms. It's these types of extremely offensive and distasteful show titles and clothing companies which should cause the Christian American Majority to bankrupt all Companies and Corporations which exhibit aforementioned behavior. Achieving this goal is quite simple; you merely stop watching their shows and discontinue using any of their products. In the case of ABC, Inc. this includes subscribing to their cable channel Showtime.

Aimonides Mishnah Torah, a code of Talmudic religious law authored by Rabbi Moshe ben Maimon (1170 and 1180), is one of history's foremost rabbis. In Chapter 10 of the English Translation, he states about Lord Jesus Christ, "It is a mitzvah [religious duty; ARC], however, to eradicate Jewish traitors, minnim, and apikorsim, and to cause them to descend to the pit of destruction, since they cause difficulty to the Jews and sway the people away from God, as did Jesus of Nazareth and his students, and Tzadok, Baithos, and their students. May the name of the wicked rot."

The Talmudic influenced Jewish Encyclopedia predicts a "Noahide" regime as a possible New World Order immediately following the universal reign of the Talmud.

The Christian American majority must understand that we are not dealing with the Noah of The Holy Bible when Talmudic worshipers refer to "Noahide law," but the Noahide law as understood and interpreted by the absolute system of falsification that constitutes the militant anti-Christian, anti-Torah Talmud.

Under the Talmud's Noahide Laws, the worship of Jesus is absolutely forbidden under penalty of death, since such worship of Christ is condemned by the Talmud as idolatry. Meanwhile various forms of incest are permitted under the Talmudic understanding of the Noahide code. (Enziklopediya Talmudit, note 1, pp. 351-352).

The Talmud also states the penalty for disobedience:

"One additional element of greater severity is that violation of any one of the seven laws subjects the Noahide to capital punishment by decapitation." - Sanh. 57A

"With the end of free will, the opportunity to earn reward and enhance one's portion in the World to Come will also cease forever." – Talmud, Sukkah 52a

The Christian American majority have been issued a clear warning of the aforementioned anti-Christian laws in The Holy Bible:

"And I saw thrones, and they sat upon them, and judgment was given unto them: and [I saw] the souls of them that were beheaded for the witness of Jesus, and for the word of God, and which had not worshipped the beast, neither his image, neither had received [his] mark upon their foreheads, or in their hands; and they lived and reigned with Christ a thousand years." - Revelations 20:4

This is why a United States Army training instructor recently listed Evangelical Christianity, Catholicism and "Orthodox Jews" e.g., conservative Torah faithful Jews, as examples of religious extremism, along with Al Qaeda and Hamas during a briefing with an Army Reserve unit based in Pennsylvania. Ron Crews, executive director of the Chaplain Alliance for Religious Liberty, states, "We find this offensive to have 279 Evangelical Christians and the Catholic Church to be listed among known terrorist groups; it is dishonorable for any U.S. military entity to allow this type of wrongheaded characterization."

Christians must be aware of the fact that Satan's Church of Babylon is comprised of those who worship the Serpent Cult of Dann, Nimrod, Baylonian Talmudism, Freemasonry, the Zohar, etc. and it's this force which is driving this militant Antichristian agenda. For example, high-level members of the Serpent Cult of Dann have deceived thousands of U.S. Military men and women into performing occult serpent rituals. Since 1980 the "Cobra Gold exercise" hosts soldiers from Thailand, U.S. Singapore, Indonesia, Japan, South Korea and Malaysia. The multi-national military training exercise teaches soldiers the occult serpent ritual of drinking fresh cobra blood because of its "nutrition for a human body." In Acts 21:25; Acts 15:19-20, 28-29; 1 Samuel 14:32-33; Deuteronomy 12:23; Leviticus 19:26, Leviticus 17:10-14 and Genesis 9:4-5, man is commanded not to eat or drink blood.

"Lest Satan [the serpent] should get an advantage of us; for we are not ignorant of his devices." – 2 Corinthians 2:11.

To better understand the Church of Babylon, all one must do is examine its fruits. The extensive history of Satanic rituals and malevolent habits of Freemasons illustrate just how wicked the tree from which freemasonry was born really is. Kabbalah is nothing more than a bastardization of the Holy Jewish Torah [Old Testament], and is thought to have been created nearly 1300 years after Jesus Christ gave us the New Testament. Its teachings come from a 23-volume book called 'The Zohar' and is very similar to the teachings of modern day esoteric Theosophy, in that it promotes an interpretation of the inner meaning of the Torah. Jesus Christ has instructed his followers to use The Holy Bible alone when researching and defining the Holy Scriptures:

"Jesus answered him, I spake openly to the world; I ever taught in the synagogue, and in the temple, whither the Jews always resort; and in secret have I said nothing." - John 18:20

Traditionally its practices were reserved for a select number of scholars who already had an advanced understanding of religious law, but for the past 500 years it has been followed more widely. What people must understand is that 'Kaballah' will not bring you closer to Jesus Christ, but in fact it will take you away. Not once does Jesus Christ cite Kabbalism or the Talmud as Christians' way into heaven, nor did he endorse mysticism:

280 "In my Father's house are many mansions: if it were not so, I would have told you. I go to prepare a place for you." – John 14:2

A CHRISTIAN VIEW
OF THE
HOLOCAUST

by Benjamin Freedman, Willard Hotel, 1961

Ladies and gentlemen, you are about to hear a very frightening speech. This speech is an explanation of the plans now being laid to throw the United States into a third world war. It was made a short time ago before a large group in the Congressional Room of the Willard Hotel in Washington, D.C. Both the speech and the question and answer period later so electrified the audience that a group of patriots has transferred it to two long-playing records which you may buy to play for friends, clubs, and your church group in your community. The speaker is Mr. Benjamin Freedman, noted authority on Zionism and all of its schemes. Mr. Freedman is a former Jew, and I mean a FORMER Jew. He has fought the Communist world conspiracy tooth and nail, and stands today as a leading American patriot. We now take you to the speaker's platform to present Benjamin Freedman.

(applause)

[Freedman's speech begins]

What I intend to tell you tonight is something that you have never been able to learn from any other source, and what I tell you now concerns not only you, but your children and the survival of this country and Christianity. I'm not here just to dish up a few facts to send up your blood pressure, but I'm here to tell you things that will help you preserve what you consider the most sacred things in the world: the liberty, and the freedom, and the right to live as Christians, where you have a little dignity, and a little right to pursue the things that your conscience tells you are the right things, as Christians.

Now, first of all, I'd like to tell you that on August 25th 1960 — that was shortly before elections — Senator Kennedy, who is now the President of the United States, went to New York, and delivered

281

an address to the Zionist Organization of America. In that address, to reduce it to its briefest form, he stated that he would use the armed forces of the United States to preserve the existence of the regime set up in Palestine by the Zionists who are now in occupation of that area.

In other words, Christian boys are going to be yanked out of their homes, away from their families, and sent abroad to fight in Palestine against the Christian and Moslem Arabs who merely want to return to their homes. And these Christian boys are going to be asked to shoot to kill these innocent [Arab Palestinians] people who only want to follow out fifteen resolutions passed by the United Nations in the last twelve years calling upon the Zionists to allow these people to return to their homes.

Now, when United States troops appear in the Middle East to fight with the Zionists as their allies to prevent the return of these people who were evicted from their homes in the 1948 armed insurrection by the Zionists who were transplanted there from Eastern Europe... when that happens, the United States will trigger World War III.

You say, when will that take place? The answer is, as soon as the difficulty between France and Algeria has been settled, that will take place. As soon as France and Algeria have been settled, that will take place. As soon as France and Algeria have settled their difficulty, and the Arab world, or the Moslem world, has no more war on their hands with France, they are going to move these people back into their homes, and when they do that and President kennedy sends your sons to fight over there to help the crooks hold on to what they stole from innocent men, women and children, we will trigger World War III; and when that starts you can be sure we cannot emerge from that war a victor. We are going to lose that war because there is not one nation in the world that will let one of their sons fight with us for such a cause.

I know and speak to these ambassadors in Washington and the United Nations — and of the ninety-nine nations there, I've consulted with maybe seventy of them — and when we go to war in Palestine to help the thieves retain possession of what they have stolen from these innocent people we're not going to have a man there to fight with us as our ally.

And who will these people have supporting them, you ask. Well, four days after President Kennedy — or he was then Senator Kennedy — made that statement on August 28, 1960, the Arab nations called a meeting in Lebanon and there they decided to resurrect, or reactivate, the government of Palestine, which has been dormant more or less, since 282 the 1948 armed insurrection by the Zionists.

Not only that... they ordered the creation of the Palestine Army, and they are now drilling maybe a half a million soldiers in that area of the world to lead these people back to their homeland. With them, they have as their allies all the nations of what is termed the Bandung Conference Group. That includes the Soviet Union and every Soviet Union satellite. It includes Red China; it includes every independent country in Asia and Africa; or eighty percent of the world's total population. Eighty percent of the world's population. Four out of five human beings on the face of the earth will be our enemies at war with us. And not alone are they four out of five human beings now on the face of this earth, but they are the non-Christian population of the world and they are the non-Caucasians... the non-white nations of the world, and that's what we face.

And what is the reason? The reason is that here in the United States, the Zionists and their co-religionists have complete control of our government. For many reasons too many and too complex to go into here at this — time I'll be glad to answer questions, however, to support that statement — the Zionists and their co-religionists rule this United States as though they were the absolute monarchs of this country.

Now, you say, 'well, that's a very broad statement to make', but let me show what happened while you were — I don't want to wear that out — let me show what happened while WE were all asleep. I'm including myself with you. We were all asleep. What happened?

World War I broke out in the summer of 1914. Nineteen-hundred and fourteen was the year in which World War One broke out. There are few people here my age who remember that. Now that war was waged on one side by Great Britain, France, and Russia; and on the other side by Germany, Austria-Hungary, and Turkey. What happened?

Within two years Germany had won that war: not alone won it nominally, but won it actually. The German submarines, which were a surprise to the world, had swept all the convoys from the Atlantic Ocean, and Great Britain stood there without ammunition for her soldiers, stood there with one week's food supply facing her — and after that, starvation.

At that time, the French army had mutinied. They lost 600,000 of the flower of French youth in the defense of Verdun on the Somme. The Russian army was defecting. They were picking up their toys and going home, they didn't want to play war anymore, they didn't like the Czar. And the Italian army had collapsed.

Now Germany — not a shot had been fired on the German 283 soil. Not an enemy soldier had crossed the border into Germany.

And yet, here was Germany offering England peace terms. They offered England a negotiated peace on what the lawyers call a status quo ante basis. That means: "Let's call the war off, and let everything be as it was before the war started."

Well, England, in the summer of 1916 was considering that. Seriously! They had no choice. It was either accepting this negotiated peace that Germany was magnanimously offering them, or going on with the war and being totally defeated.

While that was going on, the Zionists in Germany, who represented the Zionists from Eastern Europe, went to the British War Cabinet and — I am going to be brief because this is a long story, but I have all the documents to prove any statement that I make if anyone here is curious, or doesn't believe what I'm saying is at all possible — the Zionists in London went to the British war cabinet and they said: "Look here. You can yet win this war. You don't have to give up. You don't have to accept the negotiated peace offered to you now by Germany. You can win this war if the United States will come in as your ally."

The United States was not in the war at that time. We were fresh; we were young; we were rich; we were powerful. They [Zionists] told England: "We will guarantee to bring the United States into the war as your ally, to fight with you on your side, if you will promise us Palestine after you win the war."

In other words, they made this deal: "We will get the United States into this war as your ally. The price you must pay us is Palestine after you have won the war and defeated Germany, Austria-Hungary, and Turkey."

Now England had as much right to promise Palestine to anybody, as the United States would have to promise Japan to Ireland for any reason whatsoever. It's absolutely absurd that Great Britain — that never had any connection or any interest or any right in what is known as Palestine — should offer it as coin of the realm to pay the Zionists for bringing the United States into the war.

However, they made that promise, in October of 1916. October, nineteen hundred and sixteen. And shortly after that — I don't know how many here remember it — the United States, which was almost totally pro-German — totally pro-German — because the newspapers here were controlled by Jews, the bankers were Jews, all the media of mass communications in this country were controlled by Jews, and they
284 were pro-German because their people, in the majority of cases came from Germany, and they wanted to see Germany lick the Czar.

The Jews didn't like the Czar, and they didn't want Russia to win this war. So the German bankers — the German-Jews — Kuhn Loeb and the other big banking firms in the United States refused to finance France or England to the extent of one dollar. They stood aside and they said: "As long as France and England are tied up with Russia, not one cent!" But they poured money into Germany, they fought with Germany against Russia, trying to lick the Czarist regime.

Now those same Jews, when they saw the possibility of getting Palestine, they went to England and they made this deal. At that time, everything changed, like the traffic light that changes from red to green. Where the newspapers had been all pro-German, where they'd been telling the people of the difficulties that Germany was having fighting Great Britain commercially and in other respects, all of a sudden the Germans were no good. They were villains. They were Huns. They were shooting Red Cross nurses. They were cutting off babies' hands. And they were no good.

Well, shortly after that, Mr. Wilson declared war on Germany. The Zionists in London sent these cables to the United States, to Justice Brandeis: "Go to work on President Wilson. We're getting from England what we want. Now you go to work, and you go to work on President Wilson and get the United States into the war." And that did happen. That's how the United States got into the war. We had no more interest in it; we had no more right to be in it than we have to be on the moon tonight instead of in this room.

Now the war — World War One — in which the United States participated had absolutely no reason to be our war. We went in there — we were railroaded into it — if I can be vulgar, we were suckered into — that war merely so that the Zionists of the world could obtain Palestine. Now, that is something that the people in the United States have never been told. They never knew why we went into World War One. Now, what happened?

After we got into the war, the Zionists went to Great Britain and they said: "Well, we performed our part of the agreement. Let's have something in writing that shows that you are going to keep your bargain and give us Palestine after you win the war." Because they didn't know whether the war would last another year or another ten years. So they started to work out a receipt. The receipt took the form of a letter, and it was worded in very cryptic language so that the world at large wouldn't know what it was all about. And that was called the Balfour Declaration.

The Balfour Declaration was merely Great Britain's promise to pay the Zionists what they had agreed upon as a consideration for getting the United States into the war. So this great Balfour 285 Declaration, that you hear so much about, is just as phony as a three dollar bill. And I don't think I could make it more emphatic than that.

Now, that is where all the trouble started. The United States went in the war. The United States crushed Germany. We went in there, and it's history. You know what happened. Now, when the war was ended, and the Germans went to Paris, to the Paris Peace Conference in 1919, there were 117 Jews there, as a delegation representing the Jews, headed by Bernard Baruch. I was there: I ought to know. Now what happened?

The Jews at that peace conference, when they were cutting up Germany and parceling out Europe to all these nations that claimed a right to a certain part of European territory, the Jews said, "How about Palestine for us?" And they produced, for the first time to the knowledge of the Germans, this Balfour Declaration. So the Germans, for the first time realized, "Oh, that was the game! That's why the United States came into the war." And the Germans for the first time realized that they were defeated, they suffered this terrific reparation that was slapped onto them, because the Zionists wanted Palestine and they were determined to get it at any cost.

Now, that brings us to another very interesting point. When the Germans realized this, they naturally resented it. Up to that time, the Jews had never been better off in any country in the world than they had been in Germany.

You had Mr. Rathenau there, who was maybe 100 times as important in industry and finance as is Bernard Baruch in this country. You had Mr. Balin, who owned the two big steamship lines, the North German Lloyd's and the Hamburg-American Lines. You had Mr. Bleichroder, who was the banker for the Hohenzollern family. You had the Warburgs in Hamburg, who were the big merchant bankers — the biggest in the world. The Jews were doing very well in Germany. No question about that. Now, the Germans felt: "Well, that was quite a sellout."

It was a sellout that I can best compare — suppose the United States was at war today with the Soviet Union. And we were winning. And we told the Soviet Union: "Well, let's quit. We offer you peace terms. Let's forget the whole thing." And all of a sudden Red China came into the war as an ally of the Soviet Union. And throwing them into the war brought about our defeat. A crushing defeat, with reparations the likes of which man's imagination cannot encompass.

Imagine, then, after that defeat, if we found out that it was the Chinese in this country, our Chinese citizens, who all the time we 286 thought they were loyal citizens working with us, were selling us out to the Soviet Union and that it was through them that Red China was brought into the war against us. How would we feel, in the United States against Chinese? I don't think that one of them would dare show his face on any street. There wouldn't be lampposts enough, convenient, to take care of them. Imagine how we would feel.

Well, that's how the Germans felt towards these Jews. "We've been so nice to them"; and from 1905 on, when the first Communist revolution in Russia failed, and the Jews had to scramble out of Russia, they all went to Germany.

And Germany gave them refuge. And they were treated very nicely. And here they sold Germany down the river for no reason at all other than they wanted Palestine as a so-called "Jewish commonwealth."

Now, Nahum Sokolow — all the great leaders, the big names that you read about in connection with Zionism today — they, in 1919, 1920, '21, '22, and '23, they wrote in all their papers — and the press was filled with their statements — that "the feeling against the Jews in Germany is due to the fact that they realized that this great defeat was brought about by our intercession and bringing the United States into the war against them."

The Jews themselves admitted that. It wasn't that the Germans in 1919 discovered that a glass of Jewish blood tasted better than Coca-Cola or Muenschner Beer. There was no religious feeling. There was no sentiment against those people merely on account of their religious belief. It was all political. It was economic. It was anything but religious.

Nobody cared in Germany whether a Jew went home and pulled down the shades and said "Shema' Yisrael" or "Our Father." No one cared in Germany any more than they do in the United States. Now this feeling that developed later in Germany was due to one thing: that the Germans held the Jews responsible for their crushing defeat, for no reason at all, because World War One was started against Germany for no reason for which they [Germans] were responsible. They were guilty of nothing. Only of being successful. They built up a big navy. They built up world trade.

You must remember, Germany, at the time of Napoleon, at the time of the French Revolution, what was the German Reich consisted of 300 — three hundred! — small city-states, principalities, dukedoms, and so forth. Three hundred little separate political entities. And between that time, between the period of. . . between Napoleon and Bismarck, they were consolidated into one state. And within 50 years after that time they became one of the world's great powers. Their navy was rivalling Great Britain's, they were doing business all over the world, they could 287 undersell anybody and make better products. And what happened?

What happened as a result of that?

There was a conspiracy between England, France, and Russia that: "We must slap down Germany", because there isn't one historian in the world that can find a valid reason why those three countries decided to wipe Germany off the map politically. Now, what happened after that?

When Germany realized that the Jews were responsible for her defeat, they naturally resented it. But not a hair on the head of any Jew was harmed. Not a single hair. Professor Tansill, of Georgetown University, who had access to all the secret papers of the State Department, wrote in his book, and quoted from a State Department document written by Hugo Schoenfelt, a Jew who Cordell Hull sent to Europe in 1933 to investigate the so-called camps of political prisoners. And he wrote back that he found them in very fine condition.

They were in excellent shape; everybody treated well. And they were filled with Communists. Well, a lot of them were Jews, because the Jews happened to be maybe 98 per cent of the Communists in Europe at that time. And there were some priests there, and ministers, and labor leaders, Masons, and others who had international affiliations.

Now, the Jews sort of tried to keep the lid on this fact. They didn't want the world to really understand that they had sold out Germany, and that the Germans resented that.

So they did take appropriate action against them [against the Jews]. They. . . shall I say, discriminated against them wherever they could? They shunned them. The same as we would the Chinese, or the Negroes, or the Catholics, or anyone in this country who had sold us out to an enemy and brought about our defeat.

Now, after a while, the Jews of the world didn't know what to do, so they called a meeting in Amsterdam. Jews from every country in the world attended in July 1933. And they said to Germany: "You fire Hitler! And you put every Jew back into his former position, whether he was a Communist, no matter what he was. You can't treat us that way! And we, the Jews of the world, are calling upon you, and serving this ultimatum upon you." Well, the Germans told them. . . you can imagine. So what did they [the Jews] do?

They broke up, and Samuel Untermyer, if the name means anything to people here. . . (You want to ask a question? —— Uh, there were no Communists in Germany at that time. they were called 'Social Democrats.)

288

Well, I don't want to go by what they were called. We're now using English words, and what they were called in Germany is not very material. . . but they were Communists, because in 1917, the Communists took over Germany for a few days. Rosa Luxembourg and Karl Liebknecht, and a group of Jews in Germany took over the government for three days. In fact, when the Kaiser ended the war, he fled to Holland because he thought the Communists were going to take over Germany as they did Russia, and that he was going to meet the same fate that the Czar did in Russia. So he left and went to Holland for safety and for security.

Now, at that time, when the Communist threat in Germany was quashed, it was quiet, the Jews were working, still trying to get back into their former — their status — and the Germans fought them in every way they could, without hurting a hair on anyone's head. The same as one group, the Prohibitionists, fought the people who were interested in liquor, and they didn't fight one another with pistols, they did it every way they could.

Well, that's the way they were fighting the Jews in Germany. And, at that time, mind you, there were 80 to 90 million Germans and there were only 460,000 Jews. . . less than one half of one percent of Germany were Jews. And yet, they controlled all of the press, they controlled most of the economy, because they had come in and with cheap money — you know the way the Mark was devalued — they bought up practically everything.

Well, in 1933 when Germany refused to surrender, mind you, to the World Conference of Jews in Amsterdam, they broke up and Mr. Untermeyer came back to the United States — who was the head of the American delegation and the president of the whole conference — and he went from the steamer to ABC and made a radio broadcast throughout the United States in which he said:

"The Jews of the world now declare a Holy War against Germany. We are now engaged in a sacred conflict against the Germans. And we are going to starve them into surrender. We are going to use a world-wide boycott against them, that will destroy them because they are dependent upon their export business."

And it is a fact that two thirds of Germany's food supply had to be imported, and it could only be imported with the proceeds of what they exported. Their labor. So if Germany could not export, two thirds of Germany's population would have to starve. There just was not enough food for more than one third of the population.

Now in this declaration, which I have here, it was printed on page — a whole page — in the New York Times on August 7, 1933, 289

Mr. Samuel Untermyer boldly stated that: "this economic boycott is our means of self-defense. President Roosevelt has advocated its use in the NRA" . [National Recovery Administration] — which some of you may remember, where everybody was to be boycotted unless they followed the rules laid down by the New Deal, which of course was declared unconstitutional by the Supreme Court at that time.

Nevertheless, the Jews of the world declared a boycott against Germany, and it was so effective that you couldn't find one thing in any store anywhere in the world with the words "made in Germany" on it.

In fact, an executive of the Woolworth Company told me that they had to dump millions of dollars worth of crockery and dishes into the river; that their stores were boycotted. If anyone came in and found a dish marked "made in Germany," they were picketed with signs: "Hitler", "murderer", and so forth, and like — something like these sit-ins that are taking place in the South.

R. H. Macy, which is controlled by a family called Strauss who also happen to be Jews. . . a woman found stockings there which came from Chemnitz, marked "made in Germany". Well, they were cotton stockings. They may have been there 20 years, because since I've been observing women's legs in the last twenty years, I haven't seen a pair with cotton stockings on them. So Macy! I saw Macy boycotted, with hundreds of people walking around with signs saying "MURDERS" and "HITLERITES", and so forth.

Now up to that time, not one hair on the head of any Jew had been hurt in Germany. There was no suffering, there was no starvation, there was no murder, there was nothing.

Now, that. . . naturally, the Germans said, "Why, who are these people to declare a boycott against us and throw all our people out of work, and our industries come to a standstill? Who are they to do that to us?" They naturally resented it. Certainly they painted swastikas on stores owned by Jews.

Why should a German go in and give their money to a storekeeper who was part of a boycott who was going to starve Germany into surrender into the Jews of the world, who were going to dictate who their premier or chancellor was to be? Well, it was ridiculous.

That continued for some time, and it wasn't until 1938, when a young Jew from Poland walked into the German embassy in Paris and shot one of the officials [a German official] that the Germans really started to get rough with the Jews in Germany. And you found

290

them then breaking windows and having street fights and so forth.

Now, for anyone to say that — I don't like to use the word 'anti-Semitism' because it's meaningless, but it means something to you still, so I'll have to use it — the only reason that there was any feeling in Germany against Jews was that they were responsible: number one, for World War One; number two, for this world-wide boycott, and number three — did I say for World War One, they were responsible? For the boycott — and also for World War II, because after this thing got out of hand, it was absolutely necessary for the Jews and Germany to lock horns in a war to see which one was going to survive.

In the meanwhile, I had lived in Germany, and I knew that the Germans had decided [that] Europe is going to be Christian or Communist: there is no in between. It's going to be Christian or it's going to be Communist. And the Germans decided: "We're going to keep it Christian if possible". And they started to re-arm.

And there intention was — by that time the United States had recognized the Soviet Union, which they did in November, 1933 — the Soviet Union was becoming very powerful, and Germany realized: "Well, our turn is going to come soon, unless we are strong." The same as we in this country are saying today, "Our turn is going to come soon, unless we are strong."

And our government is spending 83 or 84 billion dollars of your money for defense, they say. Defense against whom? Defense against 40,000 little Jews in Moscow that took over Russia, and then, in their devious ways, took over control of many other governments of the world.

Now, for this country to now be on the verge of a Third World War, from which we cannot emerge a victor, is something that staggers my imagination. I know that nuclear bombs are measured in terms of megatons. A megaton is a term used to describe one million tons of TNT. One million tons of TNT is a megaton. Now, our nuclear bombs have a capacity of 10 megatons, or 10 million tons of TNT. That was when they were first developed five or six years ago. Now, the nuclear bombs that are being developed have a capacity of 200 megatons, and God knows how many megatons the nuclear bombs of the Soviet Union have.

So, what do we face now? If we trigger a world war that may develop into a nuclear war, humanity is finished. And why will it take place? It will take place because Act III. . . the curtain goes up on Act III. Act I was World War I. Act II was World War II. Act III is going to be World War III. 291

The Jews of the world, the Zionists and their co-religionists everywhere, are determined that they are going to again use the United States to help them permanently retain Palestine as their foothold for their world government. Now, that is just as true as I am standing here, because not alone have I read it, but many here have read it, and it's known all over the world.

Now, what are we going to do? The life you save may be your son's. Your boys may be on their way to that war tonight; and you you don't know it any more than you knew that in 1916 in London the Zionists made a deal with the British War Cabinet to send your sons to war in Europe. Did you know it at that time? Not a person in the United States knew it. You weren't permitted to know it.

Who knew it? President Wilson knew it. Colonel House knew it. Other 's knew it. Did I know it? I had a pretty good idea of what was going on: I was liaison to Henry Morgenthau, Sr., in the 1912 campaign when President Wilson was elected, and there was talk around the office there.

I was 'confidential man' to Henry Morgenthau, Sr., who was chairman of the Finance Committee, and I was liaison between him and Rollo Wells, the treasurer. So I sat in these meetings with President Wilson at the head of the table, and all the others, and I heard them drum into President Wilson's brain the graduated income tax and what has become the Federal Reserve, and also indoctrinate him with the Zionist movement.

Justice Brandeis and President Wilson were just as close as the two fingers on this hand, and President Woodrow Wilson was just as incompetent when it came to determining what was going on as a newborn baby. And that's how they got us into World War I, while we all slept.

Now, at this moment... at this moment they may be planning this World War III, in which we don't stand a chance even if they don't use nuclear bombs. How can the United States — about five percent of the world — go out and fight eighty to ninety percent of the world on their home ground? How can we do it... send our boys over there to be slaughtered? For what? So the Jews can have Palestine as their 'commonwealth'? They've fooled you so much that you don't know whether you're coming or going.

Now any judge, when he charges a jury, says, "Gentlemen, any witness that you find has told a single lie, you can disregard all his testimony." That is correct. I don't know from what state you come, but in New York state that is the way a judge addresses a jury. If that witness said one lie, disregard his testimony.

292

Now, what are the facts about the Jews? The Jews — I call them Jews to you, because they are known as Jews. I don't call them Jews. I refer to them as so-called Jews, because I know what they are. If Jesus was a Jew, there isn't a Jew in the world today, and if those people are Jews, certainly our Lord and Savior was not one of them, and I can prove that.

Now what happened? The eastern European Jews, who form 92 per cent of the world's population of those people who call themselves Jews, were originally Khazars.

They were a warlike tribe that lived deep in the heart of Asia. And they were so warlike that even the Asiatics drove them out of Asia into eastern Europe — and to reduce this so you don't get too confused about the history of Eastern Europe — they set up this big Khazar kingdom: 800,000 square miles. Only, there was no Russia, there were no other countries, and the Khazar kingdom was the biggest country in all Europe — so big and so powerful that when the other monarchs wanted to go to war, the Khazars would lend them 40,000 soldiers. That's how big and powerful they were.

Now, they were phallic worshippers, which is filthy. I don't want to go into the details of that now. It was their religion the way it was the religion of many other Pagans or Barbarians elsewhere in the world.

Now, the [Khazar] king became so disgusted with the degeneracy of his kingdom that he decided to adopt a so-called monotheistic faith — either Christianity, Islam — the Moslem faith — or what is known today as Judaism — really Talmudism. So, like spinning a top and calling out "eeny, meeny, miney, moe," he picked out so-called Judaism. And that became the state religion.

He sent down to the Talmudic schools of Pumbedita and Sura and brought up thousands of these rabbis with their teachings, and opened up synagogues and schools in his kingdom of 800,000 people — 800,000 thousand square miles — and maybe ten to twenty million people; and they became what we call Jews. There wasn't one of them that had an ancestor that ever put a toe in the Holy Land, not only in Old Testament history, but back to the beginning of time. Not one of them! And yet they come to the Christians and they ask us to support their armed insurrection in Palestine by saying:

"Well, you want to certainly help repatriate God's chosen people to their Promised Land, their ancestral homeland, It's your Christian duty. We gave you one of our boys as your Lord and Savior. You now go to church on Sunday, and kneel and you worship a Jew, and we're Jews." 293

Well, they were pagan Khazars who were converted just the same as the Irish [were converted]. And it's just as ridiculous to call them "people of the Holy Land," as it would be. . . there are 54 million Chinese Moslems. Fifty four million! And, Mohammed only died in 620 A.D., so in that time, 54 million Chinese have accepted Islam as their religious belief.

Now imagine, in China, 2,000 miles away from Arabia, where the city of Mecca is located, where Mohammed was born. . . imagine if the 54 million Chinese called themselves 'Arabs'.

Imagine! Why, you'd say they're lunatics. Anyone who believes that those 54 million Chinese are Arabs must be crazy. All they did was adopt as a religious faith; a belief that had its origin in Mecca, in Arabia.

The same as the Irish. When the Irish became Christians, nobody dumped them in the ocean and imported from the Holy Land a new crop of inhabitants that were Christians. They weren't different people. They were the same people, but they had accepted Christianity as a religious faith.

Now, these Pagans, these Asiatics, these Turko-Finns they were a Mongoloid race who were forced out of Asia into eastern Europe. They likewise, because their king took the faith — Talmudic faith — they had no choice. Just the same as in Spain: If the king was Catholic, everybody had to be a Catholic. If not, you had to get out of Spain. So everybody — they lived on the land just like the trees and the bushes; a human being belonged to the land under their feudal system — so they [Khazars] all became what we call today, Jews!

Now imagine how silly it was for the Christians. for the great Christian countries of the world to say, "We're going to use our power, our prestige to repatriate God's chosen people to their ancestral homeland, their Promised Land."

Now, could there be a bigger lie than that? Could there be a bigger lie than that?

And because they control the newspapers, the magazines, the radio, the television, the book publishing business, they have the ministers in the pulpit, they have the politicians on the soap boxes talking the same language . . . so naturally you'd believe black is white if you heard it often enough. You wouldn't call black black anymore — you'd start to call black white. And nobody could blame you.

Now, that is one of the great lies. . . that is the foundation of all the misery that has befallen the world. Because after two wars fought in Europe — World War I and World War II — if it wasn't possible for them to live in peace and harmony with the people in Europe, like their brethren are living in the United States, what were the two wars fought for? Did they have to — like you flush the toilet — because they couldn't get along, did they have to say, "Well, we're going back to our homeland and you Christians can help us"?

I can't understand yet how the Christians in Europe could have been that dumb because every theologian, every history teacher, knew the things that I'm telling you. But, they naturally bribed them, shut them up with money, stuffed their mouths with money, and now. . . I don't care whether you know all this or not. It doesn't make any difference to me whether you know all these facts or not, but it does make a difference to me. I've got, in my family, boys that will have to be in the next war, and I don't want them to go and fight and die... like they died in Korea. Like they died in Japan. Like they've died all over the world. For what?

To help crooks hold on to what they stole from innocent people who had been in peaceful possession of that land, those farms, those homes for hundreds and maybe thousands of years? Is that why the United States must go to war? Because the Democratic Party wants New York State — the electoral vote? Illinois, the electoral vote? And Pennsylvania, the electoral vote?... which are controlled by the Zionists and their co-religionists?. . . the balance of power?

In New York City there are 400,000 members of the liberal party, all Zionists and their co-religionists. And New York State went for Kennedy by 400,000 votes. Now, I don't blame Mr. Kennedy. I'm fond of Mr. Kennedy. I think he's a great man. I think he can really pull us out of this trouble if we get the facts to him. And I believe he knows a great deal more than his appointments indicate he knows. He's playing with the enemy. Like when you go fishing, you've got to play with the fish. Let 'em out and pull 'em in. Let 'em out and pull 'em in. But knowing Mr. Kennedy's father, and how well informed he is on this whole subject, and how close Kennedy is to his father, I don't think Mr. Kennedy is totally in the dark.

But I do think that it is the duty of every mother, every loyal Christian , every person that regards the defense of this country as a sacred right, that they communicate — not with their congressman, not with their senator, but with President Kennedy. And tell him, "I do not think you should send my boy, or our boys, wearing the uniform of the United States of America, and under the flag that you see here, our red, white and blue, to fight there to help keep in the hands of these that that which they have stolen". I think everyone should not alone write once, but keep writing and get your friends to write.

295

Now, I could go on endlessly, and tell you these things to support what I have just asked you to do. But I don't think it's necessary to do that. You're above the average group in intelligence and I don't think it's necessary to impress this any more.

But. . . I want to tell you one more thing. You talk about... "Oh, the Jews. Why the Jews? Christianity. Why, we got Christianity from the Jews and the Jews gave us Jesus, and the Jews gave us our religion". But do you know that on the day of atonement that you think is so sacred to them, that on that day... and I was one of them! This is not hearsay. I'm not here to be a rabble-rouser. I'm here to give you facts.

When, on the Day of Atonement, you walk into a synagogue, the very first prayer that you recite, you stand — and it's the only prayer for which you stand — and you repeat three times a short prayer. The Kol Nidre. In that prayer, you enter into an agreement with God Almighty that any oath, vow, or pledge that you may make during the next twelve months — any oath, vow or pledge that you may take during the next twelve months shall be null and void.

The oath shall not be an oath; the vow shall not be a vow; the pledge shall not be a pledge. They shall have no force and effect, and so forth and so on.

And further than that, the Talmud teaches: "Don't forget — whenever you take an oath, vow, and pledge — remember the Kol Nidre prayer that you recited on the Day of Atonement, and that exempts you from fulfilling that".

How much can you depend on their loyalty? You can depend upon their loyalty as much as the Germans depended upon it in 1916.

And we're going to suffer the same fate as Germany suffered, and for the same reason. You can't depend upon something as insecure as the leadership that is not obliged to respect an oath, vow or pledge. Now I could go on and recite many other things to you, but I would have a little respect for your time, and you want to really, uh, get through with all of this. Tomorrow's going to be a long day.

Now I want to say one thing. You ask me. . . well, you think to yourself: "well how did this fellow get mixed up in this the way he got mixed up in it." Well, I opened my mouth in 1945, and I took big pages in newspapers and tried to tell the American people what I'm telling you. And one newspaper after another refused the advertisement. And when I couldn't find a newspaper to take them — I paid cash,

296

not credit — what happened? My lawyer told me, "There's an editor over in Jersey with a paper who will take your announcement". So, I was brought together with Mr. McGinley, and that's how I met him.

So somebody told me the lawyer who introduced me, who was the son of the Dean of the Methodist Bishop, he said: "Well, I think he's a little anti-Semitic. I don't know whether I can get him over here. So he brought him over to my apartment and we hit it off wonderfully, and have since then.

Now, I say this, and I say it without any qualifications. I say it without any reservations. And I say it without any hesitation. . . if it wasn't for the work that Mr. Conley McGinley did with "Common Sense" — he's been sending out from 1,800,000 to 2,000,000 every year — if it wasn't for the work he's been doing sending those out for fifteen years now, we would already be a communist country. Nobody has done what he did to light fires. Many of the other active persons in this fight learned all about if for the first time through "Common Sense".

Now, I have been very active in helping him all I could. I'm not as flush as I was. I cannot go on spending the money. . . I'm not going to take up a collection. Don't worry. I see five people getting up to leave. (laughter)

I haven't got the money that I used to spend. I used to print a quarter of a million of them out of my own pocket and send them out. Mr. McGinley, when I first met him, had maybe 5,000 printed and circulated them locally. So I said, "With what you know and what I know, we can really do a good job". So I started printing in outside shops of big newspaper companies, a quarter of a million, and paid for them. Well, there's always a bottom to the barrel. I suppose we've all reached that at times.

I'm not so poor that I can't live without working and that's what worries the Anti-Defamation League. I can just get by without going and asking for a job or getting on the bread line. But Mr. McGinley is working. He's sick and he's going at this stronger than ever. And all I want to say is that they want to close up "Common Sense" more than any other single thing in the whole world, as a death-blow to the fight Christians are making to survive.

So I just want to tell you this. All they do is circulate rumors: "Mr. Benjamin H. Freedman is the wealthy backer of 'Common Sense'." The reason they do that is to discourage the people in the United States: don't send any money to Common Sense. They don't need it. The've got the wealthy Mr. Freedman as a backer. That all has strategy. They don't want to advertise me so that people that have real estate or securities 297 to sell will come and call on me. They just want people to lay off

"Common Sense". And all I'm telling you is, I do try to help him, but I haven't been able to. And I will be very honest. One thing I won't do is lie. In the last year I've had so much sickness in my family that I could not give him one dollar.

How he's managed to survive, I don't know. God alone knows. And he must be in God's care because how he's pulled through his sickness and with his financial troubles, I don't know. But that press is working. . . and every two weeks about a hundred or a hundred-fifty-thousand of "Common Sense" go out with a new message. And if that information could be multiplied. . . if people that now get it could buy ten or twenty five, or fifty, give them around. Plow that field. Sow those seeds, you don't know which will take root, but for God's sake, this is our last chance.

(Freedman then discusses the importance of people forgoing unnecessary purchases to 'buy more stuff', play golf, etc., and use the money to keep "Common Sense" going. He explains that the paper is going in debt; could be closed down and he (Freedman) no longer has the funds, having spent some $2,400,000 in his attempt to bring the information to the American public and elected officials. He then asks for questions from the audience.)

[Question inaudible]

Freedman: All right, I'll comment on that. This is rather deep, but you all have a very high degree of intelligence, so I'm going to make an attempt. In the time of Bible history, there was a geographic area known as Judea. Judea was a province of the Roman Empire. Now, a person who lived in Judea was known as a Judean, and in Latin it was Judaeus; in Greek it was Judaius. Those are the two words, in Greek and Latin, for a Judean.

Now, in Latin and Greek there is no such letter as 'j', and the first syllable of Judaeus and Judaius starts 'ghu'. Now, when the Bible was written, it was first written in Greek, Latin, Panantic, Syriac, Aramaic... all those languages. Never Was the word Jew in any of them because the word didn't exist. Judea was the country, and the people were Judeans, and Jesus was referred to only as a Judean. I've seen those early... the earliest scripts available.

In 1345, a man by the name of Wycliffe in England thought that it was time to translate the Bible into English. There was no English edition of the Bible because who the Devil could read? It was only the educated church people who could read Latin and Greek, Syriac, Aramaic 298 and the other languages. Anyhow, Wycliffe translated the Bible into English. But in it, he had to look around for some words for Judaeas and Judaius.

There was no English word because Judea had passed out of existence. There was no Judea. People had long ago forgotten that. So in the first translation he used the word, in referring to Jesus, as 'gyu', "jew". At the time, there was no printing press.

Then, between 1345 and the 17th century, when the press came into use, that word passed through so many changes... I have them all here. If you want I can read them to you. I will. That word 'gyu' which was in the Wycliffe Bible became. . . first it was ' gyu ', then ' giu ', then ' iu ' (because the ' i ' in Latin is pronounced like the ' j '. Julius Caesar is ' Iul ' because there is no 'j' in Latin) then ' iuw ', then ' ieuu ', then ' ieuy ', then ' iwe ', then ' iow ', then ' iewe ', all in Bibles as time went on. Then ' ieue ', then ' iue ', then ' ive ', and then ' ivw ', and finally in the 18th century... ' jew '. Jew.

All the corrupt and contracted forms for Judaius, and Judaeas in Latin. Now, there was no such thing as 'Jew', and any theologian — I've lectured in maybe 20 of the most prominent theological seminaries in this country, and two in Europe — there was no such word as Jew. There only was Judea, and Jesus was a Judean and the first English use of a word in an English bible to describe him was 'gyu' — Jew. A contracted and shortened form of Judaeus, just the same as we call a laboratory a 'lab', and gasoline 'gas'... a tendency to short up.

So, in England there were no public schools; people didn't know how to read; it looked like a scrambled alphabet so they made a short word out of it. Now for a theologian to say that you can't harm the Jews, is just ridiculous. I'd like to know where in the scriptures it says that. I'd like to know the text.

Look at what happened to Germany for touching Jews. What would you, as a citizen of the United States, do to people who did to you what the so-called Jews — the Pollacks and Litvaks and Litzianers — they weren't Jews, as I just explained to you. They were Eastern Europeans who'd been converted to Talmudism. There was no such thing as Judaism. Judaism was a name given in recent years to this religion known in Bible history as Torah [inaudible]. No Jew or no educated person ever heard of Judaism. It didn't exist. They pulled it out of the air. . . a meaningless word.

Just like 'anti-Semitic'. The Arab is a Semite. And the Christians talk about people who don't like Jews as anti-Semites, and they call all the Arabs anti-Semites. The only Semites in the world are the Arabs. There isn't one Jew who's a Semite. They're all Turkothean

Mongoloids. The Eastern european Jews. So, they brainwashed the public, and if you will invite me to meet this reverend who told you these things, I'll convince him and it'll be one step in the right direction. I'll go wherever I have to go to meet him.

Yes, ma'am. Well... I can answer that. First of all, your first premise is wrong. Your first premise that all the Jews are loyal to each other is wrong. Because, the Eastern European Jews outnumber all the rest by so many that they create the impression that they are the Jewish 'race'; that they are the Jewish nation; that they are the Jewish people. . . and the Christians swallow it like a cream puff.

But in 1844 the German rabbis called a conference of rabbis from all over the world for the purpose of abolishing the Kol Nidre from the Day of Atonement religious ceremony. In Brunswick, Germany, where that conference was held in 1844, there was almost a terrific riot. A civil war.

The Eastern Europeans said, "What the hell. We should give up Kol Nidre? That gives us our grip on our people. We give them a franchise so they can tell the Christians, 'Go to hell. We'll make any deal you want', but they don't have to carry it out. That gives us our grip on our people". So, they're not so united, and if you knew the feeling that exists. . .

Now, I'll also show you from an official document by the man responsible for. . . uh, who baptized this race. Here is a paper that we obtained from the archives of the Zionist organization in New York City, and in it is the manuscript by Sir James A. Malcolm, who — on behalf of the British Cabinet — negotiated the deal with these Zionists.

And in here he says that all the jews in England were against it. The Jews who had been there for years, the [inaudible - probably Sephardim], those who had Portuguese and Spanish ad Dutch ancestry... who were monotheists and believed in that religious belief. That was while the Eastern European Jews were still running around in the heart of Asia and then came into Europe. But they had no more to do with them than. . . can we talk about a Christian 'race'? or a Christian religion?... or are the Christians united?

So the same disunity is among the Jews. And I'll show you in this same document that when they went to France to try and get the French government to back that Zionist venture, there was only one Jew in France who was for it. That was Rothschild, and they did it because they were interested in the oil and the Suez Canal

300

[Question inaudible]

Freedman: You know why? Because if they don't, they're decked up. They come around and they tell you how much you must give, and if you don't . . . oh, you're anti-Semitic. Then none of their friends will have anything to do with them, and they start a smear campaign. . . and you have got to give.

In New York city, in the garment center, there are twelve manufacturers in the building. And when the drive is on to sell Israel Bonds, the United Jewish Drive, they put a big scoreboard with the names of the firms and opposite them, as you make the amount they put you down for, they put a gold star after the name. Then, the buyers are told, "When you come into that building to call on someone and they haven't got a gold star, tell them that you won't buy from them until they have the gold star". BLACKMAIL. I don't know what else you can call it.

Then what do they do? They tell you it's for 'humanitarian purposes' and they send maybe $8 billion dollars to Israel, tax exempt, tax deductible. So if they hadn't sent that eight billion dollars to Israel, seven billion of it would have gone into the U.S. Treasury as income tax. So what happens? That seven billion dollars deficit — that air pocket — the gullible Christians have to make up.

They put a bigger tax on gas or bread or corporation tax. Somebody has to pay the housekeeping expenses for the government. So why do you let these people send their money over there to buy guns to drive people out of their ancient homeland? And you say, "Oh, well. The poor Jews. They have no place to go and they've been persecuted all their lives". They've never been persecuted for their religion. And I wish I had two rows of Rabbis here to challenge me. Never once, in all of history, have they been persecuted for their religion.

Do you know why the Jews were driven out of England? King Edward the First in 1285 drove them out, and they never came back until the Cromwell Revolution which was financed by the Rothschilds. For four-hundred years there wasn't a Jew. But do you know why they were driven out? Because in the Christian faith and the Moslem faith it's a sin to charge 'rent' for the use of money. In other words - what we call interest [usury] is a sin.

So the Jews had a monopoly in England and they charged so much interest, and when the Lords and Dukes couldn't pay, they [Jews] foreclosed. And they were creating so much trouble that the king of England finally made himself their partner, because when they they 301 came to foreclose, some of these dukes bumped off the Jews. . . the money-lenders. So the king finally said — and this is all in history, look up Tianson [Tennyson?] or Rourke, the History of the Jews in England; two books you can find in your library. When the king found out what the trouble was all about, and how much money they were making, he declared himself a fifty-percent partner of the money lenders. Edward the First. And for many years, one-third of the revenues of the British Treasury came from the fifty-percent interest in money-lending by the Jews.

But it got worse and worse. So much worse that when the Lords and Dukes kept killing the money-lenders, the King then said, "I declare myself the heir of all the money-lenders. If they're killed you have to pay me, because I'm his sole heir". That made so much trouble, because the King had to go out and collect the money with an army, so he told the Jews to get out. There were 15,000 of them, and they had to get out, and they went across to Ireland, and that's how Ireland got to be part of the United Kingdom.

When King Edward found out what they were doing, he decided to take Ireland for himself before someone else did. He sent Robert Southgard with a mercenary army and conquered Ireland. So, show me one time where a Jew was persecuted in any country because of his religion. It has never happened. It's always their impact on the political, social, or economic customs and traditions of the community in which they settle.

[Question inaudible]

Freedman: Yes, sir. Well, they say most of those things themselves. It was unnecessary for Benjamin Franklin to say it. Most of those things they say themselves. But Benjamin Franklin observed, and by hearsay understood, what was happening in Europe.

When Russia, in 920 was formed, and gradually surrounded the Khazar Kingdom, and absorbed them, most of the well-to-do Khazars fled to Western Europe and brought with them the very things to which you object and I object and a lot of other people object. The customs, the habits, the instincts with which they were endowed.

When Benjamin Franklin referred to them as Jews because that's the name that they went by, and when the Christians first heard that these people who were fleeing from Russia — who they were — that they had practiced this Talmudic faith — the Christians in Western Europe said, "They must be the remnants of the lost ten tribes!"

And Mr. Grutz, the greatest historian amongst the Jews, said that — and he's probably as good an authority on that subject as there is. So when Ben Franklin came to Europe in the 18th century, he already saw the results of what these people had done after they left their homeland. And every word of it is true... they say it themselves. I can give you half a dozen books they've written in which they say the same thing: When they have money they become tyrants. And when they become defeated, they become ruthless. They're only barbarians. They're the descendants of Asiatic Mongols and they will do anything to accomplish their purpose.

What right did they have to take over Russia the way they did? The Czar had abdicated nine or ten months before that. There was no need for them. . . they were going to have a constitutional monarchy. But they didn't want that. When the constitutional monarchy was to assemble in November, they mowed them all down and established the Soviet Union.

There was no need for that. But they thought, "Now is the time", and if you you will look in the Encyclopedia Britannica under the word 'Bolshevism', you'll find the five laws there that Lenin put down for a successful revolution. One of them is, "Wait for the right time, and then give them everything you've got". It would pay you to read that.

You'd also find that Mr. Harold Blacktree, who wrote the article for the Encyclopedia Britannica states that the Jews conceived and created and cultivated the Communist movement. And that their energy made them the spearhead of the movement. Harold Blacktree wrote it and no one knew more about Communism than he. And the Encyclopedia Britannica for 25 years has been printing it.

[Question inaudible]

Freedman: Well, I can't advocate that you do anything that's criminal, but I can tell you this. You can start what I call an endless chain. If you can get your friends to write, objectively, here is the statement: Mr. Kennedy's office gave me this himself. Mr. Smith, who succeeded Mr. Kennedy, took over his office — was in his office — and gave me this. He delivered this on the 25th, and it says here:

"For release to AM (that means morning papers), August 25th". "Israel is here to stay. It is a national commitment, special obligation of the Democratic Party. The White House must take the lead. American intervention. We will act promptly and decisively against any nation in the Middle East which attacks its neighbor. I propose that we make clear to both Israel and the Arab states our guarantee that   303 we will act with whatever force and speed are necessary to halt any aggression by any nation".

Well, do you call the return of people to their homeland [the Arab Palestinians] aggression? Is Mr. Kennedy going to do that? Suppose three million Mexicans came into Texas and drove the six million Texans into the deserts of Arizona and New Mexico. Suppose these Mexicans were slipped in there armed — the Texans were disarmed — and one night they drove them all out of Texas and declared themselves the Republic of the Alamo. What would the United States say?

Would we say it's aggression for these Texans to try to get their homes back from the Mexican thieves? Suppose the Negroes in Alabama were secretly armed by the Soviets and overnight they rose up and drove all the whites into the swamps of Mississippi and Georgia and Florida. . . drove them out completely, and declared themselves the Republic of Ham, or the Republic of something-or-other. Would we call it aggression if these people, the whites of Alabama, tried to go back to their homes?

Would we. . . what would we think if the soviet Union said, "No, those Negroes now occupy them! Leave them there!", or "No, those Mexicans are in Texas. they declared themselves a sovereign state. Leave them there. You have plenty of room in Utah and Nevada. Settle somewhere else".

Would we call it aggression if the Alabama whites or the Texans wanted to go back to their homes? So now, you've got to write to President Kennedy and say, "We do not consider it aggression in the sense that you use the word, if these people want to return to their homes as the United Nations — fifteen times in the last twelve years — called upon the Zionists in occupation of Palestine to allow the Arab Palestinians to return to their former homes and farms".

[End of transcript of Benjamin Freedman speech, given in 1961 at the Willard Hotel in Washington, D.C., on behalf of Conde McGinley's patriotic newspaper of that time, Common Sense.]

304

THE PROTOCOLS
OF THE LEARNED ELDERS
OF ZION

PREFACE

(Conceived c.926 AD by Khazarian Babylonian Talmudists)

The author of this translation of the famous Protocols was himself a victim of the Revolution. He had lived for many years in Russia and was married to a Russian lady. Among his other activities in Russia he had been for a number of years a Russian Correspondent of the MORNING POST, a position which he occupied when the Revolution broke out, and his vivid descriptions of events in Russia will still be in the recollection of many of the readers of that Journal. Naturally he was singled out for the anger of the Soviet. On the day that Captain Cromie was murdered by Jews, Victor Marsden was arrested and thrown into the Peter-Paul Prison, expecting every day to have his name called out for execution. This, however, he escaped, and eventually he was allowed to return to England very much of a wreck in bodily health. However, he recovered under treatment and the devoted care of his wife and friends. One of the first things he undertook, as soon as he was able, was this translation of the Protocols. Mr. Marsden was eminently well qualified for the work. His intimate acquaintance with Russia, Russian life and the Russian language on the one hand, and his mastery of a terse literary English style on the other, placed him in a position of advantage which few others could claim. The consequence is that we have in his version an eminently readable work, and though the subject-matter is somewhat formless, Mr. Marsden's literary touch reveals the thread running through the twenty-four Protocols.

It may be said with truth that this work was carried out at the cost of Mr. Marsden's own life's blood. He told the writer of this Preface that he could not stand more than an hour at a time of his work on it in the British Museum, as the diabolical spirit of the matter which he was obliged to turn into English made him positively ill.

Mr. Marsden's connection with the MORNING POST was not severed by his return to England, and he was well enough to accept the post of special correspondent of that journal in the suite of H.R.H., the Prince of Wales on his Empire tour. From this he returned with the Prince, apparently in much better health, but within a few days of his landing he was taken suddenly ill, and died after a very brief illness.

May this work be his crowning monument! In it he has performed an immense service to the English-speaking world, and there can be little doubt that it will take its place in the first rank of the English versions of "THE PROTOCOLS of the Meetings of the LEARNED ELDERS OF ZION."

INTRODUCTION

Of the Protocols themselves little need be said in the way of introduction. The book in which they are embodied was first published in the year 1897 by Philip Stepanov for private circulation among his intimate friends. The first time Nilus published them was in 1901 in a book called The Great Within the Small and reprinted in 1905. A copy of this is in the British Museum bearing the date of its reception, August 10, 1906. All copies that were known to exist in Russia were destroyed in the Kerensky regime, and under his successors the possession of a copy by anyone in Soviet land was a crime sufficient to ensure the owner's of being shot on sight. The fact is in itself sufficient proof of the genuineness of the Protocols. The Jewish journals, of course, say that they are a forgery, leaving it to be understood that Professor Nilus, who embodied them in a work of his own, had concocted them for his own purposes.

Mr. Henry Ford, in an interview published in the New York WORLD, February 17th, 1921, put the case for Nilus tersely and convincingly thus:

"The only statement I care to make about the PROTOCOLS is that they fit in with what is going on. They are sixteen years old, and they have fitted the world situation up to this time. THEY FIT IT NOW."

The word "Protocol" signifies a precis gummed on to the front of a document, a draft of a document, minutes of proceedings. In this instance, "Protocol" means minutes of the proceedings of the Meetings of the Learned Elders of Zion. These Protocols give the substance of addresses delivered to the innermost circle of the Rulers of Zion. They reveal the converted plan of action of the Jewish Nation developed through the ages and edited by the Elders themselves up to date. Parts and summaries of the plan have been published from time to time during the centuries as the secrets of the Elders have leaked out. The claim of the Jews that the Protocols are forgeries is in itself an admission of their genuineness, for they NEVER ATTEMPT TO ANSWER THE FACTS corresponding to the THREATS which the Protocols contain, and, indeed, the correspondence between prophecy and fulfillment is too glaring to be set aside or obscured. This the Jews well know and therefore evade.

306

Captain A.H.M. Ramsay records in his classic, The Nameless War: "According to a letter published in "Plain English" (a weekly review published by the North British Publishing Co. and edited by the late Lord Alfred Douglas) on 3rd September, 1921:-

"The Learned Elders have been in existence for a much longer period than they have perhaps suspected. My friend, Mr. L. D. van Valckert, of Amsterdam, has recently sent me a letter containing two extracts from the Synagogue at Mulheim. The volume in which they are contained was lost at some period during the Napoleonic Wars, and has recently come into Mr. van Valckert's possession. It is written in German, and contains extracts of letters sent and received by the authorities of the Mulheim Synagogue. The first entry he sends me is of a letter received:-

16th June, 1647.

From O.C. (i.e. Oliver Cromwell), by Ebenezer Pratt.

"In return for financial support will advocate admission of Jews to England: This however impossible while Charles living.

Charles cannot be executed without trial, adequate grounds for which do not at present exist. Therefore advise that Charles be assassinated, but will have nothing to do with arrangements for procuring an assassin, though willing to help in his escape."

In reply was dispatched the following:-

12th July, 1647.

To O.C. by E. Pratt.

"Will grant financial aid as soon as Charles removed and Jews admitted. Assassination too dangerous. Charles shall be given opportunity to escape: His recapture will make trial and execution possible. The support will be liberal, but useless to discuss terms until trial commences."

Captain Ramsay quotes Isaac Disraeli, father of Benjamin, Earl of Beaconsfield, Britain's first Jewish Prime Minister, in his two volume "Life of Charles I", published in 1851: "The English Revolution under Charles I was unlike any preceding one . . . From that time and event we contemplate in our history the phases of revolution." There were many more to follow on similar lines, notably in France. In 1897 a further important clue to these mysterious happenings fell into Gentile hands in the shape of the Protocols of the Elders of Zion.

In that document we read this remarkable sentence: "Remember the French Revolution, the secrets of its preparation are well known to us for it was entirely the work of our hands." (See Protocol No. III, XIV).

In 1865 a certain Jewish Rabbi named Rzeichorn delivered a speech at Prague. It is a very accurate summary of many aspects of the Protocols which would come to light several decades later and was published eleven years later by Sir John Radcliff, who was assassinated shortly afterwards, giving testimony to the powers of the secret organisation of inner elite Jewry even then.

The presumption is strong that the Protocols were issued, or reissued, at the First Zionist Congress held at Basle in 1897 under the presidency of the Father of Modern Zionism, the late Theodore Herzl.

There has been recently published a volume of Herzl's "Diaries," a translation of some passages which appeared in the JEWISH CHRONICLE of July 14, 1922. Herzl gives an account of his first visit to England in 1895, and his conversation with Colonel Goldsmid, a Jew brought up as a Christian, an officer in the English Army, and at heart a Jew Nationalist all the time. Goldsmid suggested to Herzl that the best way of expropriating the English aristocracy, and so destroying their power to protect the people of England against Jew domination, was to put excessive taxes on the land. Herzl thought this an excellent idea, and it is now to be found definitely embodied in Protocol VI!

The above extract from Herzl's DIARY is an extremely significant bit of evidence bearing on the existence of the Jew World Plot and authenticity of the Protocols, but any reader of intelligence will be able from his own knowledge of recent history and from his own experience to confirm the genuineness of every line of them, and it is in the light of this LIVING comment that all readers are invited to study Mr. Marsden's translation of this terribly inhuman document.

Here is what Dr. Ehrenpreis, Chief Rabbi of Sweden, said in 1924, concerning the Protocols: "Long have I been well acquainted with the contents of the Protocols, indeed for many years before they were ever published in the Christian press. The Protocols of the Elders of Zion were in point of fact not the original Protocols at all, but a compressed extract of the same. Of the 70 Elders of Zion, in the matter of origin and of the existence of the original Protocols, there are only ten men in the entire world who know.

308   I participated with Dr. Herzl in the first Zionist Congress which was held in Basle in 1897. Herzl was the most prominent figure at the

Jewish World Congress. Herzl foresaw, twenty years before we experienced them, the revolution which brought the Great War, and he prepared us for that which was to happen. He foresaw the splitting up of Turkey, that England would obtain control of Palestine. We may expect important developments in the world."

And here is another very significant circumstance. The present successor of Herzl, as leader of the Zionist movement, Dr. Weizmann, quoted one of these sayings at the send-off banquet given to Chief Rabbi Hertz on October 6, 1920. The Chief Rabbi was on the point of leaving for HIS Empire tour of H.R.H., the Prince of Wales. And this is the "saying" of the Sages which Dr. Weizmann quoted: "A beneficent protection which God has instituted in the life of the Jew is that He has dispersed him all over the world." (JEWISH GUARDIAN, Oct. 8, 1920.)

Now compare this with the last clause of but one of Protocol XI.

"God has granted to us, His Chosen People, the gift of dispersion, and from this, which appears to all eyes to be our weakness, has come forth all our strength, which has now brought us to the threshold of sovereignty over all the world."

The remarkable correspondence between these passages proves several things. It proves that the Learned Elders exist. It proves that Dr. Weizmann knows all about them. It proves that the desire for a "National Home" in Palestine is only camouflage and an infinitesimal part of the Jew's real object. It proves that the Jews of the world have no intention of settling in Palestine or any separate country, and that their annual prayer that they may all meet "Next Year in Jerusalem" is merely a piece of their characteristic make-believe. It also demonstrates that the Jews are now a world menace, and that the Aryan races will have to domicile them permanently out of Europe..

WHO ARE THE ELDERS?

This is a secret which has not been revealed. They are the Hidden Hand. They are not the "Board of Deputies" (the Jewish Parliament in England) or the "Universal Israelite Alliance" which sits in Paris. But the late Walter Rathenau of the Allgemeiner Electricitaets Gesellschaft has thrown a little light on the subject and doubtless he was in possession of their names, being, in all likelihood, one of the chief leaders himself. Writing in the WIENER FREIE PRESSE, December 24, 1912, he said:

"Three hundred men, each of whom knows all the others, govern the fate of the European continent, and they elect their successors from their entourage."

In the year 1844, on the eve of the Jewish Revolution of 1848, Benjamin Disraeli, whose real name was Israel, and who was a "damped," or baptized Jew, published his novel, CONINGSBY, in which occurs this ominous passage:

"The world is governed by very different personages from what is imagined by those who are not behind the scenes."

And he went on to show that these personages were all Jews.

Now that Providence has brought to the light of day these secret Protocols all men may clearly see the hidden personages specified by Disraeli at work "behind the scenes" of all the Governments. This revelation entails on all peoples the grave responsibility of examining and revising AU FOND their attitude towards the Race and Nation which boasts of its survival over all Empires.

Notes I. - "Agentur" and "The Political."

There are two words in this translation which are unusual, the word "AGENTUR" and "political" used as a substantive, AGENTUR appears to be a word adopted from the original and it means the whole body of agents and agencies made use of by the Elders, whether members of the tribe or their Gentile tools.

By "the Political" Mr. Marsden means, not exactly the "body politic" but the entire machinery of politics.

Notes II - The Symbolic Snake of Judaism.
[The Serpent Cult of Dann]

Protocol III opens with a reference to the Symbolic Snake of Judaism. In his Epilogue to the 1905 Edition of the Protocols, Nilus gives the following interesting account of this symbol:

"According to the records of secret Jewish Zionism, Solomon and other Jewish learned men already, in 929 B.C., thought out a scheme in theory for a peaceful conquest of the whole universe by Zion. As history developed, this scheme was worked out in detail and completed by men who were subsequently initiated in this question. These learned men decided 310 by peaceful means to conquer the world for Zion with the slyness of the Symbolic Snake, whose head was to represent those who have been initiated into the plans of the Jewish administration, and the body of the Snake to represent the Jewish people - the administration was always kept secret, EVEN FROM THE JEWISH NATION ITSELF. As this Snake penetrated into the hearts of the nations which it encountered it undermined and devoured all the non-Jewish power of these States. It is foretold that the Snake has still to finish its work, strictly adhering to the designed plan, until the course which it has to run is closed by the return of its head to Zion and until, by this means, the Snake has completed its round of Europe and has encircled it - and until, by dint of enchaining Europe, it has encompassed the whole world. This it is to accomplish by using every endeavor to subdue the other countries by an ECONOMICAL CONQUEST. The return of the head of the Snake to Zion can only be accomplished after the power of all the Sovereign of Europe has been laid low, that is to say, when by means of economic crises and wholesale destruction effected everywhere, there shall have been brought about a spiritual demoralization and a moral corruption, chiefly with the assistance of Jewish women masquerading as French, Italians, etc.. These are the surest spreaders of licentiousness into the lives of the leading men at the heads of nations. A map of the course of the Symbolic Snake is shown as follows: - Its first stage in Europe was in 429 B.C. in Greece, where, about the time of Pericles, the Snake first started eating into the power of that country. The second stage was in Rome in the time of Augustus, about 69 B.C.. The third in Madrid in the time of Charles V, in A.D. 1552. The fourth in Paris about 1790, in the time of Louis XVI. The fifth in London from 1814 onwards (after the downfall of Napoleon). The sixth in Berlin in 1871 after the Franco-Prussian war. The seventh in St. Petersburg, over which is drawn the head of the Snake under the date of 1881. [This "Snake" is now being drawn through the Americas and in the United States of America, it has been partially identified as the "Council on Foreign Relations" (C.F.R.) and the "Trilateral Commission"]. All these States which the Snake traversed have had the foundations of their constitutions shaken, Germany, with its apparent power, forming no exception to the rule. In economic conditions, England and Germany are spared, but only till the conquest of Russia is accomplished by the Snake, on which at present [i.e., 1905] all its efforts are concentrated. The further course of the Snake is not shown on this map, but arrows indicate its next movement towards Moscow, Kieft and Odessa. It is now well known to us to what extent the latter cities form the centres of the militant Jewish race. Constantinople is shown as the last stage of the Snake's course before it reaches Jerusalem. (This map was drawn years before the occurrence of the "Young Turk" - i.e., Jewish - Revolution in Turkey).

311

PROTOCOL No. 1

1. ....Putting aside fine phrases we shall speak of the significance of each thought: by comparisons and deductions we shall throw light upon surrounding facts.

2. What I am about to set forth, then, is our system from the two points of view, that of ourselves and that of the GOYIM [i.e., non-Jews].

3. It must be noted that men with bad instincts are more in number than the good, and therefore the best results in governing them are attained by violence and terrorisation, and not by academic discussions. Every man aims at power, everyone would like to become a dictator if only he could, and rare indeed are the men who would not be willing to sacrifice the welfare of all for the sake of securing their own welfare.

4. What has restrained the beasts of prey who are called men? What has served for their guidance hitherto?

5. In the beginnings of the structure of society, they were subjected to brutal and blind force; afterwards - to Law, which is the same force, only disguised. I draw the conclusion that by the law of nature, right lies in force.

6. Political freedom is an idea but not a fact. This idea one must know how to apply whenever it appears necessary with this bait of an idea to attract the masses of the people to one's party for the purpose of crushing another who is in authority. This task is rendered easier if the opponent has himself been infected with the idea of freedom, SO-CALLED LIBERALISM, and, for the sake of an idea, is willing to yield some of his power. It is precisely here that the triumph of our theory appears; the slackened reins of government are immediately, by the law of life, caught up and gathered together by a new hand, because the blind might of the nation cannot for one single day exist without guidance, and the new authority merely fits into the place of the old already weakened by liberalism.

GOLD

7. In our day the power which has replaced that of the rulers who were liberal is the power of Gold. Time was when Faith ruled. The idea of freedom is impossible of realization because no one knows how to use it with moderation. It is enough to hand over a people to self-government for a certain length of time for that people to be turned into a disorganized mob. From that moment on we get internecine strife which soon develops into battles between classes, in the midst of which States burn down and their importance is reduced to that of a heap of ashes.

312

8. Whether a State exhausts itself in its own convulsions, whether its internal discord brings it under the power of external foes - in any case it can be accounted irretrievably lost: IT IS IN OUR POWER. The despotism of Capital, which is entirely in our hands, reaches out to it a straw that the State, willy-nilly, must take hold of: if not - it goes to the bottom.

9. Should anyone of a liberal mind say that such reflections as the above are immoral, I would put the following questions: If every State has two foes and if in regard to the external foe it is allowed and not considered immoral to use every manner and art of conflict, as for example to keep the enemy in ignorance of plans of attack and defense, to attack him by night or in superior numbers, then in what way can the same means in regard to a worse foe, the destroyer of the structure of society and the commonweal, be called immoral and not permissible?

10. Is it possible for any sound logical mind to hope with any success to guide crowds by the aid of reasonable counsels and arguments, when any objection or contradiction, senseless though it may be, can be made and when such objection may find more favor with the people, whose powers of reasoning are superficial? Men in masses and the men of the masses, being guided solely by petty passions, paltry beliefs, traditions and sentimental theorems, fall a prey to party dissension, which hinders any kind of agreement even on the basis of a perfectly reasonable argument. Every resolution of a crowd depends upon a chance or packed majority, which, in its ignorance of political secrets, puts forth some ridiculous resolution that lays in the administration a seed of anarchy.

11. The political has nothing in common with the moral. The ruler who is governed by the moral is not a skilled politician, and is therefore unstable on his throne. He who wishes to rule must have recourse both to cunning and to make-believe. Great national qualities, like frankness and honesty, are vices in politics, for they bring down rulers from their thrones more effectively and more certainly than the most powerful enemy. Such qualities must be the attributes of the kingdoms of the GOYIM, but we must in no wise be guided by them.

RIGHT IS MIGHT

12. Our right lies in force. The word "right" is an abstract thought and proved by nothing. The word means no more than: Give me what I want in order that thereby I may have a proof that I am stronger than you.

13. Where does right begin? Where does it end?

14. In any State in which there is a bad organization of authority, an impersonality of laws and of the rulers who have lost their personality amid the flood of rights ever multiplying out of liberalism, I find a new right - to attack by the right of the strong, and to scatter to the winds all existing forces of order and regulation, to reconstruct all institutions and to become the sovereign lord of those who have left to us the rights of their power by laying them down voluntarily in their liberalism.

15. Our power in the present tottering condition of all forms of power will be more invincible than any other, because it will remain invisible until the moment when it has gained such strength that no cunning can any longer undermine it.

16. Out of the temporary evil we are now compelled to commit will emerge the good of an unshakable rule, which will restore the regular course of the machinery of the national life, brought to naught by liberalism. The result justifies the means. Let us, however, in our plans, direct our attention not so much to what is good and moral as to what is necessary and useful.

17. Before us is a plan in which is laid down strategically the line from which we cannot deviate without running the risk of seeing the labor of many centuries brought to naught.

18. In order to elaborate satisfactory forms of action it is necessary to have regard to the rascality, the slackness, the instability of the mob, its lack of capacity to understand and respect the conditions of its own life, or its own welfare. It must be understood that the might of a mob is blind, senseless and un-reasoning force ever at the mercy of a suggestion from any side. The blind cannot lead the blind without bringing them into the abyss; consequently, members of the mob, upstarts from the people even though they should be as a genius for wisdom, yet having no understanding of the political, cannot come forward as leaders of the mob without bringing the whole nation to ruin.

19. Only one trained from childhood for independent rule can have understanding of the words that can be made up of the political alphabet.

20. A people left to itself, i.e., to upstarts from its midst, brings itself to ruin by party dissensions excited by the pursuit of power and honors and the disorders arising therefrom. Is it possible for the masses of the people calmly and without petty jealousies to form judgment, to deal with the affairs of the country, which cannot be mixed up with personal interest? Can they defend themselves from an external foe? It is unthinkable; for a plan 314 broken up into as many parts as there are heads in the mob, loses all homogeneity, and thereby becomes unintelligible and impossible of

execution.

WE ARE DESPOTS

21. It is only with a despotic ruler that plans can be elaborated extensively and clearly in such a way as to distribute the whole properly among the several parts of the machinery of the State: from this the conclusion is inevitable that a satisfactory form of government for any country is one that concentrates in the hands of one responsible person. Without an absolute despotism there can be no existence for civilization which is carried on not by the masses but by their guide, whosoever that person may be. The mob is savage, and displays its savagery at every opportunity. The moment the mob seizes freedom in its hands it quickly turns to anarchy, which in itself is the highest degree of savagery.

22. Behold the alcoholic animals, bemused with drink, the right to an immoderate use of which comes along with freedom. It is not for us and ours to walk that road. The peoples of the GOYIM are bemused with alcoholic liquors; their youth has grown stupid on classicism and from early immorality, into which it has been inducted by our special agents - by tutors, lackeys, governesses in the houses of the wealthy, by clerks and others, by our women in the places of dissipation frequented by the GOYIM. In the number of these last I count also the so-called "society ladies," voluntary followers of the others in corruption and luxury.

23. Our countersign is - Force and Make-believe. Only force conquers in political affairs, especially if it be concealed in the talents essential to statesmen. Violence must be the principle, and cunning and make-believe the rule for governments which do not want to lay down their crowns at the feet of agents of some new power. This evil is the one and only means to attain the end, the good. Therefore we must not stop at bribery, deceit and treachery when they should serve towards the attainment of our end. In politics one must know how to seize the property of others without hesitation if by it we secure submission and sovereignty.

24. Our State, marching along the path of peaceful conquest, has the right to replace the horrors of war by less noticeable and more satisfactory sentences of death, necessary to maintain the terror which tends to produce blind submission. Just but merciless severity is the greatest factor of strength in the State: not only for the sake of gain but also in the name of duty, for the sake of victory, we must keep to the programme of violence and make-believe. The doctrine of squaring accounts is precisely as strong as the means of which it makes use. Therefore it is not so much by the means themselves as by the doctrine of severity that we shall triumph   315 and bring all governments into subjection to our super-government.

It is enough for them to know that we are too merciless for all disobedience to cease.

WE SHALL END LIBERTY

25. Far back in ancient times we were the first to cry among the masses of the people the words "Liberty, Equality, Fraternity," words many times repeated since these days by stupid poll-parrots who, from all sides around, flew down upon these baits and with them carried away the well-being of the world, true freedom of the individual, formerly so well guarded against the pressure of the mob. The would-be wise men of the GOYIM, the intellectuals, could not make anything out of the uttered words in their abstractedness; did not see that in nature there is no equality, cannot be freedom: that Nature herself has established inequality of minds, of characters, and capacities, just as immutably as she has established subordination to her laws: never stopped to think that the mob is a blind thing, that upstarts elected from among it to bear rule are, in regard to the political, the same blind men as the mob itself, that the adept, though he be a fool, can yet rule, whereas the non-adept, even if he were a genius, understands nothing in the political - to all those things the GOYIM paid no regard; yet all the time it was based upon these things that dynastic rule rested: the father passed on to the son a knowledge of the course of political affairs in such wise that none should know it but members of the dynasty and none could betray it to the governed. As time went on, the meaning of the dynastic transference of the true position of affairs in the political was lost, and this aided the success of our cause.

26. In all corners of the earth the words "Liberty, Equality, Fraternity," brought to our ranks, thanks to our blind agents, whole legions who bore our banners with enthusiasm. And all the time these words were canker-worms at work boring into the well-being of the GOYIM, putting an end everywhere to peace, quiet, solidarity and destroying all the foundations of the GOY States. As you will see later, this helped us to our triumph: it gave us the possibility, among other things, of getting into our hands the master card - the destruction of the privileges, or in other words of the very existence of the aristocracy of the GOYIM, that class which was the only defense peoples and countries had against us. On the ruins of the eternal and genealogical aristocracy of the GOYIM we have set up the aristocracy of our educated class headed by the aristocracy of money. The qualifications for this aristocracy we have established in wealth, which is dependent upon us, and in knowledge, for which our learned elders provide the motive force.

27. Our triumph has been rendered easier by the fact that in our relations with the men, whom we wanted, we have always worked upon the most sensitive chords of the human mind, upon the cash account, upon the cupidity, upon the insatiability for material needs

of man; and each one of these human weaknesses, taken alone, is sufficient to paralyze initiative, for it hands over the will of men to the disposition of him who has bought their activities.

28. The abstraction of freedom has enabled us to persuade the mob in all countries that their government is nothing but the steward of the people who are the owners of the country, and that the steward may be replaced like a worn-out glove.

29. It is this possibility of replacing the representatives of the people which has placed at our disposal, and, as it were, given us the power of appointment.

PROTOCOL No. 2

1. It is indispensable for our purpose that wars, so far as possible, should not result in territorial gains: war will thus be brought on to the economic ground, where the nations will not fail to perceive in the assistance we give the strength of our predominance, and this state of things will put both sides at the mercy of our international AGENTUR; which possesses millions of eyes ever on the watch and unhampered by any limitations whatsoever. Our international rights will then wipe out national rights, in the proper sense of right, and will rule the nations precisely as the civil law of States rules the relations of their subjects among themselves.

2. The administrators, whom we shall choose from among the public, with strict regard to their capacities for servile obedience, will not be persons trained in the arts of government, and will therefore easily become pawns in our game in the hands of men of learning and genius who will be their advisers, specialists bred and reared from early childhood to rule the affairs of the whole world. As is well known to you, these specialists of ours have been drawing to fit them for rule the information they need from our political plans from the lessons of history, from observations made of the events of every moment as it passes. The GOYIM are not guided by practical use of unprejudiced historical observation, but by theoretical routine without any critical regard for consequent results. We need not, therefore, take any account of them - let them amuse themselves until the hour strikes, or live on hopes of new forms of enterprising pastime, or on the memories of all they have enjoyed. For them let that play the principal part which we have persuaded them to accept as the dictates of science (theory). It is with this object in view that we are constantly, by means of our press, arousing a blind confidence in these theories. The intellectuals of the GOYIM will puff themselves up with their knowledges and without any logical verification of them will put into effect all the information available from science, which our AGENTUR specialists have cunningly 317 pieced together for the purpose of educating their minds in the

direction we want.

DESTRUCTIVE EDUCATION

3. Do not suppose for a moment that these statements are empty words: think carefully of the successes we arranged for Darwinism, Marxism, Nietzsche-ism. To us Jews, at any rate, it should be plain to see what a disintegrating importance these directives have had upon the minds of the GOYIM.

4. It is indispensable for us to take account of the thoughts, characters, tendencies of the nations in order to avoid making slips in the political and in the direction of administrative affairs. The triumph of our system of which the component parts of the machinery may be variously disposed according to the temperament of the peoples met on our way, will fail of success if the practical application of it be not based upon a summing up of the lessons of the past in the light of the present.

5. In the hands of the States of to-day there is a great force that creates the movement of thought in the people, and that is the Press. The part played by the Press is to keep pointing our requirements supposed to be indispensable, to give voice to the complaints of the people, to express and to create discontent. It is in the Press that the triumph of freedom of speech finds its incarnation. But the GOYIM States have not known how to make use of this force; and it has fallen into our hands. Through the Press we have gained the power to influence while remaining ourselves in the shade; thanks to the Press we have got the GOLD in our hands, notwithstanding that we have had to gather it out of the oceans of blood and tears. But it has paid us, though we have sacrificed many of our people. Each victim on our side is worth in the sight of God a thousand GOYIM.

PROTOCOL No. 3

1. To-day I may tell you that our goal is now only a few steps off. There remains a small space to cross and the whole long path we have trodden is ready now to close its cycle of the Symbolic Snake, by which we symbolize our people. When this ring closes, all the States of Europe will be locked in its coil as in a powerful vice.

2. The constitution scales of these days will shortly break down, for we have established them with a certain lack of accurate balance in order that they may oscillate incessantly until they wear through the pivot on which they turn. The GOYIM are under the impression that they have welded them sufficiently strong and they have all along kept on expecting that the scales would come into equilibrium. But the pivots - the kings on their thrones - are hemmed in by their representatives, who play the

318

fool, distraught with their own uncontrolled and irresponsible power. This power they owe to the terror which has been breathed into the palaces. As they have no means of getting at their people, into their very midst, the kings on their thrones are no longer able to come to terms with them and so strengthen themselves against seekers after power. We have made a gulf between the far-seeing Sovereign Power and the blind force of the people so that both have lost all meaning, for like the blind man and his stick, both are powerless apart.

3. In order to incite seekers after power to a misuse of power we have set all forces in opposition one to another, breaking up their liberal tendencies towards independence. To this end we have stirred up every form of enterprise, we have armed all parties, we have set up authority as a target for every ambition. Of States we have made gladiatorial arenas where a lot of confused issues contend ... A little more, and disorders and bankruptcy will be universal ...

4. Babblers, inexhaustible, have turned into oratorical contests the sittings of Parliament and Administrative Boards. Bold journalists and unscrupulous pamphleteers daily fall upon executive officials. Abuses of power will put the final touch in preparing all institutions for their overthrow and everything will fly skyward under the blows of the maddened mob.

POVERTY OUR WEAPON

5. All people are chained down to heavy toil by poverty more firmly than ever. They were chained by slavery and serfdom; from these, one way and another, they might free themselves. These could be settled with, but from want they will never get away. We have included in the constitution such rights as to the masses appear fictitious and not actual rights. All these so-called "Peoples Rights" can exist only in idea, an idea which can never be realized in practical life. What is it to the proletariat laborer, bowed double over his heavy toil, crushed by his lot in life, if talkers get the right to babble, if journalists get the right to scribble any nonsense side by side with good stuff, once the proletariat has no other profit out of the constitution save only those pitiful crumbs which we fling them from our table in return for their voting in favor of what we dictate, in favor of the men we place in power, the servants of our AGENTUR ... Republican rights for a poor man are no more than a bitter piece of irony, for the necessity he is under of toiling almost all day gives him no present use of them, but the other hand robs him of all guarantee of regular and certain earnings by making him dependent on strikes by his comrades or lockouts by his masters.

319

6. The people, under our guidance, have annihilated the aristocracy, who were their one and only defense and foster-mother for the sake of their own advantage which is inseparably bound up with the well-being of the people. Nowadays, with the destruction of the aristocracy, the people have fallen into the grips of merciless money-grinding scoundrels who have laid a pitiless and cruel yoke upon the necks of the workers.

7. We appear on the scene as alleged saviours of the worker from this oppression when we propose to him to enter the ranks of our fighting forces - Socialists, Anarchists, Communists - to whom we always give support in accordance with an alleged brotherly rule (of the solidarity of all humanity) of our SOCIAL MASONRY. The aristocracy, which enjoyed by law the labor of the workers, was interested in seeing that the workers were well fed, healthy, and strong. We are interested in just the opposite - in the diminution, the KILLING OUT OF THE GOYIM. Our power is in the chronic shortness of food and physical weakness of the worker because by all that this implies he is made the slave of our will, and he will not find in his own authorities either strength or energy to set against our will. Hunger creates the right of capital to rule the worker more surely than it was given to the aristocracy by the legal authority of kings.

8. By want and the envy and hatred which it engenders we shall move the mobs and with their hands we shall wipe out all those who hinder us on our way.

9. WHEN THE HOUR STRIKES FOR OUR SOVEREIGN LORD OF ALL THE WORLD TO BE CROWNED IT IS THESE SAME HANDS WHICH WILL SWEEP AWAY EVERYTHING THAT MIGHT BE A HINDRANCE THERETO. (The Biblical "Anti-Christ?")

10. The GOYIM have lost the habit of thinking unless prompted by the suggestions of our specialists. Therefore they do not see the urgent necessity of what we, when our kingdom comes, shall adopt at once, namely this, that IT IS ESSENTIAL TO TEACH IN NATIONAL SCHOOLS ONE SIMPLE, TRUE PIECE OF KNOWLEDGE, THE BASIS OF ALL KNOWLEDGE - THE KNOWLEDGE OF THE STRUCTURE OF HUMAN LIFE, OF SOCIAL EXISTENCE, WHICH REQUIRES DIVISION OF LABOR, AND, CONSEQUENTLY, THE DIVISION OF MEN INTO CLASSES AND CONDITIONS. It is essential for all to know that OWING TO DIFFERENCE IN THE OBJECTS OF HUMAN ACTIVITY THERE CANNOT BE ANY EQUALITY, 320 that he, who by any act of his compromises a whole class, cannot be equally responsible before the law with him who affects no one but

only his own honor. The true knowledge of the structure of society, into the secrets of which we do not admit the GOYIM, would demonstrate to all men that the positions and work must be kept within a certain circle, that they may not become a source of human suffering, arising from an education which does not correspond with the work which individuals are called upon to do. After a thorough study of this knowledge, the peoples will voluntarily submit to authority and accept such position as is appointed them in the State. In the present state of knowledge and the direction we have given to its development of the people, blindly believing things in print - cherishes - thanks to promptings intended to mislead and to its own ignorance - a blind hatred towards all conditions which it considers above itself, for it has no understanding of the meaning of class and condition.

JEWS WILL BE SAFE

11. THIS HATRED WILL BE STILL FURTHER MAGNIFIED BY THE EFFECTS of an ECONOMIC CRISES, which will stop dealing on the exchanges and bring industry to a standstill. We shall create by all the secret subterranean methods open to us and with the aid of gold, which is all in our hands, A UNIVERSAL ECONOMIC CRISES WHEREBY WE SHALL THROW UPON THE STREETS WHOLE MOBS OF WORKERS SIMULTANEOUSLY IN ALL THE COUNTRIES OF EUROPE. These mobs will rush delightedly to shed the blood of those whom, in the simplicity of their ignorance, they have envied from their cradles, and whose property they will then be able to loot.

12. "OURS" THEY WILL NOT TOUCH, BECAUSE THE MOMENT OF ATTACK WILL BE KNOWN TO US AND WE SHALL TAKE MEASURES TO PROTECT OUR OWN.

13. We have demonstrated that progress will bring all the GOYIM to the sovereignty of reason. Our despotism will be precisely that; for it will know how, by wise severities, to pacificate all unrest, to cauterize liberalism out of all institutions.

14. When the populace has seen that all sorts of concessions and indulgences are yielded it, in the same name of freedom it has imagined itself to be sovereign lord and has stormed its way to power, but, naturally like every other blind man, it has come upon a host of stumbling blocks. IT HAS RUSHED TO FIND A GUIDE, IT HAS NEVER HAD THE SENSE TO RETURN TO THE FORMER STATE and it has laid down its plenipotentiary powers at OUR feet. Remember the French Revolution, to which it was we who gave the name of "Great": the secrets of its preparations are well known to us for it was wholly the work of our hands.   321

15. Ever since that time we have been leading the peoples from one disenchantment to another, so that in the end they should turn also from us in favor of that KING-DESPOT OF THE BLOOD OF ZION, WHOM WE ARE PREPARING FOR THE WORLD.

16. At the present day we are, as an international force, invincible, because if attacked by some we are supported by other States. It is the bottomless rascality of the GOYIM peoples, who crawl on their bellies to force, but are merciless towards weakness, unsparing to faults and indulgent to crimes, unwilling to bear the contradictions of a free social system but patient unto martyrdom under the violence of a bold despotism - it is those qualities which are aiding us to independence. From the premier-dictators of the present day, the GOYIM peoples suffer patiently and bear such abuses as for the least of them they would have beheaded twenty kings.

17. What is the explanation of this phenomenon, this curious inconsequence of the masses of the peoples in their attitude towards what would appear to be events of the same order?

18. It is explained by the fact that these dictators whisper to the peoples through their agents that through these abuses they are inflicting injury on the States with the highest purpose - to secure the welfare of the peoples, the international brotherhood of them all, their solidarity and equality of rights. Naturally they do not tell the peoples that this unification must be accomplished only under our sovereign rule.

19. And thus the people condemn the upright and acquit the guilty, persuaded ever more and more that it can do whatsoever it wishes. Thanks to this state of things, the people are destroying every kind of stability and creating disorders at every step.

20. The word "freedom" brings out the communities of men to fight against every kind of force, against every kind of authority even against God and the laws of nature. For this reason we, when we come into our kingdom, shall have to erase this word from the lexicon of life as implying a principle of brute force which turns mobs into bloodthirsty beasts.

21. These beasts, it is true, fall asleep again every time when they have drunk their fill of blood, and at such time can easily be riveted into their chains. But if they be not given blood they will not sleep and continue to struggle.

PROTOCOL No. 4

1. Every republic passes through several stages. The first of these is comprised in the early days of mad raging by the blind mob, tossed

322

hither and thither, right and left: the second is demagogy from which is born anarchy, and that leads inevitably to despotism - not any longer legal and overt, and therefore responsible despotism, but to unseen and secretly hidden, yet nevertheless sensibly felt despotism in the hands of some secret organization or other, whose acts are the more unscrupulous inasmuch as it works behind a screen, behind the backs of all sorts of agents, the changing of whom not only does not injuriously affect but actually aids the secret force by saving it, thanks to continual changes, from the necessity of expanding its resources on the rewarding of long services.

2. Who and what is in a position to overthrow an invisible force? And this is precisely what our force is. GENTILE masonry blindly serves as a screen for us and our objects, but the plan of action of our force, even its very abiding-place, remains for the whole people an unknown mystery.

WE SHALL DESTROY GOD

Chief Rabbi of Israel, Yona Metzger flashing "666" hand-sign. Stepped down 6/23/2013 due to criminal charges brought against him for fraud and bribery related to benefits he received from several Israeli companies.

3. But even freedom might be harmless and have its place in the State economy without injury to the well-being of the peoples if it rested upon the foundation of faith in God, upon the brotherhood of humanity, unconnected with the conception of equality, which is negatived by the very laws of creation, for they have established subordination. With such a faith as this a people might be governed by a wardship of parishes, and would walk contentedly and humbly under the guiding hand of its spiritual pastor submitting to the dispositions of God upon earth. This is the reason why IT IS INDISPENSABLE FOR US TO UNDERMINE ALL FAITH, TO TEAR OUT OF THE MIND OF THE "GOYIM" THE VERY PRINCIPLE OF GOD-HEAD AND THE SPIRIT, AND TO PUT IN ITS PLACE ARITHMETICAL CALCULATIONS AND MATERIAL NEEDS.

4. In order to give the GOYIM no time to think and take note, their minds must be diverted towards industry and trade. Thus, all the nations will be swallowed up in the pursuit of gain and in the race for it will not take note of their common foe. But again, in order 323

that freedom may once for all disintegrate and ruin the communities of the GOYIM, we must put industry on a speculative basis: the result of this will be that what is withdrawn from the land by industry will slip through the hands and pass into speculation, that is, to our classes.

5. The intensified struggle for superiority and shocks delivered to economic life will create, nay, have already created, disenchanted, cold and heartless communities. Such communities will foster a strong aversion towards the higher political and towards religion. Their only guide is gain, that is Gold, which they will erect into a veritable cult, for the sake of those material delights which it can give. Then will the hour strike when, not for the sake of attaining the good, not even to win wealth, but solely out of hatred towards the privileged, the lower classes of the GOYIM will follow our lead against our rivals for power, the intellectuals of the GOYIM.

PROTOCOL No. 5

1. What form of administrative rule can be given to communities in which corruption has penetrated everywhere, communities where riches are attained only by the clever surprise tactics of semi-swindling tricks; where loseness reigns: where morality is maintained by penal measures and harsh laws but not by voluntarily accepted principles: where the feelings towards faith and country are obligated by cosmopolitan convictions? What form of rule is to be given to these communities if not that despotism which I shall describe to you later? We shall create an intensified centralization of government in order to grip in our hands all the forces of the community. We shall regulate mechanically all the actions of the political life of our subjects by new laws. These laws will withdraw one by one all the indulgences and liberties which have been permitted by the GOYIM, and our kingdom will be distinguished by a despotism of such magnificent proportions as to be at any moment and in every place in a position to wipe out any GOYIM who oppose us by deed or word.

2. We shall be told that such a despotism as I speak of is not consistent with the progress of these days, but I will prove to you that it is.

3. In the times when the peoples looked upon kings on their thrones as on a pure manifestation of the will of God, they submitted without a murmur to the despotic power of kings: but from the day when we insinuated into their minds the conception of their own rights they began to regard the occupants of thrones as mere ordinary mortals. The holy unction of the Lord's Anointed has fallen from the heads of kings in the eyes of the people, and when we also robbed them of their faith in God the might of power was flung upon the streets into the place of public proprietorship and was seized by us.

324

4. Moreover, the art of directing masses and individuals by means of cleverly manipulated theory and verbiage, by regulations of life in common and all sorts of other quirks, in all which the GOYIM understand nothing, belongs likewise to the specialists of our administrative brain. Reared on analysis, observation, on delicacies of fine calculation, in this species of skill we have no rivals, any more than we have either in the drawing up of plans of political actions and solidarity. In this respect the Jesuits alone might have compared with us, but we have contrived to discredit them in the eyes of the unthinking mob as an overt organization, while we ourselves all the while have kept our secret organization in the shade. However, it is probably all the same to the world who is its sovereign lord, whether the head of Catholicism or our despot of the blood of Zion! But to us, the Chosen People, it is very far from being a matter of indifference.

5. FOR A TIME PERHAPS WE MIGHT BE SUCCESSFULLY DEALT WITH BY A COALITION OF THE "GOYIM" OF ALL THE WORLD: but from this danger we are secured by the discord existing among them whose roots are so deeply seated that they can never now be plucked up. We have set one against another the personal and national reckonings of the GOYIM, religious and race hatreds, which we have fostered into a huge growth in the course of the past twenty centuries. This is the reason why there is not one State which would anywhere receive support if it were to raise its arm, for every one of them must bear in mind that any agreement against us would be unprofitable to itself. We are too strong - there is no evading our power. THE NATIONS CANNOT COME TO EVEN AN INCONSIDERABLE PRIVATE AGREEMENT WITHOUT OUR SECRETLY HAVING A HAND IN IT.

6. PER ME REGES REGNANT. "It is through me that Kings reign." And it was said by the prophets that we were chosen by God Himself to rule over the whole earth. God has endowed us with genius that we may be equal to our task. Were genius in the opposite camp it would still struggle against us, but even so, a newcomer is no match for the old-established settler: the struggle would be merciless between us, such a fight as the world has never seen. Aye, and the genius on their side would have arrived too late. All the wheels of the machinery of all States go by the force of the engine, which is in our hands, and that engine of the machinery of States is - Gold. The science of political economy invented by our learned elders has for long past been giving royal prestige to capital.

7. Capital, if it is to co-operate untrammeled, must be free to establish a monopoly of industry and trade: this is already being put in execution by an unseen hand in all quarters of the world. This freedom will give political force to those engaged in industry, and that will help to oppress the people. Nowadays it is more important to disarm the peoples than to lead them into war: more important to use for our advantage the passions which have burst into flames than to quench their fire: more important to eradicate them. THE PRINCIPLE OBJECT OF OUR DIRECTORATE CONSISTS IN THIS: TO DEBILITATE THE PUBLIC MIND BY CRITICISM; TO LEAD IT AWAY FROM SERIOUS REFLECTIONS CALCULATED TO AROUSE RESISTANCE; TO DISTRACT THE FORCES OF THE MIND TOWARDS A SHAM FIGHT OF EMPTY ELOQUENCE.

8. In all ages the people of the world, equally with individuals, have accepted words for deeds, for THEY ARE CONTENT WITH A SHOW and rarely pause to note, in the public arena, whether promises are followed by performance. Therefore we shall establish show institutions which will give eloquent proof of their benefit to progress.

9. We shall assume to ourselves the liberal physiognomy of all parties, of all directions, and we shall give that physiognomy a VOICE IN ORATORS WHO WILL SPEAK SO MUCH THAT THEY WILL EXHAUST THE PATIENCE OF THEIR HEARERS AND PRODUCE AN ABHORRENCE OF ORATORY.

10. IN ORDER TO PUT PUBLIC OPINION INTO OUR HANDS WE MUST BRING IT INTO A STATE OF BEWILDERMENT BY GIVING EXPRESSION FROM ALL SIDES TO SO MANY CONTRADICTORY OPINIONS AND FOR SUCH LENGTH OF TIME AS WILL SUFFICE TO MAKE THE "GOYIM" LOSE THEIR HEADS IN THE LABYRINTH AND COME TO SEE THAT THE BEST THING IS TO HAVE NO OPINION OF ANY KIND IN MATTERS POLITICAL, which it is not given to the public to understand, because they are understood only by him who guides the public. This is the first secret.

11. The second secret requisite for the success of our government is comprised in the following: To multiply to such an extent national failings, habits, passions, conditions of civil life, that it will be impossible for anyone to know where he is in the resulting chaos, so that the people in consequence will fail to understand one another. This measure will also serve us in another way, namely, to sow discord in all parties, to dislocate all collective forces which are still unwilling to submit to us, and to discourage any kind of personal initiative which might in any degree

326

hinder our affair. THERE IS NOTHING MORE DANGEROUS THAN PERSONAL INITIATIVE: if it has genius behind it, such initiative can do more than can be done by millions of people among whom we have sown discord. We must so direct the education of the GOYIM communities that whenever they come upon a matter requiring initiative they may drop their hands in despairing impotence. The strain which results from freedom of actions saps the forces when it meets with the freedom of another. From this collision arise grave moral shocks, disenchantments, failures. BY ALL THESE MEANS WE SHALL SO WEAR DOWN THE "GOYIM" THAT THEY WILL BE COMPELLED TO OFFER US INTERNATIONAL POWER OF A NATURE THAT BY ITS POSITION WILL ENABLE US WITHOUT ANY VIOLENCE GRADUALLY TO ABSORB ALL THE STATE FORCES OF THE WORLD AND TO FORM A SUPER-GOVERNMENT. In place of the rulers of to-day we shall set up a bogey which will be called the Super-Government Administration. Its hands will reach out in all directions like nippers and its organization will be of such colossal dimensions that it cannot fail to subdue all the nations of the world. (League of Nations and subsequent United Nations Organization - Ed.).

PROTOCOL No. 6

1. We shall soon begin to establish huge monopolies, reservoirs of colossal riches, upon which even large fortunes of the GOYIM will depend to such an extent that they will go to the bottom together with the credit of the States on the day after the political smash ... (Compulsory superannuation, Social Security).

2. You gentlemen here present who are economists, just strike an estimate of the significance of this combination! ...

3. In every possible way we must develop the significance of our Super-Government by representing it as the Protector and Benefactor of all those who voluntarily submit to us.

4. The aristocracy of the GOYIM as a political force, is dead - We need not take it into account; but as landed proprietors they can still be harmful to us from the fact that they are self-sufficing in the resources upon which they live. It is essential therefore for us at whatever cost to deprive them of their land. This object will be best attained by increasing the burdens upon landed property - in loading lands with debts. These measures will check land-holding and keep it in a state of humble and unconditional submission.

5. The aristocrats of the GOYIM, being hereditarily incapable of contenting themselves with little, will rapidly burn up and fizzle out. 327

6. At the same time we must intensively patronize trade and industry, but, first and foremost, speculation, the part played by which is to provide a counterpoise to industry: the absence of speculative industry will multiply capital in private hands and will serve to restore agriculture by freeing the land from indebtedness to the land banks. What we want is that industry should drain off from the land both labor and capital and by means of speculation transfer into our hands all the money of the world, and thereby throw all the GOYIM into the ranks of the proletariat. Then the GOYIM will bow down before us, if for no other reason but to get the right to exist.

7. To complete the ruin of the industry of the GOYIM we shall bring to the assistance of speculation the luxury which we have developed among the GOYIM, that greedy demand for luxury which is swallowing up everything. WE SHALL RAISE THE RATE OF WAGES WHICH, HOWEVER, WILL NOT BRING ANY ADVANTAGE TO THE WORKERS, FOR, AT THE SAME TIME, WE SHALL PRODUCE A RISE IN PRICES OF THE FIRST NECESSARIES OF LIFE, ALLEGING THAT IT ARISES FROM THE DECLINE OF AGRICULTURE AND CATTLE-BREEDING: WE SHALL FURTHER UNDERMINE ARTFULLY AND DEEPLY SOURCES OF PRODUCTION, BY ACCUSTOMING THE WORKERS TO ANARCHY AND TO DRUNKENNESS AND SIDE BY SIDE THEREWITH TAKING ALL MEASURE TO EXTIRPATE FROM THE FACE OF THE EARTH ALL THE EDUCATED FORCES OF THE "GOYIM."

8. IN ORDER THAT THE TRUE MEANING OF THINGS MAY NOT STRIKE THE "GOYIM" BEFORE THE PROPER TIME WE SHALL MASK IT UNDER AN ALLEGED ARDENT DESIRE TO SERVE THE WORKING CLASSES AND THE GREAT PRINCIPLES OF POLITICAL ECONOMY ABOUT WHICH OUR ECONOMIC THEORIES ARE CARRYING ON AN ENERGETIC PROPAGANDA.

PROTOCOL No. 7

1. The intensification of armaments, the increase of police forces - are all essential for the completion of the aforementioned plans. What we have to get at is that there should be in all the States of the world, besides ourselves, only the masses of the proletariat, a few millionaires devoted to our interests, police and soldiers.

2. Throughout all Europe, and by means of relations with Europe, in other continents also, we must create ferments, discords and hostility. Therein we gain a double advantage. In the first place we keep in

check all countries, for they will know that we have the power whenever we like to create disorders or to restore order. All these countries are accustomed to see in us an indispensable force of coercion. In the second place, by our intrigues we shall tangle up all the threads which we have stretched into the cabinets of all States by means of the political, by economic treaties, or loan obligations. In order to succeed in this we must use great cunning and penetration during negotiations and agreements, but, as regards what is called the "official language," we shall keep to the opposite tactics and assume the mask of honesty and complacency. In this way the peoples and governments of the GOYIM, whom we have taught to look only at the outside whatever we present to their notice, will still continue to accept us as the benefactors and saviours of the human race.

UNIVERSAL WAR

3. We must be in a position to respond to every act of opposition by war with the neighbors of that country which dares to oppose us: but if these neighbors should also venture to stand collectively together against us, then we must offer resistance by a universal war.

4. The principal factor of success in the political is the secrecy of its undertakings: the word should not agree with the deeds of the diplomat.

5. We must compel the governments of the GOYIM to take action in the direction favored by our widely conceived plan, already approaching the desired consummation, by what we shall represent as public opinion, secretly promoted by us through the means of that so-called "Great Power" - THE PRESS, WHICH, WITH A FEW EXCEPTIONS THAT MAY BE DISREGARDED, IS ALREADY ENTIRELY IN OUR HANDS.

6. In a word, to sum up our system of keeping the governments of the goyim in Europe in check, we shall show our strength to one of them by terrorist attempts and to all, if we allow the possibility of a general rising against us, we shall respond with the guns of America or China or Japan. (The Russo-Japanese War of 1904-1905 - Ed.).

PROTOCOL No. 8

1. We must arm ourselves with all the weapons which our opponents might employ against us. We must search out in the very finest shades of expression and the knotty points of the lexicon of law justification for those cases where we shall have to pronounce judgments that might appear abnormally audacious and unjust, for it is important that these resolutions should be set forth in expressions that shall seem to be the most exalted moral principles cast into legal form. (Genocide Convention? U.N.

Declaration of the Rights of the Child?) Our directorate must surround itself with all these forces of civilization among which it will have to work. It will surround itself with publicists, practical jurists, administrators, diplomats and, finally, with persons prepared by a special super-educational training IN OUR SPECIAL SCHOOLS (Rhodes Scholars? London School of Economics?) These persons will have consonance of all the secrets of the social structure, they will know all the languages that can be made up by political alphabets and words; they will be made acquainted with the whole underside of human nature, with all its sensitive chords on which they will have to play. These chords are the cast of mind of the GOYIM, their tendencies, short-comings, vices and qualities, the particularities of classes and conditions. Needless to say that the talented assistants of authority, of whom I speak, will be taken not from among the GOYIM, who are accustomed to perform their administrative work without giving themselves the trouble to think what its aim is, and never consider what it is needed for. The administrators of the GOYIM sign papers without reading them, (As Margaret Thatcher signed-away British sovereignty by the Maastricht Treaty? As Australian Parliamentarians signed over 2,000 U.N. Treaties . . . unread?) and they serve either for mercenary reasons or from ambition.

2. We shall surround our government with a whole world of economists. That is the reason why economic sciences form the principal subject of the teaching given to the Jews. Around us again will be a whole constellation of bankers, industrialists, capitalists and - THE MAIN THING - MILLIONAIRES, BECAUSE IN SUBSTANCE EVERYTHING WILL BE SETTLED BY THE QUESTION OF FIGURES.

3. For a time, until there will no longer be any risk in entrusting responsible posts in our State to our brother-Jews, we shall put them in the hands of persons whose past and reputation are such that between them and the people lies an abyss, persons who, in case of disobedience to our instructions, must face criminal charges or disappear - this in order to make them defend our interests to their last gasp.

PROTOCOL No. 9

1. In applying our principles let attention be paid to the character of the people in whose country you live and act; a general, identical application of them, until such time as the people shall have been re-educated to our pattern, cannot have success. But by approaching their application cautiously you will see that not a decade will pass before the most stubborn character will change and we shall add a new people to the ranks of those already subdued by us.

2. The words of the liberal, which are in effect the words of our masonic watchword, namely, "Liberty, Equality, Fraternity," will, when we come into our kingdom, be changed by us into words no longer of a watchword, but only an expression of idealism, namely, into "The right of liberty, the duty of equality, the ideal of brotherhood." That is how we shall put it, - and so we shall catch the bull by the horns ... DE FACTO we have already wiped out every kind of rule except our own, although DE JURE there still remain a good many of them. Nowadays, if any States raise a protest against us it is only PRO FORMA at our discretion and by our direction, for THEIR ANTI-SEMITISM IS INDISPENSABLE TO US FOR THE MANAGEMENT OF OUR LESSER BRETHREN. I will not enter into further explanations, for this matter has formed the subject of repeated discussions amongst us.

JEWISH SUPER-STATE

3. For us there are not checks to limit the range of our activity. Our Super-Government subsists in extra-legal conditions which are described in the accepted terminology by the energetic and forcible word - Dictatorship. I am in a position to tell you with a clear conscience that at the proper time we, the law-givers, shall execute judgment and sentence, we shall slay and we shall spare, we, as head of all our troops, are mounted on the steed of the leader. We rule by force of will, because in our hands are the fragments of a once powerful party, now vanquished by us. AND THE WEAPONS IN OUR HANDS ARE LIMITLESS AMBITIONS, BURNING GREEDINESS, MERCILESS VENGEANCE, HATREDS AND MALICE.

4. IT IS FROM US THAT THE ALL-ENGULFING TERROR PROCEEDS. WE HAVE IN OUR SERVICE PERSONS OF ALL OPINIONS, OF ALL DOCTRINES, RESTORATING MONARCHISTS, DEMAGOGUES, SOCIALISTS, COMMUNISTS, AND UTOPIAN DREAMERS OF EVERY KIND. We have harnessed them all to the task: EACH ONE OF THEM ON HIS OWN ACCOUNT IS BORING AWAY AT THE LAST REMNANTS OF AUTHORITY, IS STRIVING TO OVERTHROW ALL ESTABLISHED FORM OF ORDER. By these acts all States are in torture; they exhort to tranquility, are ready to sacrifice everything for peace: BUT WE WILL NOT GIVE THEM PEACE UNTIL THEY OPENLY ACKNOWLEDGE OUR INTERNATIONAL SUPER-GOVERNMENT, AND WITH SUBMISSIVENESS.

5. The people have raised a howl about the necessity of settling the question of Socialism by way of an international agreement. DIVISION INTO FRACTIONAL PARTIES HAS GIVEN THEM INTO OUR HANDS, FOR, IN ORDER TO CARRY ON A CONTESTED STRUGGLE ONE MUST HAVE MONEY, AND THE MONEY IS ALL IN OUR HANDS.

6. We might have reason to apprehend a union between the "clear-sighted" force of the GOY kings on their thrones and the "blind" force of the GOY mobs, but we have taken all the needful measure against any such possibility: between the one and the other force we have erected a bulwark in the shape of a mutual terror between them. In this way the blind force of the people remains our support and we, and we only, shall provide them with a leader and, of course, direct them along the road that leads to our goal.

7. In order that the hand of the blind mob may not free itself from our guiding hand, we must every now and then enter into close communion with it, if not actually in person, at any rate through some of the most trusty of our brethren. When we are acknowledged as the only authority we shall discuss with the people personally on the market, places, and we shall instruct them on questings of the political in such wise as may turn them in the direction that suits us.

8. Who is going to verify what is taught in the village schools? But what an envoy of the government or a king on his throne himself may say cannot but become immediately known to the whole State, for it will be spread abroad by the voice of the people.

9. In order to annihilate the institutions of the GOYIM before it is time we have touched them with craft and delicacy, and have taken hold of the ends of the springs which move their mechanism. These springs lay in a strict but just sense of order; we have replaced them by the chaotic license of liberalism. We have got our hands into the administration of the law, into the conduct of elections, into the press, into liberty of the person, BUT PRINCIPALLY INTO EDUCATION AND TRAINING AS BEING THE CORNERSTONES OF A FREE EXISTENCE.

CHRISTIAN YOUTH DESTROYED

10. WE HAVE FOOLED, BEMUSED AND CORRUPTED THE YOUTH OF THE "GOYIM" BY REARING THEM IN PRINCIPLES AND THEORIES WHICH ARE KNOWN TO US TO BE FALSE ALTHOUGH IT IS THAT THEY HAVE BEEN INCULCATED.

11. Above the existing laws without substantially altering them, and by merely twisting them into contradictions of interpretations, we have erected something grandiose in the way of results. These results found expression in the fact that the INTERPRETATIONS MASKED THE LAW: afterwards they entirely hid them from the eyes of the governments owing to the impossibility of making anything out of the tangled web of legislation.

332

12. This is the origin of the theory of course of arbitration.

13. You may say that the GOYIM will rise upon us, arms in hand, if they guess what is going on before the time comes; but in the West we have against this a manoeuvre of such appalling terror that the very stoutest hearts quail - the undergrounds, metropolitans, those subterranean corridors which, before the time comes, will be driven under all the capitals and from whence those capitals will be blown into the air with all their organizations and archives.

PROTOCOL No. 10

1. To-day I begin with a repetition of what I said before, and I BEG YOU TO BEAR IN MIND THAT GOVERNMENTS AND PEOPLE ARE CONTENT IN THE POLITICAL WITH OUTSIDE APPEARANCES. And how, indeed, are the GOYIM to perceive the underlying meaning of things when their representatives give the best of their energies to enjoying themselves? For our policy it is of the greatest importance to take cognizance of this detail; it will be of assistance to us when we come to consider the division of authority of property, of the dwelling, of taxation (the idea of concealed taxes, of the reflex force of the laws. All these questions are such as ought not to be touched upon directly and openly before the people. In cases where it is indispensable to touch upon them they must not be categorically named, it must merely be declared without detailed exposition that the principles of contemporary law are acknowledged by us. The reason of keeping silence in this respect is that by not naming a principle we leave ourselves freedom of action, to drop this or that out of it without attracting notice; if they were all categorically named they would all appear to have been already given.

2. The mob cherishes a special affection and respect for the geniuses of political power and accepts all their deeds of violence with the admiring response: "rascally, well, yes, it is rascally, but it's clever! ... a trick, if you like, but how craftily played, how magnificently done, what impudent audacity!" ...

OUR GOAL - WORLD POWER

3. We count upon attracting all nations to the task of erecting the new fundamental structure, the project for which has been drawn up by us. This is why, before everything, it is indispensable for us to arm ourselves and to store up in ourselves that absolutely reckless audacity and irresistible might of the spirit which in the person of our active workers will break down all hindrances on our way.

4. WHEN WE HAVE ACCOMPLISHED OUR COUP D'ETAT WE SHALL SAY THEN TO THE VARIOUS PEOPLES: "EVERYTHING HAS GONE TERRIBLY BADLY, ALL HAVE BEEN WORN OUT WITH SUFFERING. WE ARE DESTROYING THE CAUSES OF YOUR TORMENT - NATIONALITIES, FRONTIERS, DIFFERENCES OF COINAGES. YOU ARE AT LIBERTY, OF COURSE, TO PRONOUNCE SENTENCE UPON US, BUT CAN IT POSSIBLY BE A JUST ONE IF IT IS CONFIRMED BY YOU BEFORE YOU MAKE ANY TRIAL OF WHAT WE ARE OFFERING YOU." ... THEN WILL THE MOB EXALT US AND BEAR US UP IN THEIR HANDS IN A UNANIMOUS TRIUMPH OF HOPES AND 333

EXPECTATIONS. VOTING, WHICH WE HAVE MADE THE INSTRUMENT WHICH WILL SET US ON THE THRONE OF THE WORLD BY TEACHING EVEN THE VERY SMALLEST UNITS OF MEMBERS OF THE HUMAN RACE TO VOTE BY MEANS OF MEETINGS AND AGREEMENTS BY GROUPS, WILL THEN HAVE SERVED ITS PURPOSES AND WILL PLAY ITS PART THEN FOR THE LAST TIME BY A UNANIMITY OF DESIRE TO MAKE CLOSE ACQUAINTANCE WITH US BEFORE CONDEMNING US.

5. TO SECURE THIS WE MUST HAVE EVERYBODY VOTE WITHOUT DISTINCTION OF CLASSES AND QUALIFICATIONS, in order to establish an absolute majority, which cannot be got from the educated propertied classes. In this way, by inculcating in all a sense of self-importance, we shall destroy among the GOYIM the importance of the family and its educational value and remove the possibility of individual minds splitting off, for the mob, handled by us, will not let them come to the front nor even give them a hearing; it is accustomed to listen to us only who pay it for obedience and attention. In this way we shall create a blind, mighty force which will never be in a position to move in any direction without the guidance of our agents set at its head by us as leaders of the mob. The people will submit to this regime because it will know that upon these leaders will depend its earnings, gratifications and the receipt of all kinds of benefits.

6. A scheme of government should come ready made from one brain, because it will never be clinched firmly if it is allowed to be split into fractional parts in the minds of many. It is allowable, therefore, for us to have cognizance of the scheme of action but not to discuss it lest we disturb its artfulness, the interdependence of its component parts, the practical force of the secret meaning of each clause. To discuss and make alterations in a labor of this kind by means of numerous votings is to impress upon it the stamp of all ratiocinations and misunderstandings which have failed to penetrate the depth and nexus of its plottings. We want our schemes to be forcible and suitably concocted. Therefore WE OUGHT NOT TO FLING THE WORK OF GENIUS OF OUR GUIDE to the fangs of the mob or even of a select company.

7. These schemes will not turn existing institutions upside down just yet. They will only effect changes in their economy and consequently in the whole combined movement of their progress, which will thus be directed along the paths laid down in our schemes.

POISON OF LIBERALISM

8. Under various names there exists in all countries approximately one and the same thing. Representation, Ministry, Senate, State Council, Legislative and Executive Corps. I need not explain to you the mechanism of the relation of these institutions to one another, because you are aware of all that; only take note of the fact that each of the above-named institutions corresponds to some important function of the State, and I would beg you to remark that the word "important" I apply not to the institution but to the function, consequently it is not the institutions which are important but their functions. These institutions have

334

divided up among themselves all the functions of government - administrative, legislative, executive, wherefore they have come to operate as do the organs in the human body. If we injure one part in the machinery of State, the State falls sick, like a human body, and ... will die.

9. When we introduced into the State organism the poison of Liberalism its whole political complexion underwent a change. States have been seized with a mortal illness - blood poisoning. All that remains is to await the end of their death agony.

10. Liberalism produced Constitutional States, which took the place of what was the only safeguard of the GOYIM, namely, Despotism; and A CONSTITUTION, AS YOU WELL KNOW, IS NOTHING ELSE BUT A SCHOOL OF DISCORDS, misunderstandings, quarrels, disagreements, fruitless party agitations, party whims - in a word, a school of everything that serves to destroy the personality of State activity. THE TRIBUNE OF THE "TALKERIES" HAS, NO LESS EFFECTIVELY THAN THE PRESS, CONDEMNED THE RULERS TO INACTIVITY AND IMPOTENCE, and thereby rendered them useless and superfluous, for which reason indeed they have been in many countries deposed. THEN IT WAS THAT THE ERA OF REPUBLICS BECOME POSSIBLE OF REALIZATION; AND THEN IT WAS THAT WE REPLACED THE RULER BY A CARICATURE OF A GOVERNMENT - BY A PRESIDENT, TAKEN FROM THE MOB, FROM THE MIDST OF OUR PUPPET CREATURES, OR SLAVES. This was the foundation of the mine which we have laid under the GOY people, I should rather say, under the GOY peoples.

WE NAME PRESIDENTS

11. In the near future we shall establish the responsibility of presidents.

12. By that time we shall be in a position to disregard forms in carrying through matters for which our impersonal puppet will be responsible. What do we care if the ranks of those striving for power should be thinned, if there should arise a deadlock from the impossibility of finding presidents, a deadlock which will finally disorganize the country? ...

13. In order that our scheme may produce this result we shall arrange elections in favor of such presidents as have in their past some dark, undiscovered stain, some "Panama" or other - then they will be trustworthy agents for the accomplishment of our plans out of fear of revelations and from the natural desire of everyone who has attained power, namely, the retention of the privileges, advantages and honor connected with the office of president. The chamber of deputies will provide cover for, will protect, will elect presidents, but we shall take from it the right to propose new, or make changes in existing laws, for this right will be given by us to the responsible president, a puppet in our hands. Naturally, the authority of the presidents will then become a target for every possible form of attack, but we shall provide him with a means of self-defense in the right of an appeal to the people, for the decision of the people over the heads of their representatives, that is to say, an appeal to that same blind slave of ours - the majority of the mob. Independently of this we shall invest the president with the right

of declaring a state of war. We shall justify this last right on the ground that the president as chief of the whole army of the country must have it at his disposal, in case of need for the defense of the new republican constitution, the right to defend which will belong to him as the responsible representative of this constitution. (Iran? Grenada? Kuwait? Iraq? Panama? Somalia? Bosnia? Kosovo? Indonesia?)

14. It is easy to understand that in these conditions the key of the shrine will lie in our hands, and no one outside ourselves will any longer direct the force of legislation.

15. Besides this we shall, with the introduction of the new republican constitution, take from the Chamber the right of interpolation on government measures, on the pretext of preserving political secrecy, and, further, we shall by the new constitution reduce the number of representatives to a minimum, thereby proportionately reducing political passions and the passion for politics. If, however, they should, which is hardly to be expected, burst into flame, even in this minimum, we shall nullify them by a stirring appeal and a reference to the majority of the whole people ... Upon the president will depend the appointment of presidents and vice-presidents of the Chamber and the Senate. Instead of constant sessions of Parliaments we shall reduce their sittings to a few months. Moreover, the president, as chief of the executive power, will have the right to summon and dissolve Parliament, and, in the latter case, to prolong the time for the appointment of a new parliamentary assembly. But in order that the consequences of all these acts which in substance are illegal, should not, prematurely for our plans, fall upon the responsibility established by us of the president, WE SHALL INSTIGATE MINISTERS AND OTHER OFFICIALS OF THE HIGHER ADMINISTRATION ABOUT THE PRESIDENT TO EVADE HIS DISPOSITIONS BY TAKING MEASURES OF THEIR OWN, for doing which they will be made the scapegoats in his place ... This part we especially recommend to be given to be played by the Senate, the Council of State, or the Council of Ministers, but not to an individual official.

16. The president will, at our discretion, interpret the sense of such of the existing laws as admit of various interpretation; he will further annul them when we indicate to him the necessity to do so, besides this, he will have the right to propose temporary laws, and even new departures in the government constitutional working, the pretext both for the one and the other being the requirements for the supreme welfare of the State. (Presidential Decrees such as F.D.R. employed to debase the US dollar and steal the gold and to place the U.S. under a permanent State of Emergency and War against its own citizens?)

WE SHALL DESTROY

17. By such measure we shall obtain the power of destroying little by little, step by step, all that at the outset when we enter on our rights, we are compelled to introduce into the constitutions of States to prepare for the transition to an imperceptible abolition of every kind of constitution, and then the time is come to turn every form of government into OUR DESPOTISM.

336

18. The recognition of our despot may also come before the destruction of the constitution; the moment for this recognition will come when the peoples, utterly wearied by the irregularities and incompetence - a matter which we shall arrange for - of their rulers, will clamor: "Away with them and give us one king over all the earth who will unite us and annihilate the causes of disorders - frontiers, nationalities, religions, State debts - who will give us peace and quiet which we cannot find under our rulers and representatives."

19. But you yourselves perfectly well know that TO PRODUCE THE POSSIBILITY OF THE EXPRESSION OF SUCH WISHES BY ALL THE NATIONS IT IS INDISPENSABLE TO TROUBLE IN ALL COUNTRIES THE PEOPLE'S RELATIONS WITH THEIR GOVERNMENTS SO AS TO UTTERLY EXHAUST HUMANITY WITH DISSENSION, HATRED, STRUGGLE, ENVY AND EVEN BY THE USE OF TORTURE, BY STARVATION, BY THE INOCULATION OF DISEASES, BY WANT, SO THAT THE "GOYIM" SEE NO OTHER ISSUE THAN TO TAKE REFUGE IN OUR COMPLETE SOVEREIGNTY IN MONEY AND IN ALL ELSE.

20. But if we give the nations of the world a breathing space the moment we long for is hardly likely ever to arrive.

PROTOCOL No. 11

1. The State Council has been, as it were, the emphatic expression of the authority of the ruler: it will be, as the "show" part of the Legislative Corps, what may be called the editorial committee of the laws and decrees of the ruler.

2. This, then, is the program of the new constitution. We shall make Law, Right and Justice (1) in the guise of proposals to the Legislative Corps, (2) by decrees of the president under the guise of general regulations, of orders of the Senate and of resolutions of the State Council in the guise of ministerial orders, (3) and in case a suitable occasion should arise - in the form of a revolution in the State.

3. Having established approximately the MODUS AGENDI we will occupy ourselves with details of those combinations by which we have still to complete the revolution in the course of the machinery of State in the direction already indicated. By these combinations I mean the freedom of the Press, the right of association, freedom of conscience, the voting principle, and many another that must disappear for ever from the memory of man, or undergo a radical alteration the day after the promulgation of the new constitution. It is only at the moment that we shall be able at once to announce all our orders, for, afterwards, every noticeable alteration will be dangerous, for the following reasons: if this alteration be brought in with harsh severity and in a sense of severity and limitations, it may lead to a feeling of despair caused by fear of new alterations in the same direction; if, on the other hand, it be brought in a sense of further indulgences it will be said that we have recognized our own wrong-doing and this will destroy the prestige of the infallibility of our authority, or else it will be said that we have become alarmed and are compelled to show a yielding disposition, for which we shall get no thanks because it will be supposed to be compulsory

337

... Both the one and the other are injurious to the prestige of the new constitution. What we want is that from the first moment of its promulgation, while the peoples of the world are still stunned by the accomplished fact of the revolution, still in a condition of terror and uncertainty, they should recognize once for all that we are so strong, so inexpugnable, so super-abundantly filled with power, that in no case shall we take any account of them, and so far from paying any attention to their opinions or wishes, we are ready and able to crush with irresistible power all expression or manifestation thereof at every moment and in every place, that we have seized at once everything we wanted and shall in no case divide our power with them ... Then in fear and trembling they will close their eyes to everything, and be content to await what will be the end of it all.

WE ARE WOLVES

4. The GOYIM are a flock of sheep, and we are their wolves. And you know what happens when the wolves get hold of the flock? ....

5. There is another reason also why they will close their eyes: for we shall keep promising them to give back all the liberties we have taken away as soon as we have quelled the enemies of peace and tamed all parties ....

6. It is not worth to say anything about how long a time they will be kept waiting for this return of their liberties ....

7. For what purpose then have we invented this whole policy and insinuated it into the minds of the GOY without giving them any chance to examine its underlying meaning? For what, indeed, if not in order to obtain in a roundabout way what is for our scattered tribe unattainable by the direct road? It is this which has served as the basis for our organization of SECRET MASONRY WHICH IS NOT KNOWN TO, AND AIMS WHICH ARE NOT EVEN SO MUCH AS SUSPECTED BY, THESE "GOY" CATTLE, ATTRACTED BY US INTO THE "SHOW" ARMY OF MASONIC LODGES IN ORDER TO THROW DUST IN THE EYES OF THEIR FELLOWS.

8. God has granted to us, His Chosen People, the gift of the dispersion, and in this which appears in all eyes to be our weakness, has come forth all our strength, which has now brought us to the threshold of sovereignty over all the world.

9. There now remains not much more for us to build up upon the foundation we have laid.

PROTOCOL No. 12

1. The word "freedom," which can be interpreted in various ways, is defined by us as follows -

2. Freedom is the right to do what which the law allows. This interpretation of the word will at the proper time be of service to us, because all freedom will thus be in our hands, since the laws will abolish or create only that

338

which is desirable for us according to the aforesaid program.

3. We shall deal with the press in the following way: what is the part played by the press to-day? It serves to excite and inflame those passions which are needed for our purpose or else it serves selfish ends of parties. It is often vapid, unjust, mendacious, and the majority of the public have not the slightest idea what ends the press really serves. We shall saddle and bridle it with a tight curb: we shall do the same also with all productions of the printing press, for where would be the sense of getting rid of the attacks of the press if we remain targets for pamphlets and books? The produce of publicity, which nowadays is a source of heavy expense owing to the necessity of censoring it, will be turned by us into a very lucrative source of income to our State: we shall lay on it a special stamp tax and require deposits of caution-money before permitting the establishment of any organ of the press or of printing offices; these will then have to guarantee our government against any kind of attack on the part of the press. For any attempt to attack us, if such still be possible, we shall inflict fines without mercy. Such measures as stamp tax, deposit of caution-money and fines secured by these deposits, will bring in a huge income to the government. It is true that party organs might not spare money for the sake of publicity, but these we shall shut up at the second attack upon us. No one shall with impunity lay a finger on the aureole of our government infallibility. The pretext for stopping any publication will be the alleged plea that it is agitating the public mind without occasion or justification. I BEG YOU TO NOTE THAT AMONG THOSE MAKING ATTACKS UPON US WILL ALSO BE ORGANS ESTABLISHED BY US, BUT THEY WILL ATTACK EXCLUSIVELY POINTS THAT WE HAVE PRE-DETERMINED TO ALTER.

WE CONTROL THE PRESS

4. NOT A SINGLE ANNOUNCEMENT WILL REACH THE PUBLIC WITHOUT OUR CONTROL. Even now this is already being attained by us inasmuch as all news items are received by a few agencies, in whose offices they are focused from all parts of the world. These agencies will then be already entirely ours and will give publicity only to what we dictate to them.

5. If already now we have contrived to possess ourselves of the minds of the GOY communities to such an extent the they all come near looking upon the events of the world through the colored glasses of those spectacles we are setting astride their noses; if already now there is not a single State where there exist for us any barriers to admittance into what GOY stupidity calls State secrets: what will our positions be then, when we shall be acknowledged supreme lords of the world in the person of our king of all the world....

6. Let us turn again to the FUTURE OF THE PRINTING PRESS. Every one desirous of being a publisher, librarian, or printer, will be obliged to provide himself with the diploma instituted therefore, which, in case of any fault, will be immediately impounded. With such measures THE INSTRUMENT OF THOUGHT WILL BECOME AN EDUCATIVE MEANS ON THE HANDS OF OUR GOVERNMENT, WHICH WILL NO LONGER

ALLOW THE MASS OF THE NATION TO BE LED ASTRAY IN BY-WAYS AND FANTASIES ABOUT THE BLESSINGS OF PROGRESS. Is there any one of us who does not know that these phantom blessings are the direct roads to foolish imaginings which give birth to anarchical relations of men among themselves and towards authority, because progress, or rather the idea of progress, has introduced the conception of every kind of emancipation, but has failed to establish its limits .... All the so-called liberals are anarchists, if not in fact, at any rate in thought. Every one of them in hunting after phantoms of freedom, and falling exclusively into license, that is, into the anarchy of protest for the sake of protest....

FREE PRESS DESTROYED

7. We turn to the periodical press. We shall impose on it, as on all printed matter, stamp taxes per sheet and deposits of caution-money, and books of less than 30 sheets will pay double. We shall reckon them as pamphlets in order, on the one hand, to reduce the number of magazines, which are the worst form of printed poison, and, on the other, in order that this measure may force writers into such lengthy productions that they will be little read, especially as they will be costly. At the same time what we shall publish ourselves to influence mental development in the direction laid down for our profit will be cheap and will be read voraciously. The tax will bring vapid literary ambitions within bounds and the liability to penalties will make literary men dependent upon us. And if there should be any found who are desirous of writing against us, they will not find any person eager to print their productions. Before accepting any production for publication in print, the publisher or printer will have to apply to the authorities for permission to do so. Thus we shall know beforehand of all tricks preparing against us and shall nullify them by getting ahead with explanations on the subject treated of.

8. Literature and journalism are two of the most important educative forces, and therefore our government will become proprietor of the majority of the journals. This will neutralize the injurious influence of the privately-owned press and will put us in possession of a tremendous influence upon the public mind .... If we give permits for ten journals, we shall ourselves found thirty, and so on in the same proportion. This, however, must in no wise be suspected by the public. For which reason all journals published by us will be of the most opposite, in appearance, tendencies and opinions, thereby creating confidence in us and bringing over to us quite unsuspicious opponents, who will thus fall into our trap and be rendered harmless.

9. In the front rank will stand organs of an official character. They will always stand guard over our interests, and therefore their influence will be comparatively insignificant.

10. In the second rank will be the semi-official organs, whose part it will be to attack the tepid and indifferent.

11. In the third rank we shall set up our own, to all appearance, opposition, which, in at least one of its organs, will present what looks like the very antipodes to us. Our real opponents at heart will accept this simulated

opposition as their own and will show us their cards.

12. All our newspapers will be of all possible complexions -- aristocratic, republican, revolutionary, even anarchical - for so long, of course, as the constitution exists .... Like the Indian idol "Vishnu" they will have a hundred hands, and every one of them will have a finger on any one of the public opinions as required. When a pulse quickens these hands will lead opinion in the direction of our aims, for an excited patient loses all power of judgment and easily yields to suggestion. Those fools who will think they are repeating the opinion of a newspaper of their own camp will be repeating our opinion or any opinion that seems desirable for us. In the vain belief that they are following the organ of their party they will, in fact, follow the flag which we hang out for them.

13. In order to direct our newspaper militia in this sense we must take special and minute care in organizing this matter. Under the title of central department of the press we shall institute literary gatherings at which our agents will without attracting attention issue the orders and watchwords of the day. By discussing and controverting, but always superficially, without touching the essence of the matter, our organs will carry on a sham fight fusillade with the official newspapers solely for the purpose of giving occasion for us to express ourselves more fully than could well be done from the outset in official announcements, whenever, of course, that is to our advantage.

14. THESE ATTACKS UPON US WILL ALSO SERVE ANOTHER PURPOSE, NAMELY, THAT OUR SUBJECTS WILL BE CONVINCED TO THE EXISTENCE OF FULL FREEDOM OF SPEECH AND SO GIVE OUR AGENTS AN OCCASION TO AFFIRM THAT ALL ORGANS WHICH OPPOSE US ARE EMPTY BABBLERS, since they are incapable of finding any substantial objections to our orders.

ONLY LIES PRINTED

15. Methods of organization like these, imperceptible to the public eye but absolutely sure, are the best calculated to succeed in bringing the attention and the confidence of the public to the side of our government. Thanks to such methods we shall be in a position as from time to time may be required, to excite or to tranquillize the public mind on political questions, to persuade or to confuse, printing now truth, now lies, facts or their contradictions, according as they may be well or ill received, always very cautiously feeling our ground before stepping upon it .... WE SHALL HAVE A SURE TRIUMPH OVER OUR OPPONENTS SINCE THEY WILL NOT HAVE AT THEIR DISPOSITION ORGANS OF THE PRESS IN WHICH THEY CAN GIVE FULL AND FINAL EXPRESSION TO THEIR VIEWS owing to the aforesaid methods of dealing with the press. We shall not even need to refute them except very superficially.

16. Trial shots like these, fired by us in the third rank of our press, in case of need, will be energetically refuted by us in our semi-official organs.

17. Even nowadays, already, to take only the French press, there are forms

which reveal masonic solidarity in acting on the watchword: all organs of the press are bound together by professional secrecy; like the augurs of old, not one of their numbers will give away the secret of his sources of information unless it be resolved to make announcement of them. Not one journalist will venture to betray this secret, for not one of them is ever admitted to practice literature unless his whole past has some disgraceful sore or other .... These sores would be immediately revealed. So long as they remain the secret of a few the prestige of the journalist attacks the majority of the country - the mob follow after him with enthusiasm.

18. Our calculations are especially extended to the provinces. It is indispensable for us to inflame there those hopes and impulses with which we could at any moment fall upon the capital, and we shall represent to the capitals that these expressions are the independent hopes and impulses of the provinces. Naturally, the source of them will be always one and the same - ours. WHAT WE NEED IS THAT, UNTIL SUCH TIME AS WE ARE IN THE PLENITUDE POWER, THE CAPITALS SHOULD FIND THEMSELVES STIFLED BY THE PROVINCIAL OPINION OF THE NATIONS, I.E., OF A MAJORITY ARRANGED BY OUR AGENTUR. What we need is that at the psychological moment the capitals should not be in a position to discuss an accomplished fact for the simple reason, if for no other, that it has been accepted by the public opinion of a majority in the provinces.

19. WHEN WE ARE IN THE PERIOD OF THE NEW REGIME TRANSITIONAL TO THAT OF OUR ASSUMPTION OF FULL SOVEREIGNTY WE MUST NOT ADMIT ANY REVELATION BY THE PRESS OF ANY FORM OF PUBLIC DISHONESTY; IT IS NECESSARY THAT THE NEW REGIME SHOULD BE THOUGHT TO HAVE SO PERFECTLY CONTENDED EVERYBODY THAT EVEN CRIMINALITY HAS DISAPPEARED ... Cases of the manifestation of criminality should remain known only to their victims and to chance witnesses - no more.

PROTOCOL No. 13

1. The need for daily bread forces the GOYIM to keep silence and be our humble servants. Agents taken on to our press from among the GOYIM will at our orders discuss anything which it is inconvenient for us to issue directly in official documents, and we meanwhile, quietly amid the din of the discussion so raised, shall simply take and carry through such measures as we wish and then offer them to the public as an accomplished fact. No one will dare to demand the abrogation of a matter once settled, all the more so as it will be represented as an improvement ... And immediately the press will distract the current of thought towards, new questions, (have we not trained people always to be seeking something new?). Into the discussions of these new questions will throw themselves those of the brainless dispensers of fortunes who are not able even now to understand that they have not the remotest conception about the matters which they undertake to discuss. Questions of the political are unattainable for any save those who have guided it already for many ages, the creators.

2. From all this you will see that in securing the opinion of the mob we

are only facilitating the working of our machinery, and you may remark that it is not for actions but for words issued by us on this or that question that we seem to seek approval. We are constantly making public declaration that we are guided in all our undertakings by the hope, joined to the conviction, that we are serving the common weal.

WE DECEIVE WORKERS

3. In order to distract people who may be too troublesome from discussions of questions of the political we are now putting forward what we allege to be new questions of the political, namely, questions of industry. In this sphere let them discuss themselves silly! The masses are agreed to remain inactive, to take a rest from what they suppose to be political (which we trained them to in order to use them as a means of combating the GOY governments) only on condition of being found new employments, in which we are prescribing them something that looks like the same political object. In order that the masses themselves may not guess what they are about WE FURTHER DISTRACT THEM WITH AMUSEMENTS, GAMES, PASTIMES, PASSIONS, PEOPLE'S PALACES .... SOON WE SHALL BEGIN THROUGH THE PRESS TO PROPOSE COMPETITIONS IN ART, IN SPORT IN ALL KINDS: these interests will finally distract their minds from questions in which we should find ourselves compelled to oppose them. Growing more and more unaccustomed to reflect and form any opinions of their own, people will begin to talk in the same tone as we because we alone shall be offering them new directions for thought ... of course through such persons as will not be suspected of solidarity with us.

4. The part played by the liberals, utopian dreamers, will be finally played out when our government is acknowledged. Till such time they will continue to do us good service. Therefore we shall continue to direct their minds to all sorts of vain conceptions of fantastic theories, new and apparently progressive: for have we not with complete success turned the brainless heads of the GOYIM with progress, till there is not among the GOYIM one mind able to perceive that under this word lies a departure from truth in all cases where it is not a question of material inventions, for truth is one, and in it there is no place for progress. Progress, like a fallacious idea, serves to obscure truth so that none may know it except us, the Chosen of God, its guardians.

5. When, we come into our kingdom our orators will expound great problems which have turned humanity upside down in order to bring it at the end under our beneficent rule.

6. Who will ever suspect then that ALL THESE PEOPLES WERE STAGE-MANAGED BY US ACCORDING TO A POLITICAL PLAN WHICH NO ONE HAS SO MUCH AS GUESSED AT IN THE COURSE OF MANY CENTURIES?

343

PROTOCOL No. 14

1. When we come into our kingdom it will be undesirable for us that there should exist any other religion than ours of the One God with whom our destiny is bound up by our position as the Chosen People and through whom our same destiny is united with the destinies of the world. We must therefore sweep away all other forms of belief. If this gives birth to the atheists whom we see to-day, it will not, being only a transitional stage, interfere with our views, but will serve as a warning for those generations which will hearken to our preaching of the religion of Moses, that, by its stable and thoroughly elaborated system has brought all the peoples of the world into subjection to us. Therein we shall emphasize its mystical right, on which, as we shall say, all its educative power is based .... Then at every possible opportunity we shall publish articles in which we shall make comparisons between our beneficent rule and those of past ages. The blessing of tranquillity, though it be a tranquillity forcibly brought about by centuries of agitation, will throw into higher relief the benefits to which we shall point. The errors of the GOYIM governments will be depicted by us in the most vivid hues. We shall implant such an abhorrence of them that the peoples will prefer tranquillity in a state of serfdom to those rights of vaunted freedom which have tortured humanity and exhausted the very sources of human existence, sources which have been exploited by a mob of rascally adventurers who know not what they do .... USELESS CHANGES OF FORMS OF GOVERNMENT TO WHICH WE INSTIGATED THE "GOYIM" WHEN WE WERE UNDERMINING THEIR STATE STRUCTURES, WILL HAVE SO WEARIED THE PEOPLES BY THAT TIME THAT THEY WILL PREFER TO SUFFER ANYTHING UNDER US RATHER THAN RUN THE RISK OF ENDURING AGAIN ALL THE AGITATIONS AND MISERIES THEY HAVE GONE THROUGH.

WE SHALL FORBID CHRIST

2. At the same time we shall not omit to emphasize the historical mistakes of the GOY governments which have tormented humanity for so many centuries by their lack of understanding of everything that constitutes the true good of humanity in their chase after fantastic schemes of social blessings, and have never noticed that these schemes kept on producing a worse and never a better state of the universal relations which are the basis of human life ...

3. The whole force of our principles and methods will lie in the fact that we shall present them and expound them as a splendid contrast to the dead and decomposed old order of things in social life.

4. Our philosophers will discuss all the shortcomings of the various beliefs of the "GOYIM," BUT NO ONE WILL EVER BRING UNDER DISCUSSION OUR FAITH FROM ITS TRUE POINT OF VIEW SINCE THIS WILL BE FULLY LEARNED BY NONE SAVE OURS WHO WILL NEVER DARE TO BETRAY ITS SECRETS.

344 5. IN COUNTRIES KNOWN AS PROGRESSIVE AND ENLIGHTENED WE HAVE CREATED A SENSELESS, FILTHY,

ABOMINABLE LITERATURE. For some time after our entrance to power we shall continue to encourage its existence in order to provide a telling relief by contrast to the speeches, party program, which will be distributed from exalted quarters of ours .... Our wise men, trained to become leaders of the GOYIM, will compose speeches, projects, memoirs, articles, which will be used by us to influence the minds of the GOYIM, directing them towards such understanding and forms of knowledge as have been determined by us.

Before you continue reading the next Protocol, I wanted to interject the fact that in 2000, Antichristian, Babylonian Talmudist, "Barbara Lerner Spectre" in cooperation with the Government of Sweden, set up a "non-denominational institute of Jewish learning" named "Paideia" [Greek for citizenship] in Stockholm. Spectre says that Jews have an important role to play in the elimination of Christianity throughout Europe and they will be "resented" for it. Spectre goes on to say:

"I think there's a resurgence of Antisemitism because at this point in time Europe has not yet learned how to be multicultural [codeword for Antichristian, Anti-European, pro-communist] and I think we're going to be part of the throws [death] of that transformation which must take place. Europe is not going to be the monolithic [Christian] society they once were in the last centuries. Jews [Khazarian Babylonian Talmudists] are going to be at the center of that huge transformation for Europe to make. They are now going into a multicultural [codeword for Antichristian, Anti-European, pro-communist] mode and Jews will be resented because of our leading role."

Church of Babylon member and Irishman, William Blake was influenced by what he called "supernatural visions" to create his painting titled 'Ancient of Day' [pg.346] which depicts the god of earth [Lucifer] constructing an occult pyramid with an all-seeing-eye of Satan.

"Among these dark Satanic mills? Bring me my Bow of burning gold, Bring me my Arrows of Desire, Bring me my Spear: O clouds unfold! Bring me my Chariot of fire. I will not cease from Mental Fight, Nor shall my Sword sleep in my hand Till we have built Jerusalem In England's green and pleasant Land." - William Blake (From Milton, Preface c.1804)

Just eleven years after Blake's epic poem 'Milton', the Rothschild Family would seize control of the English Banking system in 1815. One hundred two years after taking complete control of the English Banking system and three years after WWI, the Rothschild Family would construct the Balfour Declaration in 1917, one of the most revolutionary documents in the twentieth century. It committed the British people to supporting the establishment in Palestine of "a National Home for the Jewish people," [Israel]. One hundred eighty-eight years after Blake painted the occult "Ancient of Day," [pg.346] the Rothschild Family in 1992 would finance and build the Israeli supreme occult court building complete with pyramid and all-seeing-eye of Satan.

1. When we at last definitely come into our kingdom by the aid of COUPS D'ETAT prepared everywhere for one and the same day, after definitely acknowledged (and not a little time will pass before that comes about, perhaps even a whole century) we shall make it our task to see that against us such things as plots shall no longer exist. With this purpose we shall slay without mercy all who take arms (in hand, like Waco? Randy Weaver? Port Arthur? Oklahoma?) to oppose our coming into our kingdom. Every kind of new institution of anything like a secret society will also be punished with death; those of them which are now in existence, are known to us, serve us and have served us, we shall disband and send into exile to continents far removed from Europe. IN THIS WAY WE SHALL PROCEED WITH THOSE "GOY" MASONS WHO KNOW TOO MUCH; such of these as we may for some reason spare will be kept in constant fear of exile. We shall promulgate a law making all former members of secret societies liable to exile from Europe as the center of rule.

2. Resolutions of our government will be final, without appeal.

3. In the GOY societies, in which we have planted and deeply rooted discord and protestantism, the only possible way of restoring order is to employ merciless measures that prove the direct force of authority: no regard must be paid to the victims who fall, they suffer for the well-being of the future. The attainment of that well-being, even at the expense of sacrifices, is the duty of any kind of government that acknowledges as justification for its existence not only its privileges but its obligations. The principal guarantee of stability of rule is to confirm the aureole of power, and this aureole is attained only by such a majestic inflexibility of might as shall carry on its face the emblems of inviolability from mystical causes - from the choice of God. SUCH WAS, UNTIL RECENT TIMES, THE RUSSIAN AUTOCRACY, THE ONE AND ONLY SERIOUS FOE WE HAD IN THE WORLD, WITHOUT COUNTING THE PAPACY. Bear in mind the example when Italy, drenched with blood, never touched a hair of the head of Sulla who had poured forth that blood: Sulla enjoyed an apotheosis for his might in him, but his intrepid return to Italy ringed him round with inviolability. The people do not lay a finger on him who hypnotizes them by his daring and strength of mind.

SECRET SOCIETIES

4. Meantime, however, until we come into our kingdom, we shall act in the contrary way: we shall create and multiply free masonic lodges in all the countries of the world, absorb into them all who may become or who are

prominent in public activity, for these lodges we shall find our principal intelligence office and means of influence. All these lodges we shall bring under one central administration, known to us alone and to all others absolutely unknown, which will be composed of our learned elders. The lodges will have their representatives who will serve to screen the above-mentioned administration of MASONRY and from whom will issue the watchword and program. In these lodges we shall tie together the knot which binds together all revolutionary and liberal elements. Their composition will be made up of all strata of society. The most secret political plots will be known to us and fall under our guiding hands on the very day of their conception. AMONG THE MEMBERS OF THESE LODGES WILL BE ALMOST ALL THE AGENTS OF INTERNATIONAL AND NATIONAL POLICE since their service is for us irreplaceable in the respect that the police is in a position not only to use its own particular measures with the insubordinate, but also to screen our activities and provide pretexts for discontents, ET CETERA.

5. The class of people who most willingly enter into secret societies are those who live by their wits, careerists, and in general people, mostly light-minded, with whom we shall have no difficulty in dealing and in using to wind up the mechanism of the machine devised by us. If this world grows agitated the meaning of that will be that we have had to stir up in order to break up its too great solidarity. BUT IF THERE SHOULD ARISE IN ITS MIDST A PLOT, THEN AT THE HEAD OF THAT PLOT WILL BE NO OTHER THAN ONE OF OUR MOST TRUSTED SERVANTS. It is natural that we and no other should lead MASONIC activities, for we know whither we are leading, we know the final goal of every form of activity whereas the GOYIM have knowledge of nothing, not even of the immediate effect of action; they put before themselves, usually, the momentary reckoning of the satisfaction of their self-opinion in the accomplishment of their thought without even remarking that the very conception never belonged to their initiative but to our instigation of their thought ...

GENTILES ARE STUPID

6. The GOYIM enter the lodges out of curiosity or in the hope by their means to get a nibble at the public pie, and some of them in order to obtain a hearing before the public for their impracticable and groundless fantasies: they thirst for the emotion of success and applause, of which we are remarkably generous. And the reason why we give them this success is to make use of the high conceit of themselves to which it gives birth, for that insensibly disposes them to assimilate our suggestions without being on their guard against them in the fullness of their confidence that it is their own infallibility which is giving utterance to their own thoughts and that it is impossible for them to borrow those of others .... You cannot imagine to what extent the wisest of the GOYIM can be brought to a state of unconscious naivete in the presence of this condition of high conceit of themselves, and at the same time how easy it is to take the heart out of them by the slightest ill-success, though it be nothing more than the stoppage of the applause they had, and to reduce them to a slavish submission for the sake of winning a renewal of success .... BY SO MUCH AS OURS DISREGARD SUCCESS IF ONLY 347 THEY CAN CARRY THROUGH THEIR PLANS, BY SO MUCH THE

"GOYIM" ARE WILLING TO SACRIFICE ANY PLANS ONLY TO HAVE SUCCESS. This psychology of theirs materially facilitates for us the task of setting them in the required direction. These tigers in appearance have the souls of sheep and the wind blows freely through their heads. We have set them on the hobby-horse of an idea about the absorption of individuality by the symbolic unit of COLLECTIVISM .... They have never yet and they never will have the sense to reflect that this hobby-horse is a manifest violation of the most important law of nature, which has established from the very creation of the world one unit unlike another and precisely for the purpose of instituting individuality ....

7. If we have been able to bring them to such a pitch of stupid blindness is it not a proof, and an amazingly clear proof, of the degree to which the mind of the GOYIM is undeveloped in comparison with our mind? This it is, mainly, which guarantees our success.

GENTILES ARE CATTLE

8. And how far-seeing were our learned elders in ancient times when they said that to attain a serious end it behooves not to stop at any means or to count the victims sacrificed for the sake of that end .... We have not counted the victims of the seed of the GOY cattle, though we have sacrificed many of our own, but for that we have now already given them such a position on the earth as they could not even have dreamed of. The comparatively small numbers of the victims from the number of ours have preserved our nationality from destruction.

9. Death is the inevitable end for all. It is better to bring that end nearer to those who hinder our affairs than to ourselves, to the founders of this affair. WE EXECUTE MASONS IN SUCH WISE THAT NONE SAVE THE BROTHERHOOD CAN EVER HAVE A SUSPICION OF IT, NOT EVEN THE VICTIMS THEMSELVES OF OUR DEATH SENTENCE, THEY ALL DIE WHEN REQUIRED AS IF FROM A NORMAL KIND OF ILLNESS ..... Knowing this, even the brotherhood in its turn dare not protest. By such methods we have plucked out of the midst of MASONRY the very root of protest against our disposition. While preaching liberalism to the GOY we at the same time keep our own people and our agents in a state of unquestioning submission.

10. Under our influence the execution of the laws of the GOYIM has been reduced to a minimum. The prestige of the law has been exploded by the liberal interpretations introduced into this sphere. In the most important and fundamental affairs and questions, JUDGES DECIDE AS WE DICTATE TO THEM, see matters in the light wherewith we enfold them for the administration of the GOYIM, of course, through persons who are our tools though we do not appear to have anything in common with them - by newspaper opinion or by other means .... Even senators and the higher administration accept our counsels. The purely brute mind of the GOYIM is incapable of use for analysis and observation, and still more for the foreseeing whither a certain manner of setting a question may tend.

348   11. In this difference in capacity for thought between the GOYIM and ourselves may be clearly discerned the seal of our position as the Chosen

People and of our higher quality of humanness, in contradistinction to the brute mind of the GOYIM. Their eyes are open, but see nothing before them and do not invent (unless perhaps, material things). From this it is plain that nature herself has destined us to guide and rule the world.

WE DEMAND SUBMISSION

12. When comes the time of our overt rule, the time to manifest its blessing, we shall remake all legislatures, all our laws will be brief, plain, stable, without any kind of interpretations, so that anyone will be in a position to know them perfectly. The main feature which will run right through them is submission to orders, and this principle will be carried to a grandiose height. Every abuse will then disappear in consequence of the responsibility of all down to the lowest unit before the higher authority of the representative of power. Abuses of power subordinate to this last instance will be so mercilessly punished that none will be found anxious to try experiments with their own powers. We shall follow up jealously every action of the administration on which depends the smooth running of the machinery of the State, for slackness in this produces slackness everywhere; not a single case of illegality or abuse of power will be left without exemplary punishment.

13. Concealment of guilt, connivance between those in the service of the administration - all this kind of evil will disappear after the very first examples of severe punishment. The aureole of our power demands suitable, that is, cruel, punishments for the slightest infringement, for the sake of gain, of its supreme prestige. The sufferer, though his punishment may exceed his fault, will count as a soldier falling on the administrative field of battle in the interests of authority, principle and law, which do not permit that any of those who hold the reins of the public coach should turn aside from the public highway to their own private paths. FOR EXAMPLES OUR JUDGES WILL KNOW THAT WHENEVER THEY FEEL DISPOSED TO PLUME THEMSELVES ON FOOLISH CLEMENCY THEY ARE VIOLATING THE LAW OF JUSTICE WHICH IS INSTITUTED FOR THE EXEMPLARY EDIFICATION OF MEN BY PENALTIES FOR LAPSES AND NOT FOR DISPLAY OF THE SPIRITUAL QUALITIES OF THE JUDGES .... Such qualities it is proper to show in private life, but not in a public square which is the educational basis of human life.

14. Our legal staff will serve not beyond the age of 55, firstly because old men more obstinately hold to prejudiced opinions, and are less capable of submitting to new directions, and secondly because this will give us the possibility by this measure of securing elasticity in the changing of staff, which will thus the more easily bend under our pressure: he who wishes to keep his place will have to give blind obedience to deserve it. In general, our judges will be elected by us only from among those who thoroughly understand that the part they have to play is to punish and apply laws and not to dream about the manifestations of liberalism at the expense of the educational scheme of the State, as the GOYIM in these days imagine it to be .... This method of shuffling the staff will serve also to explode any collective solidarity of those in the same service and will bind all to the interests of 349 the government upon which their fate will depend. The young generation

of judges will be trained in certain views regarding the inadmissibility of any abuses that might disturb the established order of our subjects among themselves.

15. In these days the judges of the GOYIM create indulgences to every kind of crimes, not having a just understanding of their office, because the rulers of the present age in appointing judges to office take no care to inculcate in them a sense of duty and consciousness of the matter which is demanded of them. As a brute beast lets out its young in search of prey, so do the GOYIM give to them for what purpose such place was created. This is the reason why their governments are being ruined by their own forces through the acts of their own administration.

16. Let us borrow from the example of the results of these actions yet another lesson for our government.

17. We shall root out liberalism from all the important strategic posts of our government on which depends the training of subordinates for our State structure. Such posts will fall exclusively to those who have been trained by us for administrative rule. To the possible objection that the retirement of old servants will cost the Treasury heavily, I reply, firstly, they will be provided with some private service in place of what they lose, and, secondly, I have to remark that all the money in the world will be concentrated in our hands, consequently it is not our government that has to fear expense.

WE SHALL BE CRUEL

18. Our absolutism will in all things be logically consecutive and therefore in each one of its decrees our supreme will must be respected and unquestionably fulfilled: it will ignore all murmurs, all discontents of every kind and will destroy to the root every kind of manifestation of them in act by punishment of an exemplary character.

19. We shall abolish the right of appeal, which will be transferred exclusively to our disposal - to the cognizance of him who rules, for we must not allow the conception among the people of a thought that there could be such a thing as a decision that is not right of judges set up by us. If, however, anything like this should occur, we shall ourselves quash the decision, but inflict therewith such exemplary punishment on the judge for lack of understanding of his duty and the purpose of his appointment as will prevent a repetition of such cases .... I repeat that it must be born in mind that we shall know every step of our administration which only needs to be closely watched for the people to be content with us, for it has the right to demand from a good government a good official.

20. OUR GOVERNMENT WILL HAVE THE APPEARANCE OF A PATRIARCHAL PATERNAL GUARDIANSHIP ON THE PART OF OUR RULER. Our own nation and our subjects will discern in his person a father caring for their every need, their every act, their every interrelation as subjects one with another, as well as their relations to the ruler. They will then be
350 so thoroughly imbued with the thought that it is impossible for them to dispense with this wardship and guidance, if they wish to live in peace and

quiet, THAT THEY WILL ACKNOWLEDGE THE AUTOCRACY OF OUR RULER WITH A DEVOTION BORDERING ON "APOTHEOSIS," especially when they are convinced that those whom we set up do not put their own in place of authority, but only blindly execute his dictates. They will be rejoiced that we have regulated everything in their lives as is done by wise parents who desire to train children in the cause of duty and submission. For the peoples of the world in regard to the secrets of our polity are ever through the ages only children under age, precisely as are also their governments.

21. As you see, I found our despotism on right and duty: the right to compel the execution of duty is the direct obligation of a government which is a father for its subjects. It has the right of the strong that it may use it for the benefit of directing humanity towards that order which is defined by nature, namely, submission. Everything in the world is in a state of submission, if not to man, then to circumstances or its own inner character, in all cases, to what is stronger. And so shall we be this something stronger for the sake of good.

22. We are obliged without hesitation to sacrifice individuals, who commit a breach of established order, for in the exemplary punishment of evil lies a great educational problem.

23. When the King of Israel sets upon his sacred head the crown offered him by Europe he will become patriarch of the world. The indispensable victims offered by him in consequence of their suitability will never reach the number of victims offered in the course of centuries by the mania of magnificence, the emulation between the GOY governments.

24. Our King will be in constant communion with the peoples, making to them from the tribune speeches which fame will in that same hour distribute over all the world.

PROTOCOL No. 16

1. In order to effect the destruction of all collective forces except ours we shall emasculate the first stage of collectivism - the UNIVERSITIES, by re-educating them in a new direction. THEIR OFFICIALS AND PROFESSORS WILL BE PREPARED FOR THEIR BUSINESS BY DETAILED SECRET PROGRAMS OF ACTION FROM WHICH THEY WILL NOT WITH IMMUNITY DIVERGE, NOT BY ONE IOTA. THEY WILL BE APPOINTED WITH ESPECIAL PRECAUTION, AND WILL BE SO PLACED AS TO BE WHOLLY DEPENDENT UPON THE GOVERNMENT.

2. We shall exclude from the course of instruction State Law as also all that concerns the political question. These subjects will be taught to a few dozen of persons chosen for their pre-eminent capacities from among the number of the initiated. THE UNIVERSITIES MUST NO LONGER SEND OUT FROM THEIR HALLS MILK SOPS CONCOCTING PLANS FOR A CONSTITUTION, LIKE A COMEDY OR A TRAGEDY, BUSYING 351 THEMSELVES WITH QUESTIONS OF POLICY IN WHICH EVEN

3. The ill-guided acquaintance of a large number of persons with questions of polity creates utopian dreamers and bad subjects, as you can see for yourselves from the example of the universal education in this direction of the GOYIM. We must introduce into their education all those principles which have so brilliantly broken up their order. But when we are in power we shall remove every kind of disturbing subject from the course of education and shall make out of the youth obedient children of authority, loving him who rules as the support and hope of peace and quiet.

WE SHALL CHANGE HISTORY

4. Classicism as also any form of study of ancient history, in which there are more bad than good examples, we shall replace with the study of the program of the future. We shall erase from the memory of men all facts of previous centuries which are undesirable to us, and leave only those which depict all the errors of the government of the GOYIM. The study of practical life, of the obligations of order, of the relations of people one to another, of avoiding bad and selfish examples, which spread the infection of evil, and similar questions of an educative nature, will stand in the forefront of the teaching program, which will be drawn up on a separate plan for each calling or state of life, in no wise generalizing the teaching. This treatment of the question has special importance.

5. Each state of life must be trained within strict limits corresponding to its destination and work in life. The OCCASIONAL GENIUS HAS ALWAYS MANAGED AND ALWAYS WILL MANAGE TO SLIP THROUGH INTO OTHER STATES OF LIFE, BUT IT IS THE MOST PERFECT FOLLY FOR THE SAKE OF THIS RARE OCCASIONAL GENIUS TO LET THROUGH INTO RANKS FOREIGN TO THEM THE UNTALENTED WHO THUS ROB OF THEIR PLACES THOSE WHO BELONG TO THOSE RANKS BY BIRTH OR EMPLOYMENT. YOU KNOW YOURSELVES IN WHAT ALL THIS HAS ENDED FOR THE "GOYIM" WHO ALLOWED THIS CRYING ABSURDITY.

6. In order that he who rules may be seated firmly in the hearts and minds of his subjects it is necessary for the time of his activity to instruct the whole nation in the schools and on the market places about this meaning and his acts and all his beneficent initiatives.

7. We shall abolish every kind of freedom of instruction. Learners of all ages have the right to assemble together with their parents in the educational establishments as it were in a club: during these assemblies, on holidays, teachers will read what will pass as free lectures on questions of human relations, of the laws of examples, of the philosophy of new theories not yet declared to the world. These theories will be raised by us to the stage of a dogma of faith as a traditional stage towards our faith. On the completion of this exposition of our program of action in the present and the future I will read you the principles of these theories.

8. In a word, knowing by the experience of many centuries that people live and are guided by ideas, that these ideas are imbibed by people only by the aid of education provided with equal success for all ages of growth, but of course by varying methods, we shall swallow up and confiscate to our own use the last scintilla of independence of thought, which we have for long past been directing towards subjects and ideas useful for us. The system of bridling thought is already at work in the so-called system of teaching by OBJECT LESSONS, the purpose of which is to turn the GOYIM into unthinking submissive brutes waiting for things to be presented before their eyes in order to form an idea of them .... In France, one of our best agents, Bourgeois, has already made public a new program of teaching by object lessons.

PROTOCOL No. 17

1. The practice of advocacy produces men cold, cruel, persistent, unprincipled, who in all cases take up an impersonal, purely legal standpoint. They have the inveterate habit to refer everything to its value for the defense and not to the public welfare of its results. They do not usually decline to undertake any defense whatever, they strive for an acquittal at all costs, caviling over every petty crux of jurisprudence and thereby they demoralize justice. For this reason we shall set this profession into narrow frames which will keep it inside this sphere of executive public service. Advocates, equally with judges, will be deprived of the right of communication with litigants; they will receive business only from the court and will study it by notes of report and documents, defending their clients after they have been interrogated in court on facts that have appeared. They will receive an honorarium without regard to the quality of the defense. This will render them mere reporters on law-business in the interests of justice and as counterpoise to the proctor who will be the reporter in the interests of prosecution; this will shorten business before the courts. In this way will be established a practice of honest unprejudiced defense conducted not from personal interest but by conviction. This will also, by the way, remove the present practice of corrupt bargain between advocation to agree only to let that side win which pays most .....

WE SHALL DESTROY THE CLERGY

2. WE HAVE LONG PAST TAKEN CARE TO DISCREDIT THE PRIESTHOOD OF THE "GOYIM," and thereby to ruin their mission on earth which in these days might still be a great hindrance to us. Day by day its influence on the peoples of the world is falling lower. FREEDOM OF CONSCIENCE HAS BEEN DECLARED EVERYWHERE, SO THAT NOW ONLY YEARS DIVIDE US FROM THE MOMENT OF THE COMPLETE WRECKING OF THAT CHRISTIAN RELIGION: as to other religions we shall have still less difficulty in dealing with them, but it would be premature to speak of this now. We shall set clericalism and clericals into such narrow frames as to make their influence move in retrogressive proportion to its former progress.

3. When the time comes finally to destroy the papal court the finger of an invisible hand will point the nations towards this court. When, however, the

nations fling themselves upon it, we shall come forward in the guise of its defenders as if to save excessive bloodshed. By this diversion we shall penetrate to its very bowels and be sure we shall never come out again until we have gnawed through the entire strength of this place.

4. THE KING OF THE JEWS WILL BE THE REAL POPE OF THE UNIVERSE, THE PATRIARCH OF THE INTERNATIONAL CHURCH

5. But, IN THE MEANTIME, while we are re-educating youth in new traditional religions and afterwards in ours, WE SHALL NOT OVERTLY LAY A FINGER ON EXISTING CHURCHES, BUT WE SHALL FIGHT AGAINST THEM BY CRITICISM CALCULATED TO PRODUCE SCHISM . . .

6. In general, then, our contemporary press will continue to CONVICT State affairs, religions, incapacities of the GOYIM, always using the most unprincipled expressions in order by every means to lower their prestige in the manner which can only be practiced by the genius of our gifted tribe . . . (Calling the Jim Jones massacre in Guyana a mass suicide, not a C.I.A./MK-ULTRA/U.S. Government massacre? Denying the massacre of the Branch Dravidian sect at Waco, Texas, was a needless and deliberate massacre by the B.A.T.F./F.B.I/C.I.A/U.S. Government).

7. Our kingdom will be an apologia of the divinity Vishnu, in whom is found its personification - in our hundred hands will be, one in each, the springs of the machinery of social life. We shall see everything without the aid of official police which, in that scope of its rights which we elaborated for the use of the GOYIM, hinders governments from seeing. In our programs ONE-THIRD OF OUR SUBJECTS WILL KEEP THE REST UNDER OBSERVATION from a sense of duty, on the principle of volunteer service to the State. It will then be no disgrace to be a spy and informer, but a merit: unfounded denunciations, however, will be cruelly punished that there may be no development of abuses of this right.

8. Our agents will be taken from the higher as well as the lower ranks of society, from among the administrative class who spend their time in amusements, editors, printers and publishers, booksellers, clerks, and salesmen, workmen, coachmen, lackeys, et cetera. This body, having no rights and not being empowered to take any action on their own account, and consequently a police without any power, will only witness and report: verification of their reports and arrests will depend upon a responsible group of controllers of police affairs, while the actual act of arrest will be performed by the gendarmerie and the municipal police. Any person not denouncing anything seen or heard concerning questions of polity will also be charged with and made responsible for concealment, if it be proved that he is guilty of this crime.

9. JUST AS NOWADAYS OUR BRETHREN, ARE OBLIGED AT THEIR OWN RISK TO DENOUNCE TO THE KAHAL APOSTATES OF THEIR OWN FAMILY or members who have been noticed doing anything in opposition to the KAHAL, SO IN OUR KINGDOM OVER ALL THE WORLD IT WILL BE OBLIGATORY FOR ALL OUR SUBJECTS TO OBSERVE THE DUTY OF SERVICE TO THE STATE IN THIS DIRECTION.

10. Such an organization will extirpate abuses of authority, of force, of bribery, everything in fact which we by our counsels, by our theories of the superhuman rights of man, have introduced into the customs of the GOYIM .... But how else were we to procure that increase of causes predisposing to disorders in the midst of their administration? .... Among the number of those methods one of the most important is - agents for the restoration of order, so placed as to have the opportunity in their disintegrating activity of developing and displaying their evil inclinations - obstinate self-conceit, irresponsible exercise of authority, and, first and foremost, venality.

PROTOCOL No. 18

1. When it becomes necessary for us to strengthen the strict measures of secret defense (the most fatal poison for the prestige of authority) we shall arrange a simulation of disorders or some manifestation of discontents finding expression through the co-operation of good speakers. Round these speakers will assemble all who are sympathetic to his utterances. This will give us the pretext for domiciliary prerequisitions and surveillance on the part of our servants from among the number of the GOYIM police ... 2. As the majority of conspirators act out of love for the game, for the sake of talking, so, until they commit some overt act we shall not lay a finger on them but only introduce into their midst observation elements .... It must be remembered that the prestige of authority is lessened if it frequently discovers conspiracies against itself: this implies a presumption of consciousness of weakness, or, what is still worse, of injustice. You are aware that we have broken the prestige of the GOY kings by frequent attempts upon their lives through our agents, blind sheep of our flock, who are easily moved by a few liberal phrases to crimes provided only they be painted in political colors. WE HAVE COMPELLED THE RULERS TO ACKNOWLEDGE THEIR WEAKNESS IN ADVERTISING OVERT MEASURES OF SECRET DEFENSE AND THEREBY WE SHALL BRING THE PROMISE OF AUTHORITY TO DESTRUCTION.

3. Our ruler will be secretly protected only by the most insignificant guard, because we shall not admit so much as a thought that there could exist against him any sedition with which he is not strong enough to contend and is compelled to hide from it.

4. If we should admit this thought, as the GOYIM have done and are doing, we should IPSO FACTO be signing a death sentence, if not for our ruler, at any rate for his dynasty, at no distant date.

GOVERNMENT BY FEAR

5. According to strictly enforced outward appearances our ruler will employ his power only for the advantage of the nation and in no wise for his own or dynastic profits. Therefore, with the observance of this decorum, his authority will be respected and guarded by the subjects themselves, it will receive an apotheosis in the admission that with it is bound up the well-being of every citizen of the State, for upon it will depend all order in the common life of the pack ....

6. OVERT DEFENSE OF THE KIND ARGUES WEAKNESS IN THE ORGANIZATION OF HIS STRENGTH.

7. Our ruler will always be among the people and be surrounded by a mob of apparently curious men and women, who will occupy the front ranks about him, to all appearance by chance, and will restrain the ranks of the rest out of respect as it will appear for good order. This will sow an example of restraint also in others. If a petitioner appears among the people trying to hand a petition and forcing his way through the ranks, the first ranks must receive the petition and before the eyes of the petitioner pass it to the ruler, so that all may know that what is handed in reaches its destination, that consequently, there exists a control of the ruler himself. The aureole of power requires for his existence that the people may be able to say: "If the king knew of this," or: "the king will hear it."

8. WITH THE ESTABLISHMENT OF OFFICIAL DEFENSE, THE MYSTICAL PRESTIGE OF AUTHORITY DISAPPEARS: given a certain audacity, and everyone counts himself master of it, the sedition-monger is conscious of his strength, and when occasion serves watches for the moment to make an attempt upon authority .... For the GOYIM we have been preaching something else, but by that very fact we are enabled to see what measures of overt defense have brought them to ....

9. CRIMINALS WITH US WILL BE ARRESTED AT THE FIRST, more or less, well-grounded SUSPICION: it cannot be allowed that out of fear of a possible mistake an opportunity should be given of escape to persons suspected of a political lapse of crime, for in these matters we shall be literally merciless. If it is still possible, by stretching a point, to admit a reconsideration of the motive causes in simple crimes, there is no possibility of excuse for persons occupying themselves with questions in which nobody except the government can understand anything .... And it is not all governments that understand true policy.

PROTOCOL No. 19

1. If we do not permit any independent dabbling in the political we shall on the other hand encourage every kind of report or petition with proposals for the government to examine into all kinds of projects for the amelioration of the condition of the people; this will reveal to us the defects or else the fantasies of our subjects, to which we shall respond either by accomplishing them or by a wise rebuttment to prove the shortsightedness of one who judges wrongly.

2. Sedition-mongering is nothing more than the yapping of a lap-dog at an elephant. For a government well organized, not from the police but from the public point of view, the lap-dog yaps at the elephant in entire unconsciousness of its strength and importance. It needs no more than to take a good example to show the relative importance of both and the lap-dogs will cease to yap and will wag their tails the moment they set eyes on an elephant.

356   3. In order to destroy the prestige of heroism for political crime we shall send it for trial in the category of thieving, murder, and every kind of

abominable and filthy crime. Public opinion will then confuse in its conception this category of crime with the disgrace attaching to every other and will brand it with the same contempt.

4. We have done our best, and I hope we have succeeded to obtain that the GOYIM should not arrive at this means of contending with sedition. It was for this reason that through the Press and in speeches, indirectly - in cleverly compiled school-books on history, we have advertised the martyrdom alleged to have been accredited by sedition-mongers for the idea of the commonweal. This advertisement has increased the contingent of liberals and has brought thousands of GOYIM into the ranks of our livestock cattle.

PROTOCOL No. 20

1. To-day we shall touch upon the financial program, which I put off to the end of my report as being the most difficult, the crowning and the decisive point of our plans. Before entering upon it I will remind you that I have already spoken before by way of a hint when I said that the sum total of our actions is settled by the question of figures.

2. When we come into our kingdom our autocratic government will avoid, from a principle of self-preservation, sensibly burdening the masses of the people with taxes, remembering that it plays the part of father and protector. But as State organization cost dear it is necessary nevertheless to obtain the funds required for it. It will, therefore, elaborate with particular precaution the question of equilibrium in this matter.

3. Our rule, in which the king will enjoy the legal fiction that everything in his State belongs to him (which may easily be translated into fact), will be enabled to resort to the lawful confiscation of all sums of every kind for the regulation of their circulation in the State. From this follows that taxation will best be covered by a progressive tax on property. In this manner the dues will be paid without straitening or ruining anybody in the form of a percentage of the amount of property. The rich must be aware that it is their duty to place a part of their superfluities at the disposal of the State since the State guarantees them security of possession of the rest of their property and the right of honest gains, I say honest, for the control over property will do away with robbery on a legal basis.

4. This social reform must come from above, for the time is ripe for it - it is indispensable as a pledge of peace.

WE SHALL DESTROY CAPITAL

5. The tax upon the poor man is a seed of revolution and works to the detriment of the State which in hunting after the trifling is missing the big. Quite apart from this, a tax on capitalists diminishes the growth of wealth in private hands in which we have in these days concentrated it as a counterpoise to the government strength of the GOYIM - their State finances.   357

6. A tax increasing in a percentage ratio to capital will give much larger revenue than the present individual or property tax, which is useful to us now for the sole reason that it excites trouble and discontent among the GOYIM. (Now we know the purpose of the 16th Amendment!!)

7. The force upon which our king will rest consists in the equilibrium and the guarantee of peace, for the sake of which things it is indispensable that the capitalists should yield up a portion of their incomes for the sake of the secure working of the machinery of the State. State needs must be paid by those who will not feel the burden and have enough to take from.

8. Such a measure will destroy the hatred of the poor man for the rich, in whom he will see a necessary financial support for the State, will see in him the organizer of peace and well-being since he will see that it is the rich man who is paying the necessary means to attain these things.

9. In order that payers of the educated classes should not too much distress themselves over the new payments they will have full accounts given them of the destination of those payments, with the exception of such sums as will be appropriated for the needs of the throne and the administrative institutions.

10. He who reigns will not have any properties of his own once all in the State represented his patrimony, or else the one would be in contradiction to the other; the fact of holding private means would destroy the right of property in the common possessions of all.

11. Relatives of him who reigns, his heirs excepted, who will be maintained by the resources of the State, must enter the ranks of servants of the State or must work to obtain the right to property; the privilege of royal blood must not serve for the spoiling of the treasury.

12. Purchase, receipt of money or inheritance will be subject to the payment of a stamp progressive tax. Any transfer of property, whether money or other, without evidence of payment of this tax which will be strictly registered by names, will render the former holder liable to pay interest on the tax from the moment of transfer of these sums up to the discovery of his evasion of declaration of the transfer. Transfer documents must be presented weekly at the local treasury office with notifications of the name, surname and permanent place of residence of the former and the new holder of the property. This transfer with register of names must begin from a definite sum which exceeds the ordinary expenses of buying and selling necessaries, and these will be subject to payment only by a stamp impost of a definite percentage of the unit.

13. Just strike an estimate of how many times such taxes as these will cover the revenue of the GOYIM States.

WE CAUSE DEPRESSIONS

14. The State exchequer will have to maintain a definite complement of reserve sums, and all that is collected above that complement must be returned into circulation. On these sums will be organized public works. The initiative in works of this kind, proceeding from State sources, will bind the working class firmly to the interests of the State and to those who reign. From these same sums also a part will be set aside as rewards of inventiveness and productiveness.

15. On no account should so much as a single unit above the definite and freely estimated sums be retained in the State Treasuries, for money exists to be circulated and any kind of stagnation of money acts ruinously on the running of the State machinery, for which it is the lubricant; a stagnation of the lubricant may stop the regular working of the mechanism.

16. The substitution of interest-bearing paper for a part of the token of exchange has produced exactly this stagnation. The consequences of this circumstance are already sufficiently noticeable.

17. A court of account will also be instituted by us, and in it the ruler will find at any moment a full accounting for State income and expenditure, with the exception of the current monthly account, not yet made up, and that of the preceding month, which will not yet have been delivered.

18. The one and only person who will have no interest in robbing the State is its owner, the ruler. This is why his personal control will remove the possibility of leakages or extravagances.

19. The representative function of the ruler at receptions for the sake of etiquette, which absorbs so much invaluable time, will be abolished in order that the ruler may have time for control and consideration. His power will not then be split up into fractional parts among time-serving favorites who surround the throne for its pomp and splendor, and are interested only in their own and not in the common interests of the State.

20. Economic crises have been produced by us for the GOYIM by no other means than the withdrawal of money from circulation. Huge capitals have stagnated, withdrawing money from States, which were constantly obliged to apply to those same stagnant capitals for loans. These loans burdened the finances of the State with the payment of interest and made them the bond slaves of these capitals .... The concentration of industry in the hands of capitalists out of the hands of small masters has drained away all the juices of the peoples and with them also the States .... (Now we know the purpose of the Federal Reserve Bank Corporation!!)

21. The present issue of money in general does not correspond with the requirements per head, and cannot therefore satisfy all the needs of the workers. The issue of money ought to correspond with the growth of population and thereby children also must absolutely be reckoned as consumers of currency from 359 the day of their birth. The revision of issue is a material question for the

whole world.

22. YOU ARE AWARE THAT THE GOLD STANDARD HAS BEEN THE RUIN OF THE STATES WHICH ADOPTED IT, FOR IT HAS NOT BEEN ABLE TO SATISFY THE DEMANDS FOR MONEY, THE MORE SO THAT WE HAVE REMOVED GOLD FROM CIRCULATION AS FAR AS POSSIBLE.

GENTILE STATES BANKRUPT

23. With us the standard that must be introduced is the cost of working-man power, whether it be reckoned in paper or in wood. We shall make the issue of money in accordance with the normal requirements of each subject, adding to the quantity with every birth and subtracting with every death.

24. The accounts will be managed by each department (the French administrative division), each circle.

25. In order that there may be no delays in the paying out of money for State needs the sums and terms of such payments will be fixed by decree of the ruler; this will do away with the protection by a ministry of one institution to the detriment of others.

26. The budgets of income and expenditure will be carried out side by side that they may not be obscured by distance one to another.

27. The reforms projected by us in the financial institutions and principles of the GOYIM will be clothed by us in such forms as will alarm nobody. We shall point out the necessity of reforms in consequence of the disorderly darkness into which the GOYIM by their irregularities have plunged the finances. The first irregularity, as we shall point out, consists in their beginning with drawing up a single budget which year after year grows owing to the following cause: this budget is dragged out to half the year, then they demand a budget to put things right, and this they expend in three months, after which they ask for a supplementary budget, and all this ends with a liquidation budget. But, as the budget of the following year is drawn up in accordance with the sum of the total addition, the annual departure from the normal reaches as much as 50 per cent in a year, and so the annual budget is trebled in ten years. Thanks to such methods, allowed by the carelessness of the GOY States, their treasuries are empty. The period of loans supervenes, and that has swallowed up remainders and brought all the GOY States to bankruptcy. (The United States was declared "bankrupt" at the Geneva Convention of 1929! [see 31 USC 5112, 5118, and 5119).

28. You understand perfectly that economic arrangements of this kind, which have been suggested to the GOYIM by us, cannot be carried on by us.

29. Every kind of loan proves infirmity in the State and a want of understanding of the rights of the State. Loans hang like a sword of Damocles over the heads of rulers, who, instead of taking from their subjects by a temporary tax, come begging with outstretched palm to our

bankers. Foreign loans are leeches which there is no possibility of removing from the body of the State until they fall off of themselves or the State flings them off. But the GOY States do not tear them off; they go on in persisting in putting more on to themselves so that they must inevitably perish, drained by voluntary blood-letting.

TYRANNY OF USURY

30. What also indeed is, in substance, a loan, especially a foreign loan? A loan is - an issue of government bills of exchange containing a percentage obligation commensurate to the sum of the loan capital. If the loan bears a charge of 5 per cent, then in twenty years the State vainly pays away in interest a sum equal to the loan borrowed, in forty years it is paying a double sum, in sixty - treble, and all the while the debt remains an unpaid debt.

31. From this calculation it is obvious that with any form of taxation per head the State is baling out the last coppers of the poor taxpayers in order to settle accounts with wealthy foreigners, from whom it has borrowed money instead of collecting these coppers for its own needs without the additional interest.

32. So long as loans were internal the GOYIM only shuffled their money from the pockets of the poor to those of the rich, but when we bought up the necessary persons in order to transfer loans into the external sphere, (Woodrow Wilson and F.D. Roosevelt) all the wealth of States flowed into our cash-boxes and all the GOYIM began to pay us the tribute of subjects.

33. If the superficiality of GOY kings on their thrones in regard to State affairs and the venality of ministers or the want of understanding of financial matters on the part of other ruling persons have made their countries debtors to our treasuries to amounts quite impossible to pay it has not been accomplished without, on our part, heavy expenditure of trouble and money.

34. Stagnation of money will not be allowed by us and therefore there will be no State interest-bearing paper, except a one per-cent series, so that there will be no payment of interest to leeches that suck all the strength out of the State. The right to issue interest-bearing paper will be given exclusively to industrial companies who find no difficulty in paying interest out of profits, whereas the State does not make interest on borrowed money like these companies, for the State borrows to spend and not to use in operations. (Now we know why President Kennedy was assassinated in 1963 when he refused to borrow any more of the "Bank Notes" from the bankers of the Federal Reserve Bank and began circulating non-interest bearing "Notes" of the "United States of America"!!!).

35. Industrial papers will be bought also by the government which from being as now a paper of tribute by loan operations will be transformed into a lender of money at a profit. This measure will stop the stagnation of money, parasitic profits and idleness, all of which were useful for us among the GOYIM so long as they were independent but are not desirable under our rule. 361

36. How clear is the undeveloped power of thought of the purely brute brains of the GOYIM, as expressed in the fact that they have been borrowing from us with payment of interest without ever thinking that all the same these very moneys plus an addition for payment of interest must be got by them from their own State pockets in order to settle up with us. What could have been simpler than to take the money they wanted from their own people?

37. But it is a proof of the genius of our chosen mind that we have contrived to present the matter of loans to them in such a light that they have even seen in them an advantage for themselves.

38. Our accounts, which we shall present when the time comes, in the light of centuries of experience gained by experiments made by us on the GOY States, will be distinguished by clearness and definiteness and will show at a glance to all men the advantage of our innovations. They will put an end to those abuses to which we owe our mastery over the GOYIM, but which cannot be allowed in our kingdom.

39. We shall so hedge about our system of accounting that neither the ruler nor the most insignificant public servant will be in a position to divert even the smallest sum from its destination without detection or to direct it in another direction except that which will be once fixed in a definite plan of action. (Is this why a "private corporation," known as the "Internal Revenue Service," is in charge of collecting the "payments" of the "Income Taxes" and the IRS always deposits those "payments" to the Federal Reserve bank and never to the Treasury of the United States??)

40. And without a definite plan it is impossible to rule. Marching along an undetermined road and with undetermined resources brings to ruin by the way heroes and demi-gods.

41. The GOY rulers, whom we once upon a time advised should be distracted from State occupations by representative receptions, observances of etiquette, entertainments, were only screens for our rule. (Like the House of Windsor (Guelph) and the rest of the "Black Nobility"?) The accounts of favorite courtiers who replaced them in the sphere of affairs were drawn up for them by our agents, and every time gave satisfaction to short-sighted minds by promises that in the future economies and improvements were foreseen .... Economies from what? From new taxes? - were questions that might have been but were not asked by those who read our accounts and projects.

42. You know to what they have been brought by this carelessness, to what pitch of financial disorder they have arrived, notwithstanding the astonishing industry of their peoples ....

PROTOCOL No. 21

1. To what I reported to you at the last meeting I shall now add a detailed explanation of internal loans. Of foreign loans I shall say nothing more, because they have fed us with the national moneys of the GOYIM, but for our State there will be no foreigners, that is, nothing external.

2. We have taken advantage of the venality of administrators and slackness of rulers to get our moneys twice, thrice and more times over, by lending to the GOY governments moneys which were not at all needed by the States. Could anyone do the like in regard to us? .... Therefore, I shall only deal with the details of internal loans.

3. States announce that such a loan is to be concluded and open subscriptions for their own bills of exchange, that is, for their interest-bearing paper. That they may be within the reach of all the price is determined at from a hundred to a thousand; and a discount is made for the earliest subscribers. Next day by artificial means the price of them goes up, the alleged reason being that everyone is rushing to buy them. In a few days the treasury safes are, as they say, overflowing and there's more money than they can do with (why then take it?) The subscription, it is alleged, covers many times over the issue total of the loan; in this lies the whole stage effect - look you, they say, what confidence is shown in the government's bills of exchange.

4. But when the comedy is played out there emerges the fact that a debit and an exceedingly burdensome debit has been created. For the payment of interest it becomes necessary to have recourse to new loans, which do not swallow up but only add to the capital debt. And when this credit is exhausted it becomes necessary by new taxes to cover, not the loan, BUT ONLY THE INTEREST ON IT. These taxes are a debit employed to cover a debit .... (Hence THE CRY TO BALANCE THE BUDGET!)

5. Later comes the time for conversions, but they diminish the payment of interest without covering the debt, and besides they cannot be made without the consent of the lenders; on announcing a conversion a proposal is made to return the money to those who are not willing to convert their paper. If everybody expressed his unwillingness and demanded his money back, the government would be hoist on their own petard and would be found insolvent and unable to pay the proposed sums. By good luck the subjects of the GOY governments, knowing nothing about financial affairs, have always preferred losses on exchange and diminution of interest to the risk of new investments of their moneys, and have thereby many a time enabled these governments to throw off their shoulders a debit of several millions.

6. Nowadays, with external loans, these tricks cannot be played by the GOYIM for they know that we shall demand all our moneys back.

7. In this way in acknowledged bankruptcy will best prove to the various countries the absence of any means between the interests of the peoples and of those who rule them.

8. I beg you to concentrate your particular attention upon this point and upon the following: nowadays all internal loans are consolidated by so-called flying loans, that is, such as have terms of payment more or less near. These debts consist of moneys paid into the savings banks and reserve funds. If left for long at the disposition of a government these funds evaporate in the

363

payment of interest on foreign loans, and are placed by the deposit of equivalent amount of RENTS.

9. And these last it is which patch up all the leaks in the State treasuries of the GOYIM.

10. When we ascend the throne of the world all these financial and similar shifts, as being not in accord with our interests, will be swept away so as not to leave a trace, as also will be destroyed all money markets, since we shall not allow the prestige of our power to be shaken by fluctuations of prices set upon our values, which we shall announce by law at the price which represents their full worth without any possibility of lowering or raising. (Raising gives the pretext for lowering, which indeed was where we made a beginning in relation to the values of the GOYIM).

11. We shall replace the money markets by grandiose government credit institutions, the object of which will be to fix the price of industrial values in accordance with government views. These institutions will be in a position to fling upon the market five hundred millions of industrial paper in one day, or to buy up for the same amount. In this way all industrial undertakings will come into dependence upon us. You may imagine for yourselves what immense power we shall thereby secure for ourselves ....

PROTOCOL No. 22

1 In all that has so far been reported by me to you, I have endeavored to depict with care the secret of what is coming, of what is past, and of what is going on now, rushing into the flood of the great events coming already in the near future, the secret of our relations to the GOYIM and of financial operations. On this subject there remains still a little for me to add.

2. IN OUR HANDS IS THE GREATEST POWER OF OUR DAY - GOLD: IN TWO DAYS WE CAN PROCURE FROM OUR STOREHOUSES ANY QUANTITY WE MAY PLEASE.

3. Surely there is no need to seek further proof that our rule is predestined by God? Surely we shall not fail with such wealth to prove that all that evil which for so many centuries we have had to commit has served at the end of ends the cause of true well-being - the bringing of everything into order? Though it be even by the exercise of some violence, yet all the same it will be established. (The motto of the Freemasons - "Out of Chaos, Order"). We shall contrive to prove that we are benefactors who have restored to the rent and mangled earth the true good and also freedom of the person, and therewith we shall enable it to be enjoyed in peace and quiet, with proper dignity of relations, on the condition, of course, of strict observance of the laws established by us. We shall make plain therewith that freedom does not consist in dissipation and in the right of unbridled license any more than the dignity and force of a man do not consist in the right of everyone to promulgate destructive principles in the nature of freedom of conscience, equality and the like, that freedom of the person in no wise consists in the right to agitate oneself and others by abominable speeches

before disorderly mobs, and that true freedom consists in the inviolability of the person who honorably and strictly observes all the laws of life in common, that human dignity is wrapped up in consciousness of the rights and also of the absence of rights of each, and not wholly and solely in fantastic imaginings about the subject of one's EGO.

4. One authority will be glorious because it will be all-powerful, will rule and guide, and not muddle along after leaders and orators shrieking themselves hoarse with senseless words which they call great principles and which are nothing else, to speak honestly, but utopian .... Our authority will be the crown of order, and in that is included the whole happiness of man. The aureole of this authority will inspire a mystical bowing of the knee before it and a reverent fear before it of all the peoples. True force makes no terms with any right, not even with that of God: none dare come near to it so as to take so much as a span from it away.

PROTOCOL No. 23

1. That the peoples may become accustomed to obedience it is necessary to inculcate lessons of humility and therefore to reduce the production of articles of luxury. By this we shall improve morals which have been debased by emulation in the sphere of luxury. We shall re-establish small master production which will mean laying a mine under the private capital of manufactures. This is indispensable also for the reason that manufacturers on the grand scale often move, though not always consciously, the thoughts of the masses in directions against the government. A people of small masters knows nothing of unemployment and this binds him closely with existing order, and consequently with the firmness of authority. For us its part will have been played out the moment authority is transferred into our hands. Drunkenness also will be prohibited by law and punishable as a crime against the humanness of man who is turned into a brute under the influence of alcohol.

2. Subjects, I repeat once more, give blind obedience only to the strong hand which is absolutely independent of them, for in it they feel the sword of defense and support against social scourges .... What do they want with an angelic spirit in a king? What they have to see in him is the personification of force and power.

3. The supreme lord who will replace all now existing rulers, dragging in their existence among societies demoralized by us, societies that have denied even the authority of God, from whose midst breeds out on all sides the fire of anarchy, must first of all proceed to quench this all-devouring flame. Therefore he will be obliged to kill off those existing societies, though he should drench them with his own blood, that he may resurrect them again in the form of regularly organized troops fighting consciously with every kind of infection that may cover the body of the State with sores.

4. This Chosen One of God is chosen from above to demolish the senseless forces moved by instinct and not reason, by brutishness and not humanness. These forces now triumph in manifestations of robbery and every kind of violence under the mask of principles of freedom and rights. They have overthrown all forms of social order to erect on the ruins the throne of the

365

King of the Jews; but their part will be played out the moment he enters into his kingdom. Then it will be necessary to sweep them away from his path, on which must be left no knot, no splinter.

5. Then will it be possible for us to say to the peoples of the world: "Give thanks to God and bow the knee before him who bears on his front the seal of the predestination of man, to which God himself has led his star that none other but Him might free us from all the before-mentioned forces and evils".

PROTOCOL No. 24

1. I pass now to the method of confirming the dynastic roots of King David to the last strata of the earth.

2. This confirmation will first and foremost be included in that which to this day has rested the force of conservatism by our learned elders of the conduct of the affairs of the world, in the directing of the education of thought of all humanity.

3. Certain members of the seed of David will prepare the kings and their heirs, selecting not by right of heritage but by eminent capacities, inducting them into the most secret mysteries of the political, into schemes of government, but providing always that none may come to knowledge of the secrets. The object of this mode of action is that all may know that government cannot be entrusted to those who have not been inducted into the secret places of its art ....

4. To these persons only will be taught the practical application of the aforenamed plans by comparison of the experiences of many centuries, all the observations on the politico-economic moves and social sciences - in a word, all the spirit of laws which have been unshakably established by nature herself for the regulation of the relations of humanity.

5. Direct heirs will often be set aside from ascending the throne if in their time of training they exhibit frivolity, softness and other qualities that are the ruin of authority, which render them incapable of governing and in themselves dangerous for kingly office.

6. Only those who are unconditionally capable for firm, even if it be to cruelty, direct rule will receive the reins of rule from our learned elders.

7. In case of falling sick with weakness of will or other form of incapacity. kings must by law hand over the reins of rule to new and capable hands.

8. The king's plan of action for the current moment, and all the more so for the future, will be unknown, even to those who are called his closest counselors.

KING OF THE JEWS

9. Only the king and the three who stood sponsor for him will know what is coming.

10. In the person of the king who with unbending will is master of himself and of humanity all will discern as it were fate with its mysterious ways. None will know what the king wishes to attain by his dispositions, and therefore none will dare to stand across an unknown path.

11. It is understood that the brain reservoir of the king must correspond in capacity to the plan of government it has to contain. It is for this reason that he will ascend the throne not otherwise than after examination of his mind by the aforesaid learned elders.

12. That the people may know and love their king, it is indispensable for him to converse in the market-places with his people. This ensures the necessary clinching of the two forces which are now divided one from another by us by the terror.

13. This terror was indispensable for us till the time comes for both these forces separately to fall under our influence.

14. The king of the Jews must not be at the mercy of his passions, and especially of sensuality: on no side of his character must he give brute instincts power over his mind. Sensuality worse than all else disorganizes the capacities of the mind and clearness of views, distracting the thoughts to the worst and most brutal side of human activity.

15. The prop of humanity in the person of the supreme lord of all the world of the holy seed of David must sacrifice to his people all personal inclinations.

16. Our supreme lord must be of an exemplary irreproachability.

Signed by the representative of
Zion, of the 33rd Degree

Scottish American Louis Thomas McFadden was poisoned to death on 10/1/1936, aged 60. Louis was a Pennsylvania Republican Congressman and Chairman of the House Banking & Currency Committee, from 1920-1931. There were three attempts on McFadden's life including one gunman and two poisonings. McFadden was a "vociferous foe of the Federal Reserve" which he claimed was created and operated by Jewish banking interests who conspired to economically control the United States. On 6/10/1932, McFadden made a 25-minute speech before House of Representatives, in which he accused the Federal Reserve of deliberately causing the Great Depression. McFadden also claimed that he had proof that Wall Street bankers funded the Jewish created and controlled Bolshevik Revolution through the Federal Reserve banks and the European central banks with which it cooperated. McFadden was, "virtually read out of his party... [had] his committee posts...taken away from him...was ostracized by Republicans [and] called crazy..." Senator David A. Reed (R-PA) said, "We intend to act to all practical purposes as though McFadden had died." McFadden was the chief sponsor of the, "McFadden Act," of 1927 which limited the federal branch banks to the city in which the main branch operates. The Scottish McFadden family is derived from the personal name, "Paidean." The Gaelic forms of the surname are Mac Phadein or Mac Phaidin, both of which mean son of Paiden. First found in Kintyre, where they held a family seat from very ancient times, the McFadden's were from the Irish Christian Dalriadan clans of the mountainous west coast of Scotland.

Now that you've had the opportunity to examine my entire thesis, Mr. Benjamin Freedman's, "Christian View of the Holocaust," and "The Protocols of the Learned Elders of Zion," it doesn't take a Masonic Einstein to figure out the clear and present danger posed to Americans by Babylonian Talmudist destroyers. However, I suspect there will be a minute group of individuals desperately clinging to the hope that none of the preceding facts directly correlate with Talmudist leaders, headquartered inside of modern day Israel, which is why I've put aside the subsequent information for last.

On 10/08/2013, The Prime Minister of Israel, Benjamin Netanyahu [left] called the late Chief Rabbi of Israel [1973-1983] and Talmudic scholar, "Ovadia Yosef" [left], "a great scholar," and that Yosef, "uniquely combined Judaism and humanity," indicating an admiration on Netanyahu's part for Rabbi Yosef's understanding of the Talmud and the writings contained therein. It will be remembered from previous discussions that the Talmud, which Netanyahu and Rabbi Yosef's nation and religion are synonymous, contains the following edicts concerning all non-Jews, including:

"Jesus is in hell where he is boiling in hot excrement."
- Bablyonian Talmud, Gitten 57a

"A pregnant non-Jew is no better than a pregnant animal."
- Coschen Hamischpat 405

"Gentile [Christian] girls are in a state of niddah (filth) from birth. Christian women are regarded as slaves, heathen and whores.
- Abodah Zarah 36b

"All gentile chidren are animals."
- Yebamoth 98a

368

"The Jews are called human beings, but the non-Jews are not humans. They are beasts." - Talmud: Baba Mezia 114b

"The Akum [Christian] is like a dog. Yes, the scripture teaches to honor the dog more than the Akum." - Ereget Raschi Erod. 22 30

"Every Jew, who spills the blood of the godless (non-Jew), is doing the same as making a sacrifice to God." - Bammidber Raba, c 21 & Jalkut 772

"It is permitted to take the body and the life of a non-Jew." - Sepher Ikkarim IIIc, 25

"violation of any one of the seven [Noahide] laws subjects the Noahide to capital punishment by decapitation - Sanhedrin 57A."

Presumably Netanyahu was referring to the following weekly sermon delivered by Rabbi Yosef. While you're reading this sermon, please keep in mind that this is the very same Prime Minister Netanyahu who has repeatedly begged American men and women to fight, bleed and die in the Middle East for Antichristian Talmudists while they pray inside of their synagogues of Satan.

"Goyim were born only to serve us. Without that, they have no place in the world; only to serve the People of Israel... Why are gentiles needed? They will work, they will plow, they will reap. We will sit like an effendi and eat."

While Rabbi Josef was making the above-mentioned comments the exclusively Jewish audience laughed in accordance with his proclamation.

Rabbi Yosef's Antichristian vitriol continued when he stated, "With gentiles, it will be like any person: They need to die, but God will give them longevity. Why? Imagine that one's donkey would die, they'd lose their money. This is his servant. That's why he gets a long life, to work well for this Jew." - Jewish Telegraph Agency, [www.jta.org] 10/18/2010

Israel's Chief Rabbi continued by stating that the Babylonian Talmud endorses the genocide of every non-Jewish man, woman and child: "...waste their seed and exterminate them, devastate them and vanish them from this world..."

Chief Rabbi Yosef endorsing the deliberate devastation of a Nation's food supply with the goal in mind of bringing about a genocidal level event is psychopathic at best. His rhetoric, which was inspired by generational inbreeding, advanced syphilitic delirium and demonic possession, brings to mind the leading manufacturer of Genetically

369

Modification Organisms [GMOs] in the world, "Monsanto Corporation". This organization was founded by Scottish American, John Francis Queeny, who worked for the Jewish-owned, Meyer Brothers Drug Company, one of the largest wholesale pharmaceutical companies at the time.

Queeny married a Jewess named, Olga Mendez Monsanto, the daughter of Don Emmanuel Mendes de Monsanto. The Monsantos were one of many Jewish families involved in the enslavement and ownership of Black Africans. Monsanto was the first modern day group to

Genetically modify a plant cell [1982] and five years later Monsanto planted their toxic GMO seed into U.S. soil. In accordance with Chief Rabbi Yosef proclamation, Monsantos techno-seed will in fact destroy all organic seed and replace it with toxic GMO seeds that cause mental and physical illness and if allowed to continue will inflict a famine upon the U.S. of biblical proporations ultimately leading to the extermination of all non-Jews living inside of the U.S.

The following are organizations associated with Monsanto company: BASF, aspartame, NutraSweet Company, DEKALB Genetics Corporation, Solutia, Inc. Pharmacia & Upjohn, mergent Genetics, Stoneville, NexGen Cotton brands, Delta and Pine Land Company cotton seed breeder, Bayer, Dutch seed company De Ruiter Seeds, Eli Lily, President of South Dakota State University, Cisco Systems, Inc., Sara Lee Corporation, MPI Research, Inc., McDonalds USA, Health Technology Networks and The Proctor & Gamble Company.

In 2013 President Barack Hussein Obama supported the, Consolidation and Further Continuing Appropriations Act, which prevents the courts from stopping Monsanto's cancer causing GMO toxins from being grown in U.S. soil. Obama further strengthened Monsanto Corporation by appointing former Monsanto VP Michael R. Taylor as head of the FDA.

Dear Reader,

Thank you for investing your valuable time and energy into reading my book. I created this resource, to warn the American people of the very real threat facing our Nation. My aim is to strengthen the United States by exposing the seditious, covert campaign which seeks to destroy our Nation from within. I hope that in some measure I've achieved this goal.

If what you've read has inspired you in any way please recommend its content, to those you care about, in person and on social media. I would be grateful if you would consider leaving a positive review at www.killingireland.com regarding this book.

If you are currently part of the Christian American majority, I challenge you to get directly involved in auditing your local, regional and National Christian leadership today to ensure they are in fact sharing the true message of Jesus Christ and not promoting any of the deceptions I've exposed throughout this book.

If you're a Christian parent please begin to apply the deciphering techniques that you've learned throughout this book to identify Church of Babylon cryptography in your child's cartoons, television programs, toys, food containers, clothing, theme parks and what's being promoted as a whole throughout their peer group.

If you are a non-Christian and this information has opened your eyes, to the deception of Satan and has inspired you to know the real message and meaning of Lord Jesus Christ, please pray with me now.

"Father, I know that I have broken your laws and my sins have separated me from you. I am truly sorry. I want to turn away from my past sinful life toward you. Please forgive me, and help me avoid sinning again. I believe that your son, Jesus Christ died for my sins, was resurrected from the dead, is alive, and hears my prayer. I invite Jesus Christ, to become the Lord of my life, to rule and reign in my heart from this day forward. Please send your Holy Ghost to help me obey You, and to do Your will for the rest of my life. In Jesus' name I pray, Amen."

"For whosoever shall call upon the name of the Lord shall be saved." – Romans 10:13

"Neither is there salvation in any other: for there is none other name under heaven given among men, whereby we must be saved." - Acts 4:12

Index

T

The Church of Babylon's Holy War

www. acts17. net

www marchingtozion . com
the Legacy of Arab Islam in Africa
        John Alembillah Azumah
Libertygunrights . com
    Xendrius "Demon Magician"
            you tube p 84
China - Rockefeller p 98

89960090R00214

Made in the USA
Middletown, DE
19 September 2018